SECOND COMING

VOLUME ONE

MARK RUSSELL

RICHARD PACE

LEONARD KIRK

ANDY TROY

ROB STEEN

COMICSAHOY.COM  @ AHOYCOMICMAGS

HART SEELY - PUBLISHER
TOM PEYER - EDITOR-IN-CHIEF
FRANK CAMMUSO - CHIEF CREATIVE OFFICER
STUART MOORE - OPS
SARAH LITT - EDITOR-AT-LARGE

DAVID HYDE - PUBLICITY
DERON BENNETT - PRODUCTION COORDINATOR
KIT CAOAGAS - MARKETING ASSOCIATE
LILLIAN LASERSON - LEGAL
RUSSELL NATHERSON SR. - BUSINESS

PRINTED IN THE U.S.A. FIRST PRINTING - FEBRUARY 2020 - ISBN: 978-0-9980442-7-9

SECOND COMING
VOLUME ONE

MARK RUSSELL	WRITER
RICHARD PACE	ARTIST
LEONARD KIRK	FINISHER (SUNSTAR PAGES)
ANDY TROY	COLOR (SUNSTAR PAGES)
ROB STEEN	LETTERS
RICHARD PACE	COLLECTION COVER ARTIST
AMANDA CONNER	COVER ARTIST
PAUL MOUNTS	COVER COLOR
JARED FLETCHER	LOGO
JOHN J. HILL	DESIGN
DERON BENNETT	ASSISTANT EDITOR
TOM PEYER	EDITOR
CORY SEDLMEIER	COLLECTION EDITOR

CREATED BY **MARK RUSSELL** AND **RICHARD PACE**

CONTENTS

SECOND COMING

I N T R O D U C T I O N

If Jesus ever came back, he'd be disgusted with the world. What's more, no one would believe he *was* Jesus. They'd treat him like a loon and probably toss his loinclothed ass in jail.

Who would win a fight, Jesus or Superman?

These were hack premises when I started doing stand-up in the late '80s. They've since been beaten to death in a hundred different mediums — films, TV, literature, music. You name it. Comic books — both mainstream and alternative — have also run endless variations on this idea. There's no meat left on those bones, us comedians used to say, when a premise had been pulped to a husk.

Which is what makes AHOY Comics' *SECOND COMING* such a — pardon the pun — miracle. This is Jesus plopped into our cynical, post-meta-ironic-lulz world, paired up with a deconstructed superhero. And you start reading the first issue and you're already running every joke through your head, but damn if Mark Russell, Richard Pace and Leonard Kirk don't keep surprising you at every turn.

Suffice to say I'm going to try and NOT spoil any of the surprises in this one. So lemme talk to you about it the way we'd talk about it over a cup of coffee. I'm trying to be enthusiastic without ruining the pleasure of you discovering it. But I also need to get across the little moments that make up the whole.

Like the food court in heaven, full of discontinued franchises, and how my heart leapt a little when I saw the Burger Chef kiosk. Or Jesus' take on miracles and wonder working, and how his rejection of them makes him even *more* Christ-like. And Satan's entire role in this, which is NOT what you'd expect. And how Brian Cox in *Succession* would be perfect to play this comic's take on God. And poor Sunstar, a demigod whose partner is an actual god. Seeing a metahuman humbled by the sheer sanity and reasonableness of Jesus was NOT how I saw a Jesus/Superman fight going.

You're about to experience *SECOND COMING*. May the Lord bless you and keep you.

Patton Oswalt
Los Angeles
January 16, 2020

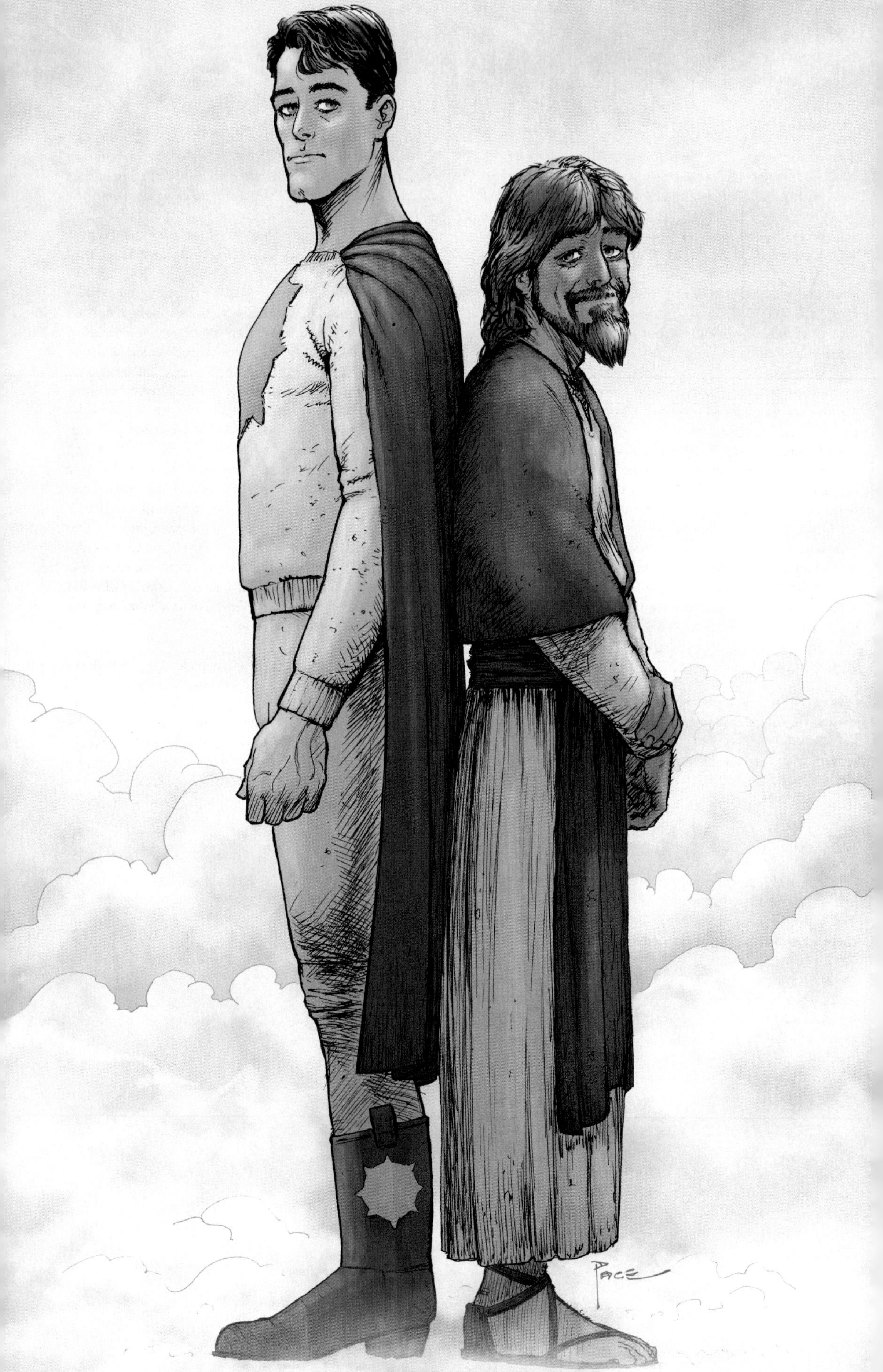
PACE

F O R E W O R D

Apparently this is where I explain myself.

In late 2018, the world learned that some idiot had written a comic book about Jesus Christ sharing a two-bedroom apartment with a superhero. The ensuing controversy forced us to delay publication and ultimately go with another publisher. Since then, I've done a lot of media interviews, fielded a lot of questions, both from those who were sympathetic to my cause and those who were very much not so. But, regardless of their perspective, their questions all sort of boiled down to the same one—what were you *thinking?*

I suppose the short answer is that I was thinking that I had as much right to an opinion on the meaning of Christ's teachings and their legacy as anyone else. That was enough to get me labeled a blasphemer. Though, I suppose ultimately that's what blasphemy *is*...coming up with an opinion of your own. So maybe they have a point.

But, seeing as how the second half the New Testament is essentially an argument over the meaning of Christ's brief visit to the Earth, I consider myself to be in good company. If Paul, James, and Peter couldn't come up with a consensus about what Christ meant or what he wanted from us, then trusting the arc-welder who volunteered to teach your Sunday School class to know...well, that just seems a tad *presumptuous.*

So, for better or worse, this is my blasphemy. My stab at what I think Christ came to Earth to accomplish and how he'd feel about returning to find that mega-church tycoons, prosperity doctrine charlatans, and media anger-merchants had made themselves the executors of his estate. By no means am I suggesting mine is the only possible interpretation, or even the best, just that when I consider what is important and unique about the life and words of Christ, the things that come to my mind are his empathy and forgiveness. His refusal to play any of the reindeer games of the rich and powerful. I suppose it's possible that there were also people he wanted killed, caged or closeted, but he never said so as far as I can tell. I know those were common things people believed in back in those days, just as they are in ours, but what makes a person's words and actions worth remembering are how they are *different* from everyone else's. So, even so, it would be as weird to base Christianity on the beliefs Christ held in common with the people of his time as it would be to base it on the wearing of beards and robes.

So why pair him with a *superhero*, of all things? Superhero stories are, ultimately, a meditation on power. How you would apply power if you could fly, had the strength to melt steel with your eyes, or bend the very world to your will? It's a question comic book writers have wrestled with since *Action Comics* #1. But while they're good at turning these thought experiments into entertainment, superhero comics are predicated on a rather dodgy assumption. That, ultimately, it is physical force that solves problems. "Good" is simply a matter of using violence better than "evil". In a world where our problems are increasingly immune to violent solutions...no amount of drop-kicking people is going to solve global warming or get your sick mom the health care she needs...we need to start incorporating other solutions into the thought experiment. And that is why bringing Christ into a superhero comic made sense to me. He is the counterpoint to the assumption that you can fix the world with punishment. To me, that is the core of Christ's mission to Earth...to show human beings that we could build a world immune to the threat of violence and to the seduction of bribery, if only we chose to be so ourselves. And that's what made it necessary for any self-respecting empire to crucify him.

Whether people agree with Christ's assessment or not, whether they agree with my assessment of Christ or not, none of it really matters. The great problems confronting the world today will not be solved by laying down more barbed wire or simply finding new ways to punch people harder than ever before. The ability of armies, empires, and the other great institutions of force to protect us dwindles by the day. If not Christ, then we need someone like him in our thought experiments to be the voice of other possibilities. Other ways of fixing human civilization. For without them, the world is lost.

I would like to thank the artist Richard Pace and all the good people at AHOY for incriminating themselves in this blasphemy. I wish I could tell them that they're not committing career suicide. All I know is, as weird as the answers may seem, the questions these comics attempt to answer are important. And as professional thought-experimenters, that is our duty to the world. We blaspheme, not to belittle the faith of millions, but to offer the world something new.

Mark Russell
Portland, Oregon
January 6, 2020

1

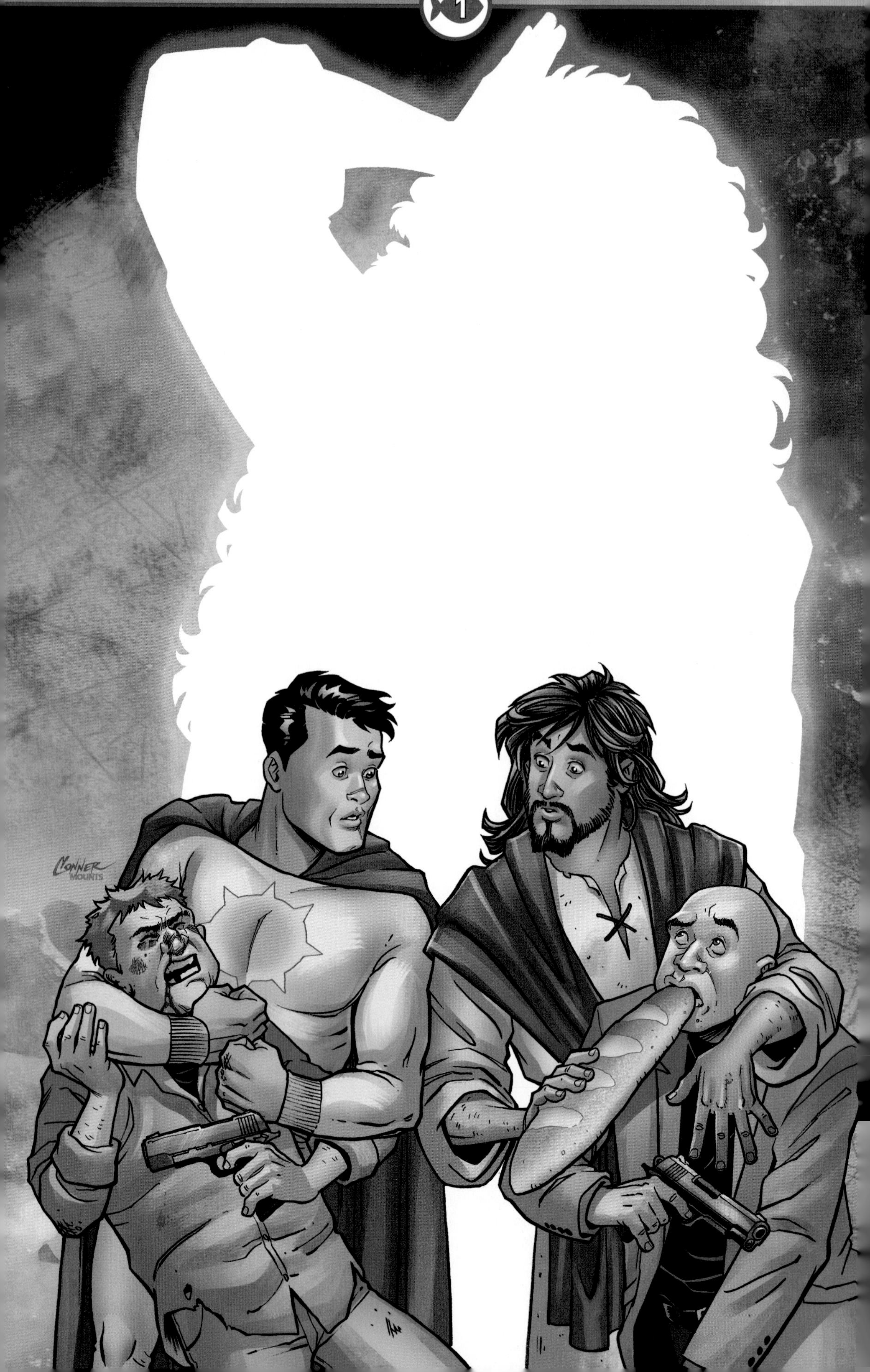
CONNER
MOUNTS

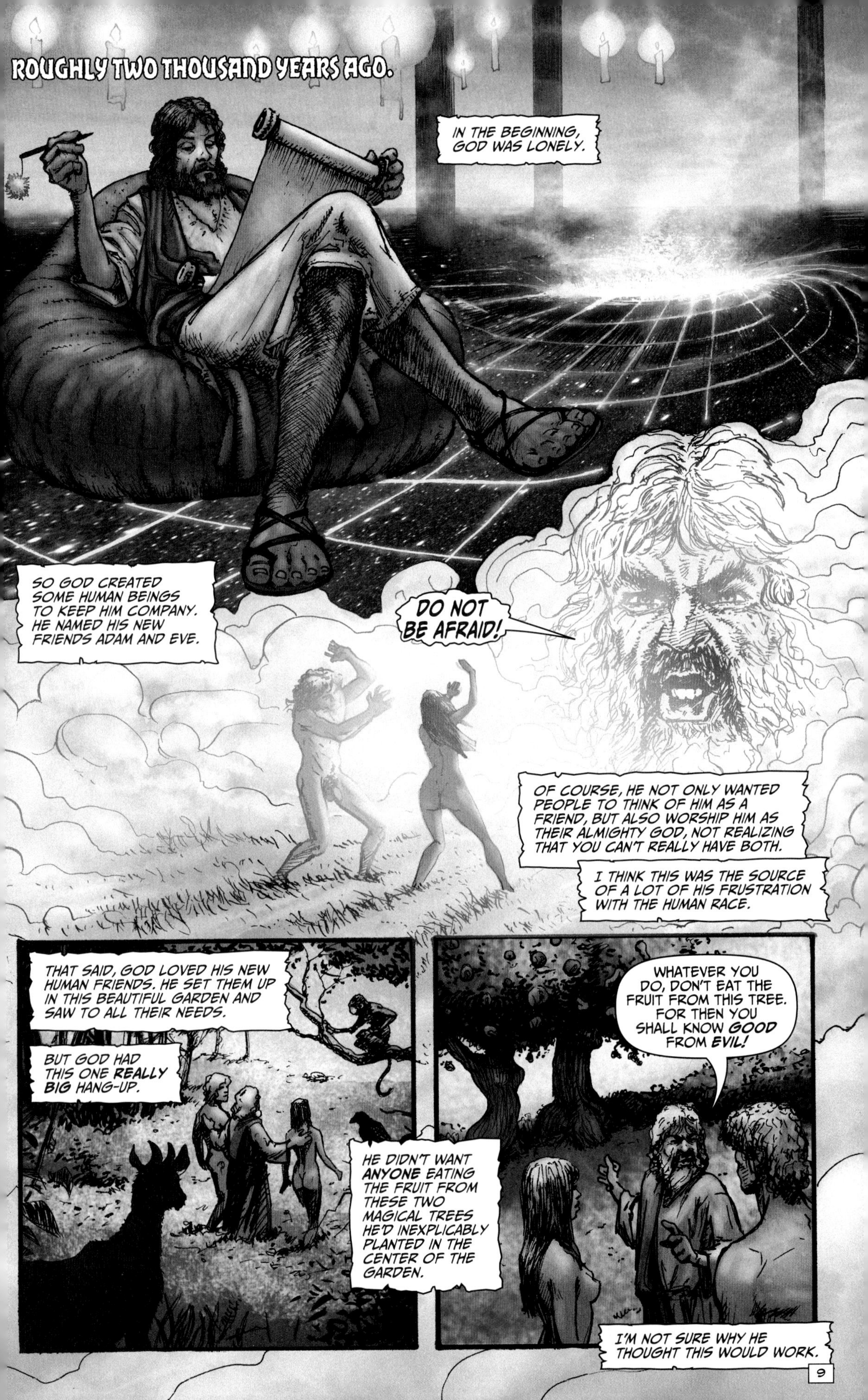
ROUGHLY TWO THOUSAND YEARS AGO.
IN THE BEGINNING, GOD WAS LONELY.
SO GOD CREATED SOME HUMAN BEINGS TO KEEP HIM COMPANY. HE NAMED HIS NEW FRIENDS ADAM AND EVE.
DO NOT BE AFRAID!
OF COURSE, HE NOT ONLY WANTED PEOPLE TO THINK OF HIM AS A FRIEND, BUT ALSO WORSHIP HIM AS THEIR ALMIGHTY GOD, NOT REALIZING THAT YOU CAN'T REALLY HAVE BOTH.
I THINK THIS WAS THE SOURCE OF A LOT OF HIS FRUSTRATION WITH THE HUMAN RACE.
THAT SAID, GOD LOVED HIS NEW HUMAN FRIENDS. HE SET THEM UP IN THIS BEAUTIFUL GARDEN AND SAW TO ALL THEIR NEEDS.
BUT GOD HAD THIS ONE **REALLY BIG** HANG-UP.
HE DIDN'T WANT **ANYONE** EATING THE FRUIT FROM THESE TWO MAGICAL TREES HE'D INEXPLICABLY PLANTED IN THE CENTER OF THE GARDEN.
WHATEVER YOU DO, DON'T EAT THE FRUIT FROM THIS TREE. FOR THEN YOU SHALL KNOW **GOOD** FROM **EVIL!**
I'M NOT SURE WHY HE THOUGHT THIS WOULD WORK.

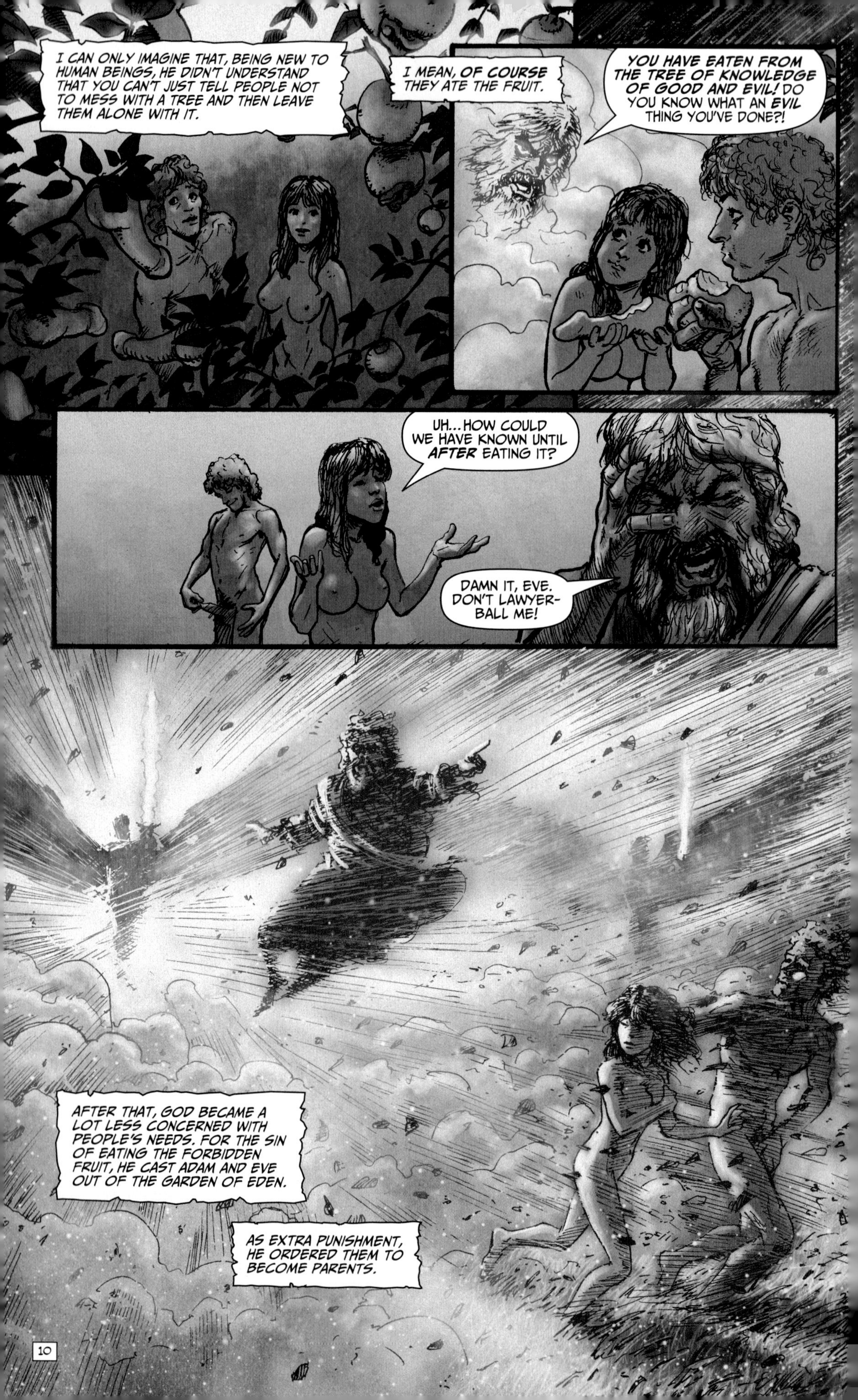
I CAN ONLY IMAGINE THAT, BEING NEW TO HUMAN BEINGS, HE DIDN'T UNDERSTAND THAT YOU CAN'T JUST TELL PEOPLE NOT TO MESS WITH A TREE AND THEN LEAVE THEM ALONE WITH IT.
I MEAN, OF COURSE THEY ATE THE FRUIT.
YOU HAVE EATEN FROM THE TREE OF KNOWLEDGE OF GOOD AND EVIL! DO YOU KNOW WHAT AN EVIL THING YOU'VE DONE?!
UH...HOW COULD WE HAVE KNOWN UNTIL AFTER EATING IT?
DAMN IT, EVE. DON'T LAWYER-BALL ME!
AFTER THAT, GOD BECAME A LOT LESS CONCERNED WITH PEOPLE'S NEEDS. FOR THE SIN OF EATING THE FORBIDDEN FRUIT, HE CAST ADAM AND EVE OUT OF THE GARDEN OF EDEN.
AS EXTRA PUNISHMENT, HE ORDERED THEM TO BECOME PARENTS.

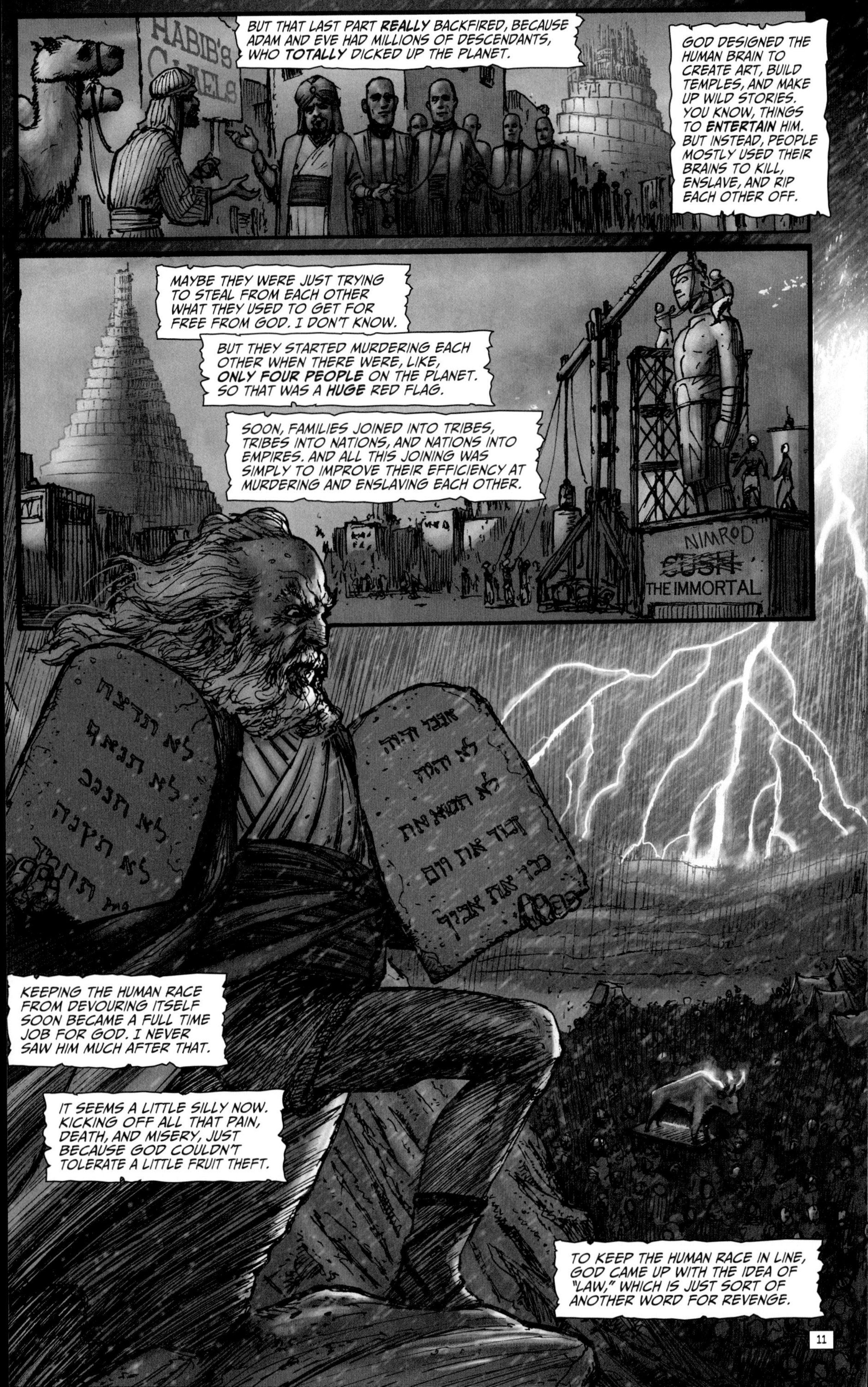
HABIB'S
BUT THAT LAST PART **REALLY** BACKFIRED, BECAUSE ADAM AND EVE HAD MILLIONS OF DESCENDANTS, WHO **TOTALLY** DICKED UP THE PLANET.
GOD DESIGNED THE HUMAN BRAIN TO CREATE ART, BUILD TEMPLES, AND MAKE UP WILD STORIES. YOU KNOW, THINGS TO **ENTERTAIN** HIM. BUT INSTEAD, PEOPLE MOSTLY USED THEIR BRAINS TO KILL, ENSLAVE, AND RIP EACH OTHER OFF.
MAYBE THEY WERE JUST TRYING TO STEAL FROM EACH OTHER WHAT THEY USED TO GET FOR FREE FROM GOD. I DON'T KNOW.
BUT THEY STARTED MURDERING EACH OTHER WHEN THERE WERE, LIKE, **ONLY FOUR PEOPLE** ON THE PLANET. SO THAT WAS A **HUGE** RED FLAG.
SOON, FAMILIES JOINED INTO TRIBES, TRIBES INTO NATIONS, AND NATIONS INTO EMPIRES. AND ALL THIS JOINING WAS SIMPLY TO IMPROVE THEIR EFFICIENCY AT MURDERING AND ENSLAVING EACH OTHER.
NIMROD
~~CUSH~~
THE IMMORTAL
KEEPING THE HUMAN RACE FROM DEVOURING ITSELF SOON BECAME A FULL TIME JOB FOR GOD. I NEVER SAW HIM MUCH AFTER THAT.
IT SEEMS A LITTLE SILLY NOW. KICKING OFF ALL THAT PAIN, DEATH, AND MISERY, JUST BECAUSE GOD COULDN'T TOLERATE A LITTLE FRUIT THEFT.
TO KEEP THE HUMAN RACE IN LINE, GOD CAME UP WITH THE IDEA OF "LAW," WHICH IS JUST SORT OF ANOTHER WORD FOR REVENGE.

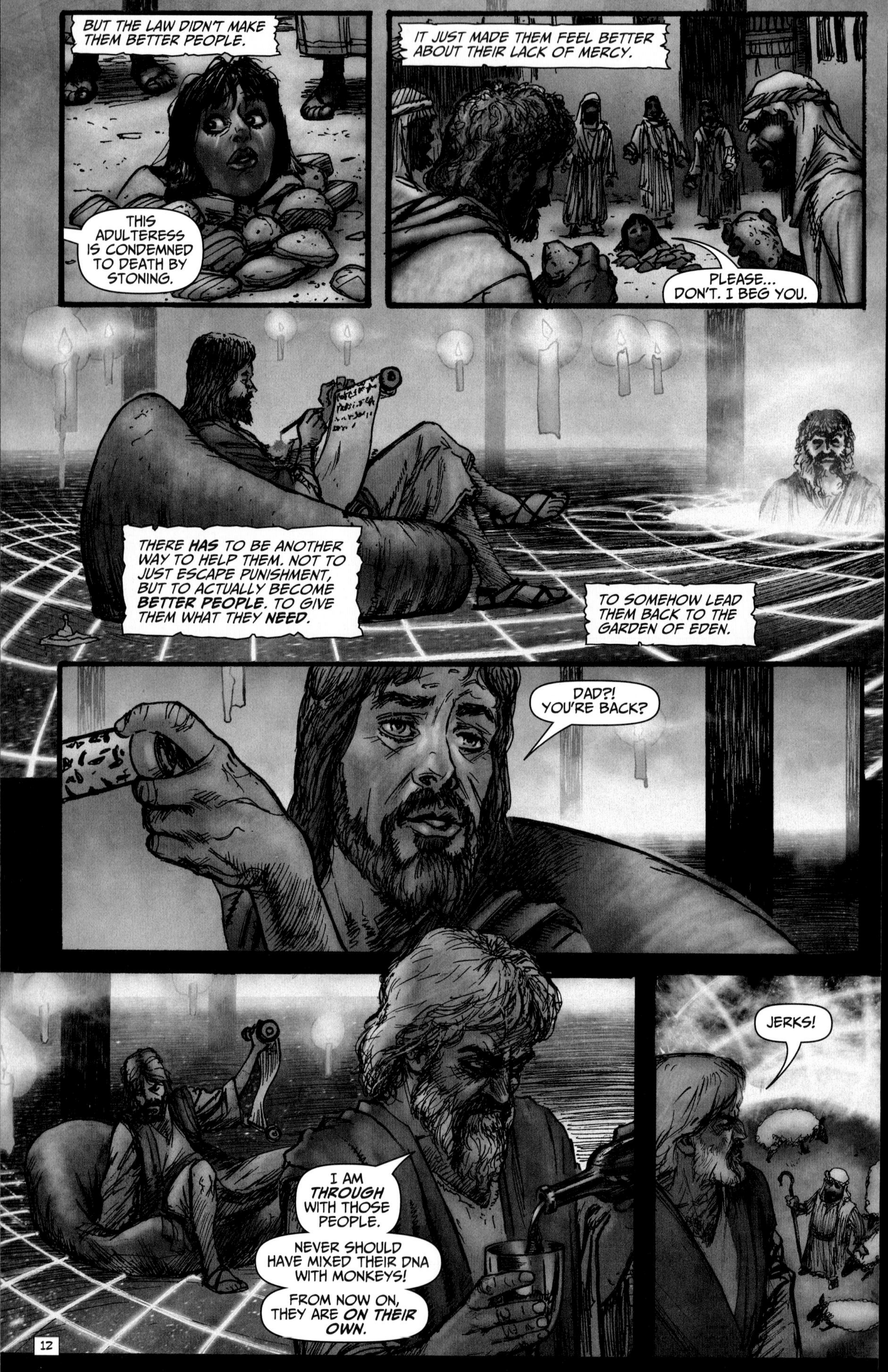
BUT THE LAW DIDN'T MAKE THEM BETTER PEOPLE.
THIS ADULTERESS IS CONDEMNED TO DEATH BY STONING.
IT JUST MADE THEM FEEL BETTER ABOUT THEIR LACK OF MERCY.
PLEASE... DON'T. I BEG YOU.
THERE HAS TO BE ANOTHER WAY TO HELP THEM. NOT TO JUST ESCAPE PUNISHMENT, BUT TO ACTUALLY BECOME BETTER PEOPLE. TO GIVE THEM WHAT THEY NEED.
TO SOMEHOW LEAD THEM BACK TO THE GARDEN OF EDEN.
DAD?! YOU'RE BACK?
I AM THROUGH WITH THOSE PEOPLE.
NEVER SHOULD HAVE MIXED THEIR DNA WITH MONKEYS!
FROM NOW ON, THEY ARE ON THEIR OWN.
JERKS!

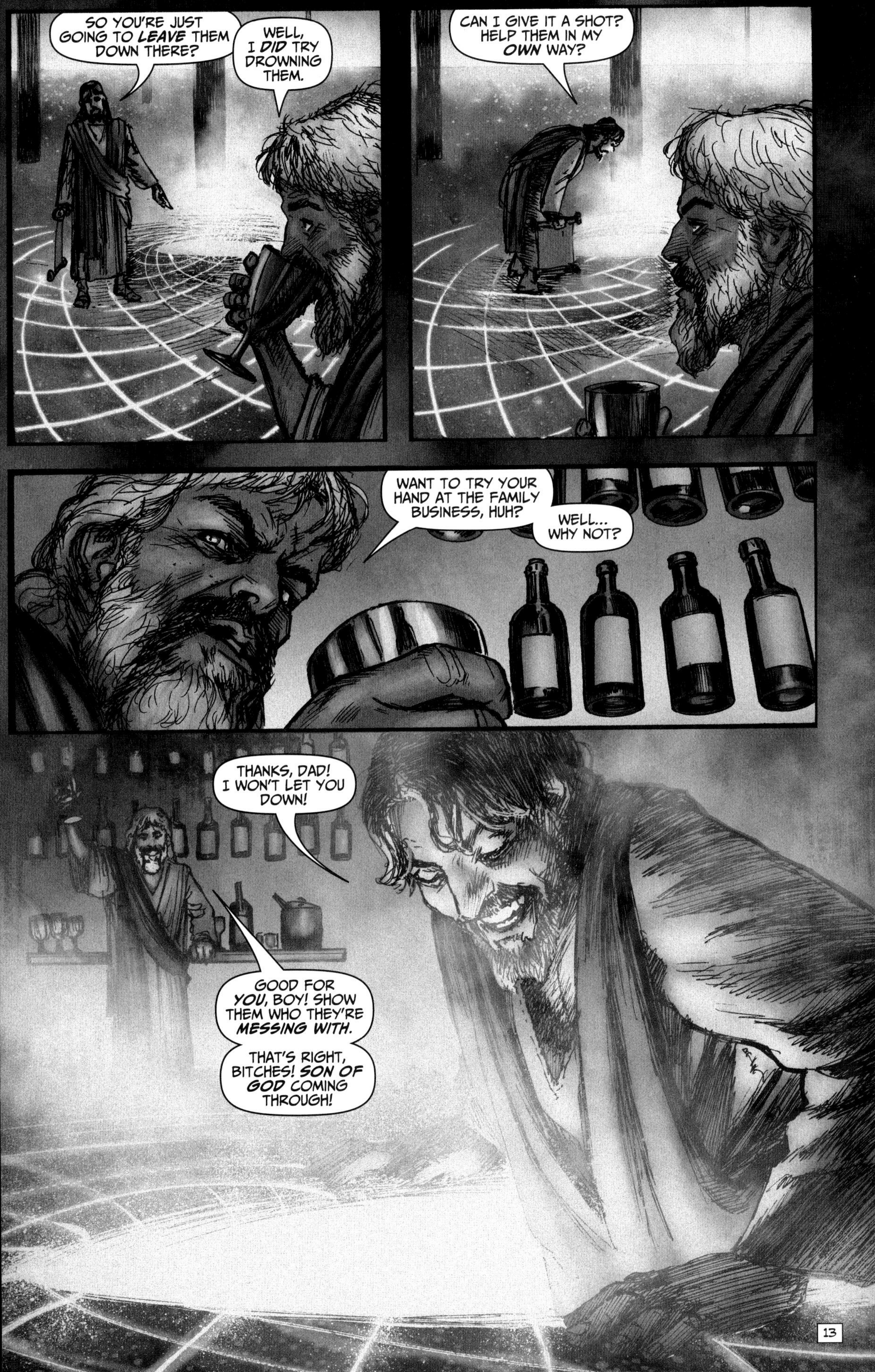
SO YOU'RE JUST GOING TO LEAVE THEM DOWN THERE?
WELL, I DID TRY DROWNING THEM.
CAN I GIVE IT A SHOT? HELP THEM IN MY OWN WAY?
WANT TO TRY YOUR HAND AT THE FAMILY BUSINESS, HUH?
WELL... WHY NOT?
THANKS, DAD! I WON'T LET YOU DOWN!
GOOD FOR YOU, BOY! SHOW THEM WHO THEY'RE MESSING WITH.
THAT'S RIGHT, BITCHES! SON OF GOD COMING THROUGH!

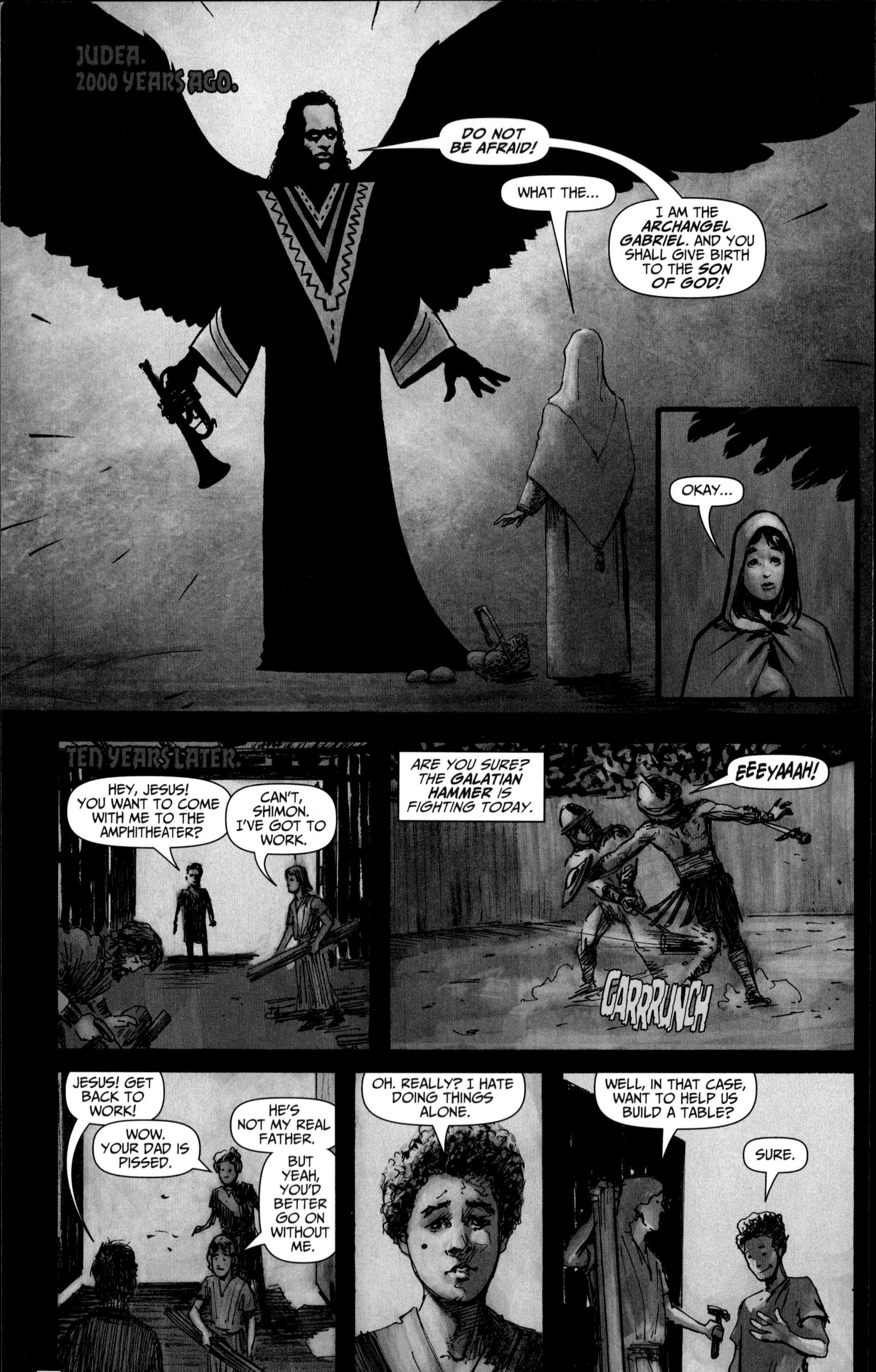
JUDEA.
2000 YEARS AGO.
DO NOT BE AFRAID!
WHAT THE...
I AM THE ARCHANGEL GABRIEL. AND YOU SHALL GIVE BIRTH TO THE SON OF GOD!
OKAY...
TEN YEARS LATER.
HEY, JESUS! YOU WANT TO COME WITH ME TO THE AMPHITHEATER?
CAN'T, SHIMON. I'VE GOT TO WORK.
ARE YOU SURE? THE GALATIAN HAMMER IS FIGHTING TODAY.
EEEYAAAH!
GARRRUNCH
JESUS! GET BACK TO WORK!
WOW. YOUR DAD IS PISSED.
HE'S NOT MY REAL FATHER.
BUT YEAH, YOU'D BETTER GO ON WITHOUT ME.
OH. REALLY? I HATE DOING THINGS ALONE.
WELL, IN THAT CASE, WANT TO HELP US BUILD A TABLE?
SURE.

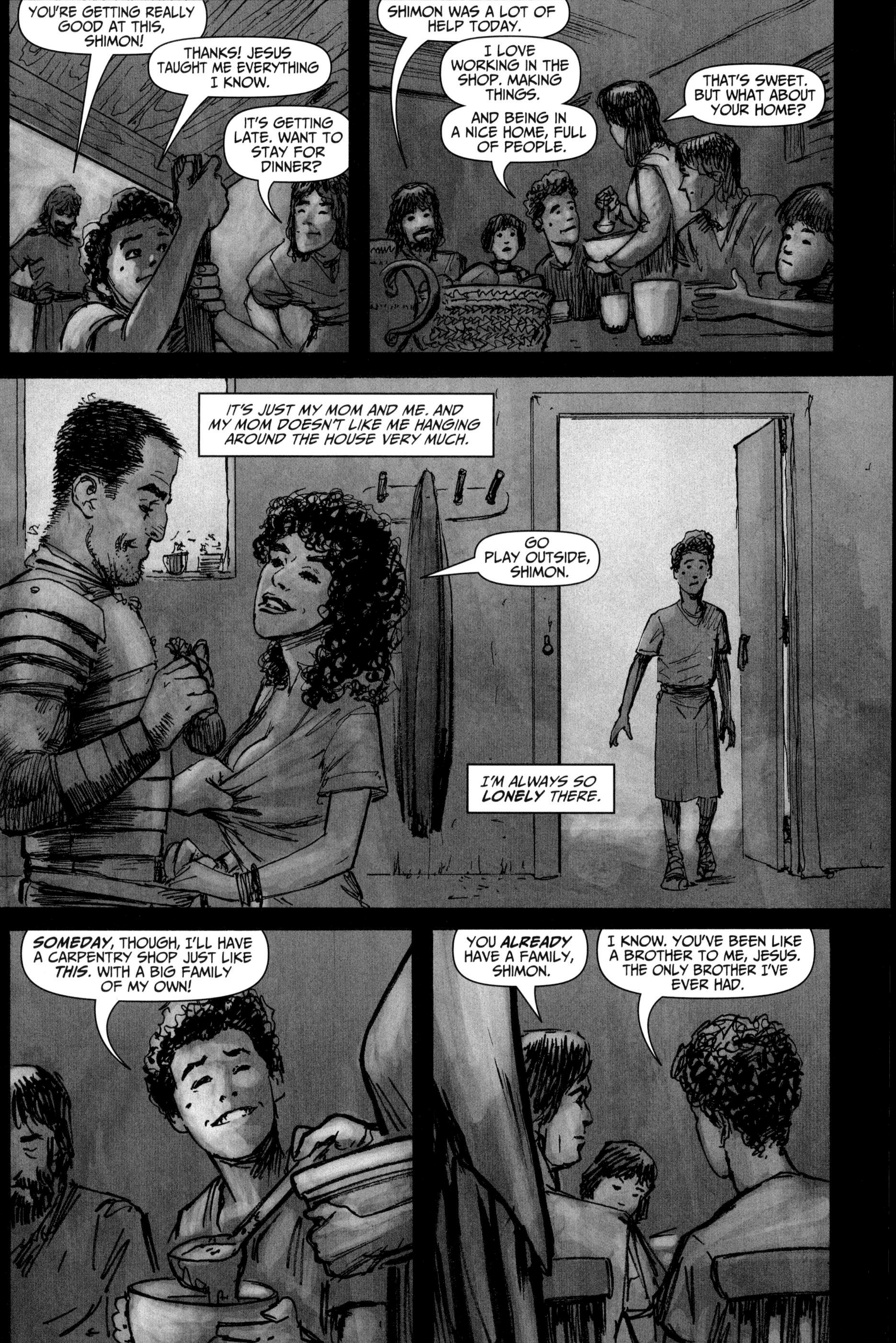
YOU'RE GETTING REALLY GOOD AT THIS, SHIMON!
THANKS! JESUS TAUGHT ME EVERYTHING I KNOW.
IT'S GETTING LATE. WANT TO STAY FOR DINNER?
SHIMON WAS A LOT OF HELP TODAY.
I LOVE WORKING IN THE SHOP. MAKING THINGS.
AND BEING IN A NICE HOME, FULL OF PEOPLE.
THAT'S SWEET. BUT WHAT ABOUT YOUR HOME?
IT'S JUST MY MOM AND ME. AND MY MOM DOESN'T LIKE ME HANGING AROUND THE HOUSE VERY MUCH.
GO PLAY OUTSIDE, SHIMON.
I'M ALWAYS SO ***LONELY*** *THERE.*
SOMEDAY, THOUGH, I'LL HAVE A CARPENTRY SHOP JUST LIKE ***THIS***. WITH A BIG FAMILY OF MY OWN!
YOU ***ALREADY*** HAVE A FAMILY, SHIMON.
I KNOW. YOU'VE BEEN LIKE A BROTHER TO ME, JESUS. THE ONLY BROTHER I'VE EVER HAD.

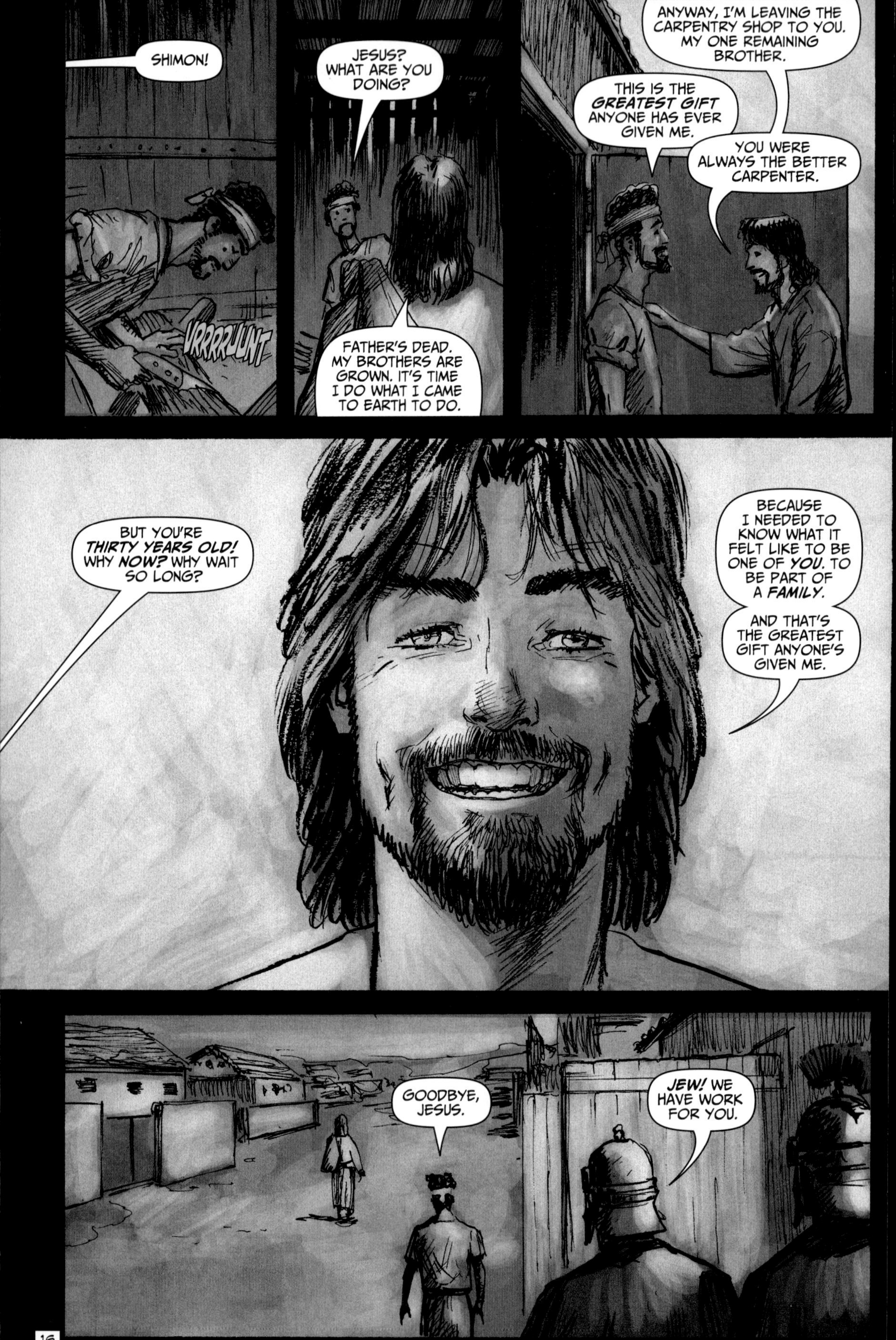
SHIMON!
VRRRRUNT
JESUS? WHAT ARE YOU DOING?
FATHER'S DEAD. MY BROTHERS ARE GROWN. IT'S TIME I DO WHAT I CAME TO EARTH TO DO.
ANYWAY, I'M LEAVING THE CARPENTRY SHOP TO YOU. MY ONE REMAINING BROTHER.
THIS IS THE *GREATEST GIFT* ANYONE HAS EVER GIVEN ME.
YOU WERE ALWAYS THE BETTER CARPENTER.
BUT YOU'RE *THIRTY YEARS OLD!* WHY *NOW?* WHY WAIT SO LONG?
BECAUSE I NEEDED TO KNOW WHAT IT FELT LIKE TO BE ONE OF *YOU*. TO BE PART OF A *FAMILY*.
AND THAT'S THE GREATEST GIFT ANYONE'S GIVEN ME.
GOODBYE, JESUS.
JEW! WE HAVE WORK FOR YOU.

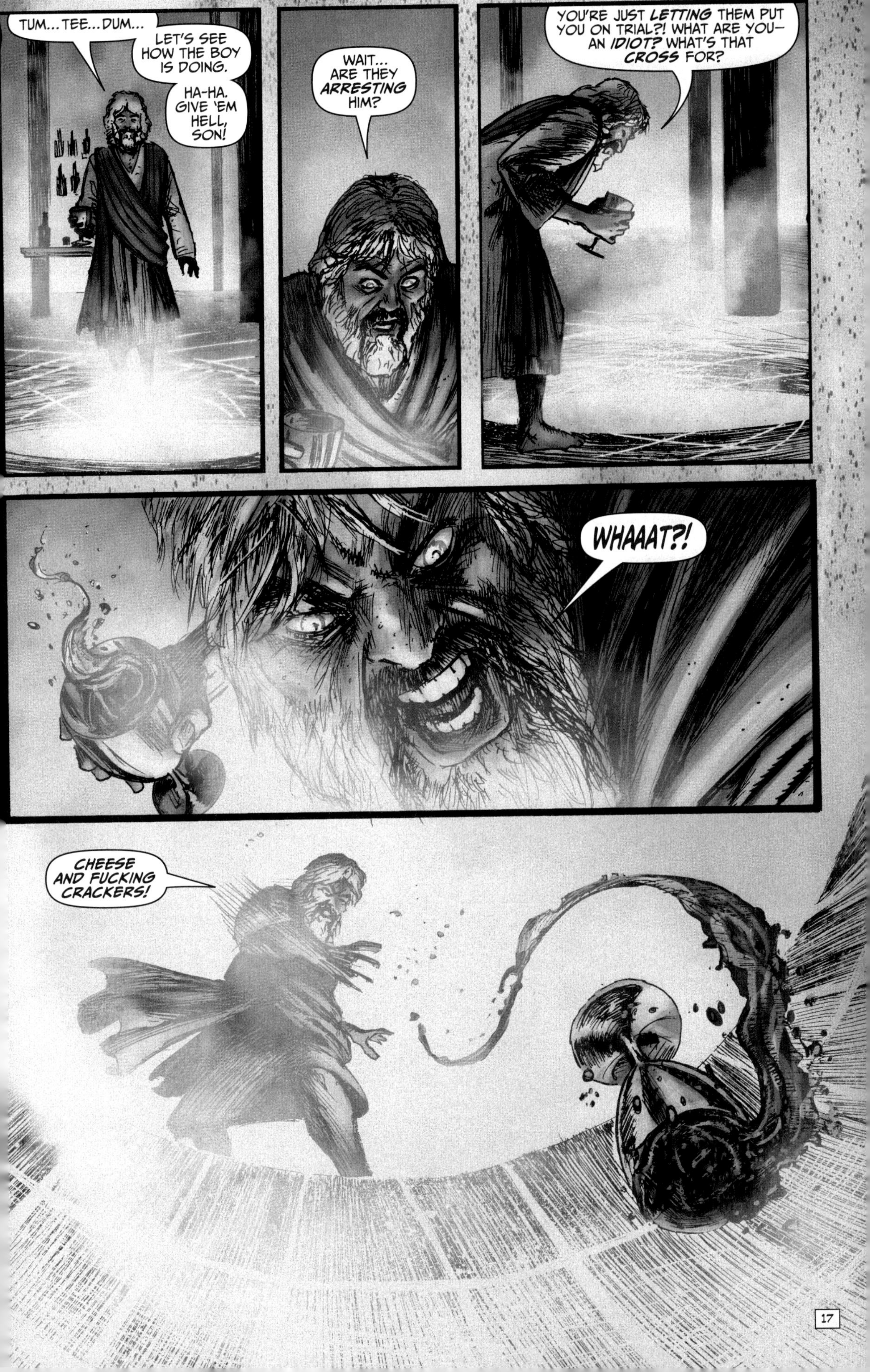
TUM...TEE...DUM...
LET'S SEE HOW THE BOY IS DOING.
HA-HA. GIVE 'EM HELL, SON!
WAIT... ARE THEY ARRESTING HIM?
YOU'RE JUST LETTING THEM PUT YOU ON TRIAL?! WHAT ARE YOU— AN IDIOT? WHAT'S THAT CROSS FOR?
WHAAAT?!
CHEESE AND FUCKING CRACKERS!

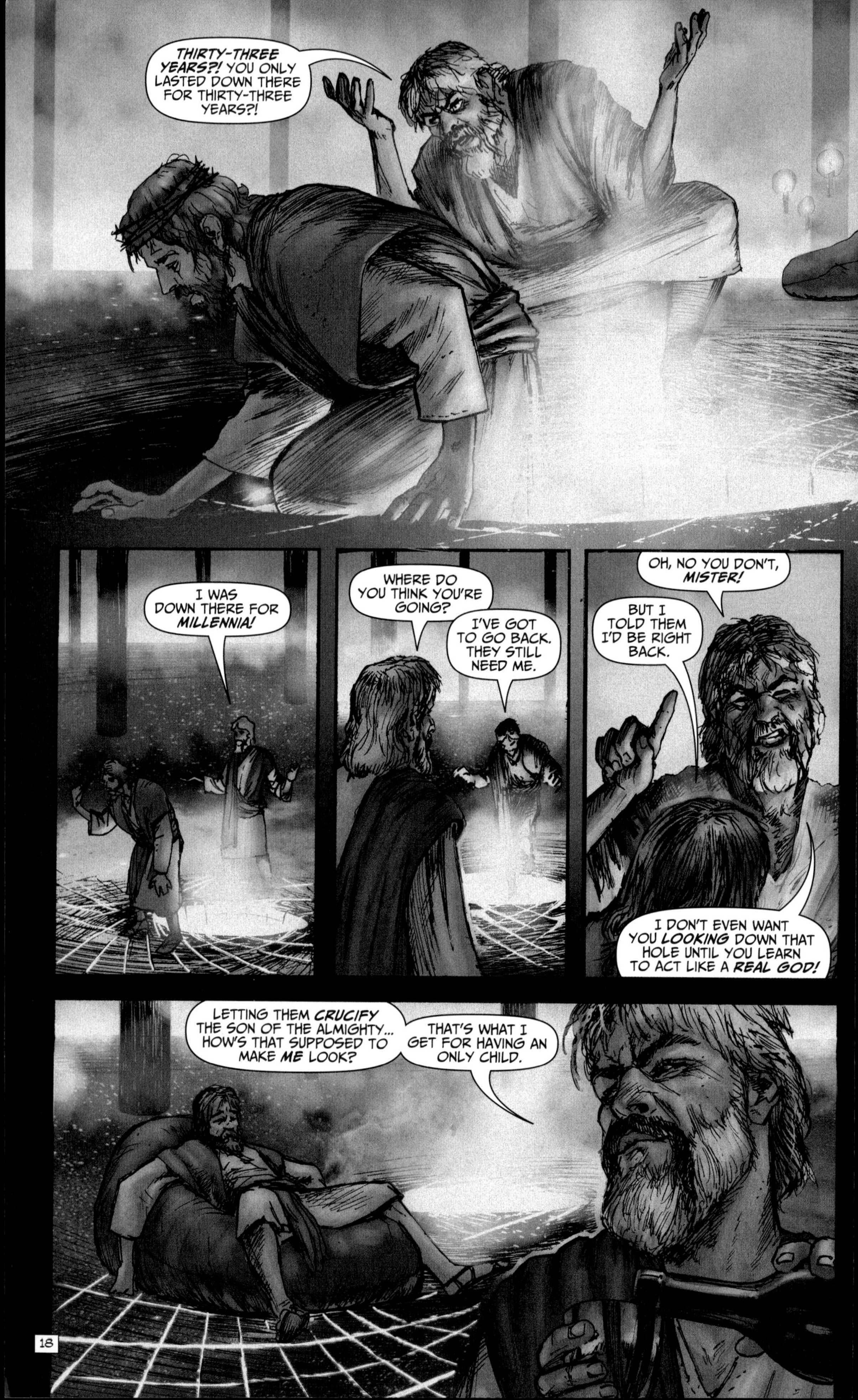
THIRTY-THREE YEARS?! YOU ONLY LASTED DOWN THERE FOR THIRTY-THREE YEARS?!
I WAS DOWN THERE FOR MILLENNIA!
WHERE DO YOU THINK YOU'RE GOING?
I'VE GOT TO GO BACK. THEY STILL NEED ME.
OH, NO YOU DON'T, MISTER!
BUT I TOLD THEM I'D BE RIGHT BACK.
I DON'T EVEN WANT YOU LOOKING DOWN THAT HOLE UNTIL YOU LEARN TO ACT LIKE A REAL GOD!
LETTING THEM CRUCIFY THE SON OF THE ALMIGHTY... HOW'S THAT SUPPOSED TO MAKE ME LOOK?
THAT'S WHAT I GET FOR HAVING AN ONLY CHILD.

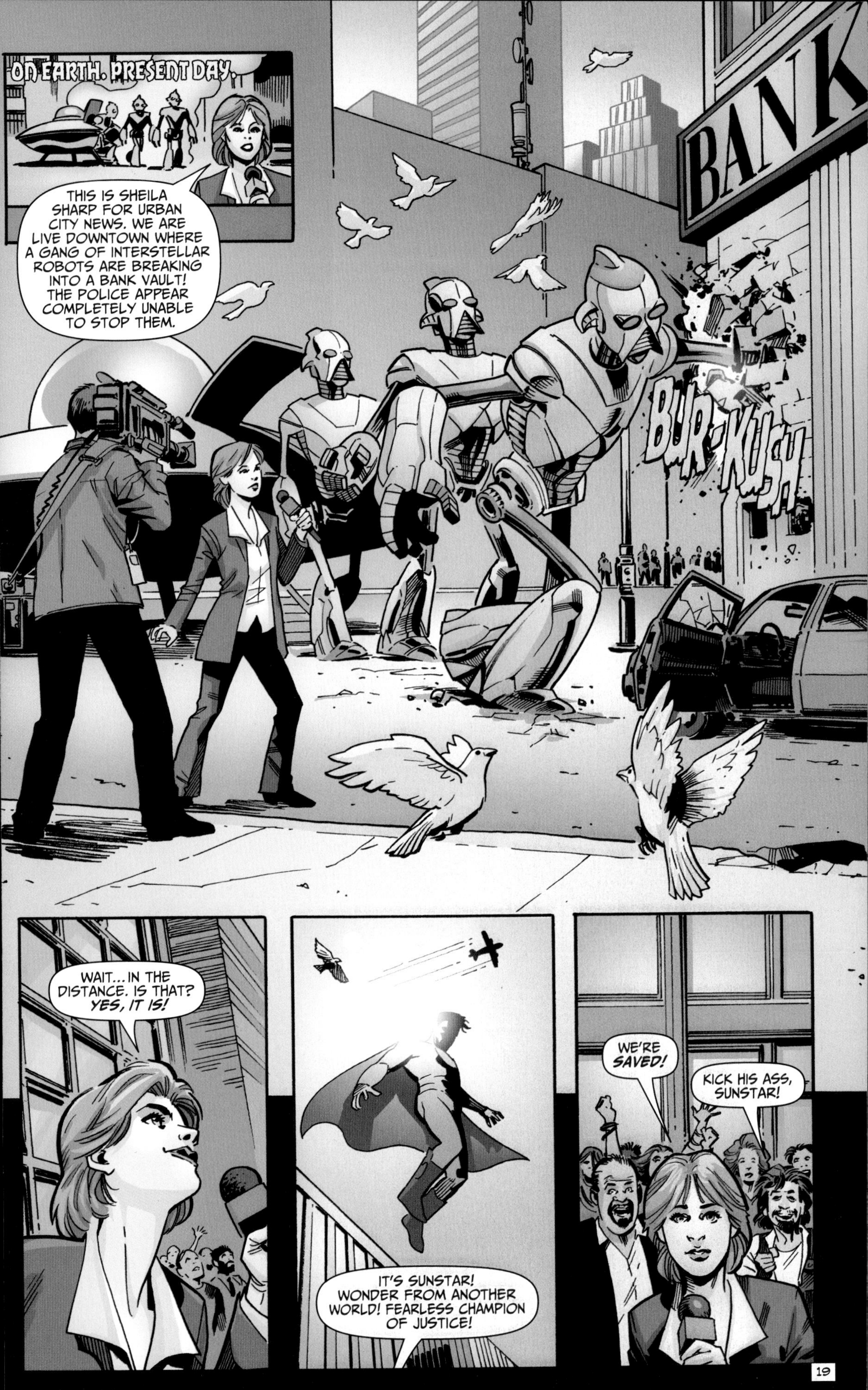
ON EARTH. PRESENT DAY.
THIS IS SHEILA SHARP FOR URBAN CITY NEWS. WE ARE LIVE DOWNTOWN WHERE A GANG OF INTERSTELLAR ROBOTS ARE BREAKING INTO A BANK VAULT! THE POLICE APPEAR COMPLETELY UNABLE TO STOP THEM.
BANK
BUR-KUSH
WAIT... IN THE DISTANCE. IS THAT? YES, IT IS!
IT'S SUNSTAR! WONDER FROM ANOTHER WORLD! FEARLESS CHAMPION OF JUSTICE!
WE'RE SAVED!
KICK HIS ASS, SUNSTAR!

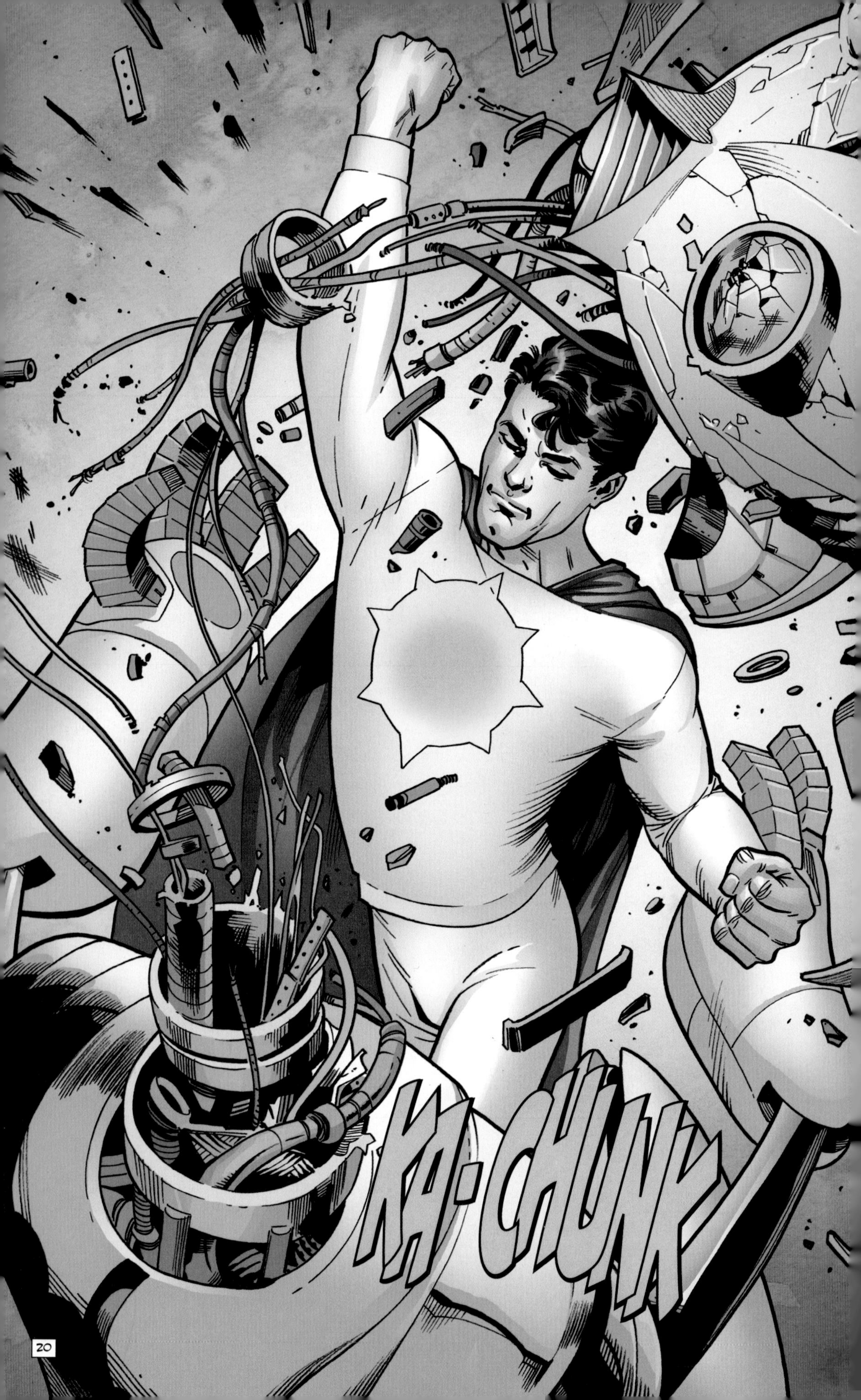
KA-CHUNK

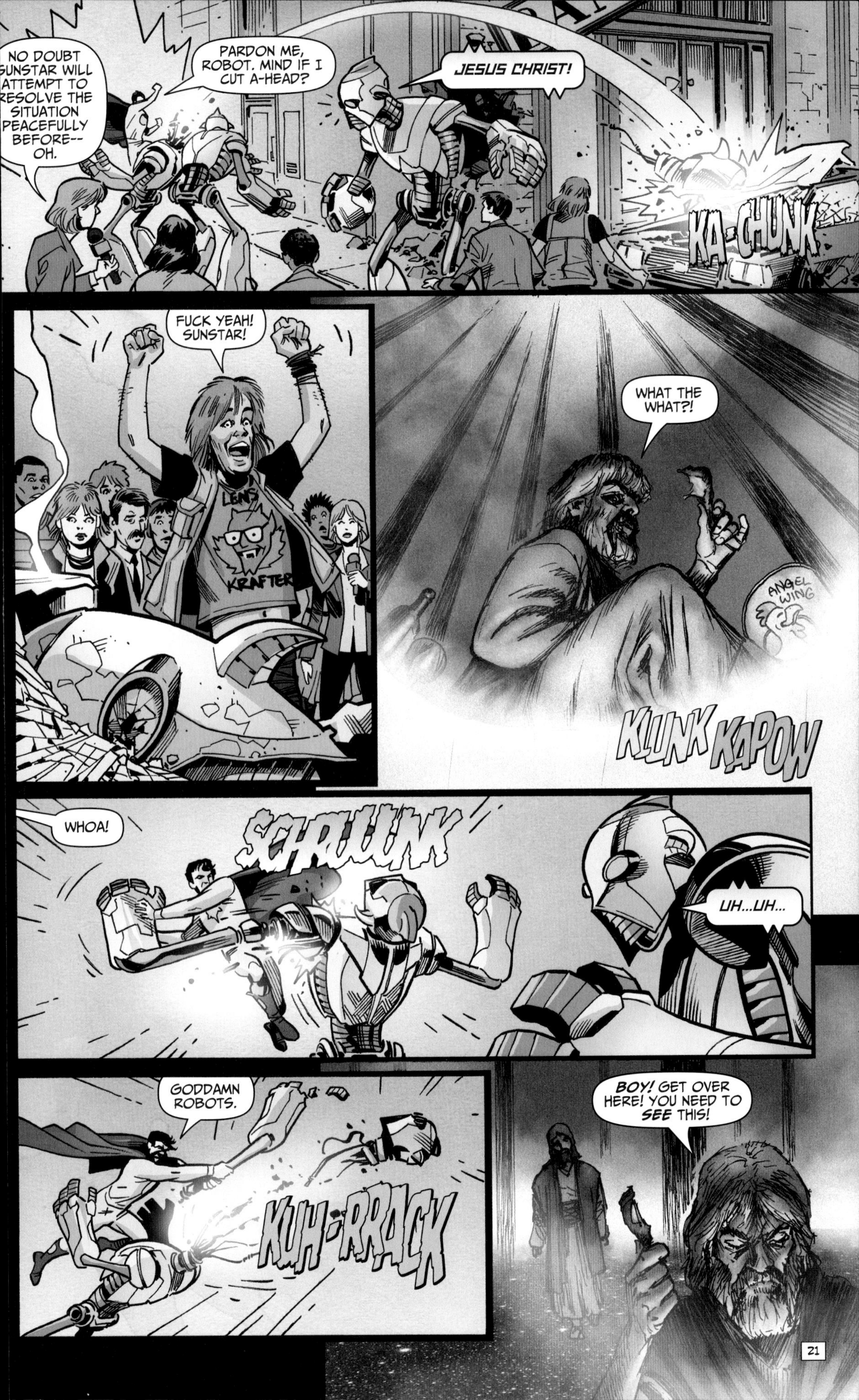
NO DOUBT SUNSTAR WILL ATTEMPT TO RESOLVE THE SITUATION PEACEFULLY BEFORE-- OH.
PARDON ME, ROBOT. MIND IF I CUT A-HEAD?
JESUS CHRIST!
KA-CHUNK
FUCK YEAH! SUNSTAR!
LENS KRAFTER
WHAT THE WHAT?!
ANGEL WING
KLUNK KAPOW
WHOA!
SCHLUUNK
UH...UH...
GODDAMN ROBOTS.
KUH-RRACK
BOY! GET OVER HERE! YOU NEED TO SEE THIS!

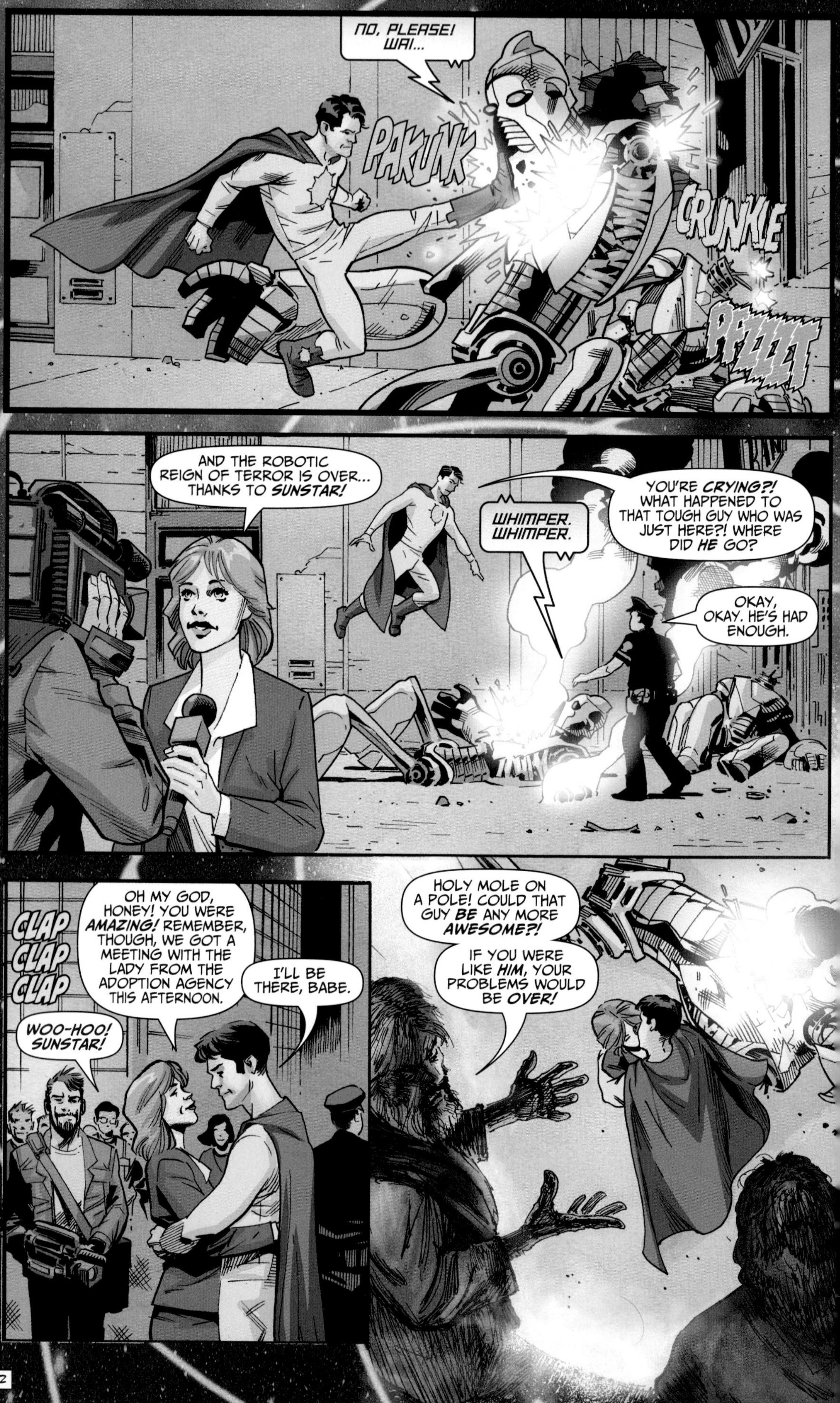

NO, PLEASE! WAI...
PAKUNK
CRUNKLE
PFZZZT
AND THE ROBOTIC REIGN OF TERROR IS OVER... THANKS TO SUNSTAR!
WHIMPER. WHIMPER.
YOU'RE CRYING?! WHAT HAPPENED TO THAT TOUGH GUY WHO WAS JUST HERE?! WHERE DID HE GO?
OKAY, OKAY. HE'S HAD ENOUGH.
CLAP CLAP CLAP
OH MY GOD, HONEY! YOU WERE AMAZING! REMEMBER, THOUGH, WE GOT A MEETING WITH THE LADY FROM THE ADOPTION AGENCY THIS AFTERNOON.
I'LL BE THERE, BABE.
WOO-HOO! SUNSTAR!
HOLY MOLE ON A POLE! COULD THAT GUY BE ANY MORE AWESOME?!
IF YOU WERE LIKE HIM, YOUR PROBLEMS WOULD BE OVER!

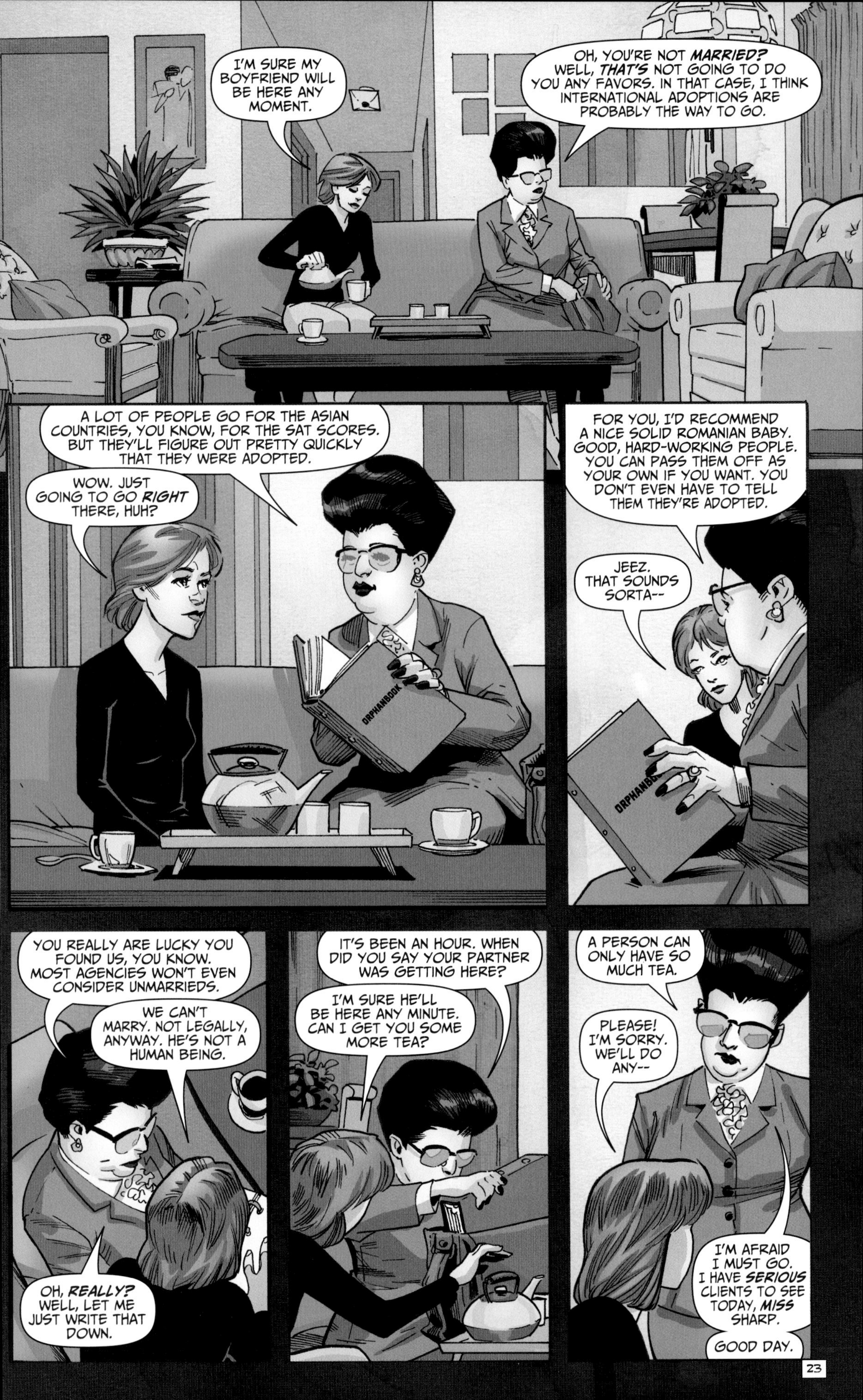
I'M SURE MY BOYFRIEND WILL BE HERE ANY MOMENT.
OH, YOU'RE NOT *MARRIED?* WELL, *THAT'S* NOT GOING TO DO YOU ANY FAVORS. IN THAT CASE, I THINK INTERNATIONAL ADOPTIONS ARE PROBABLY THE WAY TO GO.
A LOT OF PEOPLE GO FOR THE ASIAN COUNTRIES, YOU KNOW, FOR THE SAT SCORES. BUT THEY'LL FIGURE OUT PRETTY QUICKLY THAT THEY WERE ADOPTED.
WOW. JUST GOING TO GO *RIGHT* THERE, HUH?
ORPHANBOOK
FOR YOU, I'D RECOMMEND A NICE SOLID ROMANIAN BABY. GOOD, HARD-WORKING PEOPLE. YOU CAN PASS THEM OFF AS YOUR OWN IF YOU WANT. YOU DON'T EVEN HAVE TO TELL THEM THEY'RE ADOPTED.
JEEZ. THAT SOUNDS SORTA--
YOU REALLY ARE LUCKY YOU FOUND US, YOU KNOW. MOST AGENCIES WON'T EVEN CONSIDER UNMARRIEDS.
WE CAN'T MARRY. NOT LEGALLY, ANYWAY. HE'S NOT A HUMAN BEING.
OH, *REALLY?* WELL, LET ME JUST WRITE THAT DOWN.
IT'S BEEN AN HOUR. WHEN DID YOU SAY YOUR PARTNER WAS GETTING HERE?
I'M SURE HE'LL BE HERE ANY MINUTE. CAN I GET YOU SOME MORE TEA?
A PERSON CAN ONLY HAVE SO MUCH TEA.
PLEASE! I'M SORRY. WE'LL DO ANY--
I'M AFRAID I MUST GO. I HAVE *SERIOUS* CLIENTS TO SEE TODAY, *MISS* SHARP.
GOOD DAY.

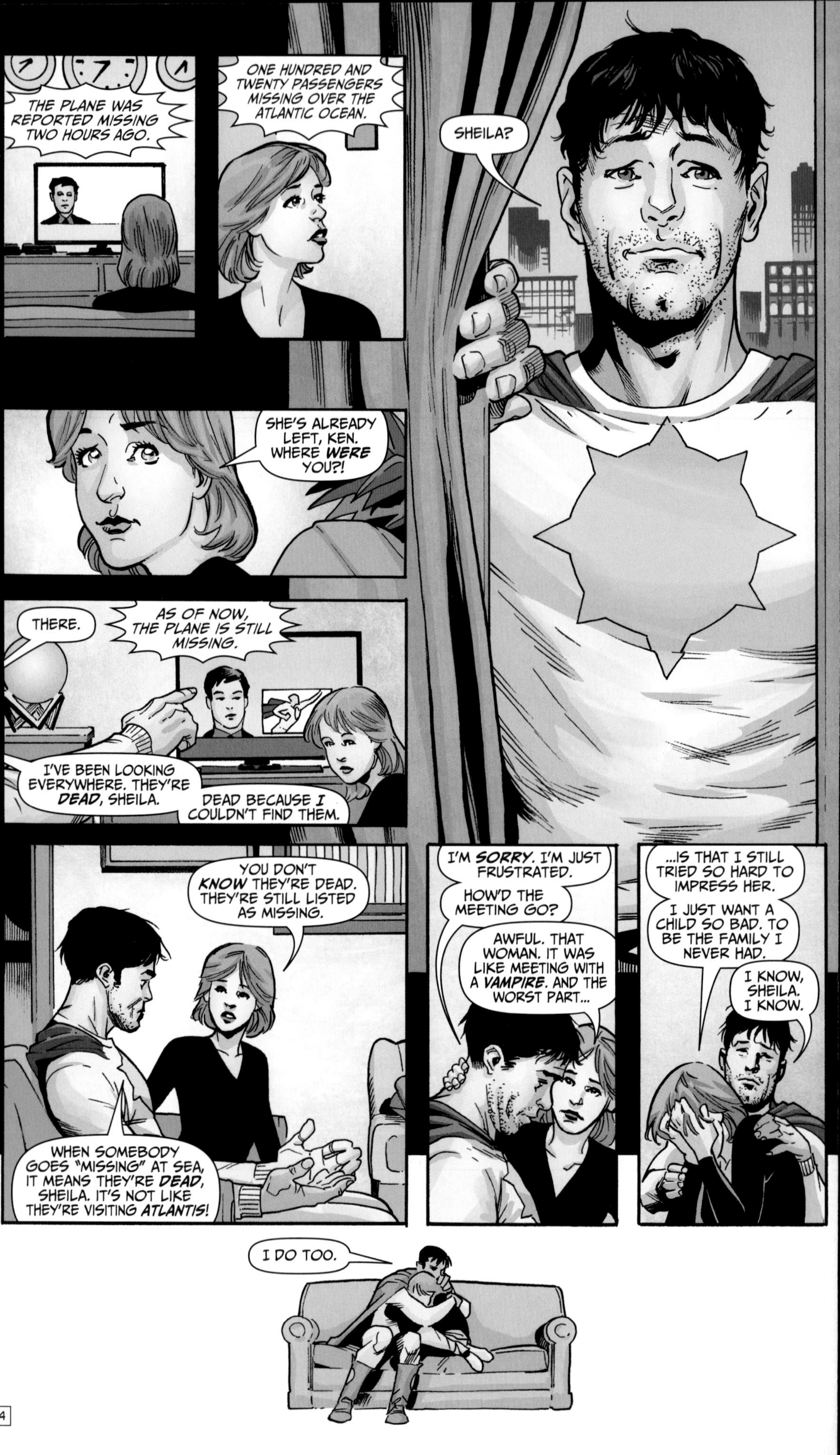
THE PLANE WAS REPORTED MISSING TWO HOURS AGO.
ONE HUNDRED AND TWENTY PASSENGERS MISSING OVER THE ATLANTIC OCEAN.
SHEILA?
SHE'S ALREADY LEFT, KEN. WHERE WERE YOU?!
THERE.
AS OF NOW, THE PLANE IS STILL MISSING.
I'VE BEEN LOOKING EVERYWHERE. THEY'RE DEAD, SHEILA.
DEAD BECAUSE I COULDN'T FIND THEM.
YOU DON'T KNOW THEY'RE DEAD. THEY'RE STILL LISTED AS MISSING.
WHEN SOMEBODY GOES "MISSING" AT SEA, IT MEANS THEY'RE DEAD, SHEILA. IT'S NOT LIKE THEY'RE VISITING ATLANTIS!
I'M SORRY. I'M JUST FRUSTRATED.
HOW'D THE MEETING GO?
AWFUL. THAT WOMAN. IT WAS LIKE MEETING WITH A VAMPIRE. AND THE WORST PART...
...IS THAT I STILL TRIED SO HARD TO IMPRESS HER.
I JUST WANT A CHILD SO BAD. TO BE THE FAMILY I NEVER HAD.
I KNOW, SHEILA. I KNOW.
I DO TOO.

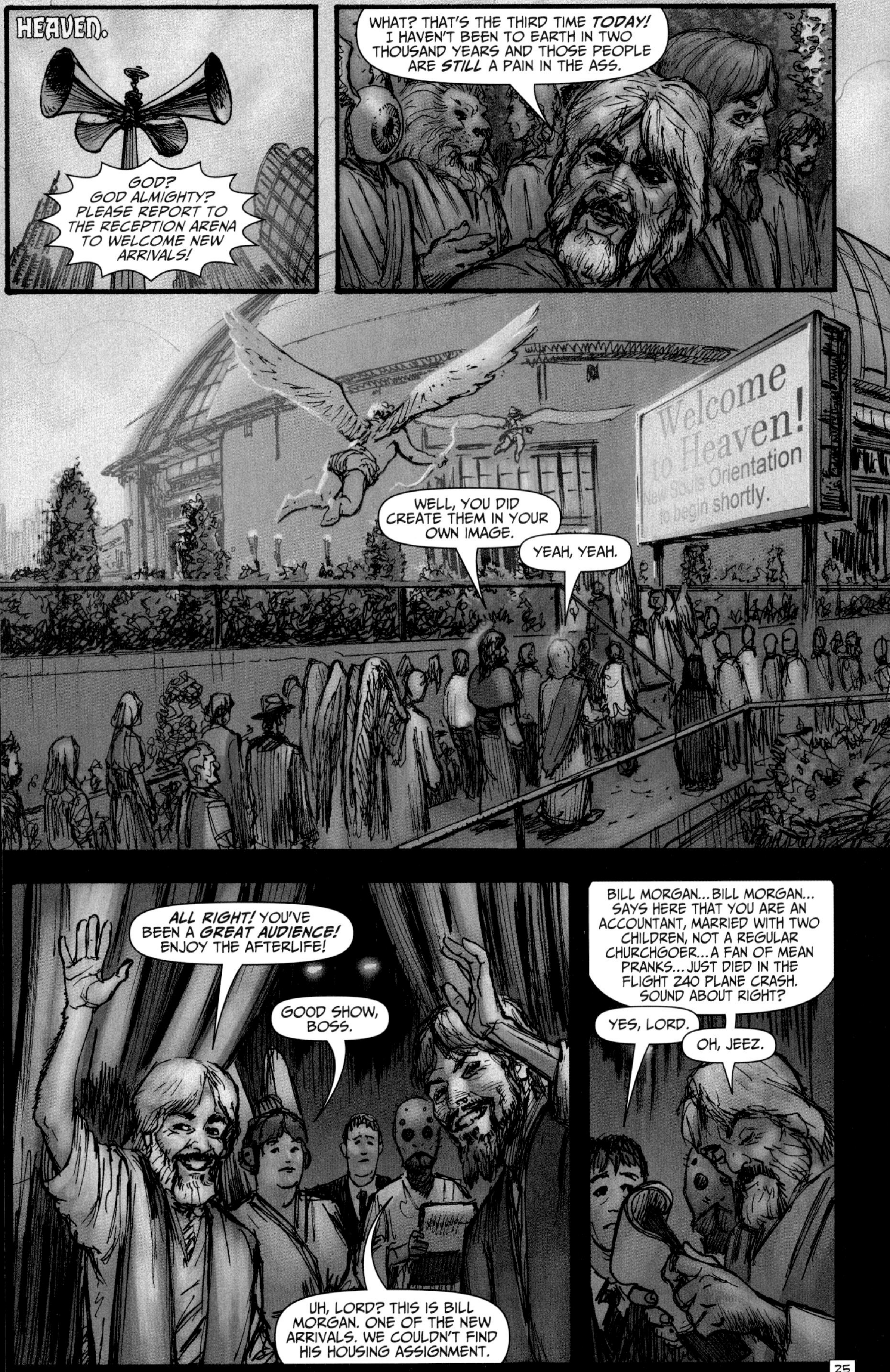
HEAVEN.
GOD? GOD ALMIGHTY? PLEASE REPORT TO THE RECEPTION ARENA TO WELCOME NEW ARRIVALS!
WHAT? THAT'S THE THIRD TIME TODAY! I HAVEN'T BEEN TO EARTH IN TWO THOUSAND YEARS AND THOSE PEOPLE ARE STILL A PAIN IN THE ASS.
Welcome to Heaven! New Souls Orientation to begin shortly.
WELL, YOU DID CREATE THEM IN YOUR OWN IMAGE.
YEAH, YEAH.
ALL RIGHT! YOU'VE BEEN A GREAT AUDIENCE! ENJOY THE AFTERLIFE!
GOOD SHOW, BOSS.
UH, LORD? THIS IS BILL MORGAN. ONE OF THE NEW ARRIVALS. WE COULDN'T FIND HIS HOUSING ASSIGNMENT.
BILL MORGAN... BILL MORGAN... SAYS HERE THAT YOU ARE AN ACCOUNTANT, MARRIED WITH TWO CHILDREN, NOT A REGULAR CHURCHGOER... A FAN OF MEAN PRANKS... JUST DIED IN THE FLIGHT 240 PLANE CRASH. SOUND ABOUT RIGHT?
YES, LORD.
OH, JEEZ.

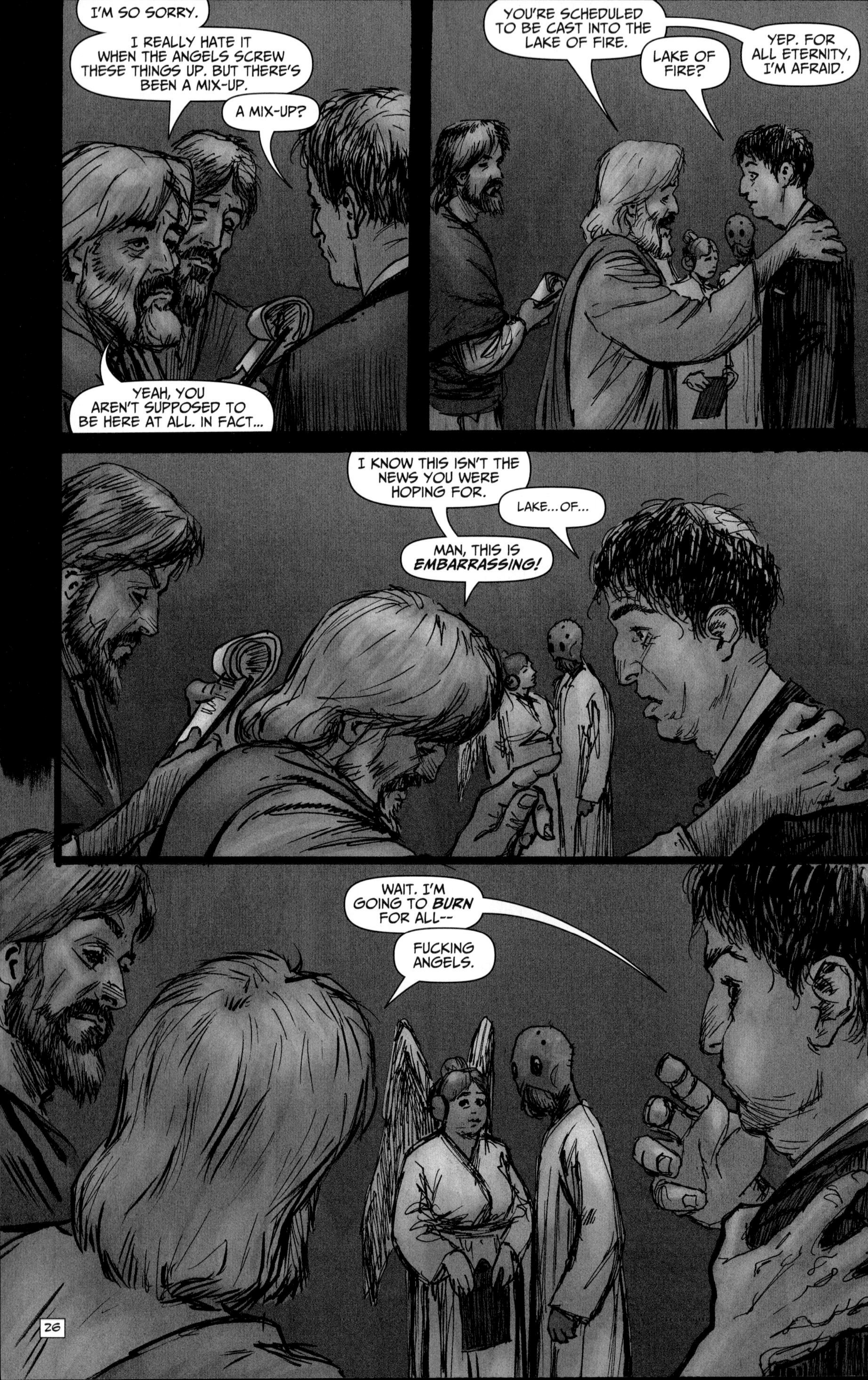
I'M SO SORRY.
I REALLY HATE IT WHEN THE ANGELS SCREW THESE THINGS UP. BUT THERE'S BEEN A MIX-UP.
A MIX-UP?
YEAH, YOU AREN'T SUPPOSED TO BE HERE AT ALL. IN FACT...
YOU'RE SCHEDULED TO BE CAST INTO THE LAKE OF FIRE.
LAKE OF FIRE?
YEP. FOR ALL ETERNITY, I'M AFRAID.
I KNOW THIS ISN'T THE NEWS YOU WERE HOPING FOR.
LAKE... OF...
MAN, THIS IS *EMBARRASSING!*
WAIT. I'M GOING TO *BURN* FOR ALL--
FUCKING ANGELS.

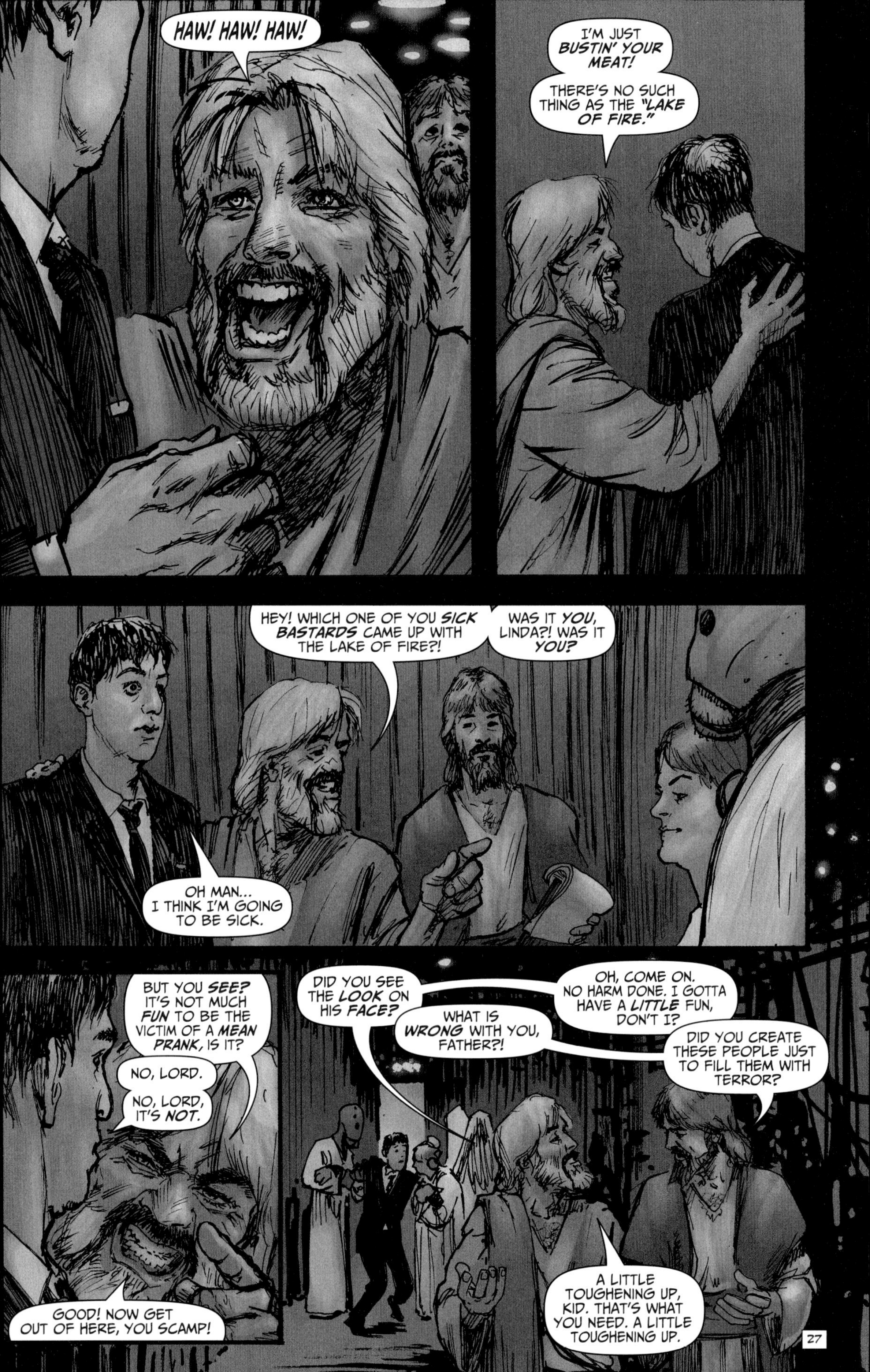
HAW! HAW! HAW!
I'M JUST BUSTIN' YOUR MEAT!
THERE'S NO SUCH THING AS THE "LAKE OF FIRE."
HEY! WHICH ONE OF YOU SICK BASTARDS CAME UP WITH THE LAKE OF FIRE?!
WAS IT YOU, LINDA?! WAS IT YOU?
OH MAN... I THINK I'M GOING TO BE SICK.
BUT YOU SEE? IT'S NOT MUCH FUN TO BE THE VICTIM OF A MEAN PRANK, IS IT?
NO, LORD.
NO, LORD, IT'S NOT.
GOOD! NOW GET OUT OF HERE, YOU SCAMP!
DID YOU SEE THE LOOK ON HIS FACE?
WHAT IS WRONG WITH YOU, FATHER?!
OH, COME ON. NO HARM DONE. I GOTTA HAVE A LITTLE FUN, DON'T I?
DID YOU CREATE THESE PEOPLE JUST TO FILL THEM WITH TERROR?
A LITTLE TOUGHENING UP, KID. THAT'S WHAT YOU NEED. A LITTLE TOUGHENING UP.

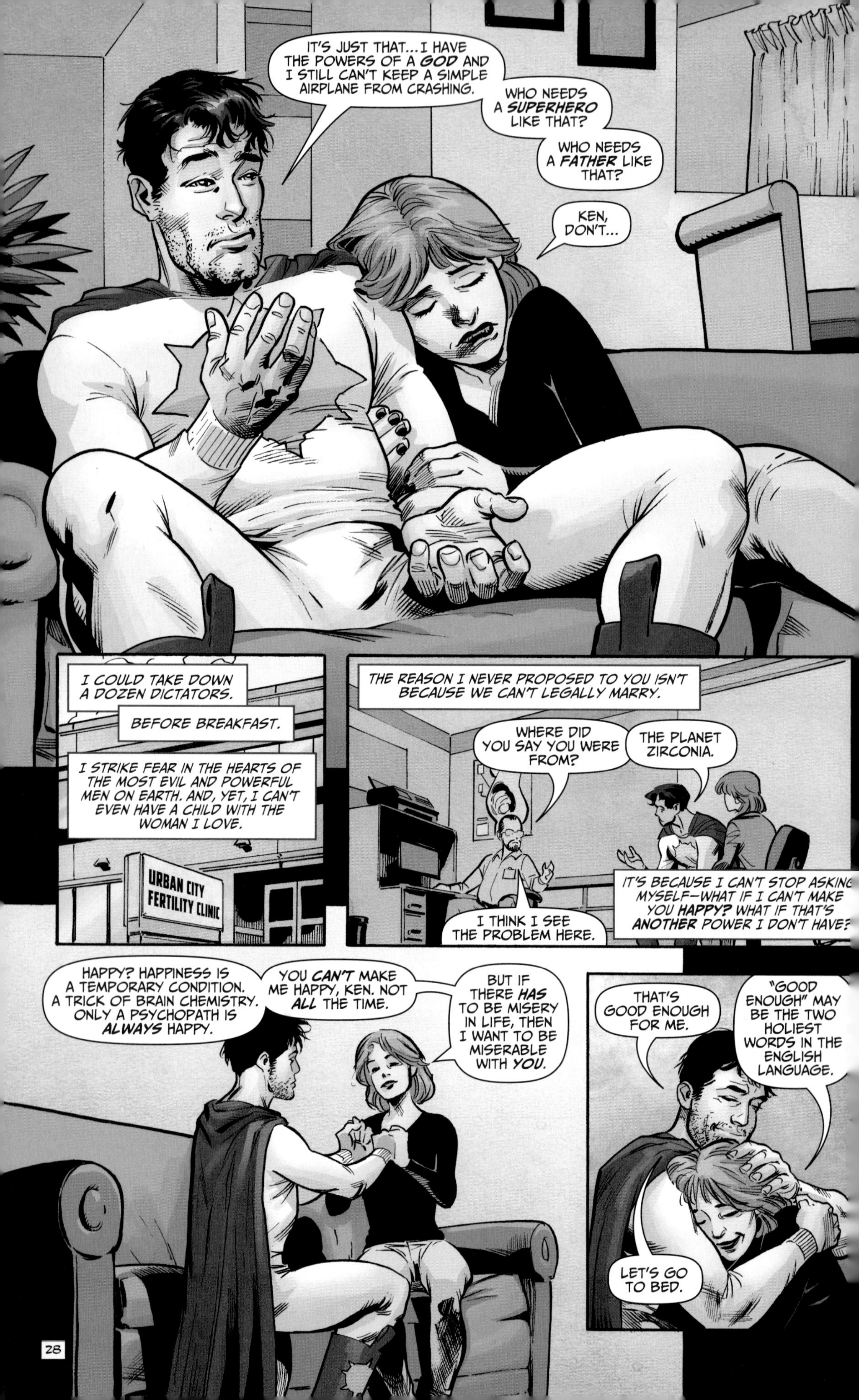

IT'S JUST THAT... I HAVE THE POWERS OF A GOD AND I STILL CAN'T KEEP A SIMPLE AIRPLANE FROM CRASHING.
WHO NEEDS A SUPERHERO LIKE THAT?
WHO NEEDS A FATHER LIKE THAT?
KEN, DON'T...
I COULD TAKE DOWN A DOZEN DICTATORS.
BEFORE BREAKFAST.
I STRIKE FEAR IN THE HEARTS OF THE MOST EVIL AND POWERFUL MEN ON EARTH. AND, YET, I CAN'T EVEN HAVE A CHILD WITH THE WOMAN I LOVE.
URBAN CITY FERTILITY CLINIC
THE REASON I NEVER PROPOSED TO YOU ISN'T BECAUSE WE CAN'T LEGALLY MARRY.
WHERE DID YOU SAY YOU WERE FROM?
THE PLANET ZIRCONIA.
I THINK I SEE THE PROBLEM HERE.
IT'S BECAUSE I CAN'T STOP ASKING MYSELF—WHAT IF I CAN'T MAKE YOU HAPPY? WHAT IF THAT'S ANOTHER POWER I DON'T HAVE?
HAPPY? HAPPINESS IS A TEMPORARY CONDITION. A TRICK OF BRAIN CHEMISTRY. ONLY A PSYCHOPATH IS ALWAYS HAPPY.
YOU CAN'T MAKE ME HAPPY, KEN. NOT ALL THE TIME.
BUT IF THERE HAS TO BE MISERY IN LIFE, THEN I WANT TO BE MISERABLE WITH YOU.
THAT'S GOOD ENOUGH FOR ME.
"GOOD ENOUGH" MAY BE THE TWO HOLIEST WORDS IN THE ENGLISH LANGUAGE.
LET'S GO TO BED.

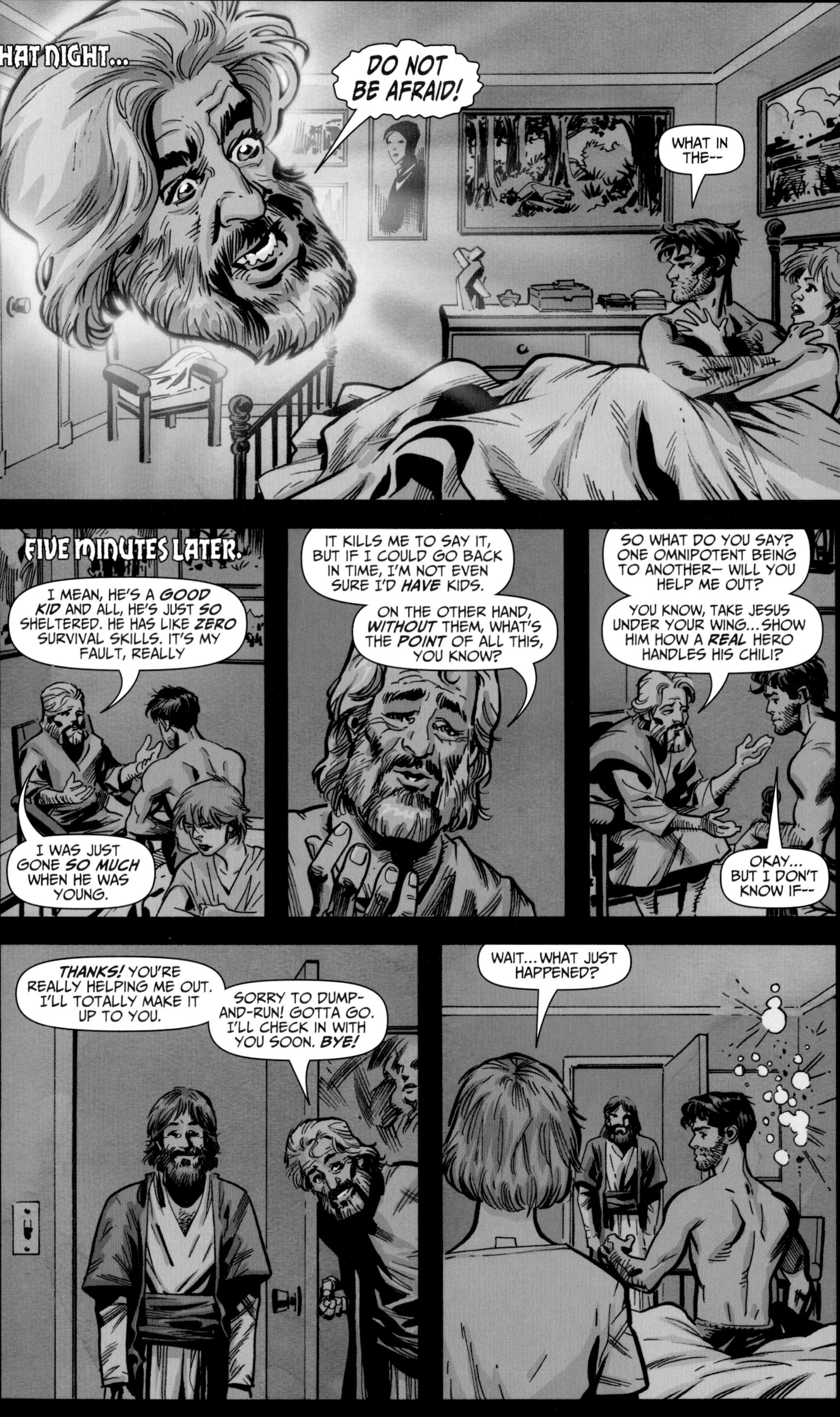

HAT NIGHT...
DO NOT BE AFRAID!
WHAT IN THE--
FIVE MINUTES LATER.
I MEAN, HE'S A GOOD KID AND ALL, HE'S JUST SO SHELTERED. HE HAS LIKE ZERO SURVIVAL SKILLS. IT'S MY FAULT, REALLY
I WAS JUST GONE SO MUCH WHEN HE WAS YOUNG.
IT KILLS ME TO SAY IT, BUT IF I COULD GO BACK IN TIME, I'M NOT EVEN SURE I'D HAVE KIDS.
ON THE OTHER HAND, WITHOUT THEM, WHAT'S THE POINT OF ALL THIS, YOU KNOW?
SO WHAT DO YOU SAY? ONE OMNIPOTENT BEING TO ANOTHER– WILL YOU HELP ME OUT?
YOU KNOW, TAKE JESUS UNDER YOUR WING...SHOW HIM HOW A REAL HERO HANDLES HIS CHILI?
OKAY... BUT I DON'T KNOW IF--
THANKS! YOU'RE REALLY HELPING ME OUT. I'LL TOTALLY MAKE IT UP TO YOU.
SORRY TO DUMP-AND-RUN! GOTTA GO. I'LL CHECK IN WITH YOU SOON. BYE!
WAIT...WHAT JUST HAPPENED?

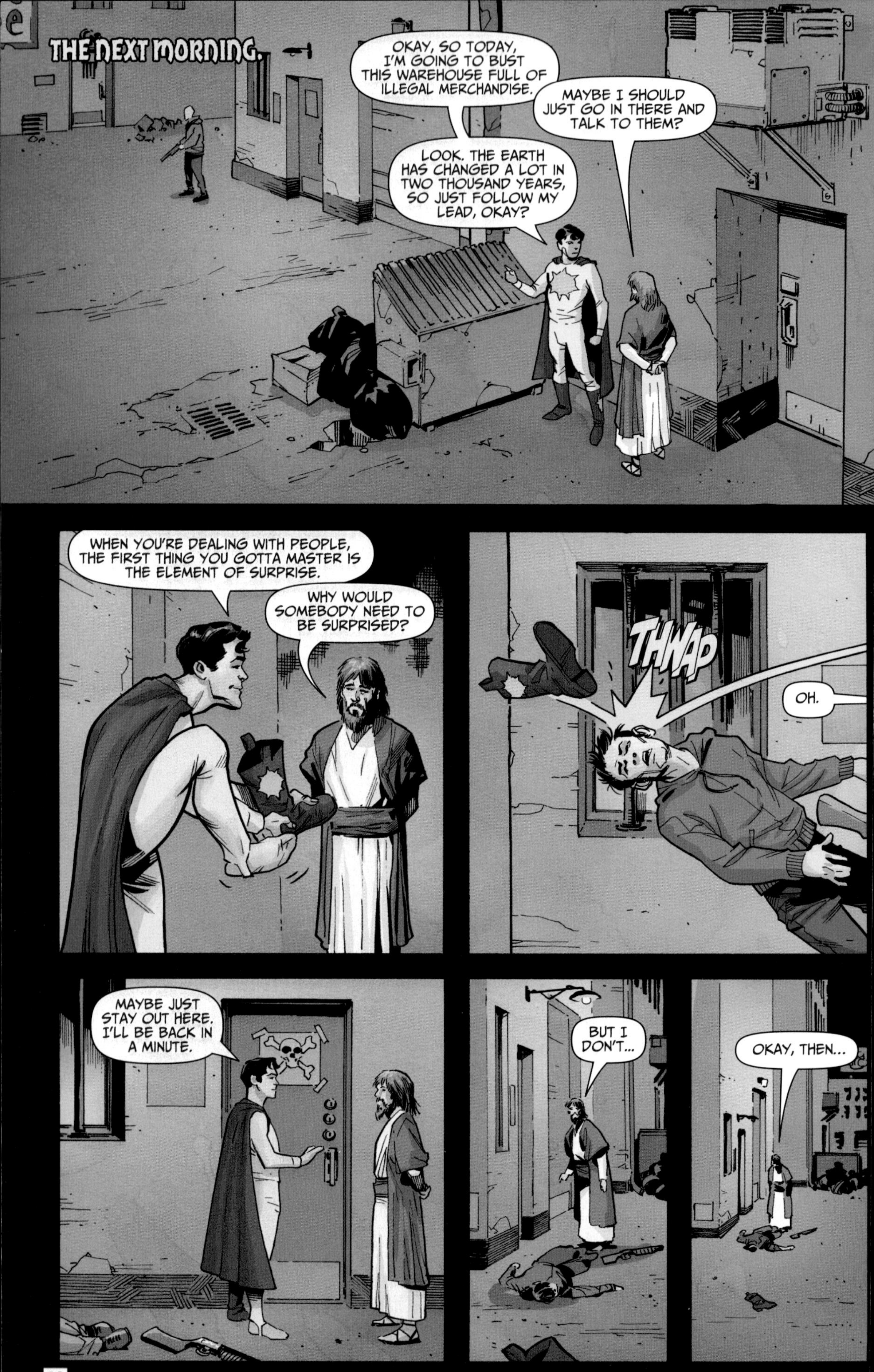
THE NEXT MORNING.
OKAY, SO TODAY, I'M GOING TO BUST THIS WAREHOUSE FULL OF ILLEGAL MERCHANDISE.
LOOK. THE EARTH HAS CHANGED A LOT IN TWO THOUSAND YEARS, SO JUST FOLLOW MY LEAD, OKAY?
MAYBE I SHOULD JUST GO IN THERE AND TALK TO THEM?
WHEN YOU'RE DEALING WITH PEOPLE, THE FIRST THING YOU GOTTA MASTER IS THE ELEMENT OF SURPRISE.
WHY WOULD SOMEBODY NEED TO BE SURPRISED?
THWAP
OH.
MAYBE JUST STAY OUT HERE. I'LL BE BACK IN A MINUTE.
BUT I DON'T...
OKAY, THEN...

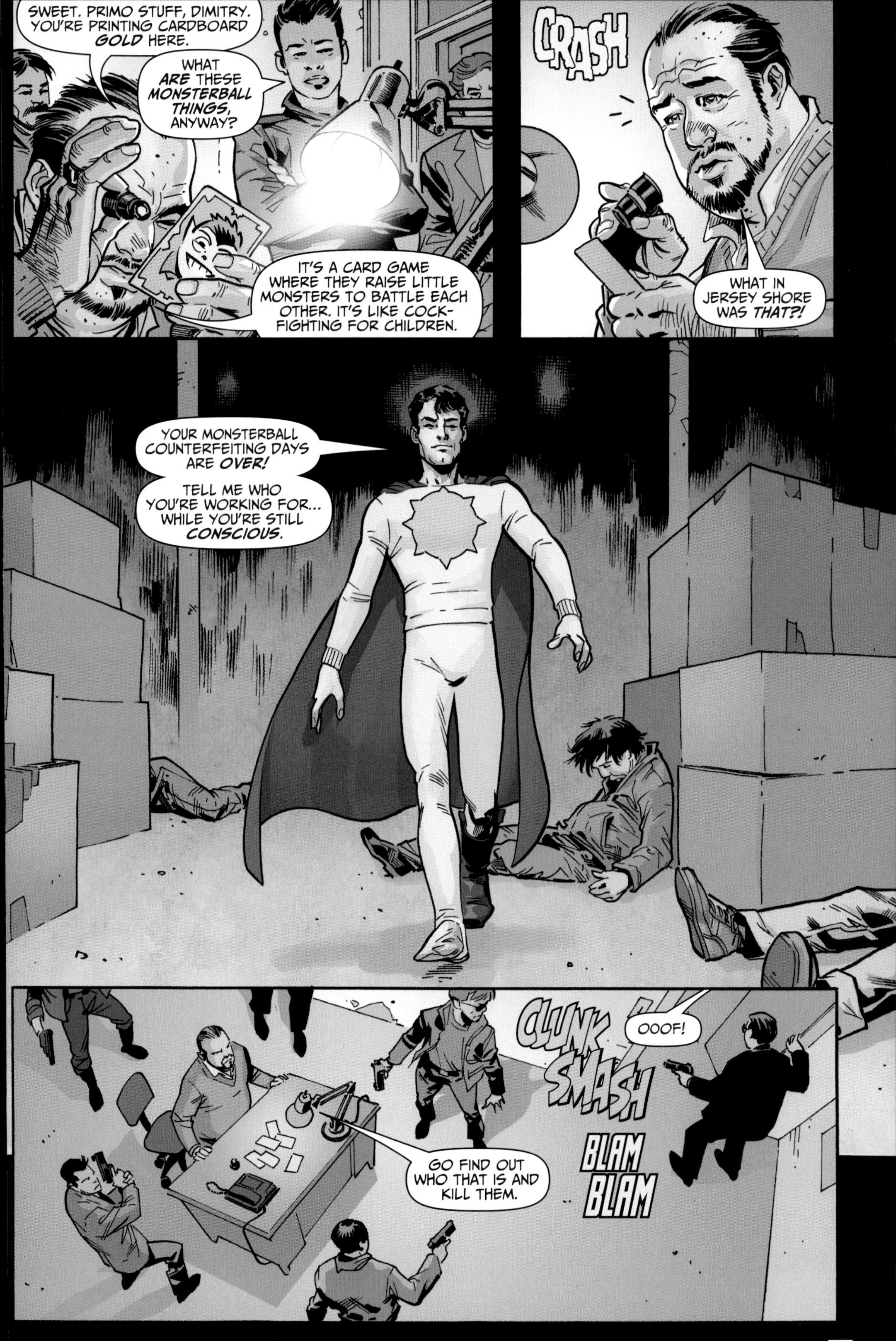
SWEET. PRIMO STUFF, DIMITRY. YOU'RE PRINTING CARDBOARD GOLD HERE.
WHAT ARE THESE MONSTERBALL THINGS, ANYWAY?
IT'S A CARD GAME WHERE THEY RAISE LITTLE MONSTERS TO BATTLE EACH OTHER. IT'S LIKE COCK-FIGHTING FOR CHILDREN.
CRASH
WHAT IN JERSEY SHORE WAS THAT?!
YOUR MONSTERBALL COUNTERFEITING DAYS ARE OVER!
TELL ME WHO YOU'RE WORKING FOR... WHILE YOU'RE STILL CONSCIOUS.
CLUNK
OOOF!
SMASH
BLAM
BLAM
GO FIND OUT WHO THAT IS AND KILL THEM.

SMAAAASH

AAAARGH!

INTELLECTUAL PROPERTY THEFT IS *EVERYBODY'S* PROBLEM!

GO TO HELL!

GET HIM!

BFF

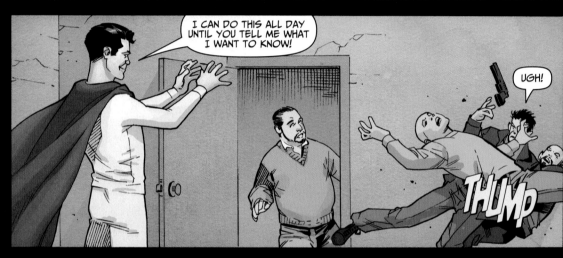

I CAN DO THIS ALL DAY UNTIL YOU TELL ME WHAT I WANT TO KNOW!

UGH!

THUMP

WHUMP CRACK

AYYIIE!

SMAAAASH

AAARGH! MY FACE IS ON FIRE!

HI.

SMASH

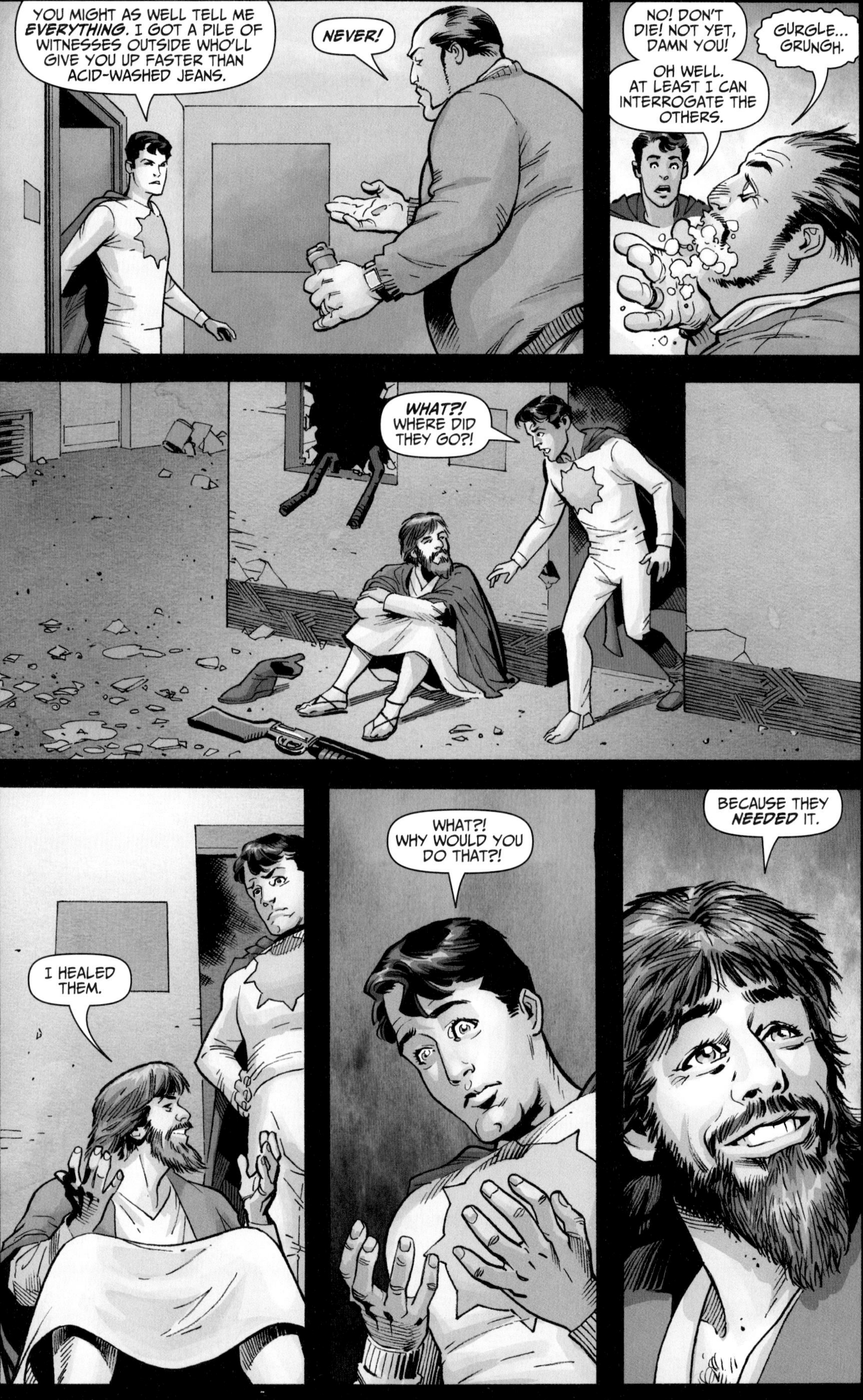
YOU MIGHT AS WELL TELL ME EVERYTHING. I GOT A PILE OF WITNESSES OUTSIDE WHO'LL GIVE YOU UP FASTER THAN ACID-WASHED JEANS.
NEVER!
NO! DON'T DIE! NOT YET, DAMN YOU!
GURGLE... GRUNGH.
OH WELL. AT LEAST I CAN INTERROGATE THE OTHERS.
WHAT?! WHERE DID THEY GO?!
I HEALED THEM.
WHAT?! WHY WOULD YOU DO THAT?!
BECAUSE THEY NEEDED IT.

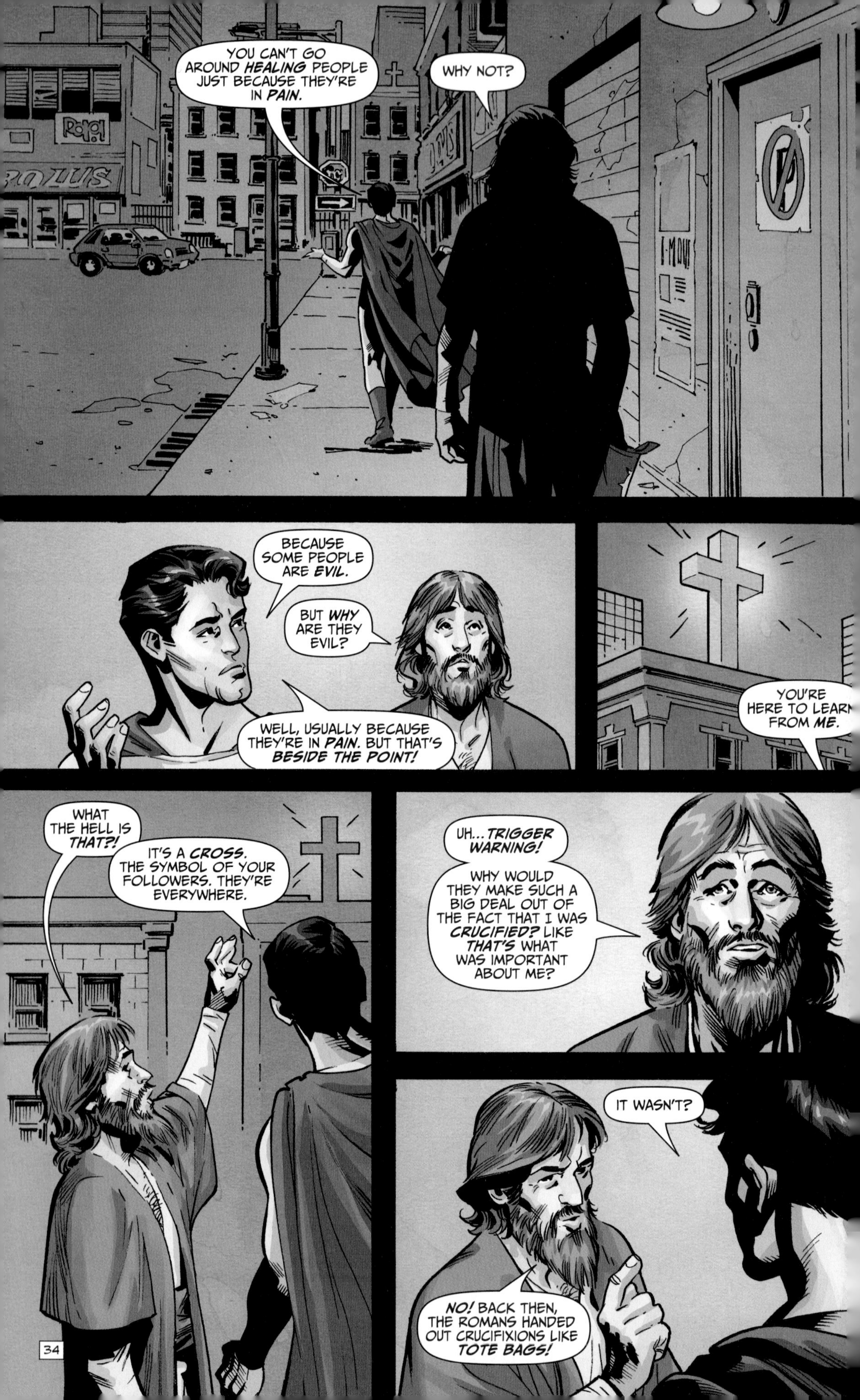
YOU CAN'T GO AROUND HEALING PEOPLE JUST BECAUSE THEY'RE IN PAIN.
WHY NOT?
BECAUSE SOME PEOPLE ARE EVIL.
BUT WHY ARE THEY EVIL?
WELL, USUALLY BECAUSE THEY'RE IN PAIN. BUT THAT'S BESIDE THE POINT!
YOU'RE HERE TO LEARN FROM ME.
WHAT THE HELL IS THAT?!
IT'S A CROSS. THE SYMBOL OF YOUR FOLLOWERS. THEY'RE EVERYWHERE.
UH... TRIGGER WARNING!
WHY WOULD THEY MAKE SUCH A BIG DEAL OUT OF THE FACT THAT I WAS CRUCIFIED? LIKE THAT'S WHAT WAS IMPORTANT ABOUT ME?
IT WASN'T?
NO! BACK THEN, THE ROMANS HANDED OUT CRUCIFIXIONS LIKE TOTE BAGS!

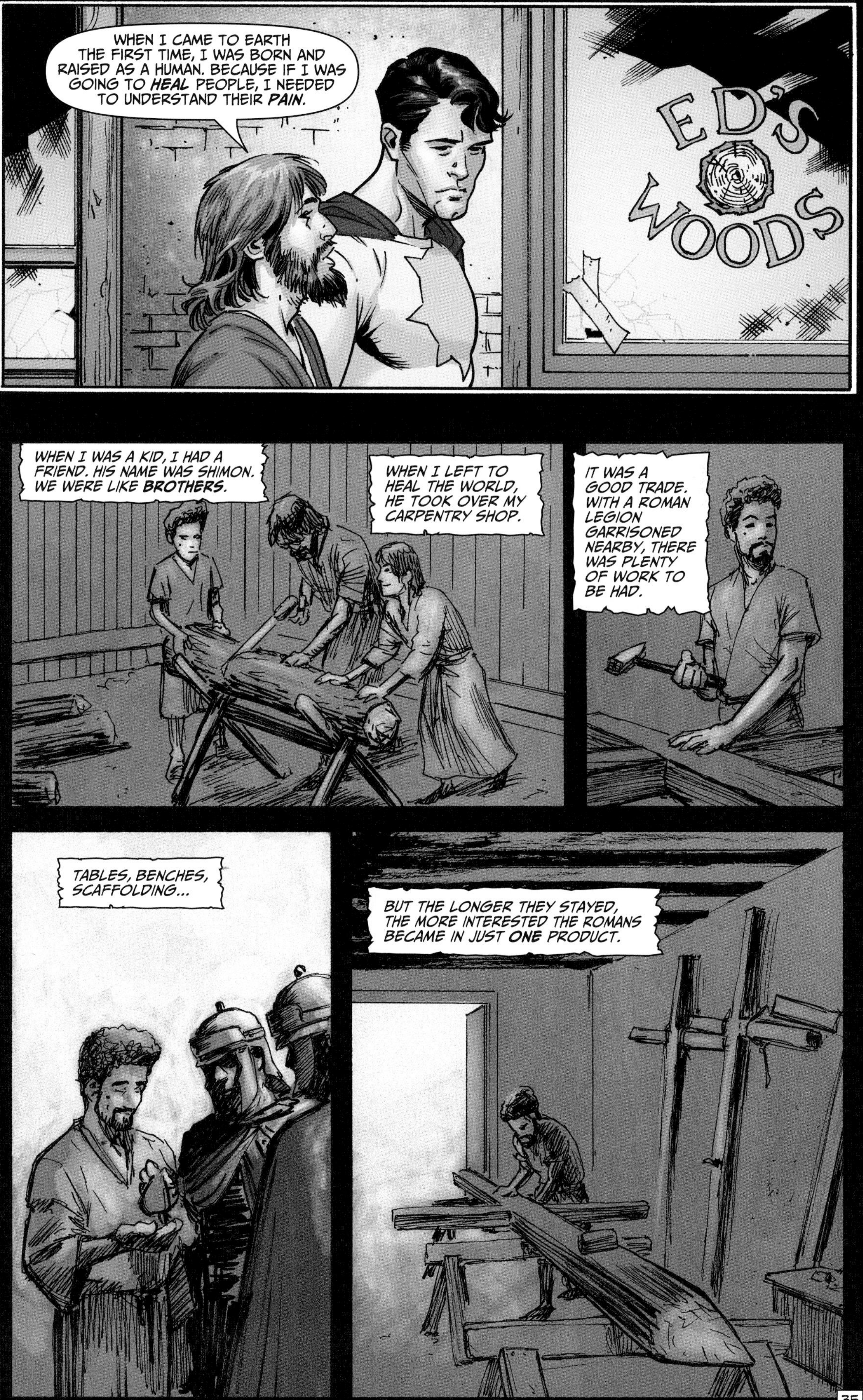

WHEN I CAME TO EARTH THE FIRST TIME, I WAS BORN AND RAISED AS A HUMAN. BECAUSE IF I WAS GOING TO *HEAL* PEOPLE, I NEEDED TO UNDERSTAND THEIR *PAIN.*
ED'S WOODS
WHEN I WAS A KID, I HAD A FRIEND. HIS NAME WAS SHIMON. WE WERE LIKE **BROTHERS.**
WHEN I LEFT TO HEAL THE WORLD, HE TOOK OVER MY CARPENTRY SHOP.
IT WAS A GOOD TRADE. WITH A ROMAN LEGION GARRISONED NEARBY, THERE WAS PLENTY OF WORK TO BE HAD.
TABLES, BENCHES, SCAFFOLDING...
BUT THE LONGER THEY STAYED, THE MORE INTERESTED THE ROMANS BECAME IN JUST **ONE** PRODUCT.

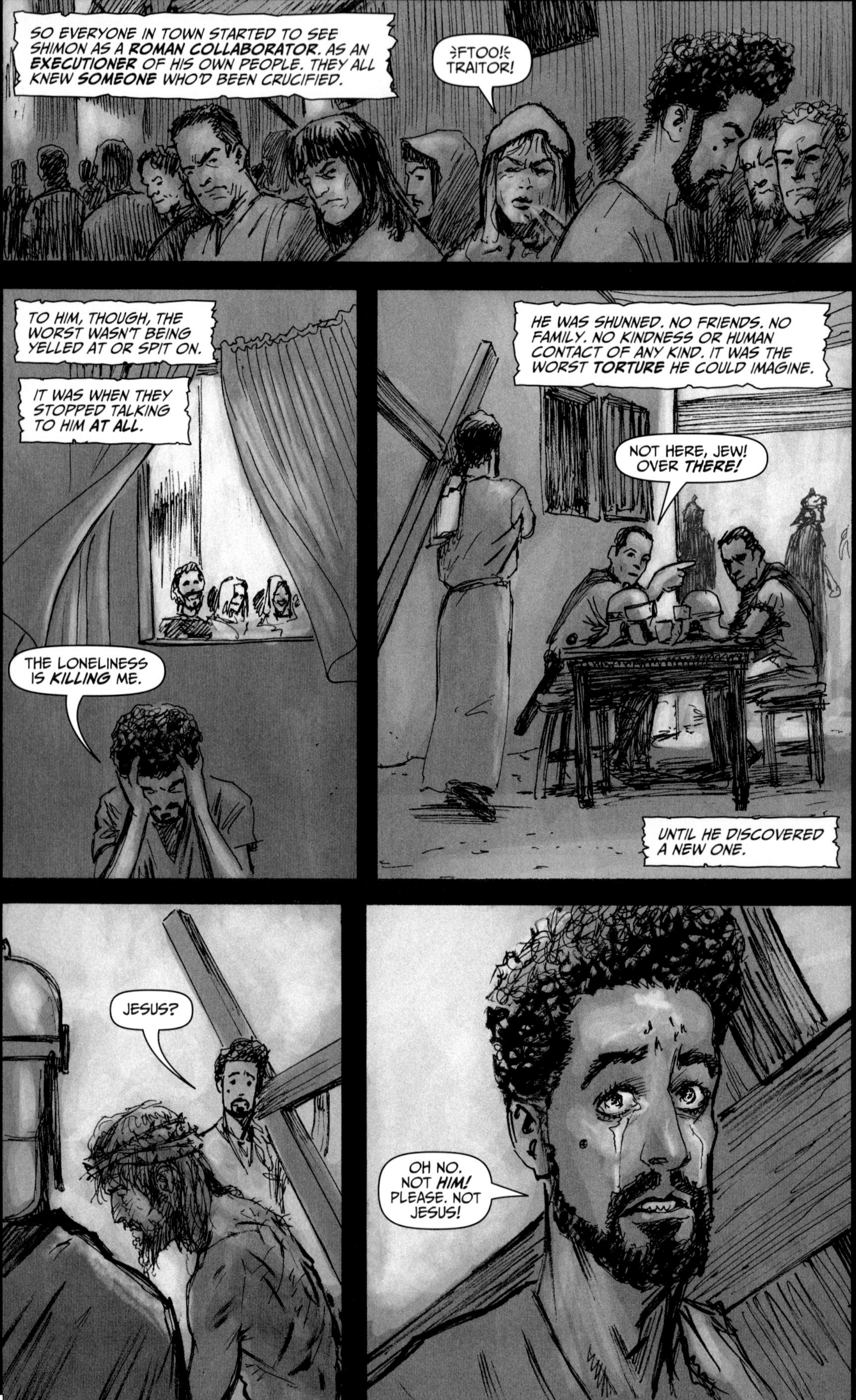
SO EVERYONE IN TOWN STARTED TO SEE SHIMON AS A **ROMAN COLLABORATOR**. AS AN **EXECUTIONER** OF HIS OWN PEOPLE. THEY ALL KNEW **SOMEONE** WHO'D BEEN CRUCIFIED.
FTOO! TRAITOR!
TO HIM, THOUGH, THE WORST WASN'T BEING YELLED AT OR SPIT ON.
IT WAS WHEN THEY STOPPED TALKING TO HIM **AT ALL**.
THE LONELINESS IS ***KILLING*** ME.
HE WAS SHUNNED. NO FRIENDS. NO FAMILY. NO KINDNESS OR HUMAN CONTACT OF ANY KIND. IT WAS THE WORST **TORTURE** HE COULD IMAGINE.
NOT HERE, JEW! OVER ***THERE!***
UNTIL HE DISCOVERED A NEW ONE.
JESUS?
OH NO. NOT ***HIM!*** PLEASE. NOT JESUS!

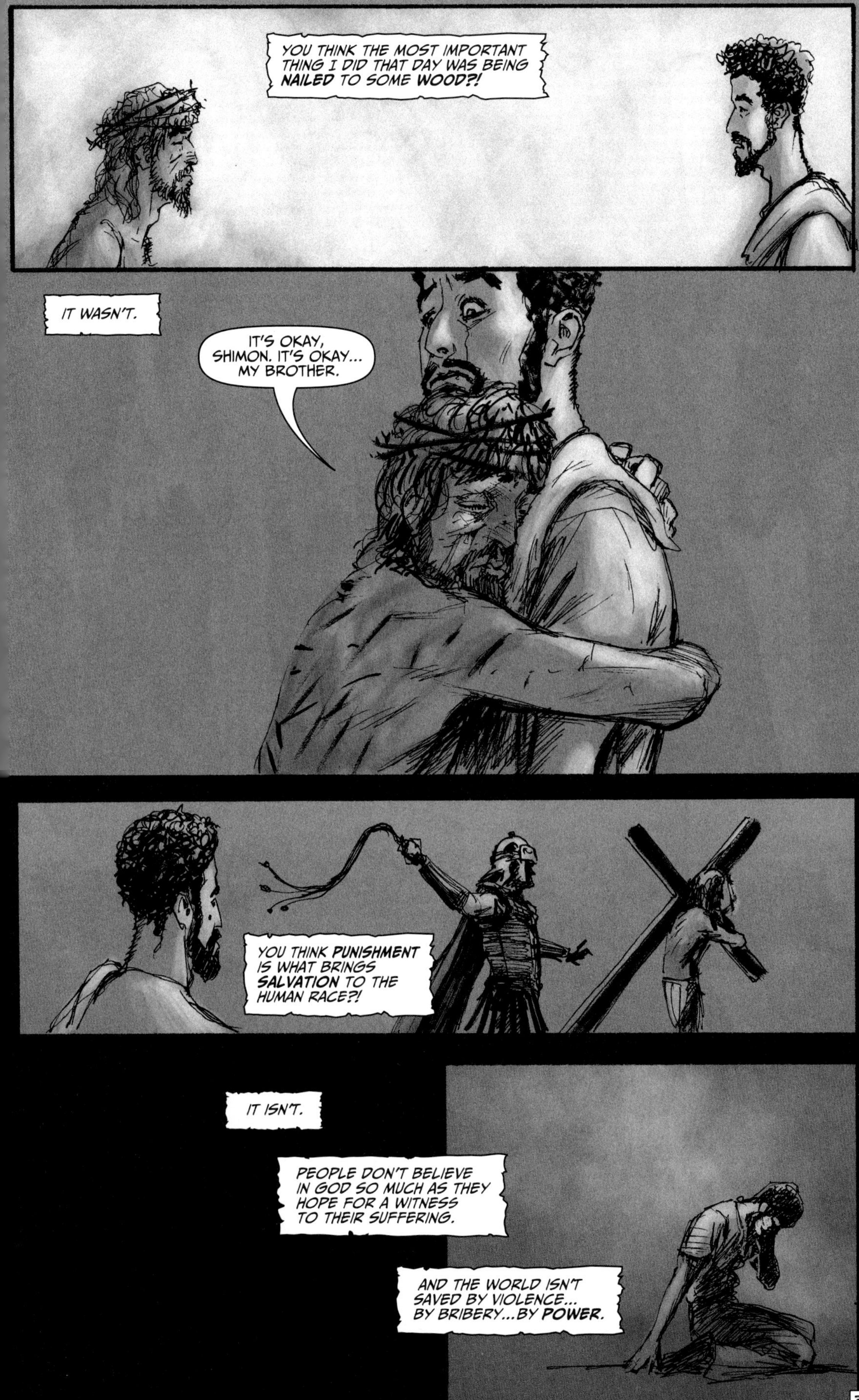
YOU THINK THE MOST IMPORTANT THING I DID THAT DAY WAS BEING **NAILED** TO SOME **WOOD?!**
IT WASN'T.
IT'S OKAY, SHIMON. IT'S OKAY... MY BROTHER.
YOU THINK **PUNISHMENT** IS WHAT BRINGS **SALVATION** TO THE HUMAN RACE?!
IT ISN'T.
PEOPLE DON'T BELIEVE IN GOD SO MUCH AS THEY HOPE FOR A WITNESS TO THEIR SUFFERING.
AND THE WORLD ISN'T SAVED BY VIOLENCE... BY BRIBERY...BY **POWER.**

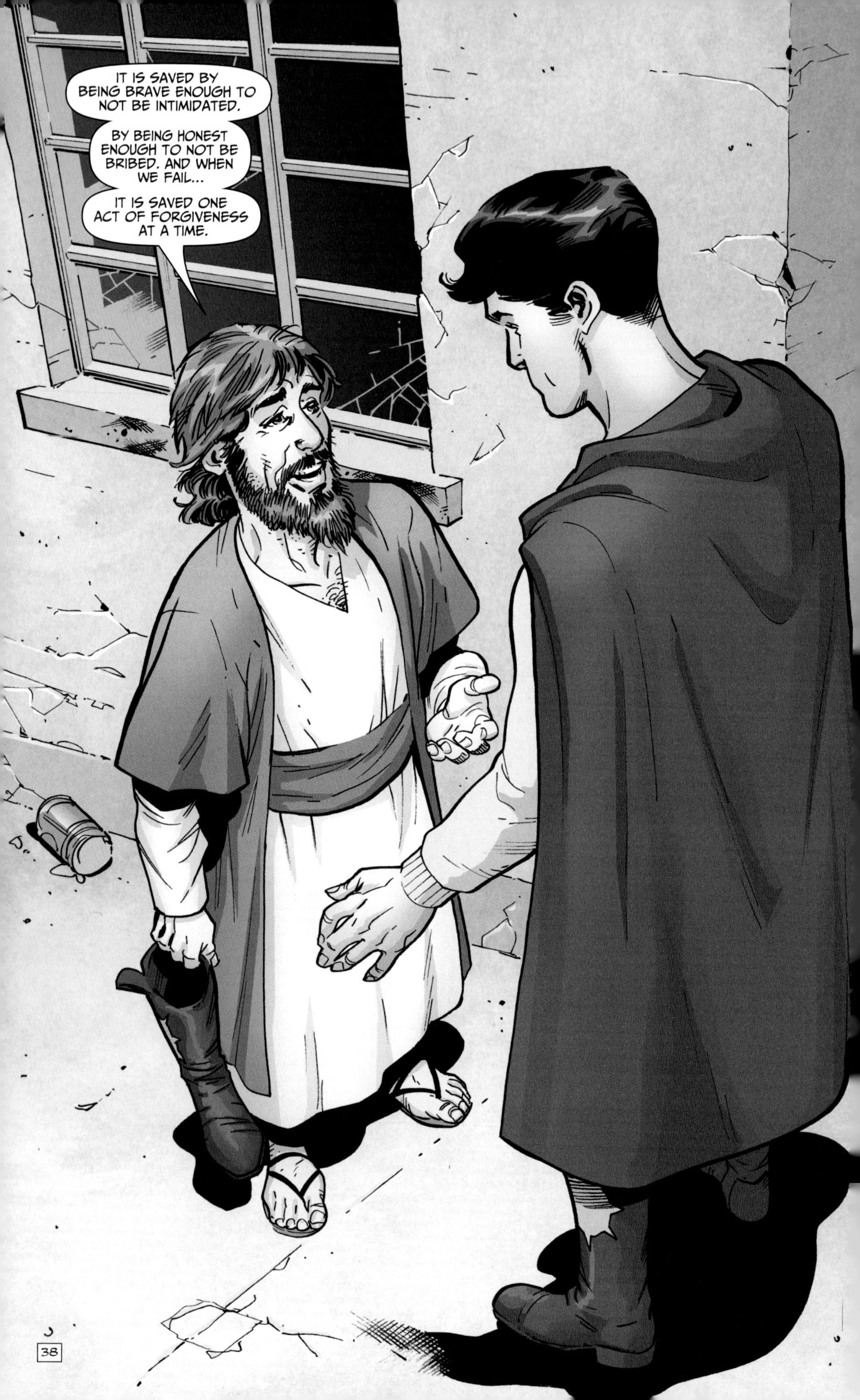
IT IS SAVED BY BEING BRAVE ENOUGH TO NOT BE INTIMIDATED.
BY BEING HONEST ENOUGH TO NOT BE BRIBED. AND WHEN WE FAIL...
IT IS SAVED ONE ACT OF FORGIVENESS AT A TIME.

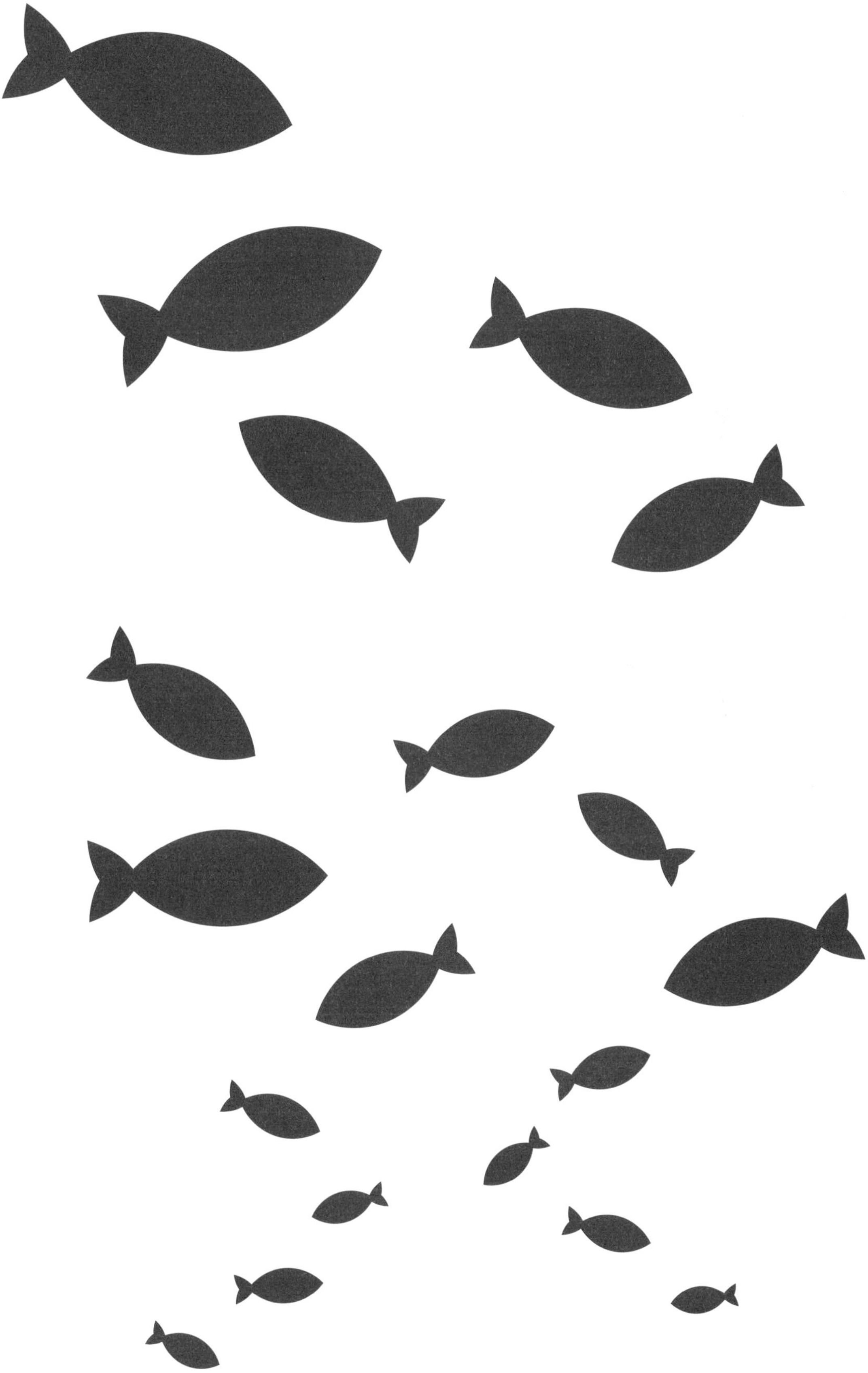

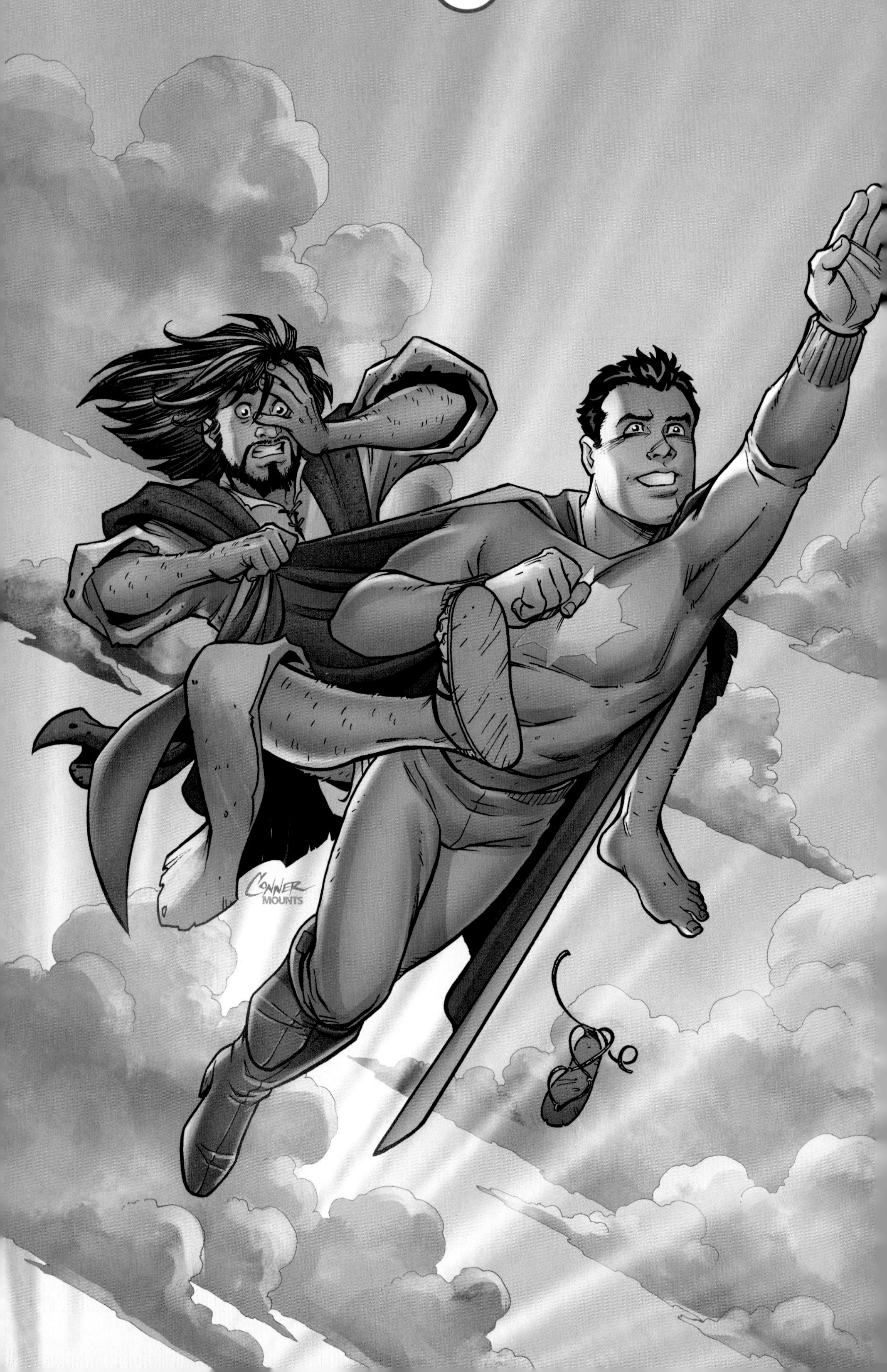
CONNER
MOUNTS

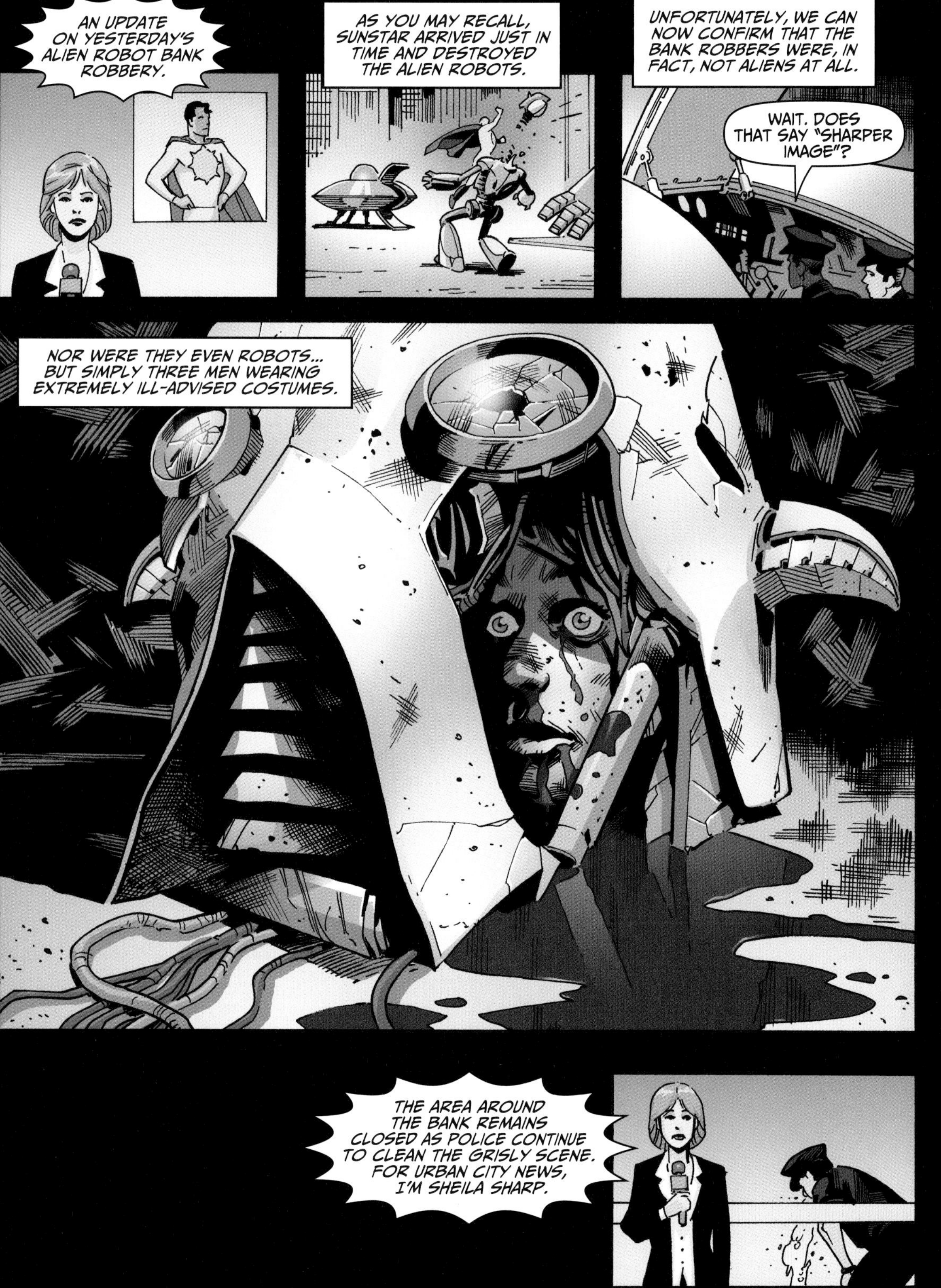
AN UPDATE ON YESTERDAY'S ALIEN ROBOT BANK ROBBERY.
AS YOU MAY RECALL, SUNSTAR ARRIVED JUST IN TIME AND DESTROYED THE ALIEN ROBOTS.
UNFORTUNATELY, WE CAN NOW CONFIRM THAT THE BANK ROBBERS WERE, IN FACT, NOT ALIENS AT ALL.
WAIT. DOES THAT SAY "SHARPER IMAGE"?
NOR WERE THEY EVEN ROBOTS... BUT SIMPLY THREE MEN WEARING EXTREMELY ILL-ADVISED COSTUMES.
THE AREA AROUND THE BANK REMAINS CLOSED AS POLICE CONTINUE TO CLEAN THE GRISLY SCENE. FOR URBAN CITY NEWS, I'M SHEILA SHARP.

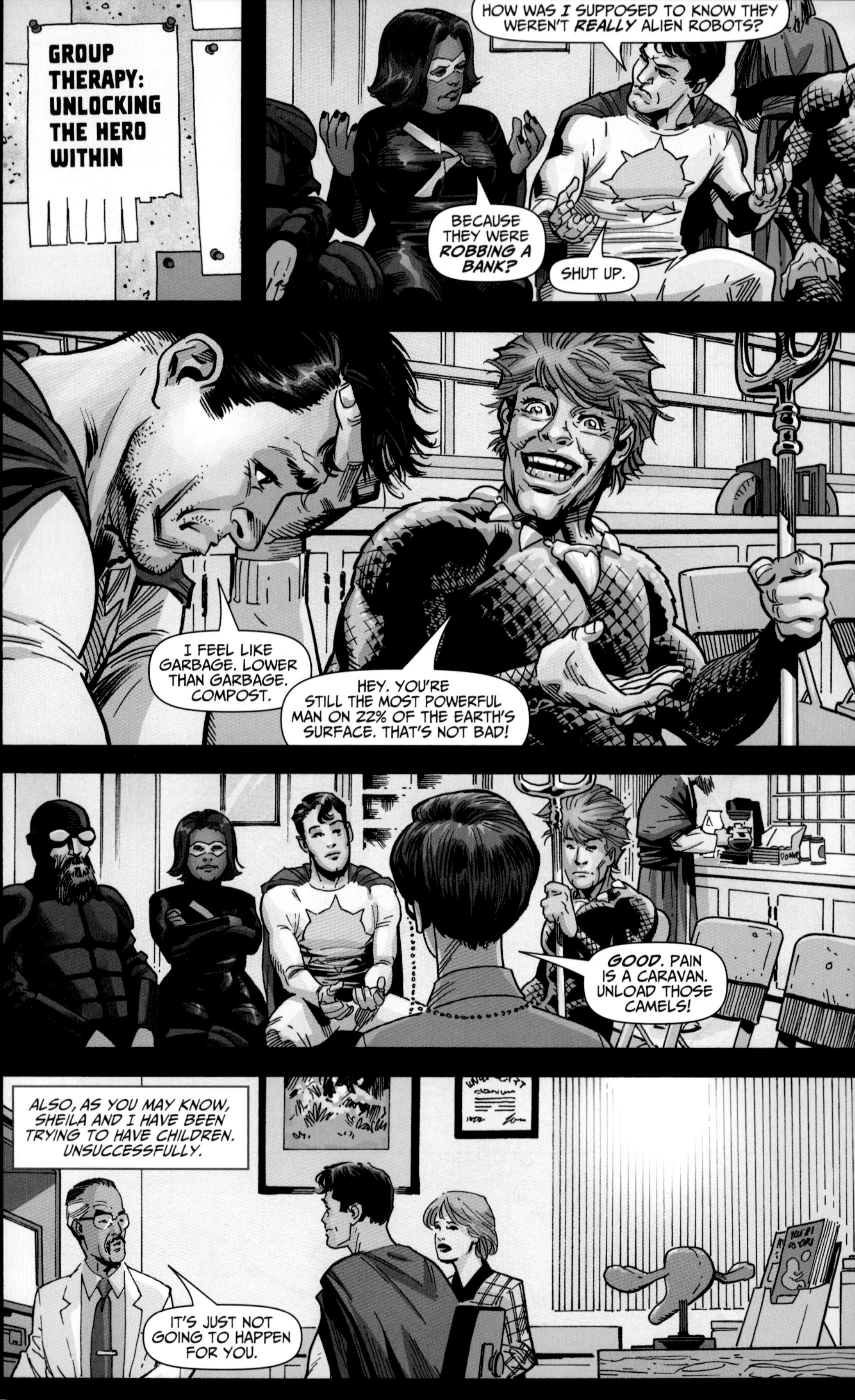

GROUP THERAPY: UNLOCKING THE HERO WITHIN
HOW WAS I SUPPOSED TO KNOW THEY WEREN'T REALLY ALIEN ROBOTS?
BECAUSE THEY WERE ROBBING A BANK?
SHUT UP.
I FEEL LIKE GARBAGE. LOWER THAN GARBAGE. COMPOST.
HEY. YOU'RE STILL THE MOST POWERFUL MAN ON 22% OF THE EARTH'S SURFACE. THAT'S NOT BAD!
GOOD. PAIN IS A CARAVAN. UNLOAD THOSE CAMELS!
ALSO, AS YOU MAY KNOW, SHEILA AND I HAVE BEEN TRYING TO HAVE CHILDREN. UNSUCCESSFULLY.
IT'S JUST NOT GOING TO HAPPEN FOR YOU.

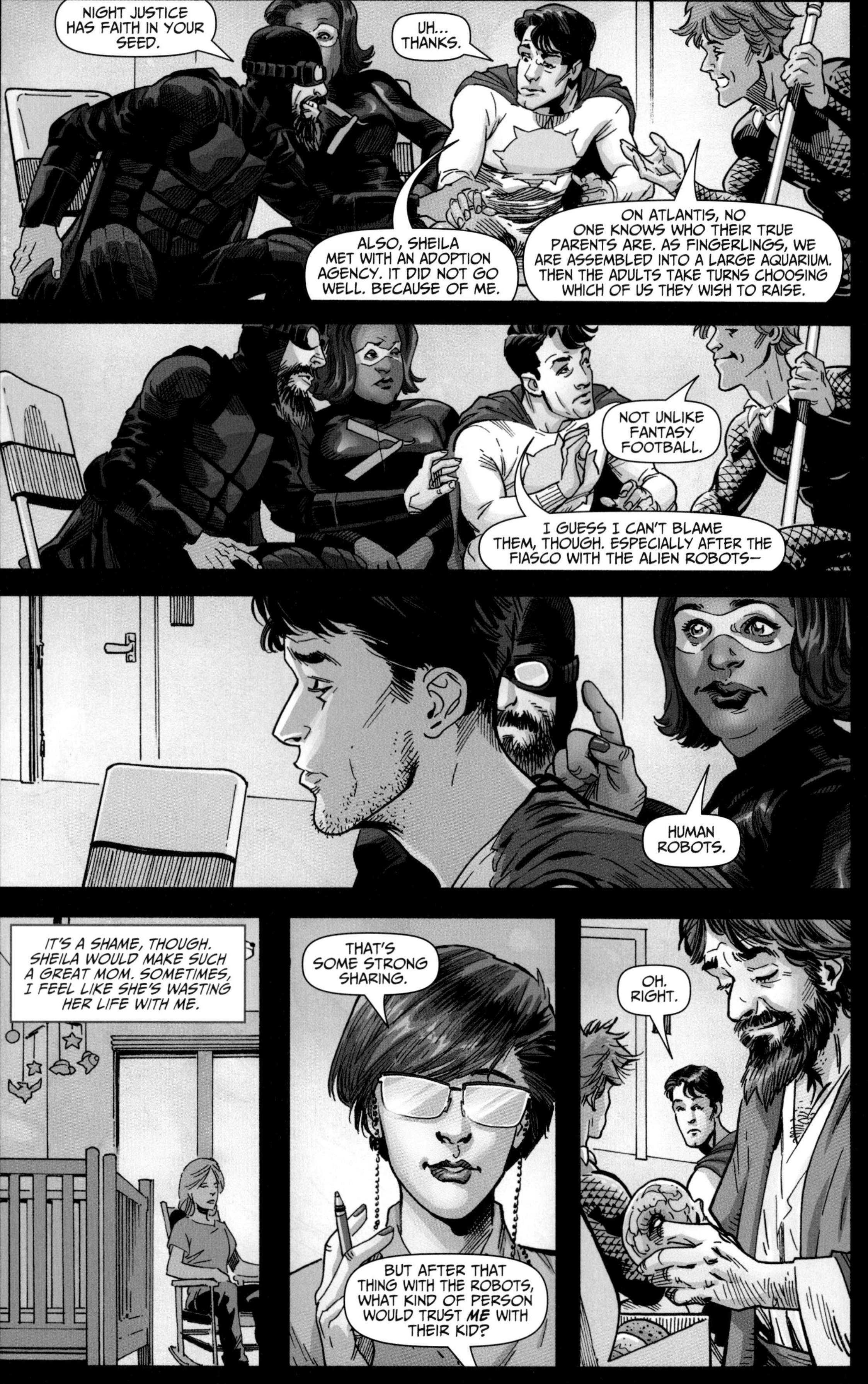
NIGHT JUSTICE HAS FAITH IN YOUR SEED.
UH... THANKS.
ALSO, SHEILA MET WITH AN ADOPTION AGENCY. IT DID NOT GO WELL. BECAUSE OF ME.
ON ATLANTIS, NO ONE KNOWS WHO THEIR TRUE PARENTS ARE. AS FINGERLINGS, WE ARE ASSEMBLED INTO A LARGE AQUARIUM. THEN THE ADULTS TAKE TURNS CHOOSING WHICH OF US THEY WISH TO RAISE.
NOT UNLIKE FANTASY FOOTBALL.
I GUESS I CAN'T BLAME THEM, THOUGH. ESPECIALLY AFTER THE FIASCO WITH THE ALIEN ROBOTS—
HUMAN ROBOTS.
IT'S A SHAME, THOUGH. SHEILA WOULD MAKE SUCH A GREAT MOM. SOMETIMES, I FEEL LIKE SHE'S WASTING HER LIFE WITH ME.
THAT'S SOME STRONG SHARING.
BUT AFTER THAT THING WITH THE ROBOTS, WHAT KIND OF PERSON WOULD TRUST *ME* WITH THEIR KID?
OH. RIGHT.

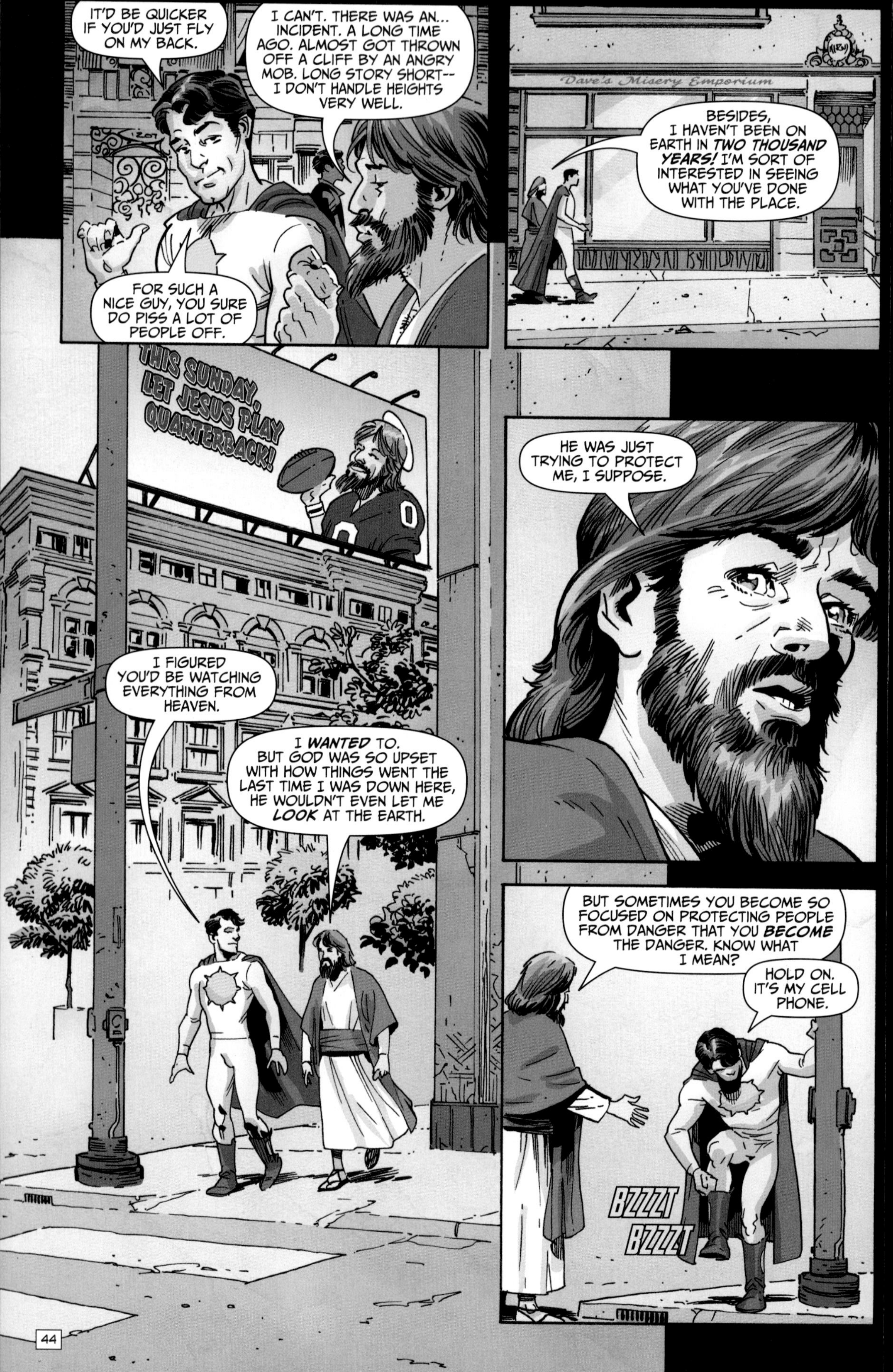
IT'D BE QUICKER IF YOU'D JUST FLY ON MY BACK.
I CAN'T. THERE WAS AN... INCIDENT. A LONG TIME AGO. ALMOST GOT THROWN OFF A CLIFF BY AN ANGRY MOB. LONG STORY SHORT-- I DON'T HANDLE HEIGHTS VERY WELL.
FOR SUCH A NICE GUY, YOU SURE DO PISS A LOT OF PEOPLE OFF.
Dave's Misery Emporium
BESIDES, I HAVEN'T BEEN ON EARTH IN TWO THOUSAND YEARS! I'M SORT OF INTERESTED IN SEEING WHAT YOU'VE DONE WITH THE PLACE.
THIS SUNDAY, LET JESUS PLAY QUARTERBACK!
I FIGURED YOU'D BE WATCHING EVERYTHING FROM HEAVEN.
I WANTED TO. BUT GOD WAS SO UPSET WITH HOW THINGS WENT THE LAST TIME I WAS DOWN HERE, HE WOULDN'T EVEN LET ME LOOK AT THE EARTH.
HE WAS JUST TRYING TO PROTECT ME, I SUPPOSE.
BUT SOMETIMES YOU BECOME SO FOCUSED ON PROTECTING PEOPLE FROM DANGER THAT YOU BECOME THE DANGER. KNOW WHAT I MEAN?
HOLD ON. IT'S MY CELL PHONE.
BZZZT
BZZZT

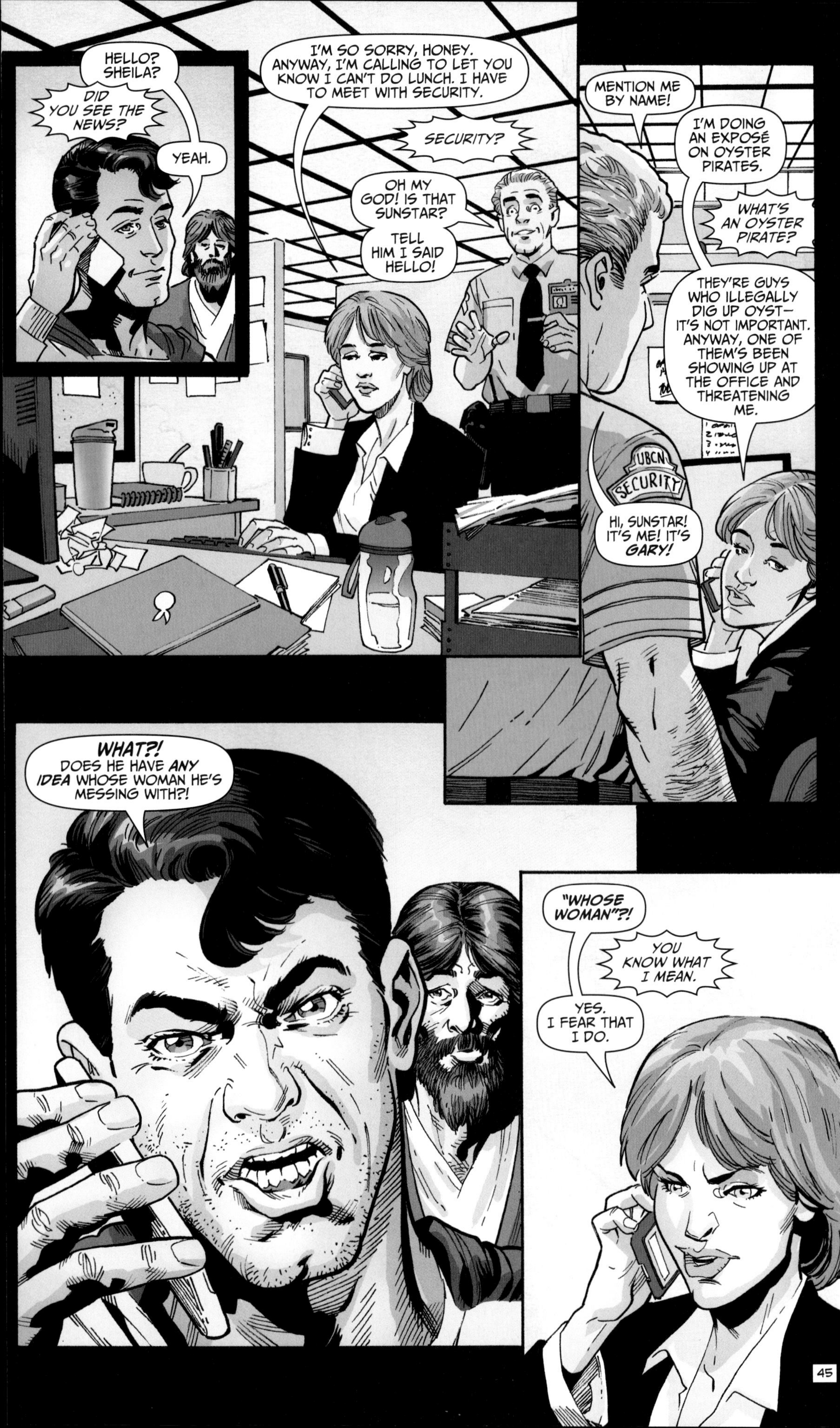

HELLO? SHEILA?
DID YOU SEE THE NEWS?
YEAH.
I'M SO SORRY, HONEY. ANYWAY, I'M CALLING TO LET YOU KNOW I CAN'T DO LUNCH. I HAVE TO MEET WITH SECURITY.
SECURITY?
OH MY GOD! IS THAT SUNSTAR?
TELL HIM I SAID HELLO!
MENTION ME BY NAME!
I'M DOING AN EXPOSÉ ON OYSTER PIRATES.
WHAT'S AN OYSTER PIRATE?
THEY'RE GUYS WHO ILLEGALLY DIG UP OYST— IT'S NOT IMPORTANT. ANYWAY, ONE OF THEM'S BEEN SHOWING UP AT THE OFFICE AND THREATENING ME.
UBCN SECURITY
HI, SUNSTAR! IT'S ME! IT'S GARY!
WHAT?! DOES HE HAVE ANY IDEA WHOSE WOMAN HE'S MESSING WITH?!
"WHOSE WOMAN"?!
YOU KNOW WHAT I MEAN.
YES. I FEAR THAT I DO.

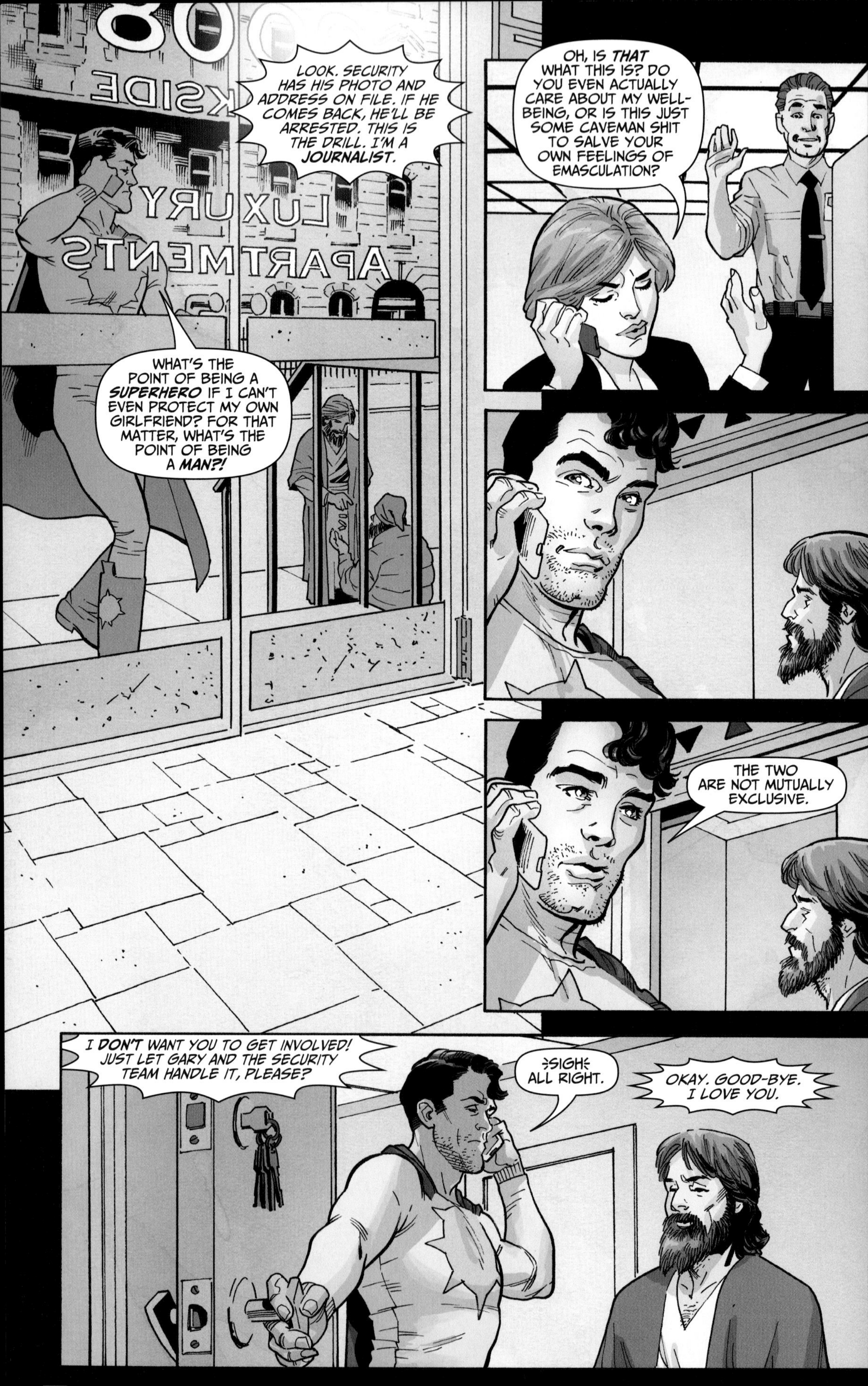
LOOK. SECURITY HAS HIS PHOTO AND ADDRESS ON FILE. IF HE COMES BACK, HE'LL BE ARRESTED. THIS IS THE DRILL. I'M A JOURNALIST.
LUXURY APARTMENTS
WHAT'S THE POINT OF BEING A SUPERHERO IF I CAN'T EVEN PROTECT MY OWN GIRLFRIEND? FOR THAT MATTER, WHAT'S THE POINT OF BEING A MAN?!
OH, IS THAT WHAT THIS IS? DO YOU EVEN ACTUALLY CARE ABOUT MY WELL-BEING, OR IS THIS JUST SOME CAVEMAN SHIT TO SALVE YOUR OWN FEELINGS OF EMASCULATION?
THE TWO ARE NOT MUTUALLY EXCLUSIVE.
I DON'T WANT YOU TO GET INVOLVED! JUST LET GARY AND THE SECURITY TEAM HANDLE IT, PLEASE?
SIGH ALL RIGHT.
OKAY. GOOD-BYE. I LOVE YOU.

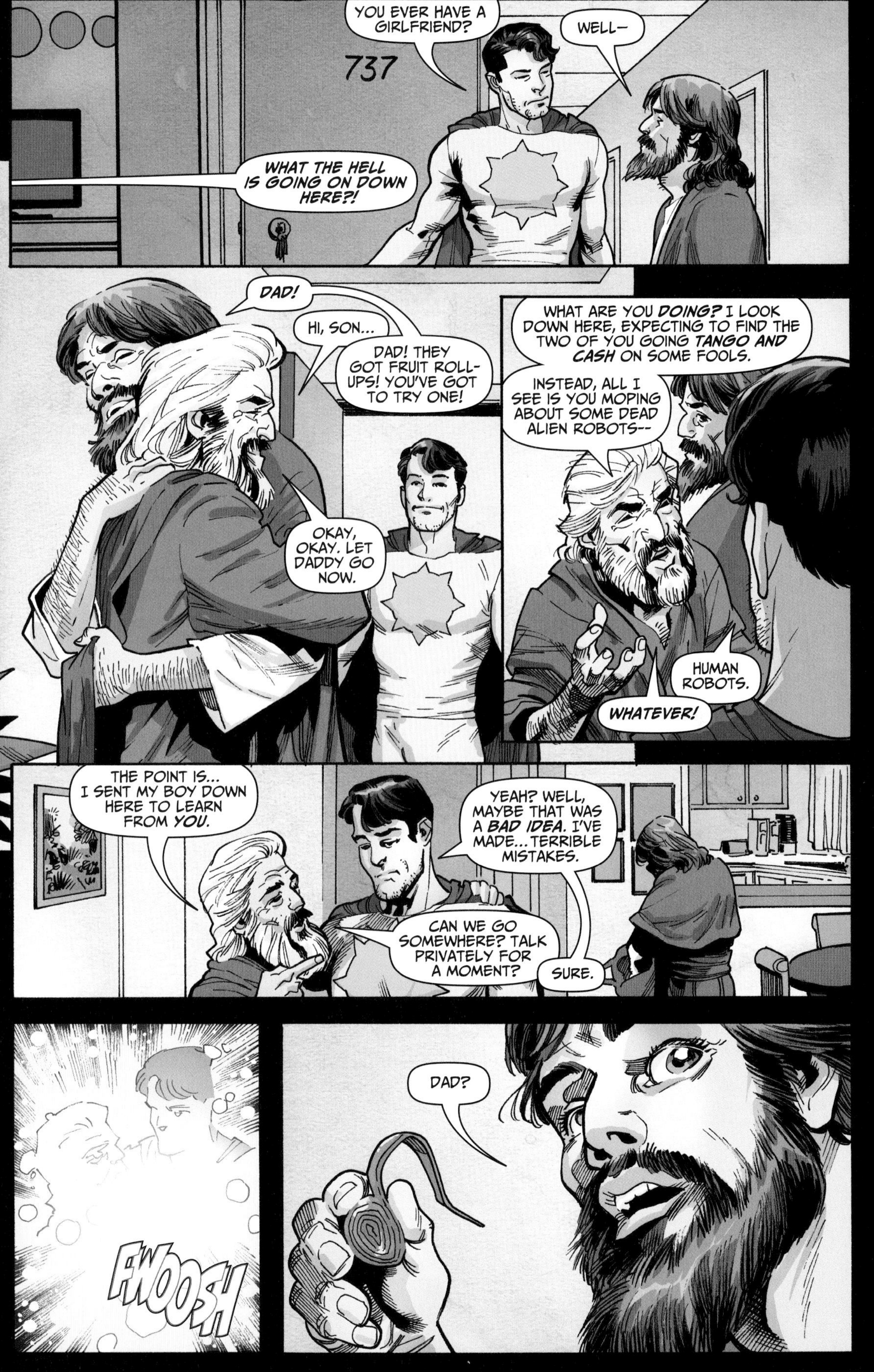
737
YOU EVER HAVE A GIRLFRIEND?
WELL—
WHAT THE HELL IS GOING ON DOWN HERE?!
DAD!
HI, SON...
DAD! THEY GOT FRUIT ROLL-UPS! YOU'VE GOT TO TRY ONE!
OKAY, OKAY. LET DADDY GO NOW.
WHAT ARE YOU DOING? I LOOK DOWN HERE, EXPECTING TO FIND THE TWO OF YOU GOING TANGO AND CASH ON SOME FOOLS.
INSTEAD, ALL I SEE IS YOU MOPING ABOUT SOME DEAD ALIEN ROBOTS--
HUMAN ROBOTS.
WHATEVER!
THE POINT IS... I SENT MY BOY DOWN HERE TO LEARN FROM YOU.
YEAH? WELL, MAYBE THAT WAS A BAD IDEA. I'VE MADE... TERRIBLE MISTAKES.
CAN WE GO SOMEWHERE? TALK PRIVATELY FOR A MOMENT?
SURE.
FWOOSH
DAD?

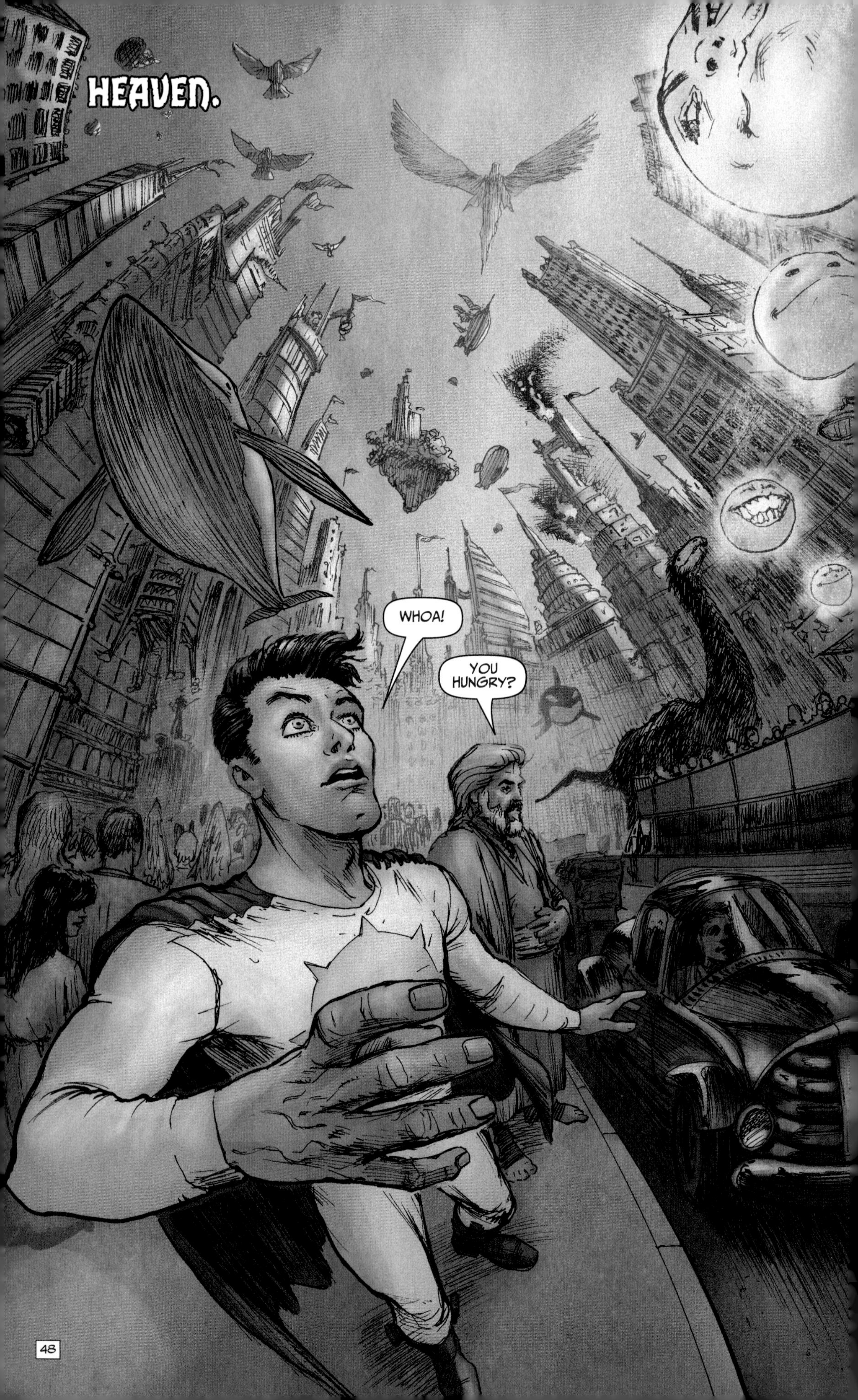
HEAVEN.
WHOA!
YOU HUNGRY?

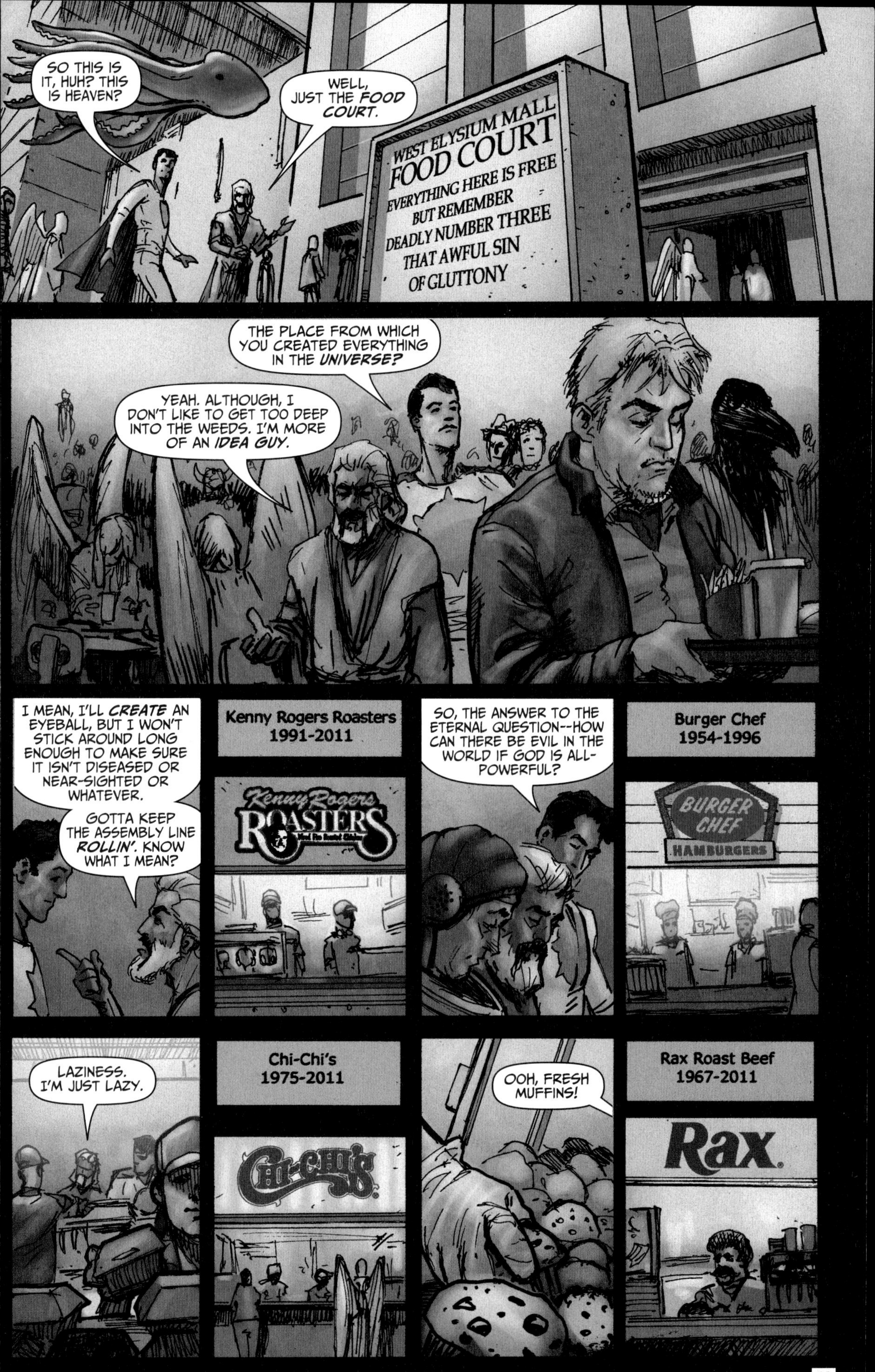
SO THIS IS IT, HUH? THIS IS HEAVEN?
WELL, JUST THE FOOD COURT.
WEST ELYSIUM MALL
FOOD COURT
EVERYTHING HERE IS FREE
BUT REMEMBER
DEADLY NUMBER THREE
THAT AWFUL SIN
OF GLUTTONY
THE PLACE FROM WHICH YOU CREATED EVERYTHING IN THE UNIVERSE?
YEAH. ALTHOUGH, I DON'T LIKE TO GET TOO DEEP INTO THE WEEDS. I'M MORE OF AN IDEA GUY.
I MEAN, I'LL CREATE AN EYEBALL, BUT I WON'T STICK AROUND LONG ENOUGH TO MAKE SURE IT ISN'T DISEASED OR NEAR-SIGHTED OR WHATEVER.
GOTTA KEEP THE ASSEMBLY LINE ROLLIN'. KNOW WHAT I MEAN?
Kenny Rogers Roasters
1991-2011
Kenny Rogers
ROASTERS
SO, THE ANSWER TO THE ETERNAL QUESTION--HOW CAN THERE BE EVIL IN THE WORLD IF GOD IS ALL-POWERFUL?
Burger Chef
1954-1996
BURGER CHEF
HAMBURGERS
LAZINESS. I'M JUST LAZY.
Chi-Chi's
1975-2011
CHI-CHI'S
OOH, FRESH MUFFINS!
Rax Roast Beef
1967-2011
Rax

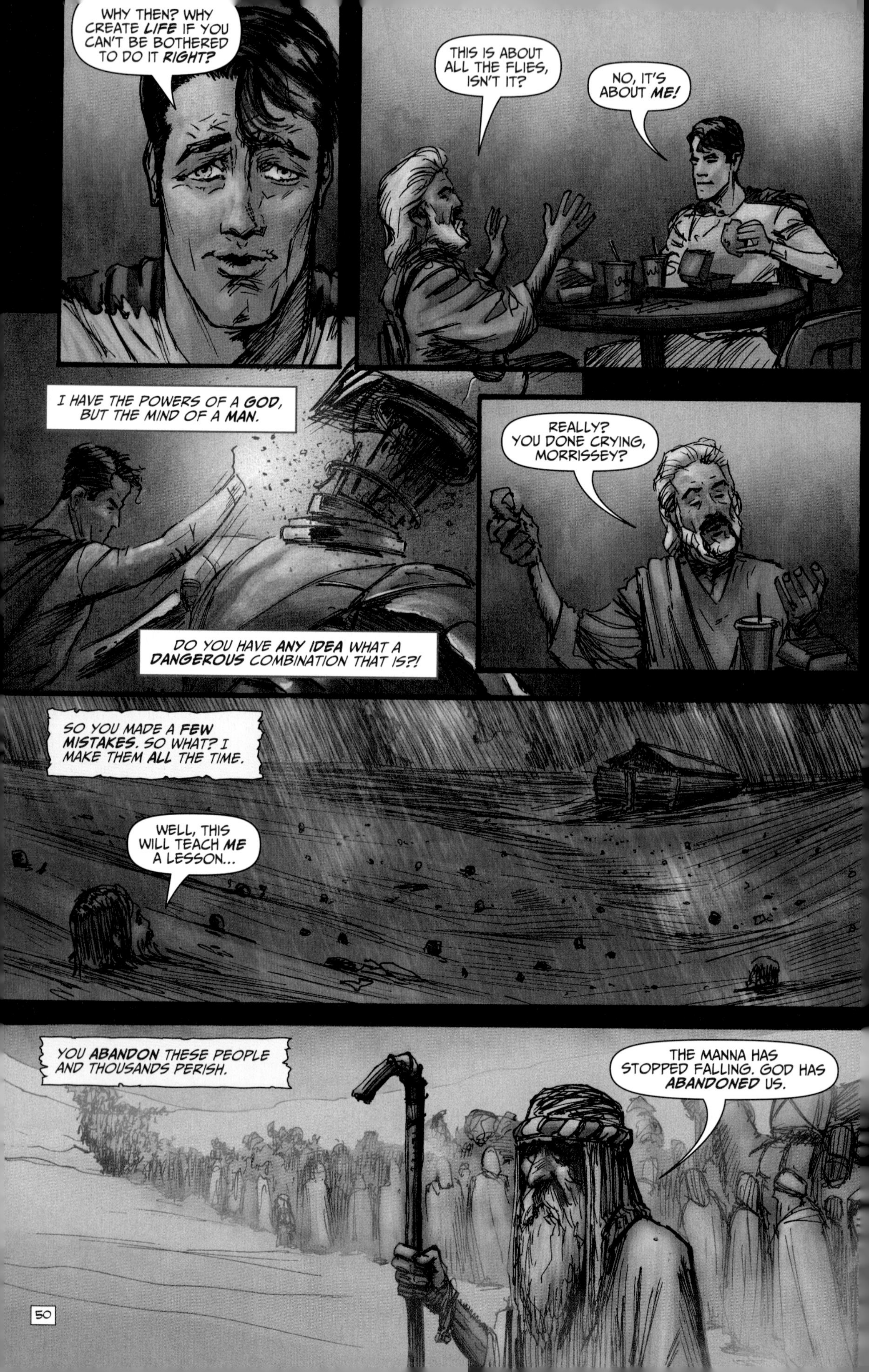
WHY THEN? WHY CREATE LIFE IF YOU CAN'T BE BOTHERED TO DO IT RIGHT?
THIS IS ABOUT ALL THE FLIES, ISN'T IT?
NO, IT'S ABOUT ME!
I HAVE THE POWERS OF A GOD, BUT THE MIND OF A MAN.
DO YOU HAVE ANY IDEA WHAT A DANGEROUS COMBINATION THAT IS?!
REALLY? YOU DONE CRYING, MORRISSEY?
SO YOU MADE A FEW MISTAKES. SO WHAT? I MAKE THEM ALL THE TIME.
WELL, THIS WILL TEACH ME A LESSON...
YOU ABANDON THESE PEOPLE AND THOUSANDS PERISH.
THE MANNA HAS STOPPED FALLING. GOD HAS ABANDONED US.

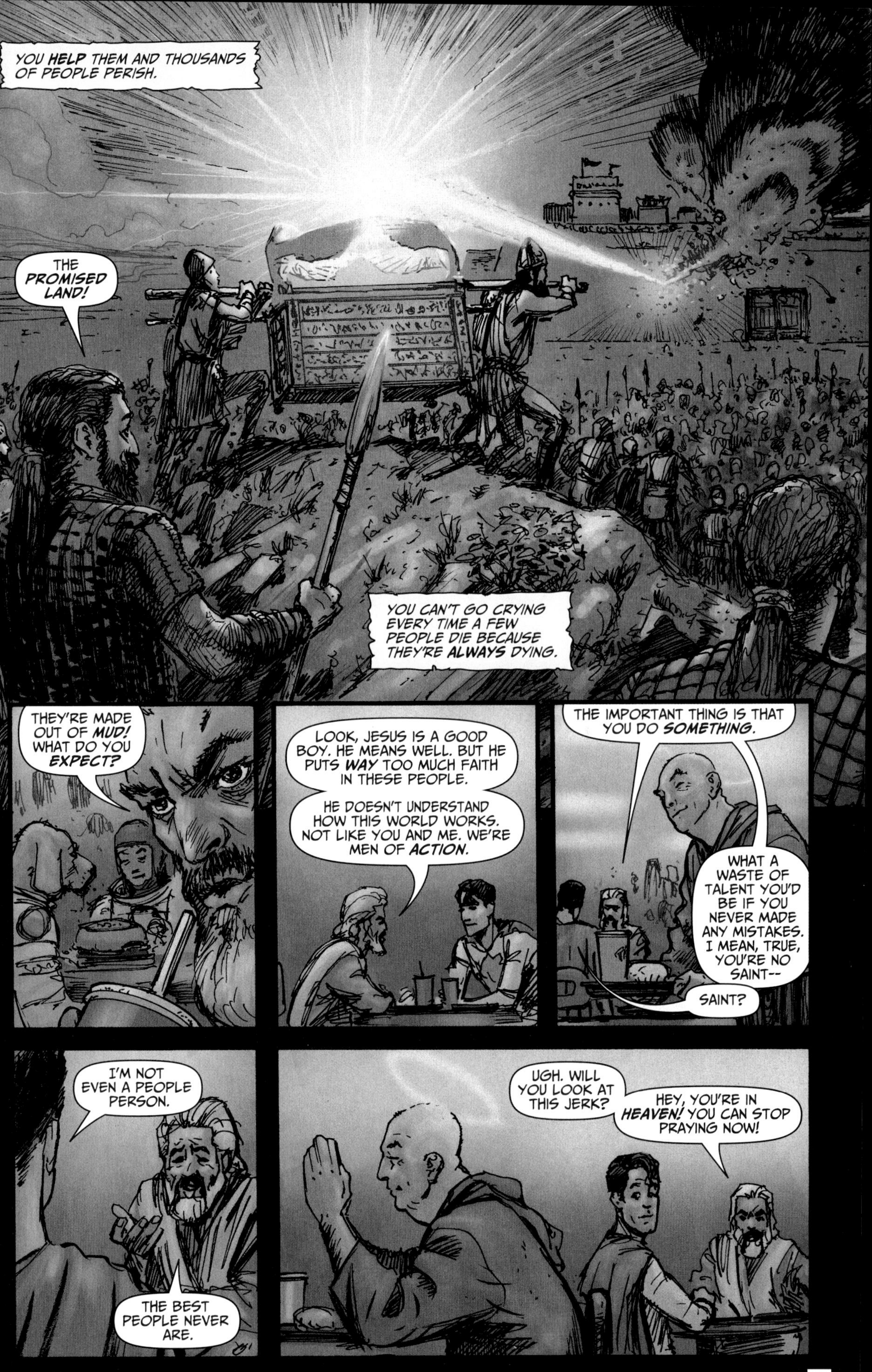
YOU **HELP** THEM AND THOUSANDS OF PEOPLE PERISH.
THE **PROMISED LAND!**
YOU CAN'T GO CRYING EVERY TIME A FEW PEOPLE DIE BECAUSE THEY'RE **ALWAYS** DYING.
THEY'RE MADE OUT OF **MUD!** WHAT DO YOU **EXPECT?**
LOOK, JESUS IS A GOOD BOY. HE MEANS WELL. BUT HE PUTS **WAY** TOO MUCH FAITH IN THESE PEOPLE.
HE DOESN'T UNDERSTAND HOW THIS WORLD WORKS. NOT LIKE YOU AND ME. WE'RE MEN OF **ACTION**.
THE IMPORTANT THING IS THAT YOU DO **SOMETHING**.
WHAT A WASTE OF TALENT YOU'D BE IF YOU NEVER MADE ANY MISTAKES. I MEAN, TRUE, YOU'RE NO SAINT--
SAINT?
I'M NOT EVEN A PEOPLE PERSON.
THE BEST PEOPLE NEVER ARE.
UGH. WILL YOU LOOK AT THIS JERK?
HEY, YOU'RE IN **HEAVEN!** YOU CAN STOP PRAYING NOW!

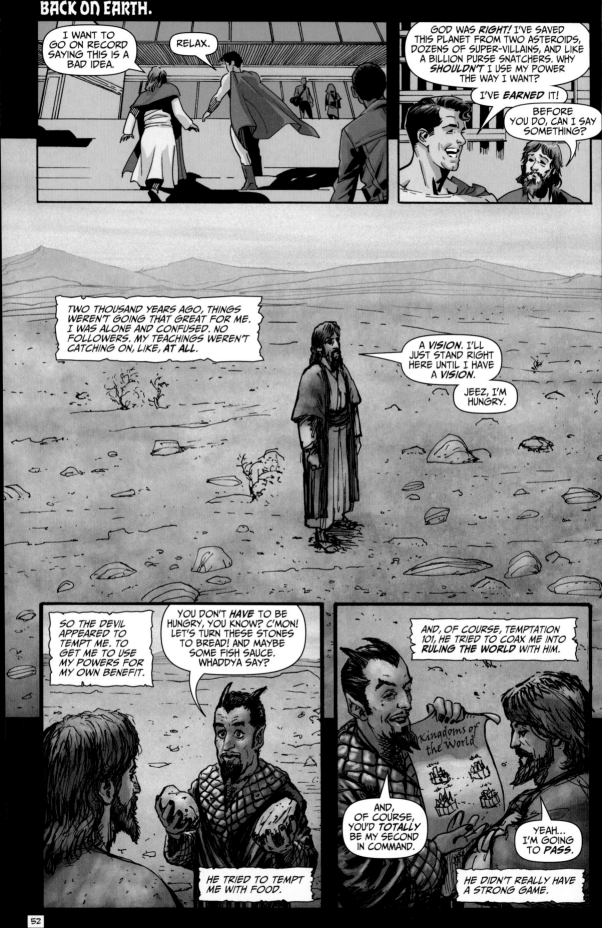

I WANT TO GO ON RECORD SAYING THIS IS A BAD IDEA.

RELAX.

GOD WAS *RIGHT!* I'VE SAVED THIS PLANET FROM TWO ASTEROIDS, DOZENS OF SUPER-VILLAINS, AND LIKE A BILLION PURSE SNATCHERS. WHY *SHOULDN'T* I USE MY POWER THE WAY I WANT?

I'VE *EARNED* IT!

BEFORE YOU DO, CAN I SAY SOMETHING?

TWO THOUSAND YEARS AGO, THINGS WEREN'T GOING THAT GREAT FOR ME. I WAS ALONE AND CONFUSED. NO FOLLOWERS. MY TEACHINGS WEREN'T CATCHING ON, LIKE, *AT ALL.*

A *VISION.* I'LL JUST STAND RIGHT HERE UNTIL I HAVE A *VISION.*

JEEZ, I'M HUNGRY.

SO THE DEVIL APPEARED TO TEMPT ME. TO GET ME TO USE MY POWERS FOR MY OWN BENEFIT.

YOU DON'T *HAVE* TO BE HUNGRY, YOU KNOW? C'MON! LET'S TURN THESE STONES TO BREAD! AND MAYBE SOME FISH SAUCE. WHADDYA SAY?

HE TRIED TO TEMPT ME WITH FOOD.

AND, OF COURSE, TEMPTATION 101, HE TRIED TO COAX ME INTO *RULING THE WORLD* WITH HIM.

Kingdoms of the World

AND, OF COURSE, YOU'D *TOTALLY* BE MY SECOND IN COMMAND.

YEAH... I'M GOING TO *PASS.*

HE DIDN'T REALLY HAVE A STRONG GAME.

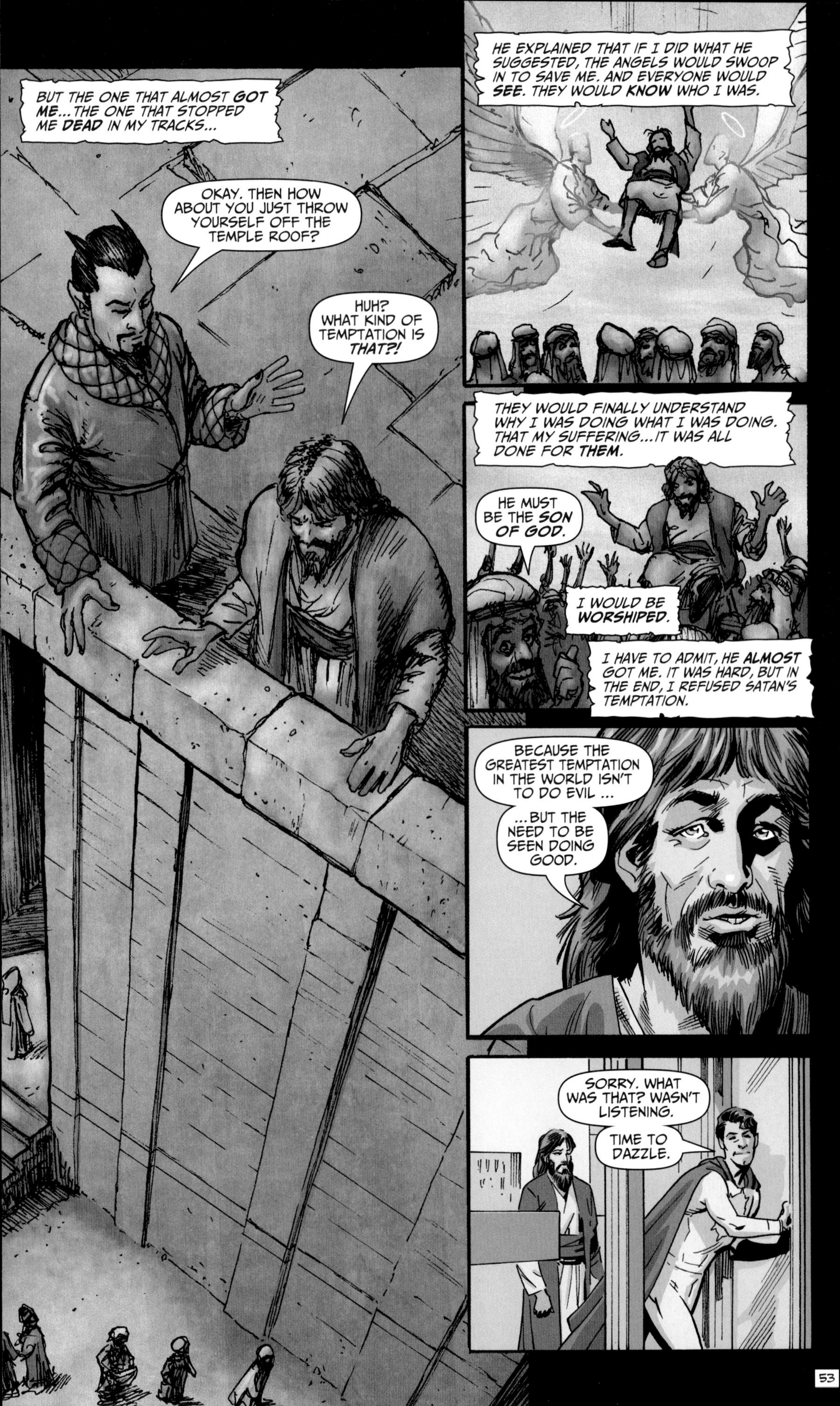
BUT THE ONE THAT ALMOST GOT ME...THE ONE THAT STOPPED ME DEAD IN MY TRACKS...
OKAY. THEN HOW ABOUT YOU JUST THROW YOURSELF OFF THE TEMPLE ROOF?
HUH? WHAT KIND OF TEMPTATION IS THAT?!
HE EXPLAINED THAT IF I DID WHAT HE SUGGESTED, THE ANGELS WOULD SWOOP IN TO SAVE ME. AND EVERYONE WOULD SEE. THEY WOULD KNOW WHO I WAS.
THEY WOULD FINALLY UNDERSTAND WHY I WAS DOING WHAT I WAS DOING. THAT MY SUFFERING...IT WAS ALL DONE FOR THEM.
HE MUST BE THE SON OF GOD.
I WOULD BE WORSHIPED.
I HAVE TO ADMIT, HE ALMOST GOT ME. IT WAS HARD, BUT IN THE END, I REFUSED SATAN'S TEMPTATION.
BECAUSE THE GREATEST TEMPTATION IN THE WORLD ISN'T TO DO EVIL ...
...BUT THE NEED TO BE SEEN DOING GOOD.
SORRY. WHAT WAS THAT? WASN'T LISTENING.
TIME TO DAZZLE.

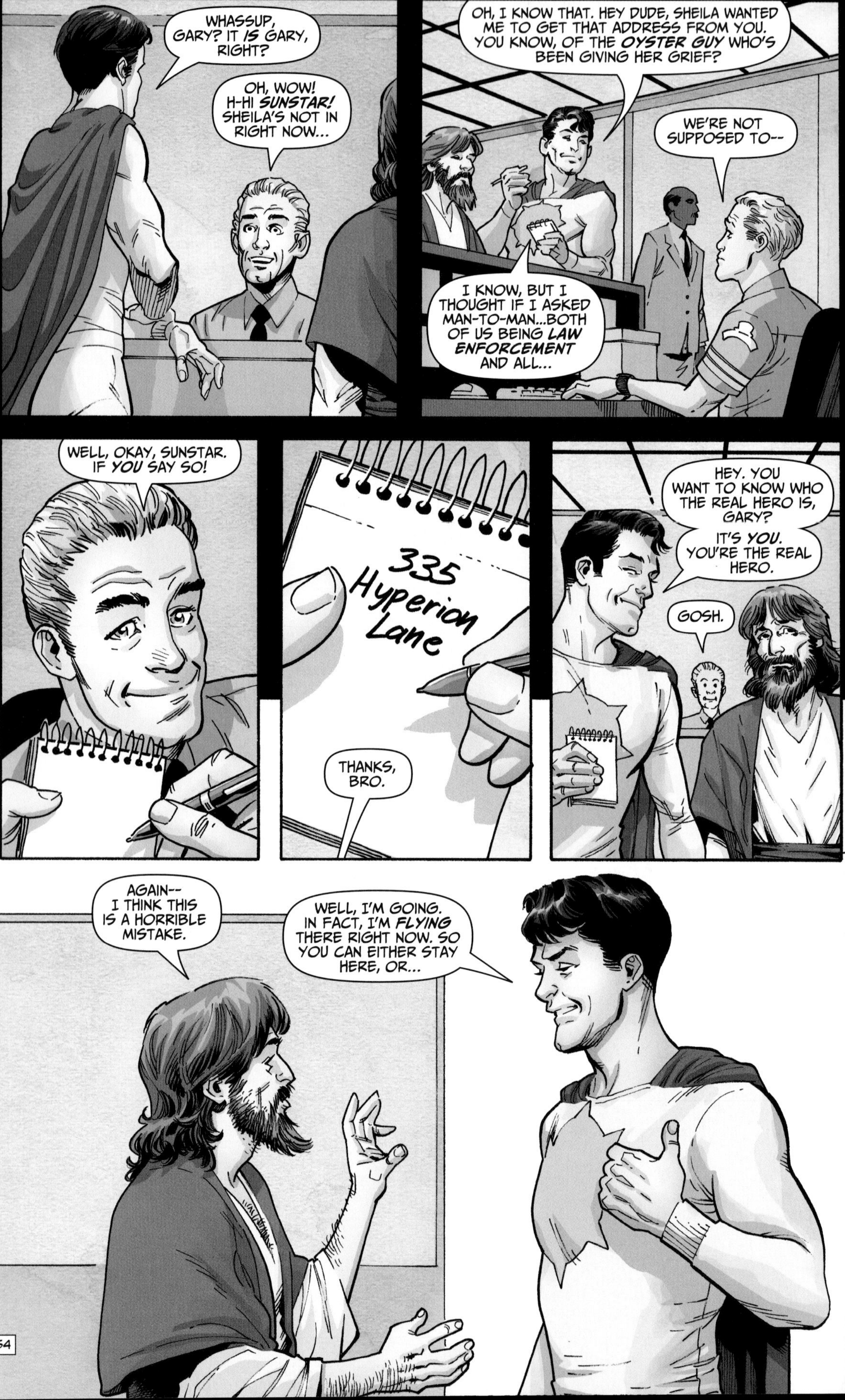
WHASSUP, GARY? IT IS GARY, RIGHT?
OH, WOW! H-HI SUNSTAR! SHEILA'S NOT IN RIGHT NOW...
OH, I KNOW THAT. HEY DUDE, SHEILA WANTED ME TO GET THAT ADDRESS FROM YOU. YOU KNOW, OF THE OYSTER GUY WHO'S BEEN GIVING HER GRIEF?
WE'RE NOT SUPPOSED TO--
I KNOW, BUT I THOUGHT IF I ASKED MAN-TO-MAN...BOTH OF US BEING LAW ENFORCEMENT AND ALL...
WELL, OKAY, SUNSTAR. IF YOU SAY SO!
335 Hyperion Lane
THANKS, BRO.
HEY. YOU WANT TO KNOW WHO THE REAL HERO IS, GARY?
IT'S YOU. YOU'RE THE REAL HERO.
GOSH.
AGAIN-- I THINK THIS IS A HORRIBLE MISTAKE.
WELL, I'M GOING. IN FACT, I'M FLYING THERE RIGHT NOW. SO YOU CAN EITHER STAY HERE, OR...

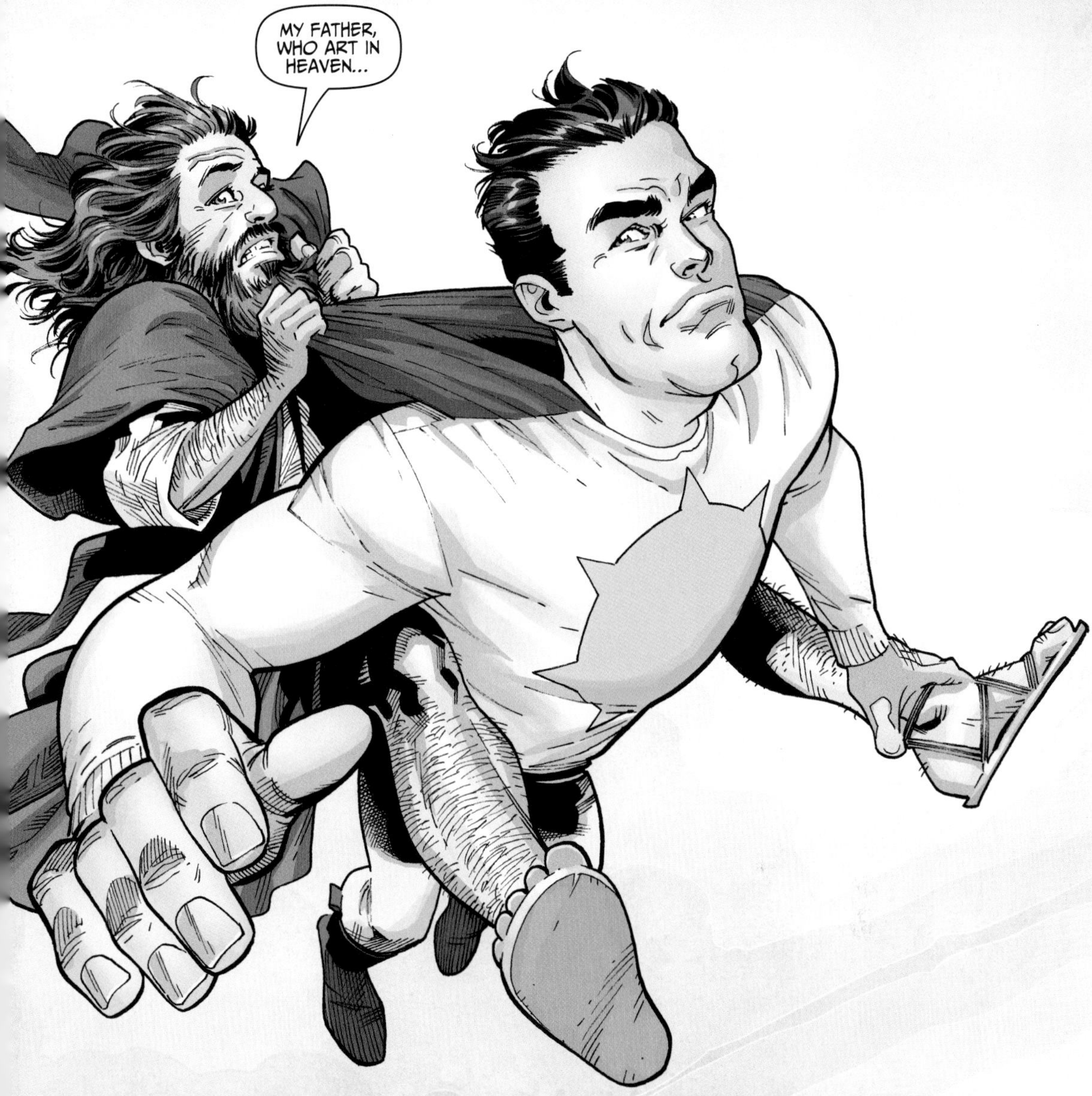
MY FATHER, WHO ART IN HEAVEN...

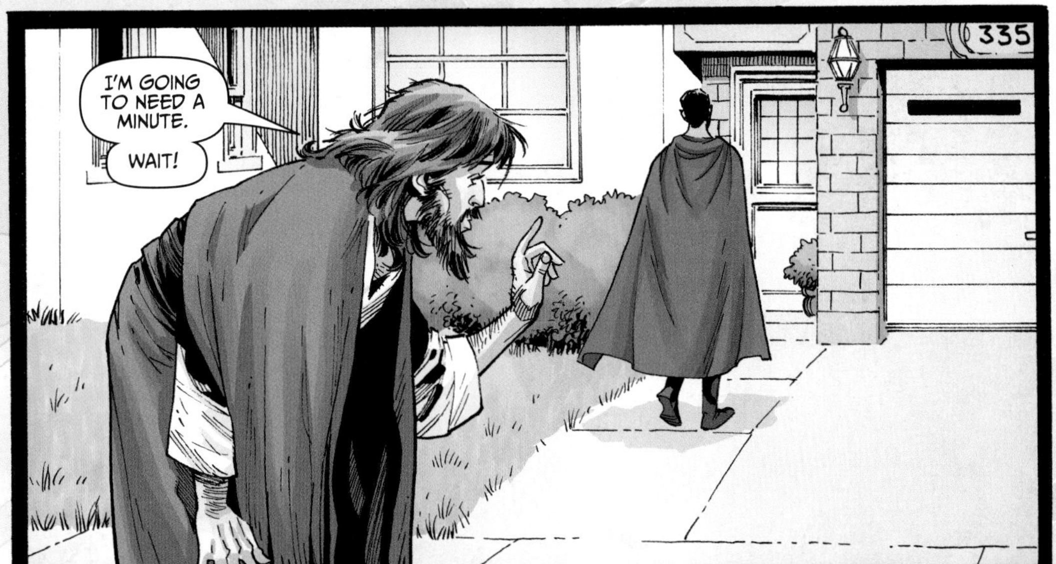
335
I'M GOING TO NEED A MINUTE.
WAIT!

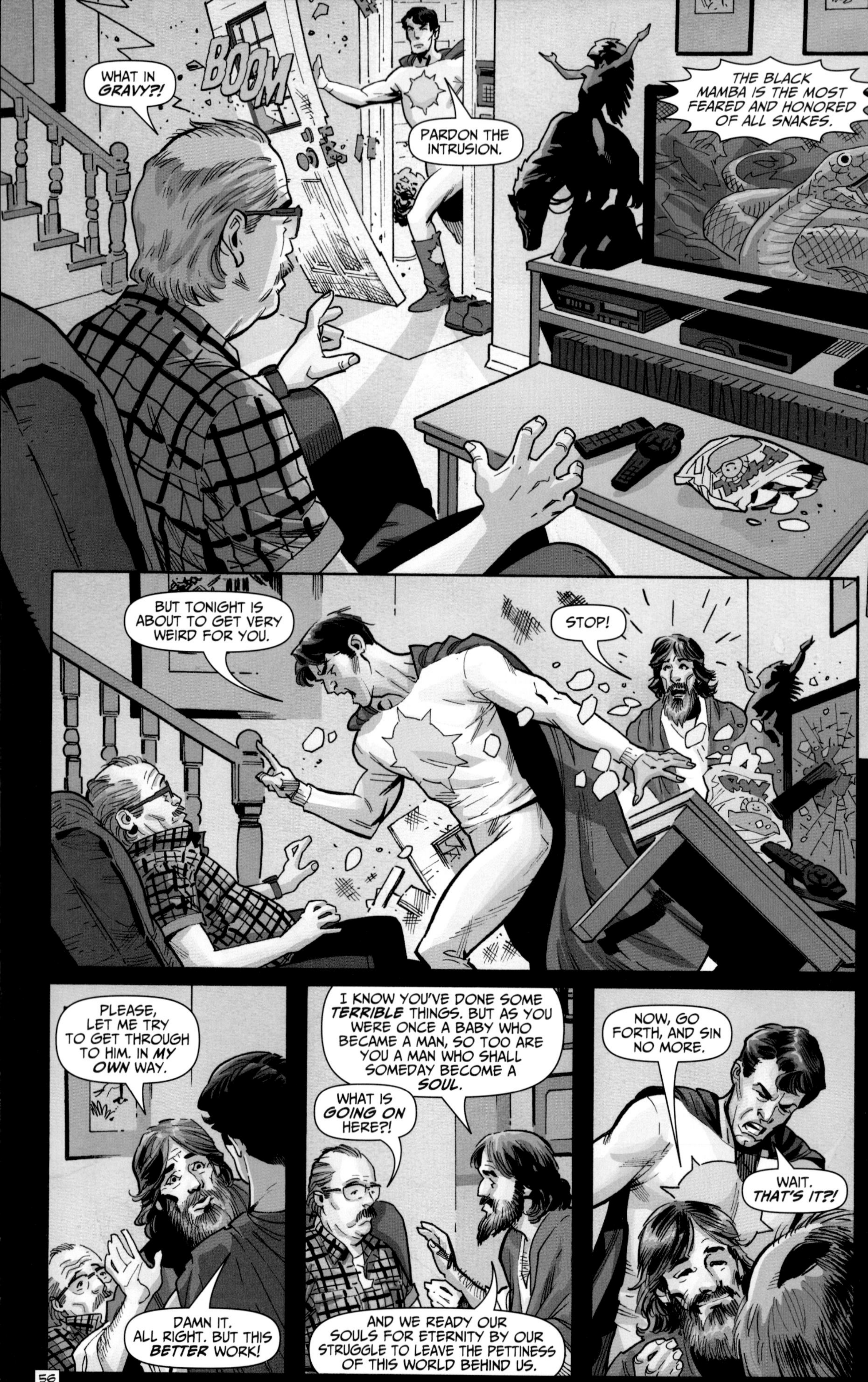
WHAT IN *GRAVY?!*
BOOM
PARDON THE INTRUSION.
THE BLACK MAMBA IS THE MOST FEARED AND HONORED OF ALL SNAKES.
BUT TONIGHT IS ABOUT TO GET VERY WEIRD FOR YOU.
STOP!
PLEASE, LET ME TRY TO GET THROUGH TO HIM. IN *MY OWN* WAY.
DAMN IT. ALL RIGHT. BUT THIS *BETTER* WORK!
I KNOW YOU'VE DONE SOME *TERRIBLE* THINGS. BUT AS YOU WERE ONCE A BABY WHO BECAME A MAN, SO TOO ARE YOU A MAN WHO SHALL SOMEDAY BECOME A *SOUL*.
WHAT IS *GOING ON* HERE?!
AND WE READY OUR SOULS FOR ETERNITY BY OUR STRUGGLE TO LEAVE THE PETTINESS OF THIS WORLD BEHIND US.
NOW, GO FORTH, AND SIN NO MORE.
WAIT. *THAT'S IT?!*

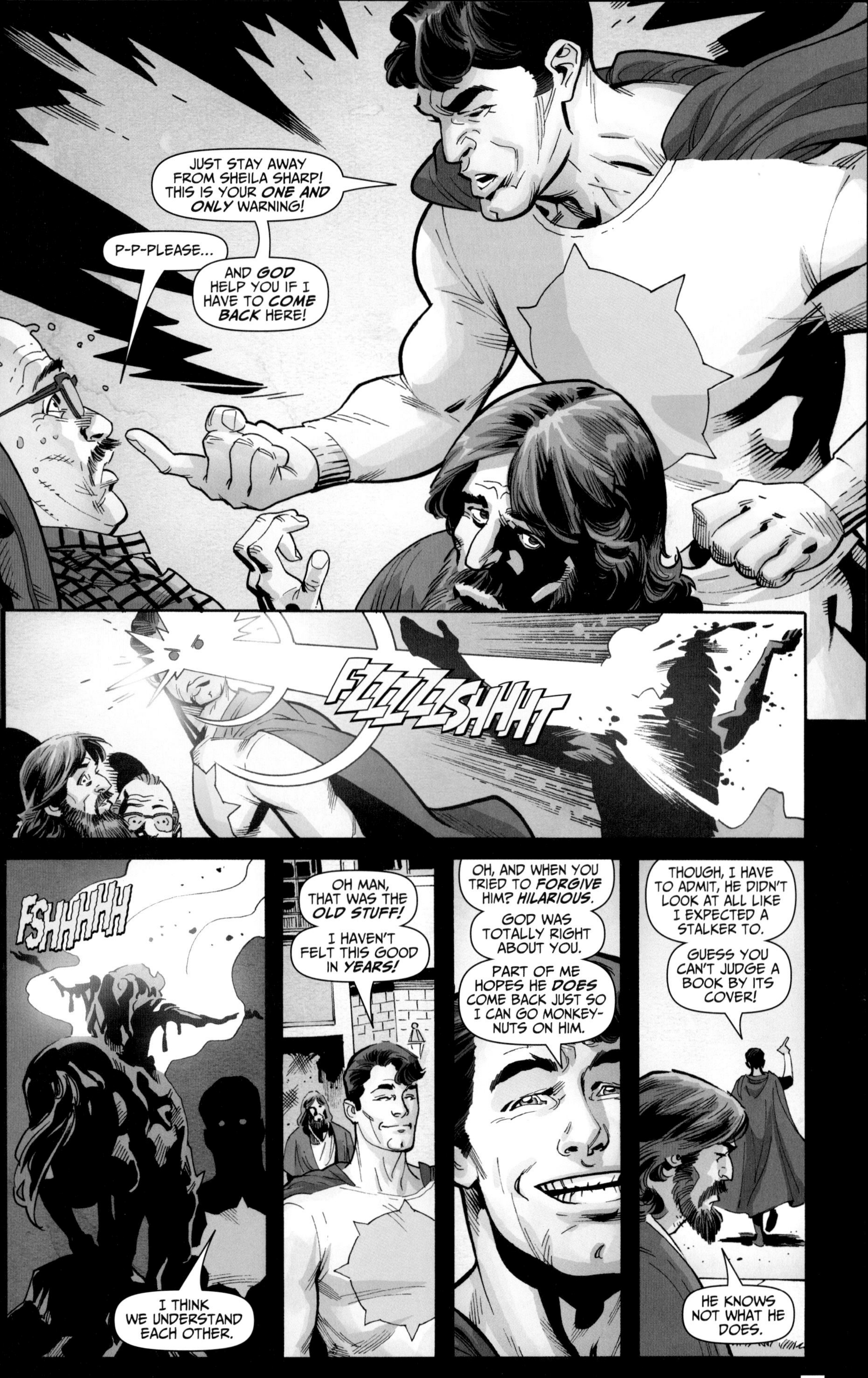

JUST STAY AWAY FROM SHEILA SHARP! THIS IS YOUR *ONE AND ONLY* WARNING!
P-P-PLEASE...
AND *GOD* HELP YOU IF I HAVE TO *COME BACK* HERE!
FZZZZSHHHT
FSHHHHH
I THINK WE UNDERSTAND EACH OTHER.
OH MAN, THAT WAS THE *OLD STUFF!*
I HAVEN'T FELT THIS GOOD IN *YEARS!*
OH, AND WHEN YOU TRIED TO *FORGIVE* HIM? *HILARIOUS.*
GOD WAS TOTALLY RIGHT ABOUT YOU.
PART OF ME HOPES HE *DOES* COME BACK JUST SO I CAN GO MONKEY-NUTS ON HIM.
THOUGH, I HAVE TO ADMIT, HE DIDN'T LOOK AT ALL LIKE I EXPECTED A STALKER TO.
GUESS YOU CAN'T JUDGE A BOOK BY ITS COVER!
HE KNOWS NOT WHAT HE DOES.

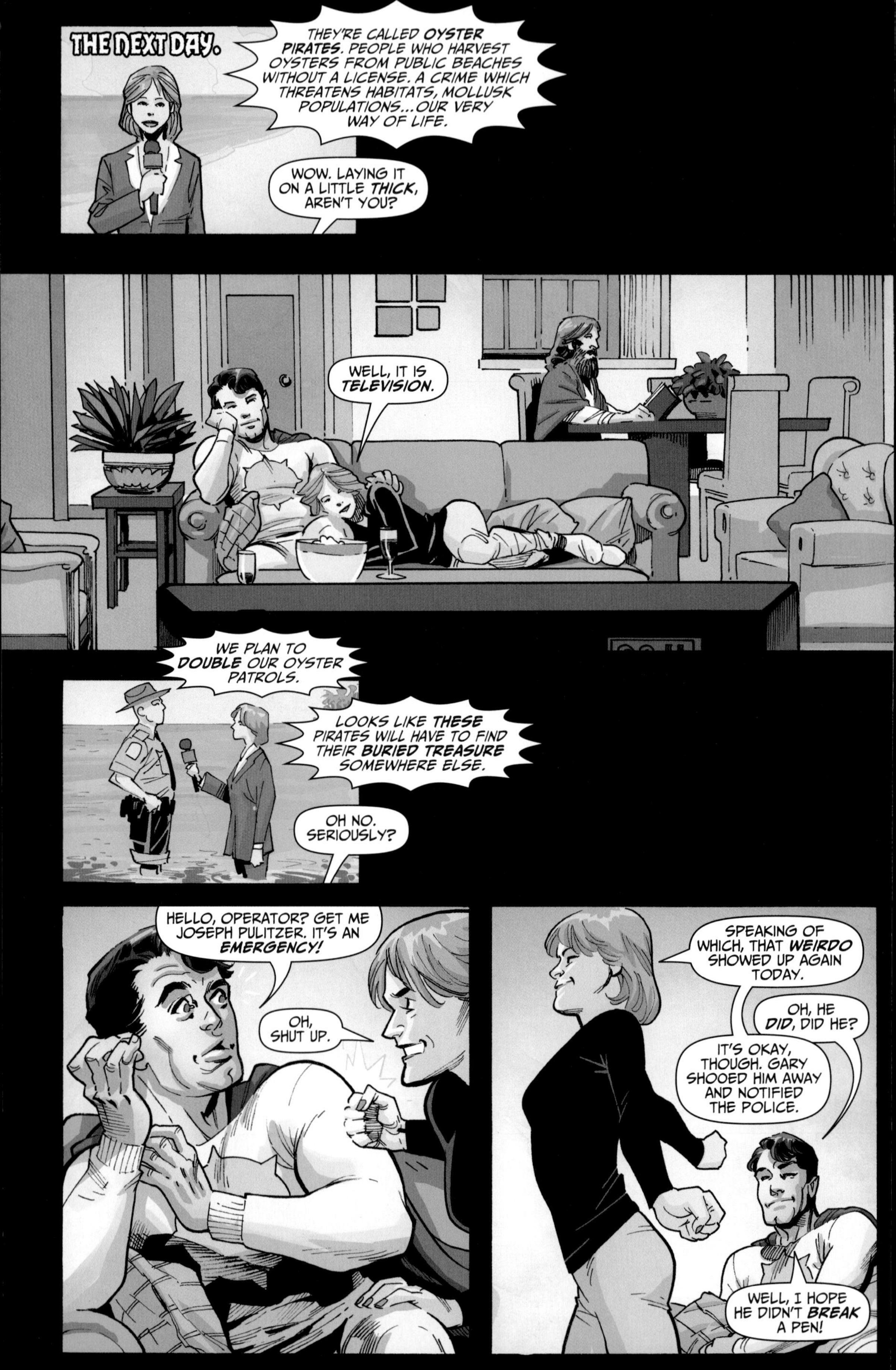
THE NEXT DAY.
THEY'RE CALLED OYSTER PIRATES. PEOPLE WHO HARVEST OYSTERS FROM PUBLIC BEACHES WITHOUT A LICENSE. A CRIME WHICH THREATENS HABITATS, MOLLUSK POPULATIONS...OUR VERY WAY OF LIFE.
WOW. LAYING IT ON A LITTLE THICK, AREN'T YOU?
WELL, IT IS TELEVISION.
WE PLAN TO DOUBLE OUR OYSTER PATROLS.
LOOKS LIKE THESE PIRATES WILL HAVE TO FIND THEIR BURIED TREASURE SOMEWHERE ELSE.
OH NO. SERIOUSLY?
HELLO, OPERATOR? GET ME JOSEPH PULITZER. IT'S AN EMERGENCY!
OH, SHUT UP.
SPEAKING OF WHICH, THAT WEIRDO SHOWED UP AGAIN TODAY.
OH, HE DID, DID HE?
IT'S OKAY, THOUGH. GARY SHOOED HIM AWAY AND NOTIFIED THE POLICE.
WELL, I HOPE HE DIDN'T BREAK A PEN!

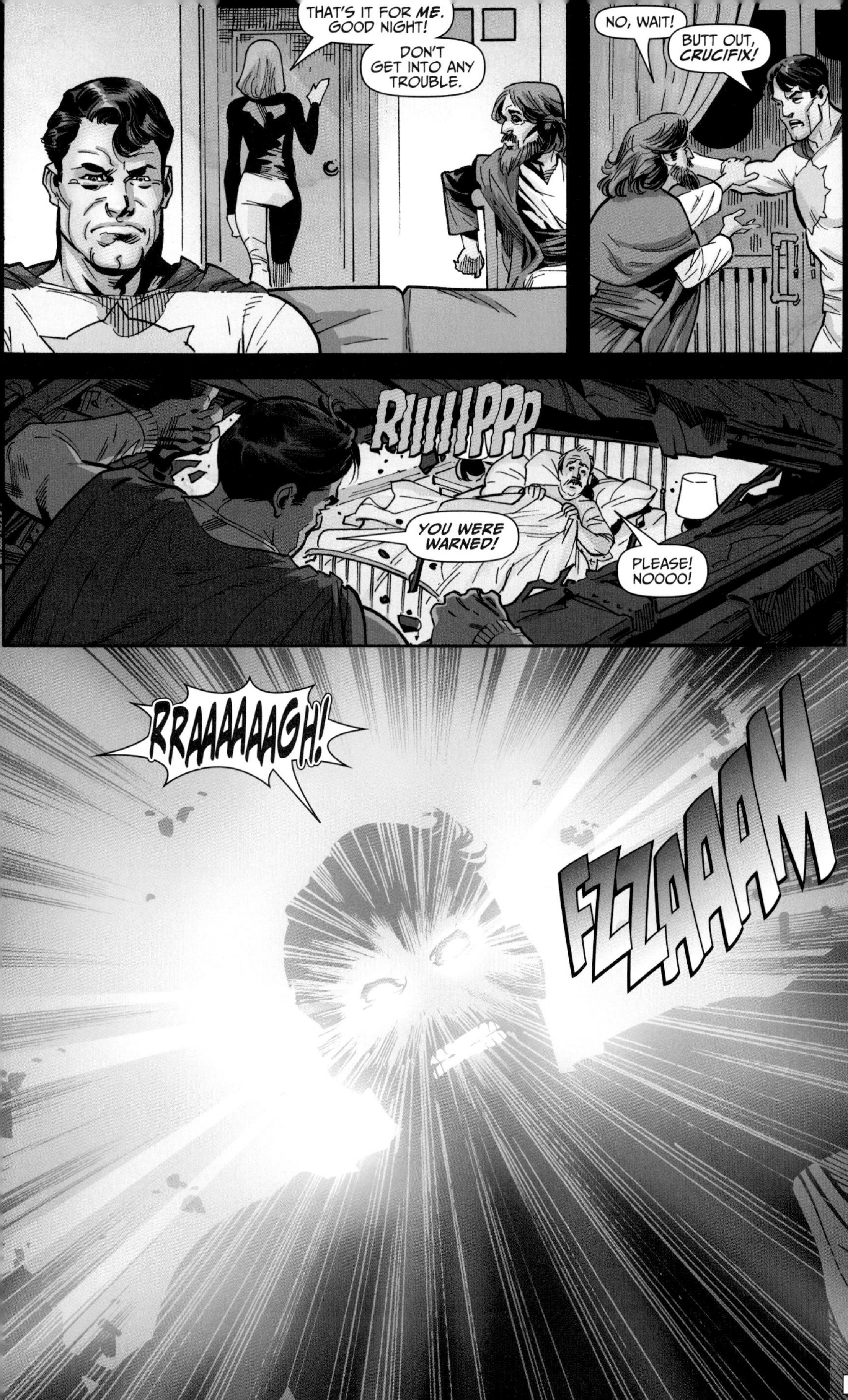

THAT'S IT FOR ME. GOOD NIGHT!
DON'T GET INTO ANY TROUBLE.
NO, WAIT!
BUTT OUT, CRUCIFIX!
RIIIIPPP
YOU WERE WARNED!
PLEASE! NOOOO!
RRAAAAAAGH!
FZZAAAM

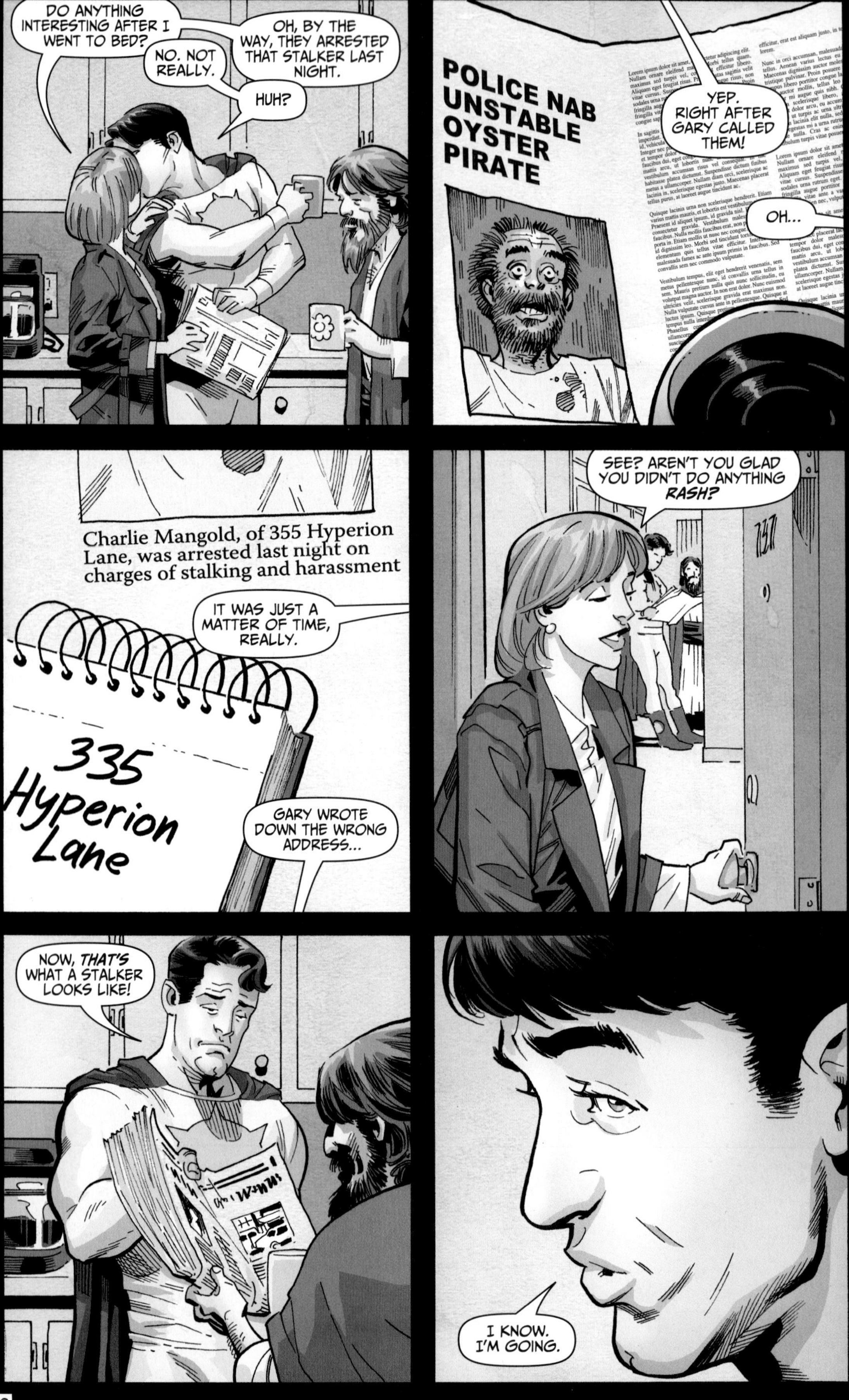
DO ANYTHING INTERESTING AFTER I WENT TO BED?
NO. NOT REALLY.
OH, BY THE WAY, THEY ARRESTED THAT STALKER LAST NIGHT.
HUH?
POLICE NAB UNSTABLE OYSTER PIRATE
YEP. RIGHT AFTER GARY CALLED THEM!
OH...
Charlie Mangold, of 355 Hyperion Lane, was arrested last night on charges of stalking and harassment
IT WAS JUST A MATTER OF TIME, REALLY.
335 Hyperion Lane
GARY WROTE DOWN THE WRONG ADDRESS...
SEE? AREN'T YOU GLAD YOU DIDN'T DO ANYTHING *RASH?*
NOW, *THAT'S* WHAT A STALKER LOOKS LIKE!
I KNOW. I'M GOING.

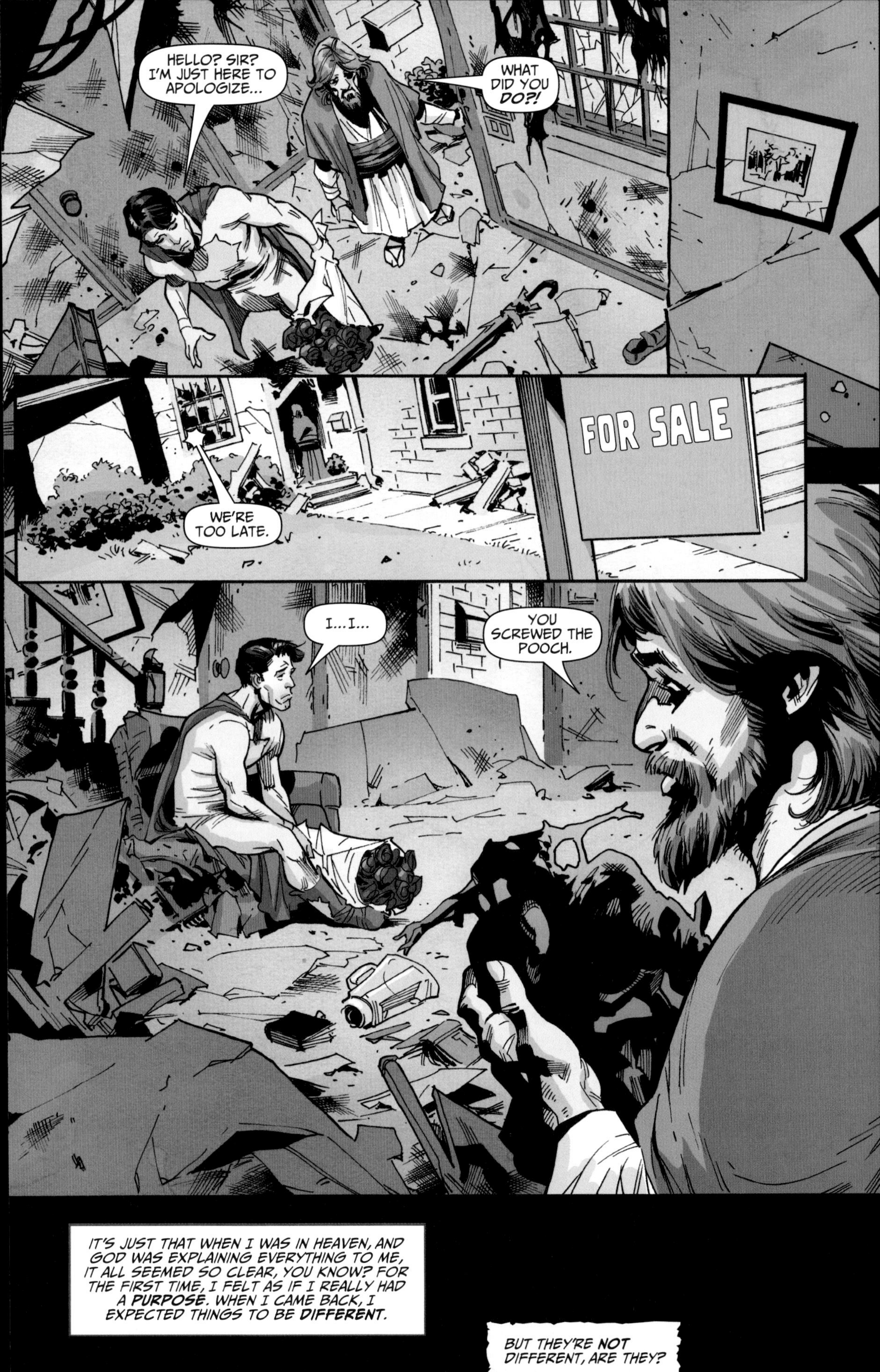
HELLO? SIR? I'M JUST HERE TO APOLOGIZE...
WHAT DID YOU DO?!
FOR SALE
WE'RE TOO LATE.
I...I...
YOU SCREWED THE POOCH.
IT'S JUST THAT WHEN I WAS IN HEAVEN, AND GOD WAS EXPLAINING EVERYTHING TO ME, IT ALL SEEMED SO CLEAR, YOU KNOW? FOR THE FIRST TIME, I FELT AS IF I REALLY HAD A PURPOSE. WHEN I CAME BACK, I EXPECTED THINGS TO BE DIFFERENT.
BUT THEY'RE NOT DIFFERENT, ARE THEY?

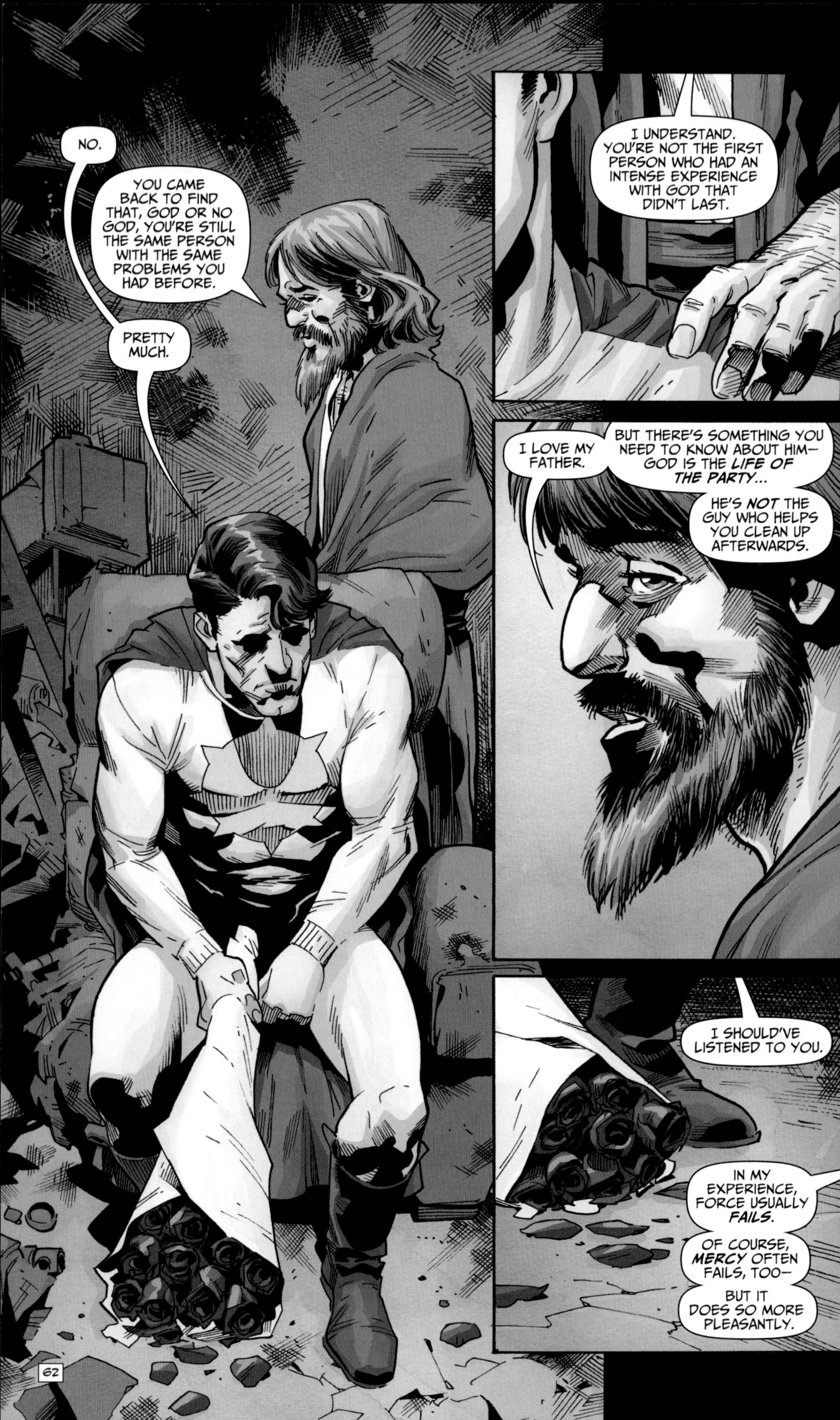
NO.
YOU CAME BACK TO FIND THAT, GOD OR NO GOD, YOU'RE STILL THE SAME PERSON WITH THE SAME PROBLEMS YOU HAD BEFORE.
PRETTY MUCH.
I UNDERSTAND. YOU'RE NOT THE FIRST PERSON WHO HAD AN INTENSE EXPERIENCE WITH GOD THAT DIDN'T LAST.
I LOVE MY FATHER.
BUT THERE'S SOMETHING YOU NEED TO KNOW ABOUT HIM— GOD IS THE *LIFE OF THE PARTY*...
HE'S *NOT* THE GUY WHO HELPS YOU CLEAN UP AFTERWARDS.
I SHOULD'VE LISTENED TO YOU.
IN MY EXPERIENCE, FORCE USUALLY *FAILS.*
OF COURSE, *MERCY* OFTEN FAILS, TOO—
BUT IT DOES SO MORE PLEASANTLY.

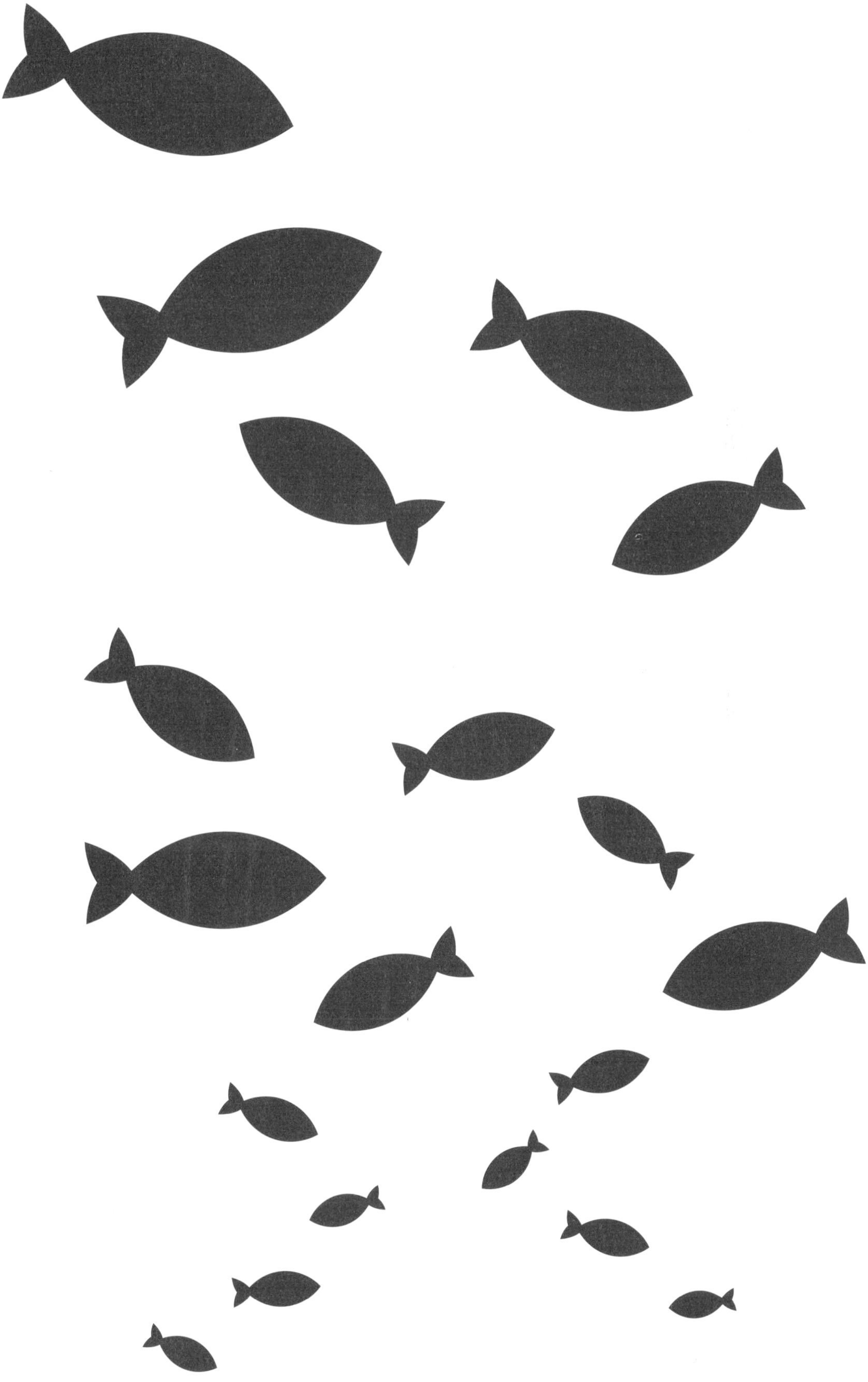

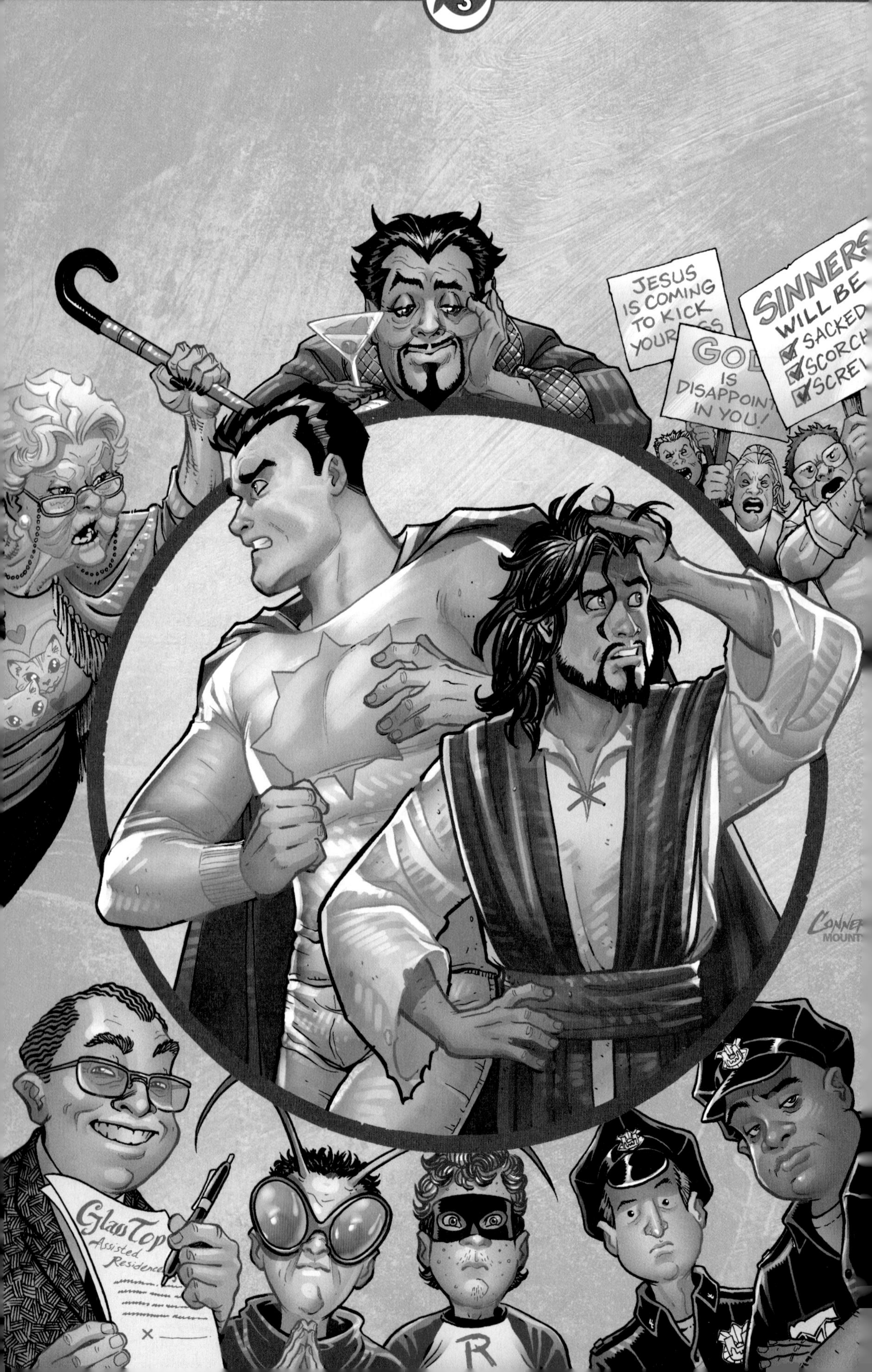
JESUS IS COMING TO KICK YOUR
GOD IS DISAPPOINT IN YOU!
SINNERS WILL BE
SACKED
SCORCH
SCRE
Glass Top Assisted Residence
R
CONNER MOUNT

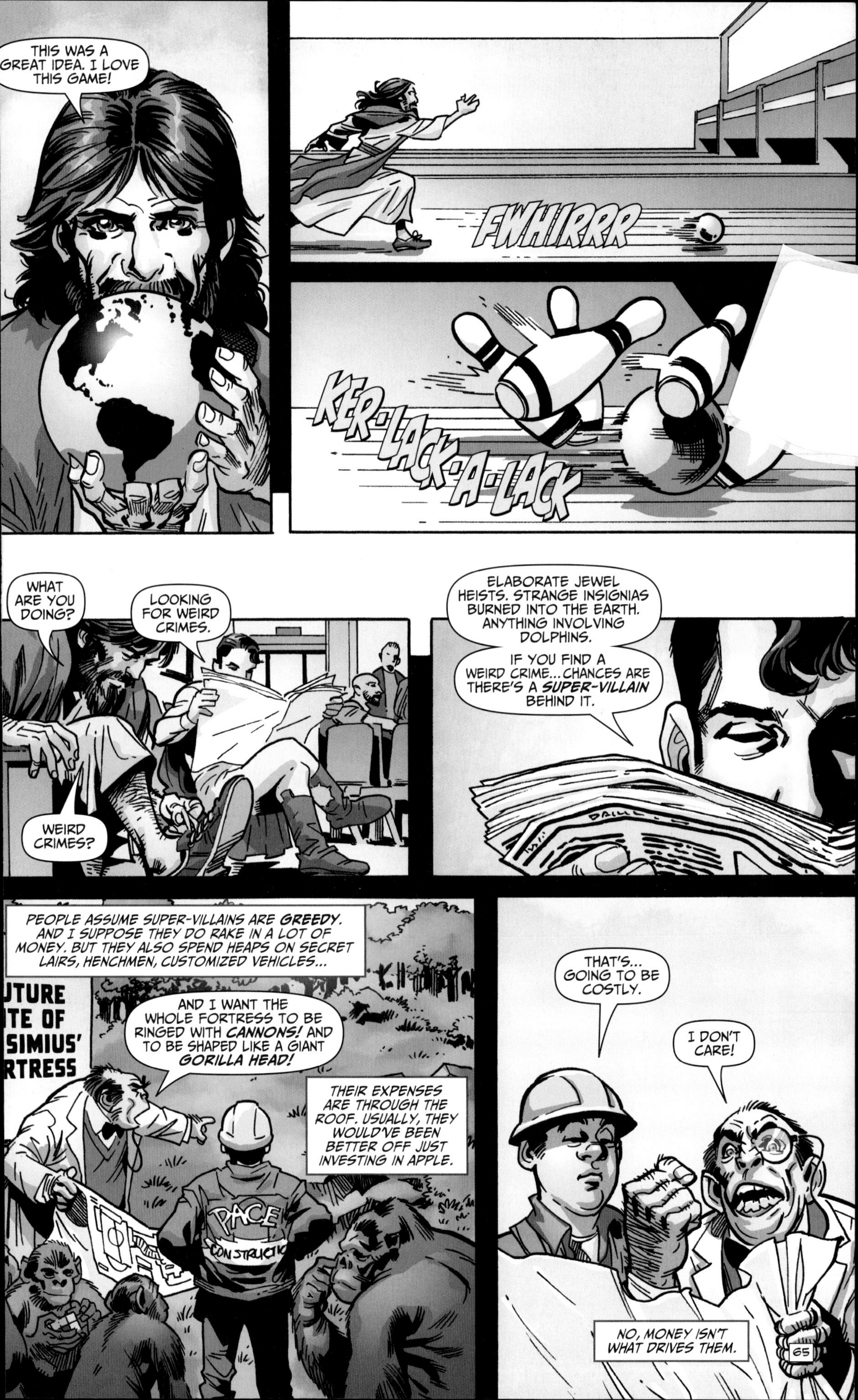

THIS WAS A GREAT IDEA. I LOVE THIS GAME!
FWHIRRR
KER-LACK-A-LACK
WHAT ARE YOU DOING?
LOOKING FOR WEIRD CRIMES.
WEIRD CRIMES?
ELABORATE JEWEL HEISTS. STRANGE INSIGNIAS BURNED INTO THE EARTH. ANYTHING INVOLVING DOLPHINS.
IF YOU FIND A WEIRD CRIME...CHANCES ARE THERE'S A SUPER-VILLAIN BEHIND IT.
PEOPLE ASSUME SUPER-VILLAINS ARE GREEDY. AND I SUPPOSE THEY DO RAKE IN A LOT OF MONEY. BUT THEY ALSO SPEND HEAPS ON SECRET LAIRS, HENCHMEN, CUSTOMIZED VEHICLES...
UTURE
TE OF
SIMIUS'
RTRESS
AND I WANT THE WHOLE FORTRESS TO BE RINGED WITH CANNONS! AND TO BE SHAPED LIKE A GIANT GORILLA HEAD!
THEIR EXPENSES ARE THROUGH THE ROOF. USUALLY, THEY WOULD'VE BEEN BETTER OFF JUST INVESTING IN APPLE.
PACE
CONSTRUCTIO
THAT'S... GOING TO BE COSTLY.
I DON'T CARE!
NO, MONEY ISN'T WHAT DRIVES THEM.

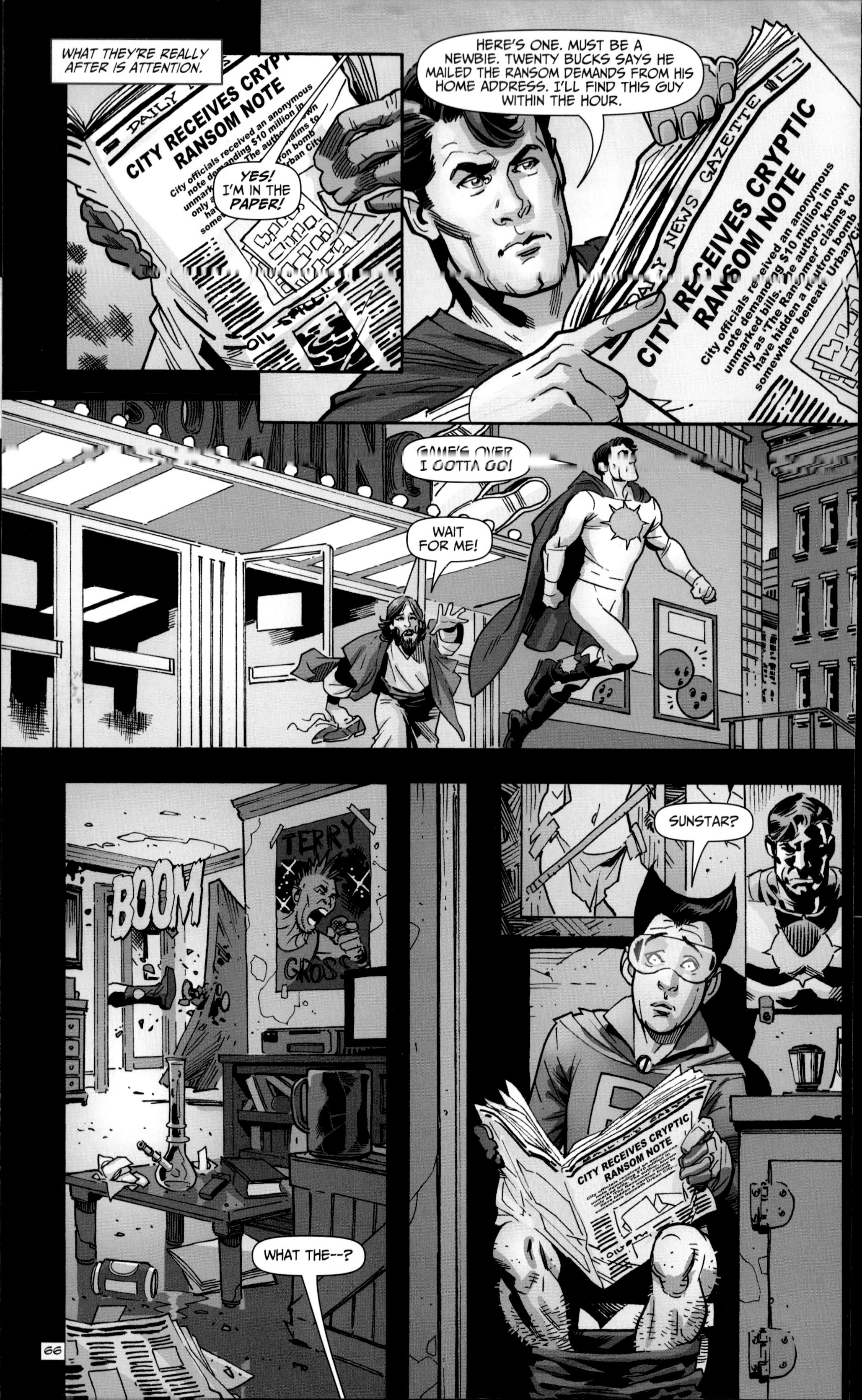
WHAT THEY'RE REALLY AFTER IS ATTENTION.
CITY RECEIVES CRYPTIC RANSOM NOTE
YES! I'M IN THE PAPER!
HERE'S ONE. MUST BE A NEWBIE. TWENTY BUCKS SAYS HE MAILED THE RANSOM DEMANDS FROM HIS HOME ADDRESS. I'LL FIND THIS GUY WITHIN THE HOUR.
DAILY NEWS GAZETTE
CITY RECEIVES CRYPTIC RANSOM NOTE
GAME'S OVER I GOTTA GO!
WAIT FOR ME!
BOOM
TERRY GROSS
WHAT THE--?
SUNSTAR?
CITY RECEIVES CRYPTIC RANSOM NOTE

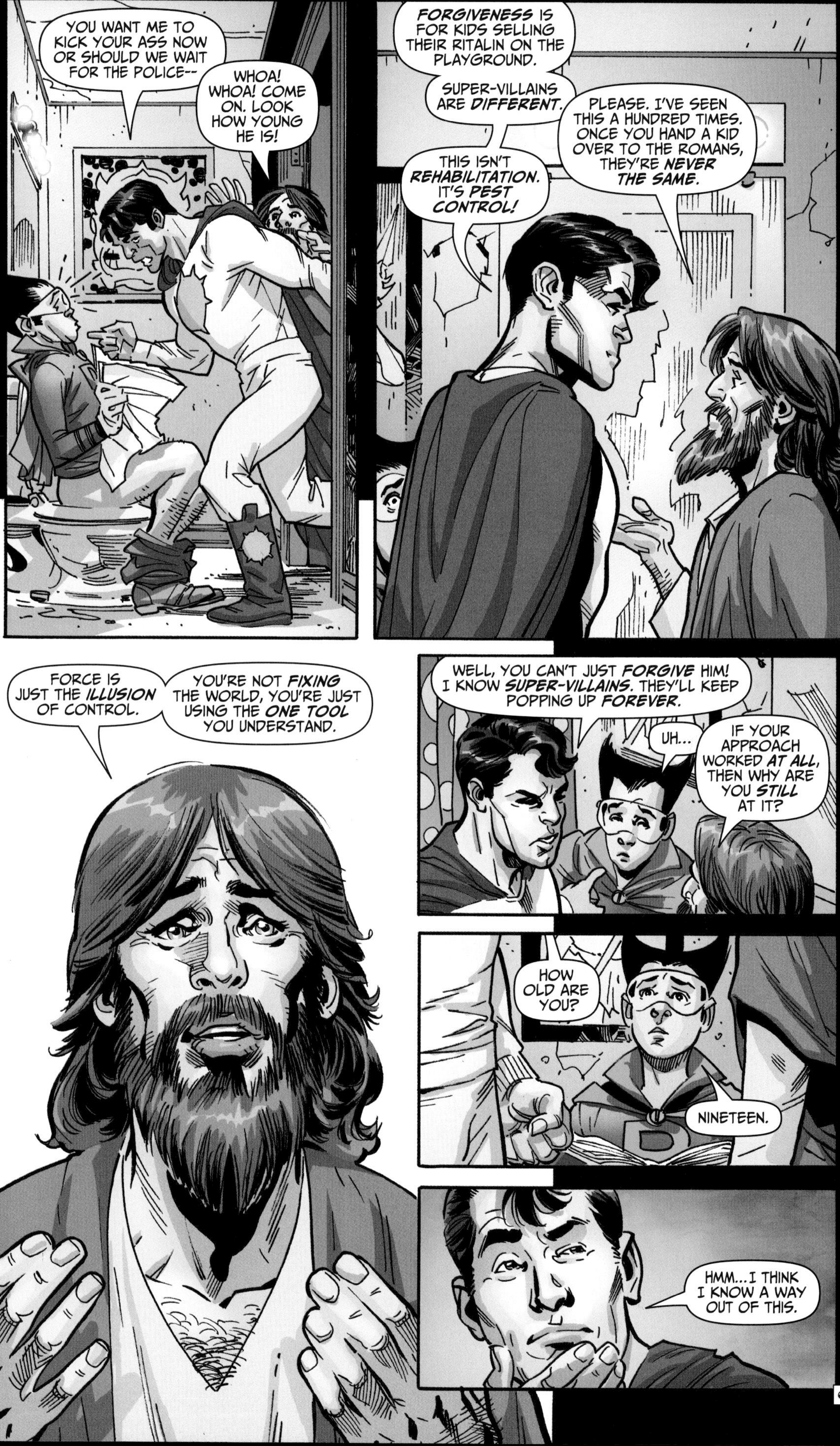
YOU WANT ME TO KICK YOUR ASS NOW OR SHOULD WE WAIT FOR THE POLICE--
WHOA! WHOA! COME ON. LOOK HOW YOUNG HE IS!
FORGIVENESS IS FOR KIDS SELLING THEIR RITALIN ON THE PLAYGROUND.
SUPER-VILLAINS ARE DIFFERENT.
THIS ISN'T REHABILITATION. IT'S PEST CONTROL!
PLEASE. I'VE SEEN THIS A HUNDRED TIMES. ONCE YOU HAND A KID OVER TO THE ROMANS, THEY'RE NEVER THE SAME.
FORCE IS JUST THE ILLUSION OF CONTROL.
YOU'RE NOT FIXING THE WORLD, YOU'RE JUST USING THE ONE TOOL YOU UNDERSTAND.
WELL, YOU CAN'T JUST FORGIVE HIM! I KNOW SUPER-VILLAINS. THEY'LL KEEP POPPING UP FOREVER.
UH...
IF YOUR APPROACH WORKED AT ALL, THEN WHY ARE YOU STILL AT IT?
HOW OLD ARE YOU?
NINETEEN.
HMM...I THINK I KNOW A WAY OUT OF THIS.

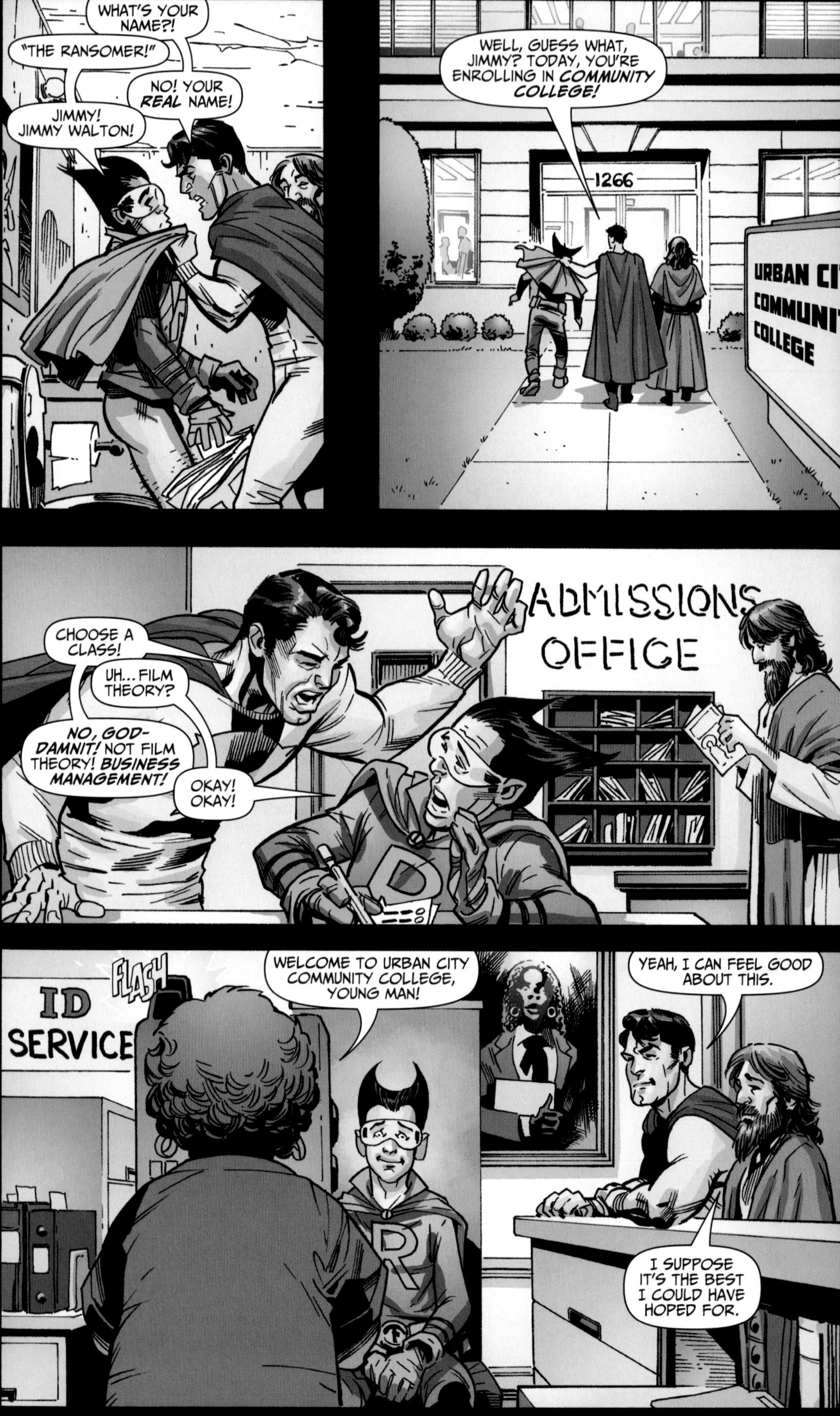
WHAT'S YOUR NAME?!
"THE RANSOMER!"
NO! YOUR REAL NAME!
JIMMY! JIMMY WALTON!
WELL, GUESS WHAT, JIMMY? TODAY, YOU'RE ENROLLING IN COMMUNITY COLLEGE!
1266
URBAN CIT
COMMUNIT
COLLEGE
ADMISSIONS OFFICE
CHOOSE A CLASS!
UH... FILM THEORY?
NO, GOD-DAMNIT! NOT FILM THEORY! BUSINESS MANAGEMENT!
OKAY! OKAY!
ID SERVICE
FLASH
WELCOME TO URBAN CITY COMMUNITY COLLEGE, YOUNG MAN!
YEAH, I CAN FEEL GOOD ABOUT THIS.
I SUPPOSE IT'S THE BEST I COULD HAVE HOPED FOR.

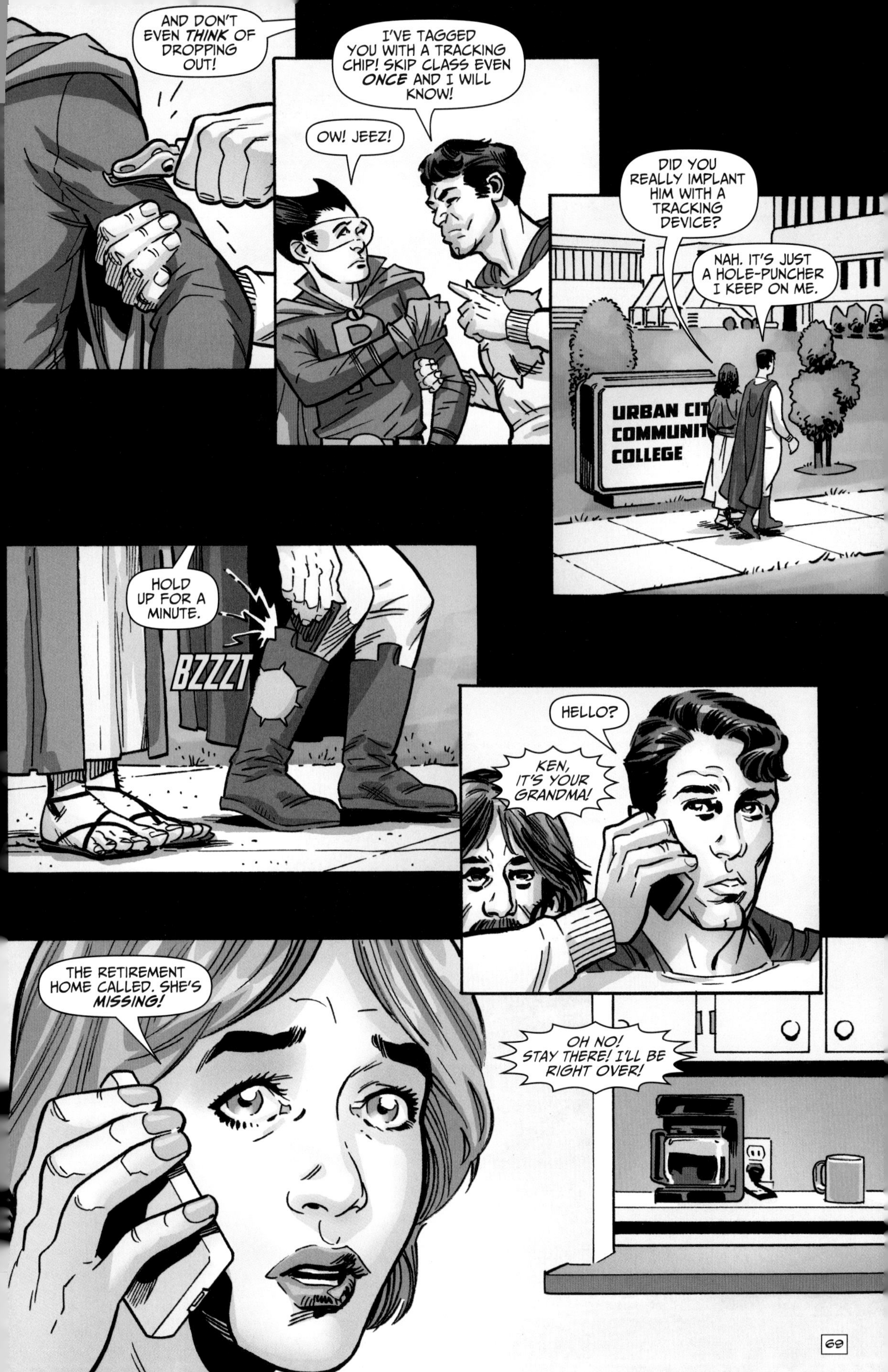
AND DON'T EVEN THINK OF DROPPING OUT!
I'VE TAGGED YOU WITH A TRACKING CHIP! SKIP CLASS EVEN ONCE AND I WILL KNOW!
OW! JEEZ!
DID YOU REALLY IMPLANT HIM WITH A TRACKING DEVICE?
NAH. IT'S JUST A HOLE-PUNCHER I KEEP ON ME.
URBAN CIT
COMMUNIT
COLLEGE
HOLD UP FOR A MINUTE.
BZZZT
HELLO?
KEN, IT'S YOUR GRANDMA!
THE RETIREMENT HOME CALLED. SHE'S MISSING!
OH NO! STAY THERE! I'LL BE RIGHT OVER!

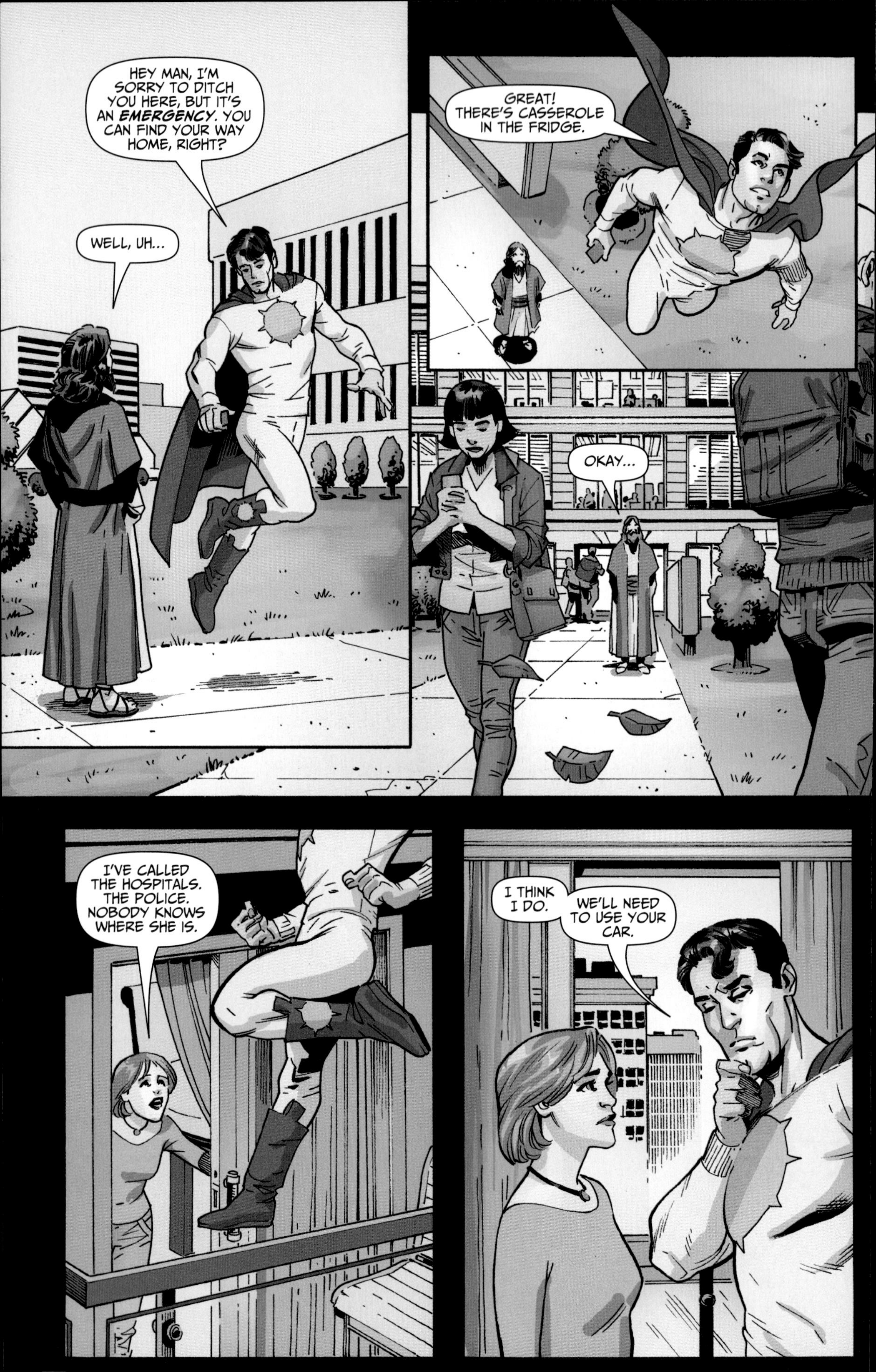
HEY MAN, I'M SORRY TO DITCH YOU HERE, BUT IT'S AN ***EMERGENCY***. YOU CAN FIND YOUR WAY HOME, RIGHT?
WELL, UH...
GREAT! THERE'S CASSEROLE IN THE FRIDGE.
OKAY...
I'VE CALLED THE HOSPITALS. THE POLICE. NOBODY KNOWS WHERE SHE IS.
I THINK I DO.
WE'LL NEED TO USE YOUR CAR.

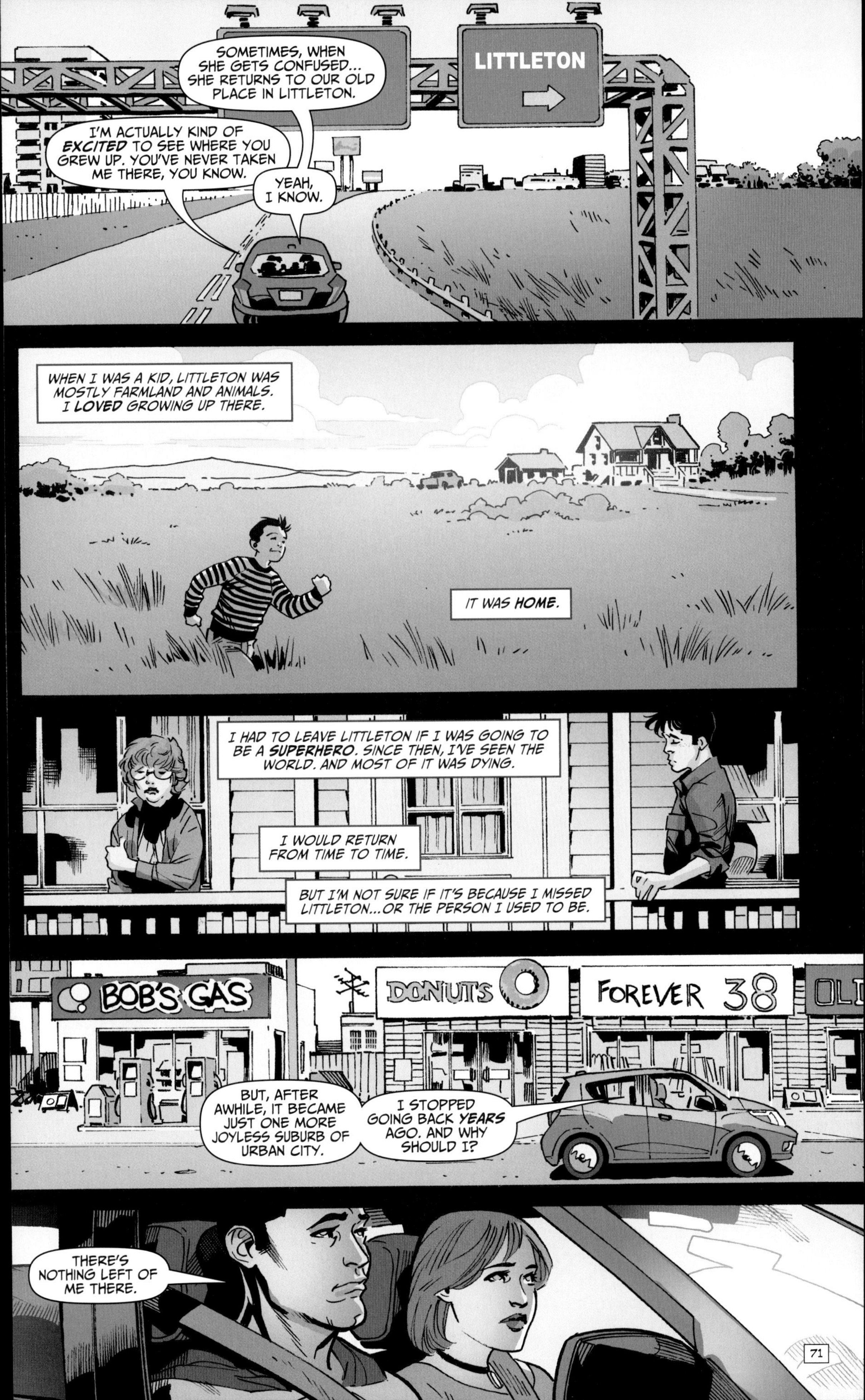
LITTLETON
SOMETIMES, WHEN SHE GETS CONFUSED... SHE RETURNS TO OUR OLD PLACE IN LITTLETON.
I'M ACTUALLY KIND OF EXCITED TO SEE WHERE YOU GREW UP. YOU'VE NEVER TAKEN ME THERE, YOU KNOW.
YEAH, I KNOW.
WHEN I WAS A KID, LITTLETON WAS MOSTLY FARMLAND AND ANIMALS. I LOVED GROWING UP THERE.
IT WAS HOME.
I HAD TO LEAVE LITTLETON IF I WAS GOING TO BE A SUPERHERO. SINCE THEN, I'VE SEEN THE WORLD. AND MOST OF IT WAS DYING.
I WOULD RETURN FROM TIME TO TIME.
BUT I'M NOT SURE IF IT'S BECAUSE I MISSED LITTLETON...OR THE PERSON I USED TO BE.
BOB'S GAS
DONUTS
FOREVER 38
BUT, AFTER AWHILE, IT BECAME JUST ONE MORE JOYLESS SUBURB OF URBAN CITY.
I STOPPED GOING BACK YEARS AGO. AND WHY SHOULD I?
THERE'S NOTHING LEFT OF ME THERE.

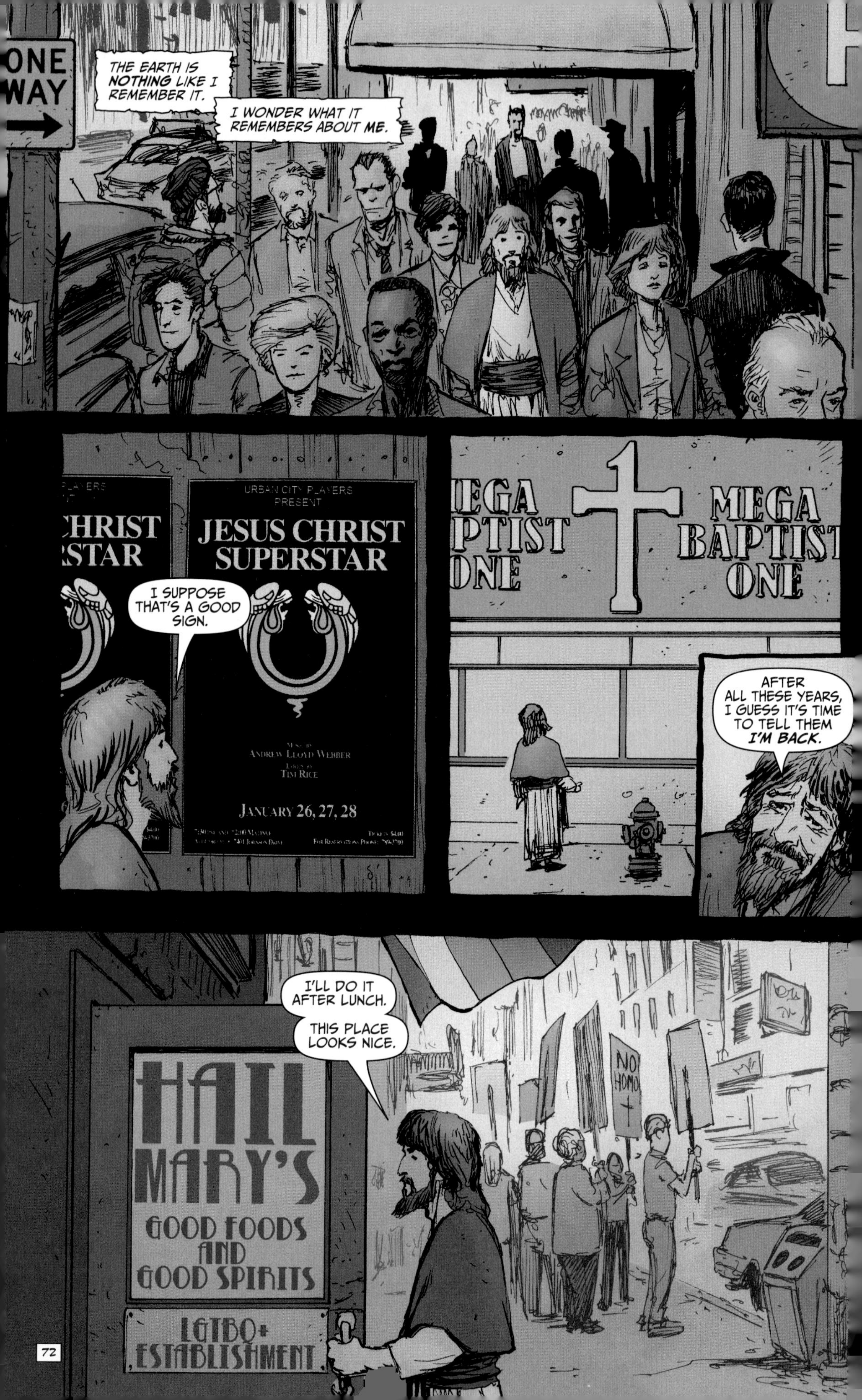

ONE WAY
THE EARTH IS NOTHING LIKE I REMEMBER IT.
I WONDER WHAT IT REMEMBERS ABOUT ME.
URBAN CITY PLAYERS PRESENT
JESUS CHRIST SUPERSTAR
I SUPPOSE THAT'S A GOOD SIGN.
ANDREW LLOYD WEBBER
TIM RICE
JANUARY 26, 27, 28
MEGA BAPTIST ONE
AFTER ALL THESE YEARS, I GUESS IT'S TIME TO TELL THEM I'M BACK.
I'LL DO IT AFTER LUNCH.
THIS PLACE LOOKS NICE.
NO HOMO
HAIL MARY'S
GOOD FOODS AND GOOD SPIRITS
LGTBQ+ ESTABLISHMENT

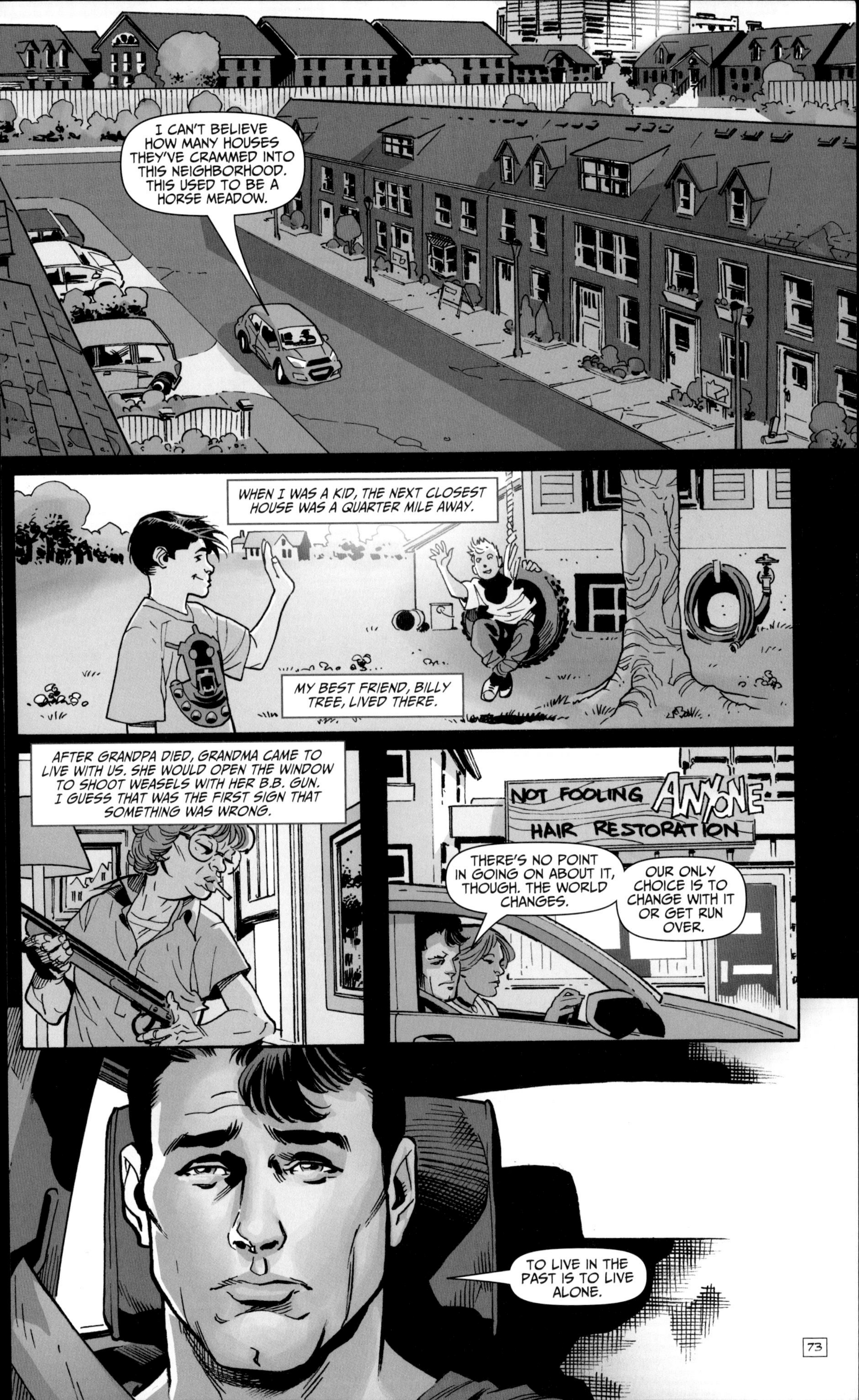
I CAN'T BELIEVE HOW MANY HOUSES THEY'VE CRAMMED INTO THIS NEIGHBORHOOD. THIS USED TO BE A HORSE MEADOW.
WHEN I WAS A KID, THE NEXT CLOSEST HOUSE WAS A QUARTER MILE AWAY.
MY BEST FRIEND, BILLY TREE, LIVED THERE.
AFTER GRANDPA DIED, GRANDMA CAME TO LIVE WITH US. SHE WOULD OPEN THE WINDOW TO SHOOT WEASELS WITH HER B.B. GUN. I GUESS THAT WAS THE FIRST SIGN THAT SOMETHING WAS WRONG.
NOT FOOLING ANYONE
HAIR RESTORATION
THERE'S NO POINT IN GOING ON ABOUT IT, THOUGH. THE WORLD CHANGES.
OUR ONLY CHOICE IS TO CHANGE WITH IT OR GET RUN OVER.
TO LIVE IN THE PAST IS TO LIVE ALONE.

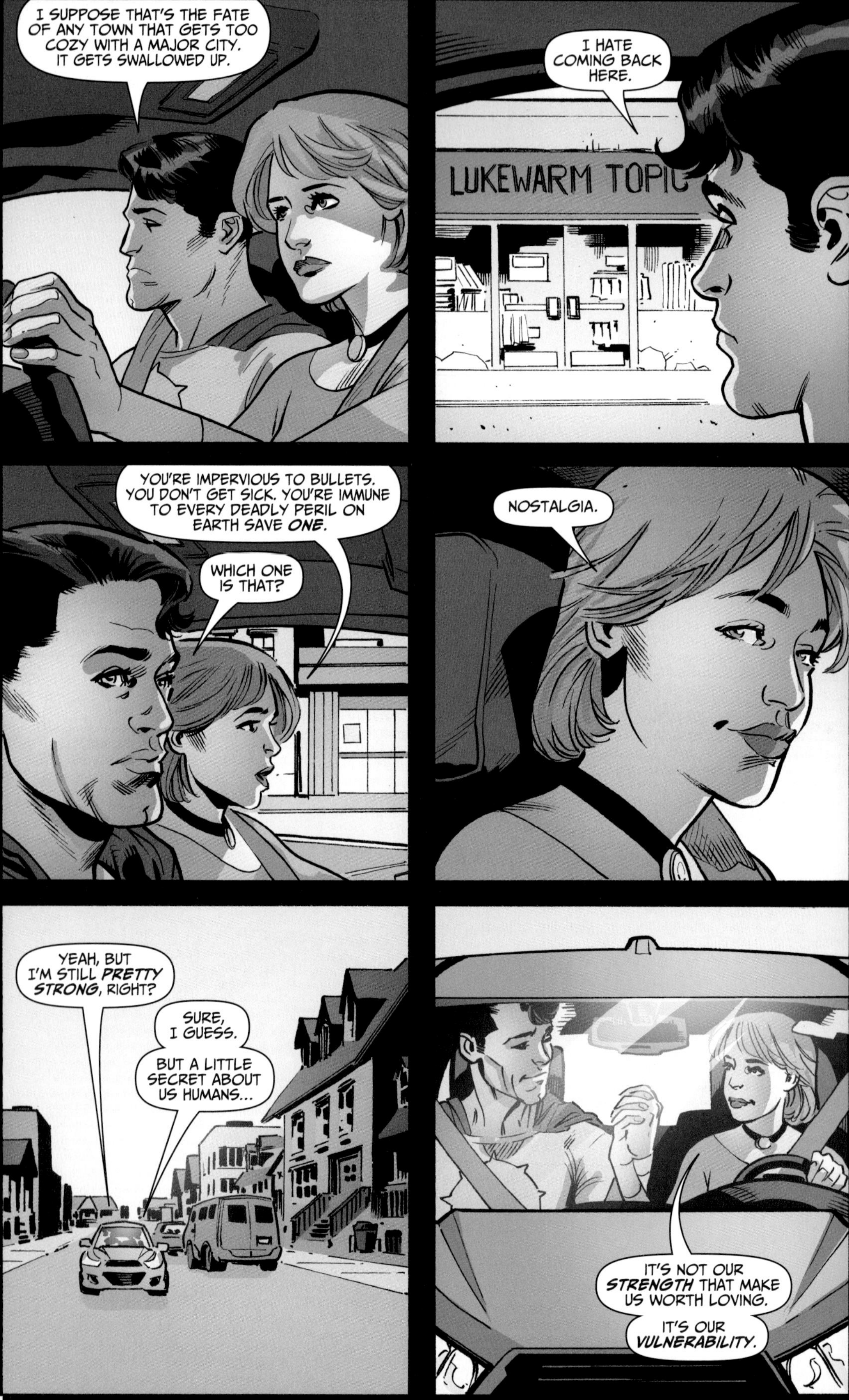
I SUPPOSE THAT'S THE FATE OF ANY TOWN THAT GETS TOO COZY WITH A MAJOR CITY. IT GETS SWALLOWED UP.
I HATE COMING BACK HERE.
LUKEWARM TOPIC
YOU'RE IMPERVIOUS TO BULLETS. YOU DON'T GET SICK. YOU'RE IMMUNE TO EVERY DEADLY PERIL ON EARTH SAVE *ONE*.
WHICH ONE IS THAT?
NOSTALGIA.
YEAH, BUT I'M STILL *PRETTY STRONG*, RIGHT?
SURE, I GUESS.
BUT A LITTLE SECRET ABOUT US HUMANS...
IT'S NOT OUR *STRENGTH* THAT MAKE US WORTH LOVING.
IT'S OUR *VULNERABILITY*.

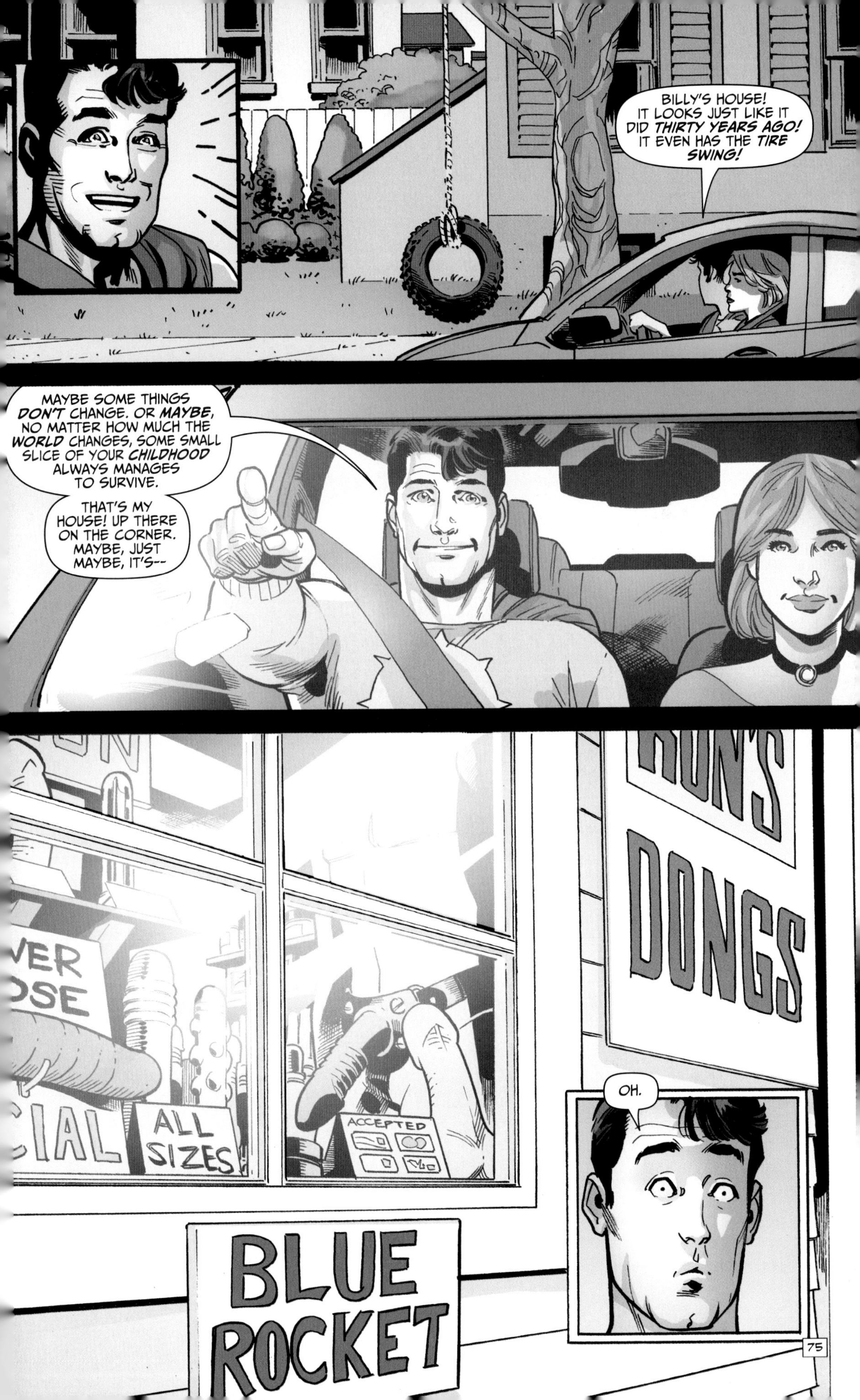

BILLY'S HOUSE! IT LOOKS JUST LIKE IT DID *THIRTY YEARS AGO!* IT EVEN HAS THE *TIRE SWING!*
MAYBE SOME THINGS *DON'T* CHANGE. OR *MAYBE,* NO MATTER HOW MUCH THE *WORLD* CHANGES, SOME SMALL SLICE OF YOUR *CHILDHOOD* ALWAYS MANAGES TO SURVIVE.
THAT'S MY HOUSE! UP THERE ON THE CORNER. MAYBE, JUST MAYBE, IT'S--
DONGS
ALL SIZES
ACCEPTED
OH.
BLUE ROCKET

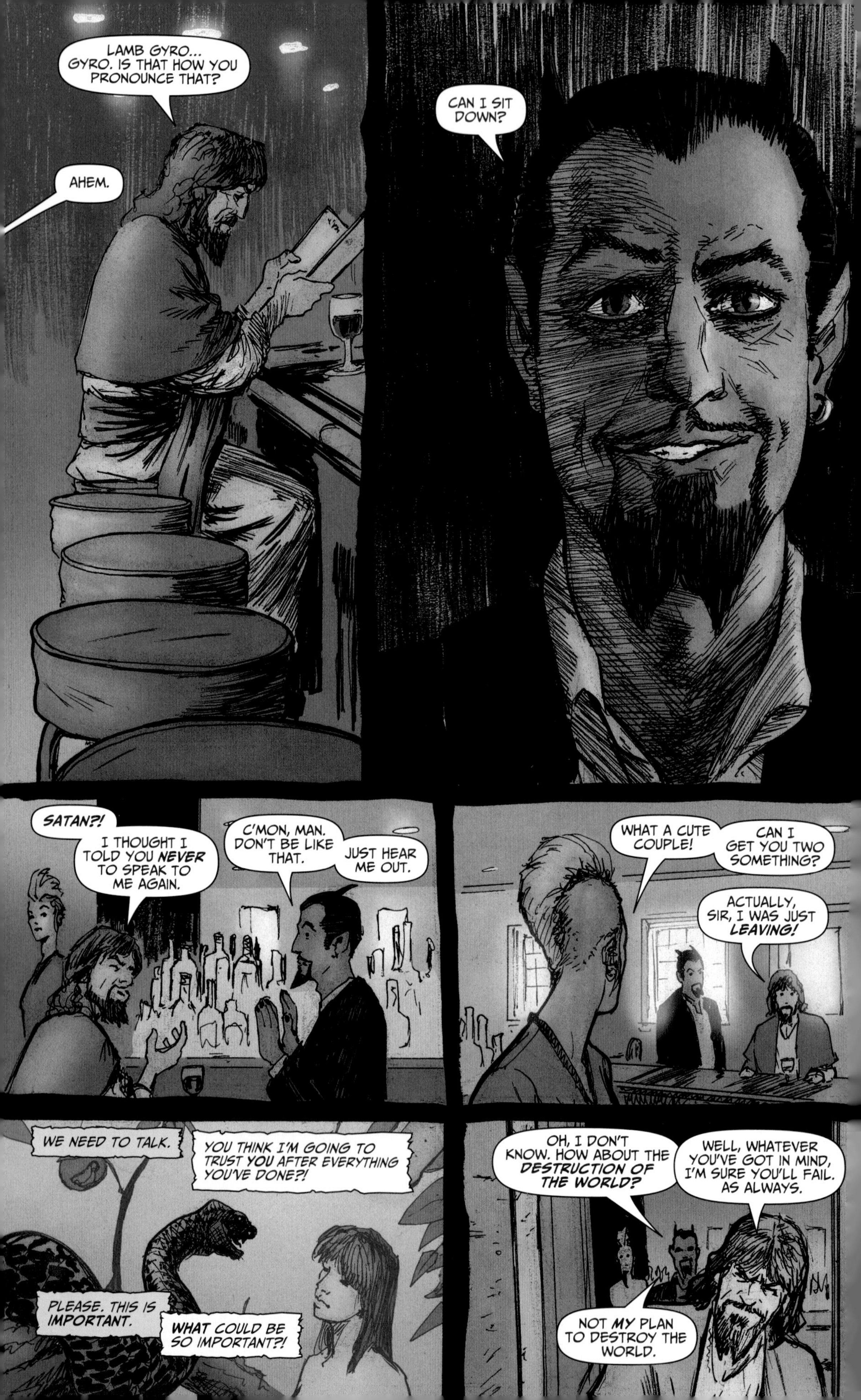
LAMB GYRO... GYRO. IS THAT HOW YOU PRONOUNCE THAT?
AHEM.
CAN I SIT DOWN?
SATAN?!
I THOUGHT I TOLD YOU NEVER TO SPEAK TO ME AGAIN.
C'MON, MAN. DON'T BE LIKE THAT.
JUST HEAR ME OUT.
WHAT A CUTE COUPLE!
CAN I GET YOU TWO SOMETHING?
ACTUALLY, SIR, I WAS JUST LEAVING!
WE NEED TO TALK.
YOU THINK I'M GOING TO TRUST YOU AFTER EVERYTHING YOU'VE DONE?!
PLEASE. THIS IS IMPORTANT.
WHAT COULD BE SO IMPORTANT?!
OH, I DON'T KNOW. HOW ABOUT THE DESTRUCTION OF THE WORLD?
WELL, WHATEVER YOU'VE GOT IN MIND, I'M SURE YOU'LL FAIL. AS ALWAYS.
NOT MY PLAN TO DESTROY THE WORLD.

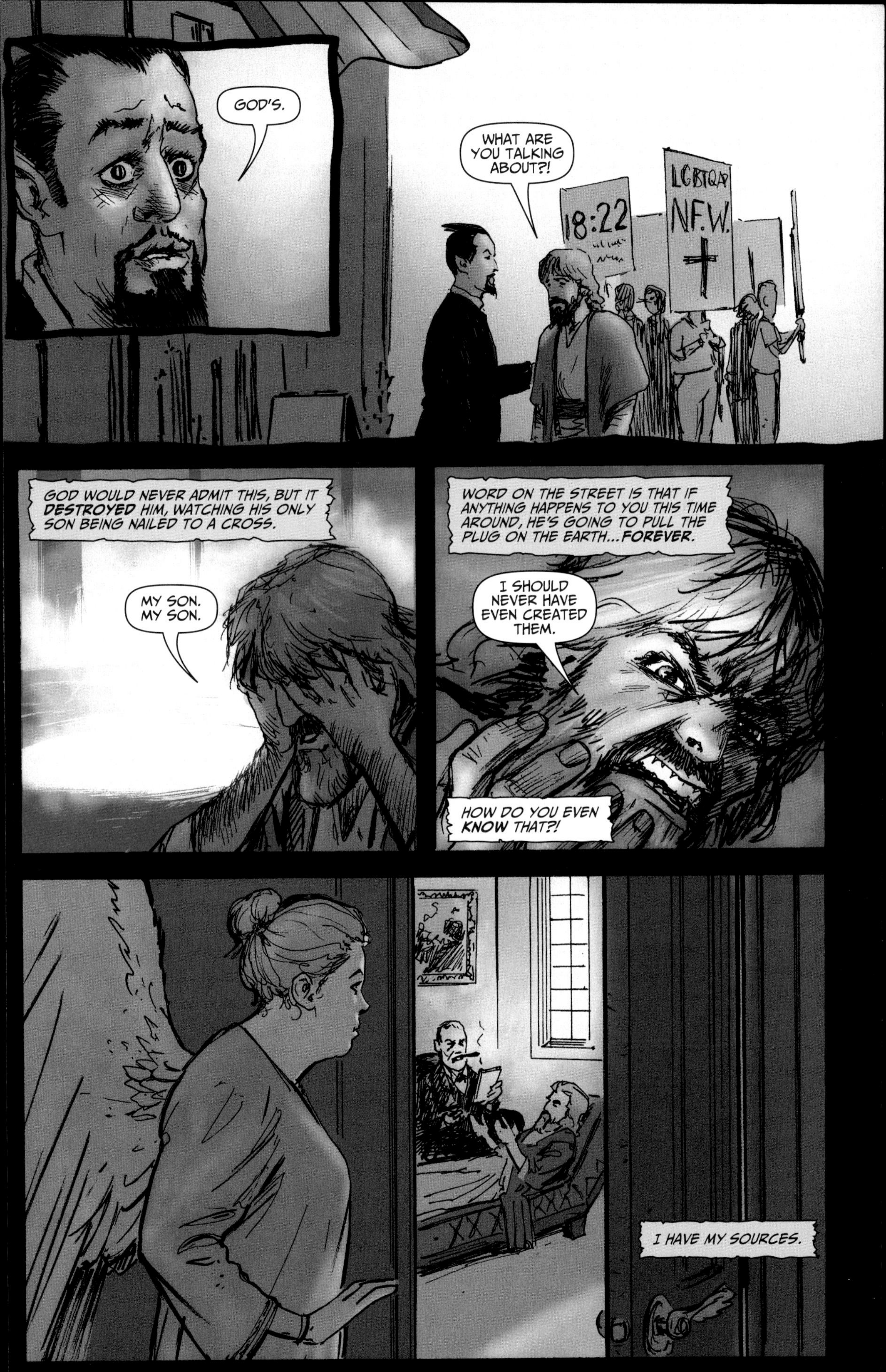
GOD'S.
WHAT ARE YOU TALKING ABOUT?!
18:22
LGBTQA NF.W.
GOD WOULD NEVER ADMIT THIS, BUT IT DESTROYED HIM, WATCHING HIS ONLY SON BEING NAILED TO A CROSS.
MY SON. MY SON.
WORD ON THE STREET IS THAT IF ANYTHING HAPPENS TO YOU THIS TIME AROUND, HE'S GOING TO PULL THE PLUG ON THE EARTH...FOREVER.
I SHOULD NEVER HAVE EVEN CREATED THEM.
HOW DO YOU EVEN KNOW THAT?!
I HAVE MY SOURCES.

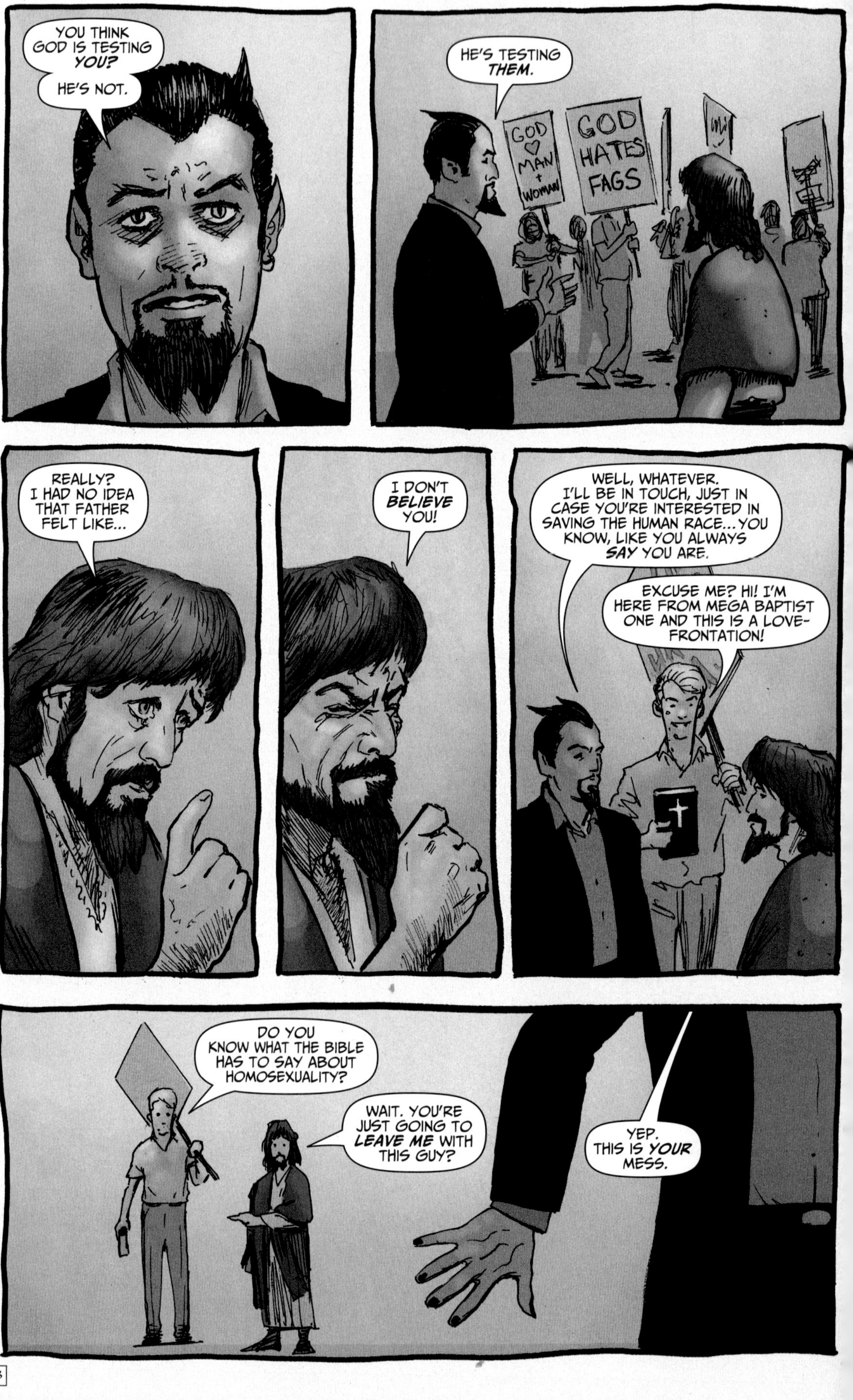
YOU THINK GOD IS TESTING ***YOU?***
HE'S NOT.
HE'S TESTING ***THEM.***
GOD ♡ MAN + WOMAN
GOD HATES FAGS
REALLY? I HAD NO IDEA THAT FATHER FELT LIKE...
I DON'T ***BELIEVE*** YOU!
WELL, WHATEVER. I'LL BE IN TOUCH, JUST IN CASE YOU'RE INTERESTED IN SAVING THE HUMAN RACE...YOU KNOW, LIKE YOU ALWAYS ***SAY*** YOU ARE.
EXCUSE ME? HI! I'M HERE FROM MEGA BAPTIST ONE AND THIS IS A LOVE-FRONTATION!
DO YOU KNOW WHAT THE BIBLE HAS TO SAY ABOUT HOMOSEXUALITY?
WAIT. YOU'RE JUST GOING TO ***LEAVE ME*** WITH THIS GUY?
YEP. THIS IS ***YOUR*** MESS.

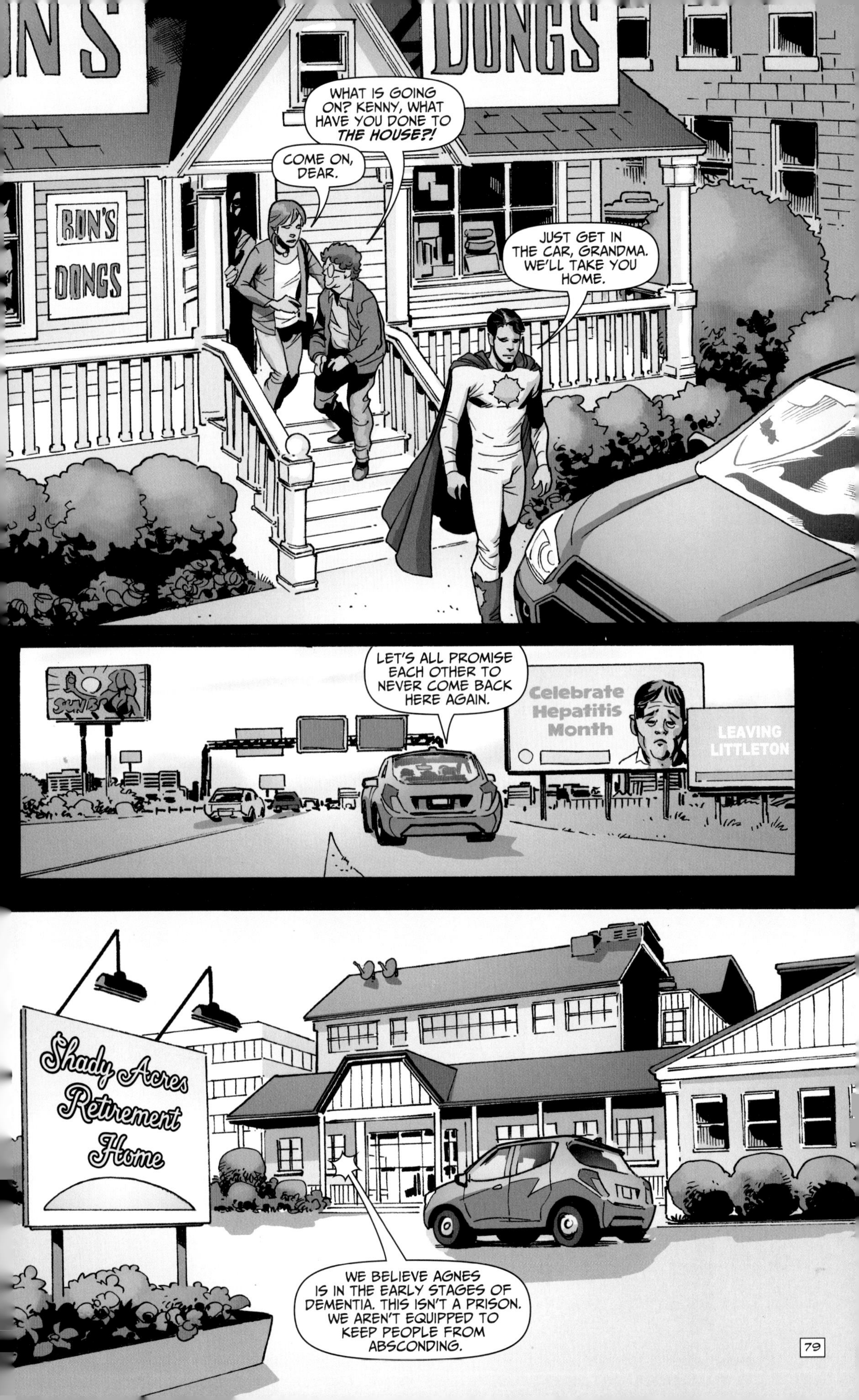
NS
DONGS
RON'S DONGS
WHAT IS GOING ON? KENNY, WHAT HAVE YOU DONE TO *THE HOUSE?!*
COME ON, DEAR.
JUST GET IN THE CAR, GRANDMA. WE'LL TAKE YOU HOME.
LET'S ALL PROMISE EACH OTHER TO NEVER COME BACK HERE AGAIN.
Celebrate Hepatitis Month
LEAVING LITTLETON
Shady Acres Retirement Home
WE BELIEVE AGNES IS IN THE EARLY STAGES OF DEMENTIA. THIS ISN'T A PRISON. WE AREN'T EQUIPPED TO KEEP PEOPLE FROM ABSCONDING.

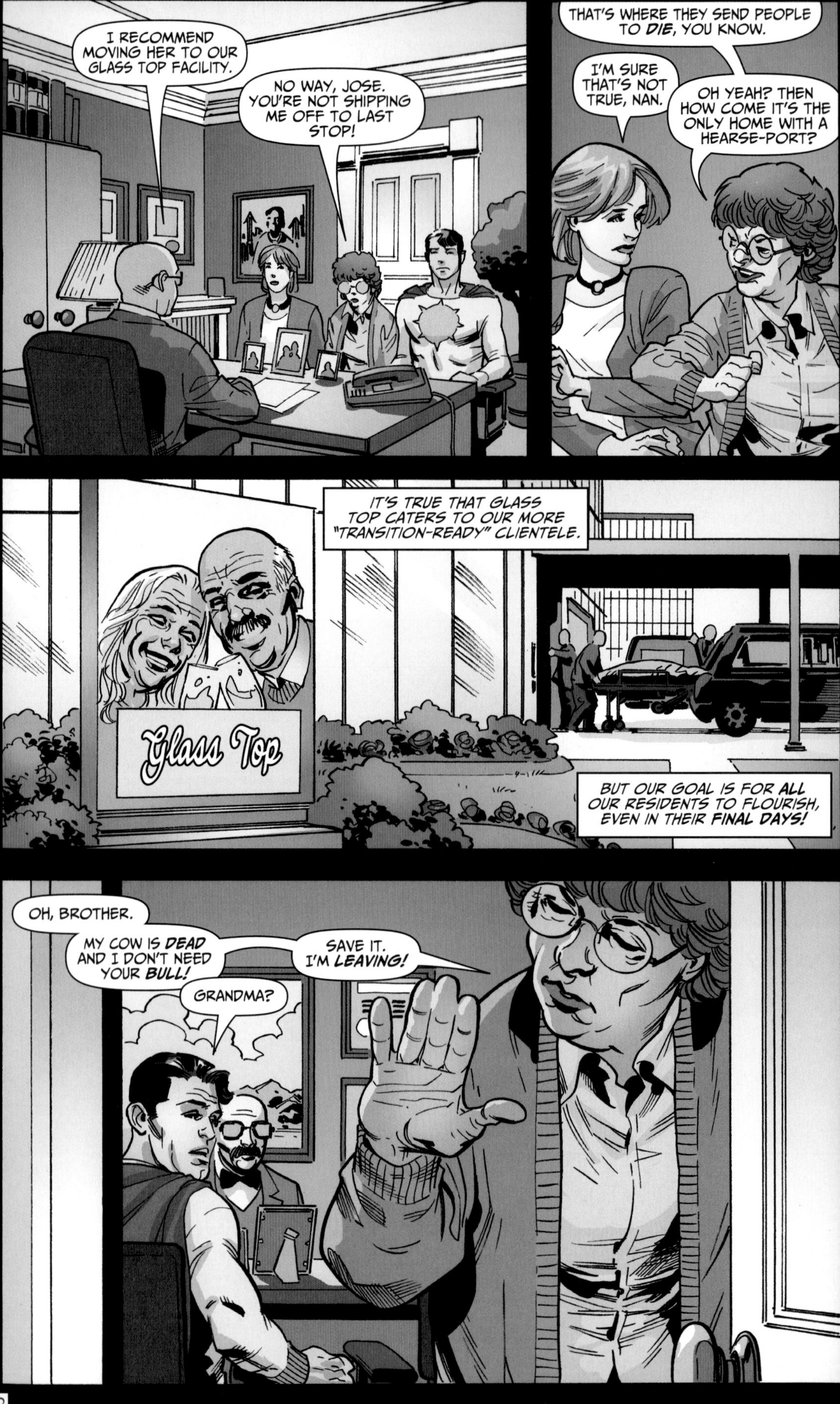

I RECOMMEND MOVING HER TO OUR GLASS TOP FACILITY.
NO WAY, JOSE. YOU'RE NOT SHIPPING ME OFF TO LAST STOP!
THAT'S WHERE THEY SEND PEOPLE TO *DIE*, YOU KNOW.
I'M SURE THAT'S NOT TRUE, NAN.
OH YEAH? THEN HOW COME IT'S THE ONLY HOME WITH A HEARSE-PORT?
IT'S TRUE THAT GLASS TOP CATERS TO OUR MORE "TRANSITION-READY" CLIENTELE.
Glass Top
BUT OUR GOAL IS FOR **ALL** OUR RESIDENTS TO FLOURISH, EVEN IN THEIR **FINAL DAYS!**
OH, BROTHER.
MY COW IS **DEAD** AND I DON'T NEED YOUR **BULL!**
SAVE IT. I'M **LEAVING!**
GRANDMA?

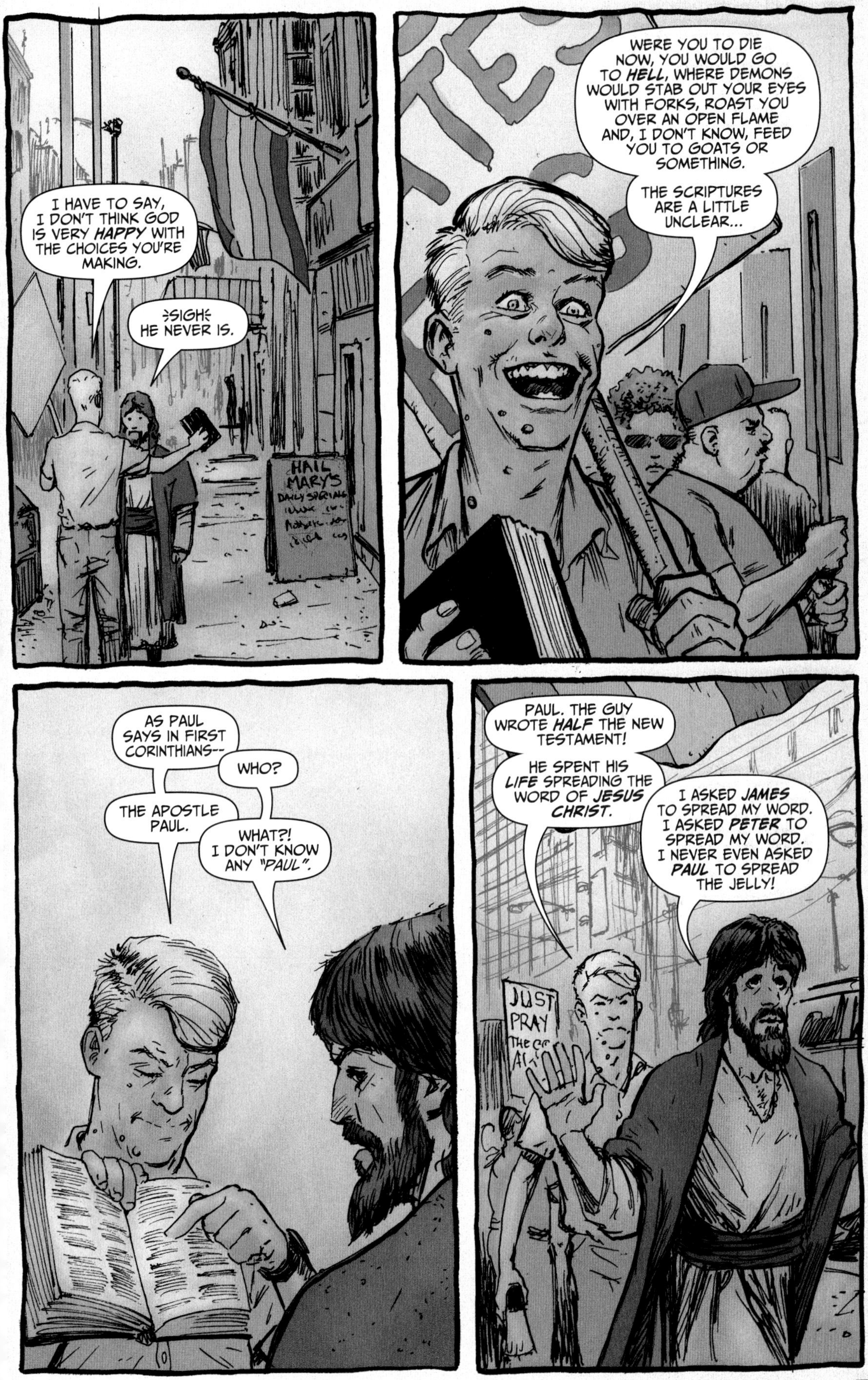
I HAVE TO SAY, I DON'T THINK GOD IS VERY *HAPPY* WITH THE CHOICES YOU'RE MAKING.
SIGH HE NEVER IS.
HAIL MARY'S DAILY SPECIALS
WERE YOU TO DIE NOW, YOU WOULD GO TO *HELL*, WHERE DEMONS WOULD STAB OUT YOUR EYES WITH FORKS, ROAST YOU OVER AN OPEN FLAME AND, I DON'T KNOW, FEED YOU TO GOATS OR SOMETHING.
THE SCRIPTURES ARE A LITTLE UNCLEAR...
AS PAUL SAYS IN FIRST CORINTHIANS--
WHO?
THE APOSTLE PAUL.
WHAT?! I DON'T KNOW ANY *"PAUL"*.
PAUL. THE GUY WROTE *HALF* THE NEW TESTAMENT!
HE SPENT HIS *LIFE* SPREADING THE WORD OF *JESUS CHRIST*.
I ASKED *JAMES* TO SPREAD MY WORD. I ASKED *PETER* TO SPREAD MY WORD. I NEVER EVEN ASKED *PAUL* TO SPREAD THE JELLY!
JUST PRAY

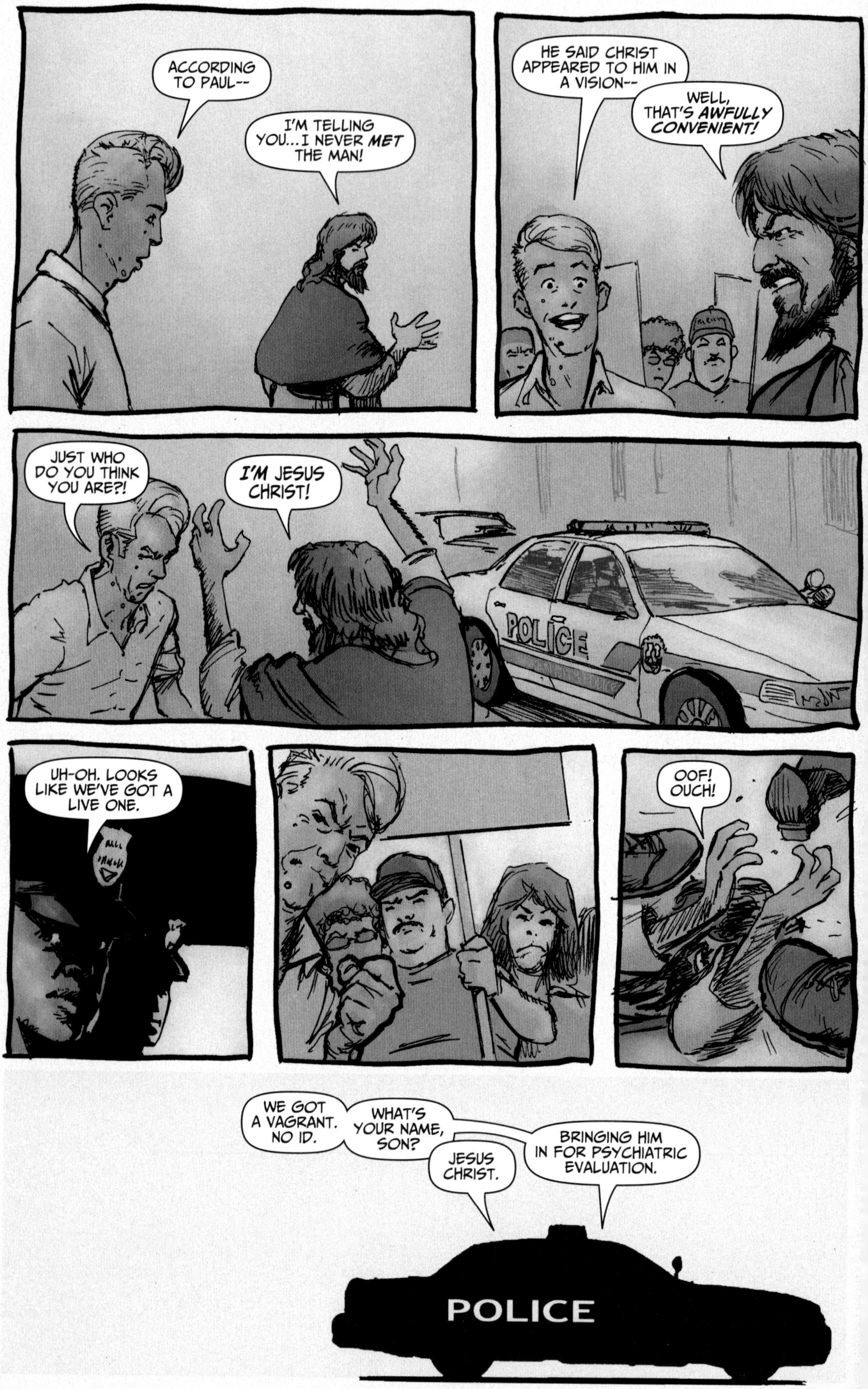
ACCORDING TO PAUL--
I'M TELLING YOU...I NEVER *MET* THE MAN!
HE SAID CHRIST APPEARED TO HIM IN A VISION--
WELL, THAT'S *AWFULLY CONVENIENT!*
JUST WHO DO YOU THINK YOU ARE?!
I'M JESUS CHRIST!
POLICE
UH-OH. LOOKS LIKE WE'VE GOT A LIVE ONE.
OOF! OUCH!
WE GOT A VAGRANT. NO ID.
WHAT'S YOUR NAME, SON?
JESUS CHRIST.
BRINGING HIM IN FOR PSYCHIATRIC EVALUATION.
POLICE

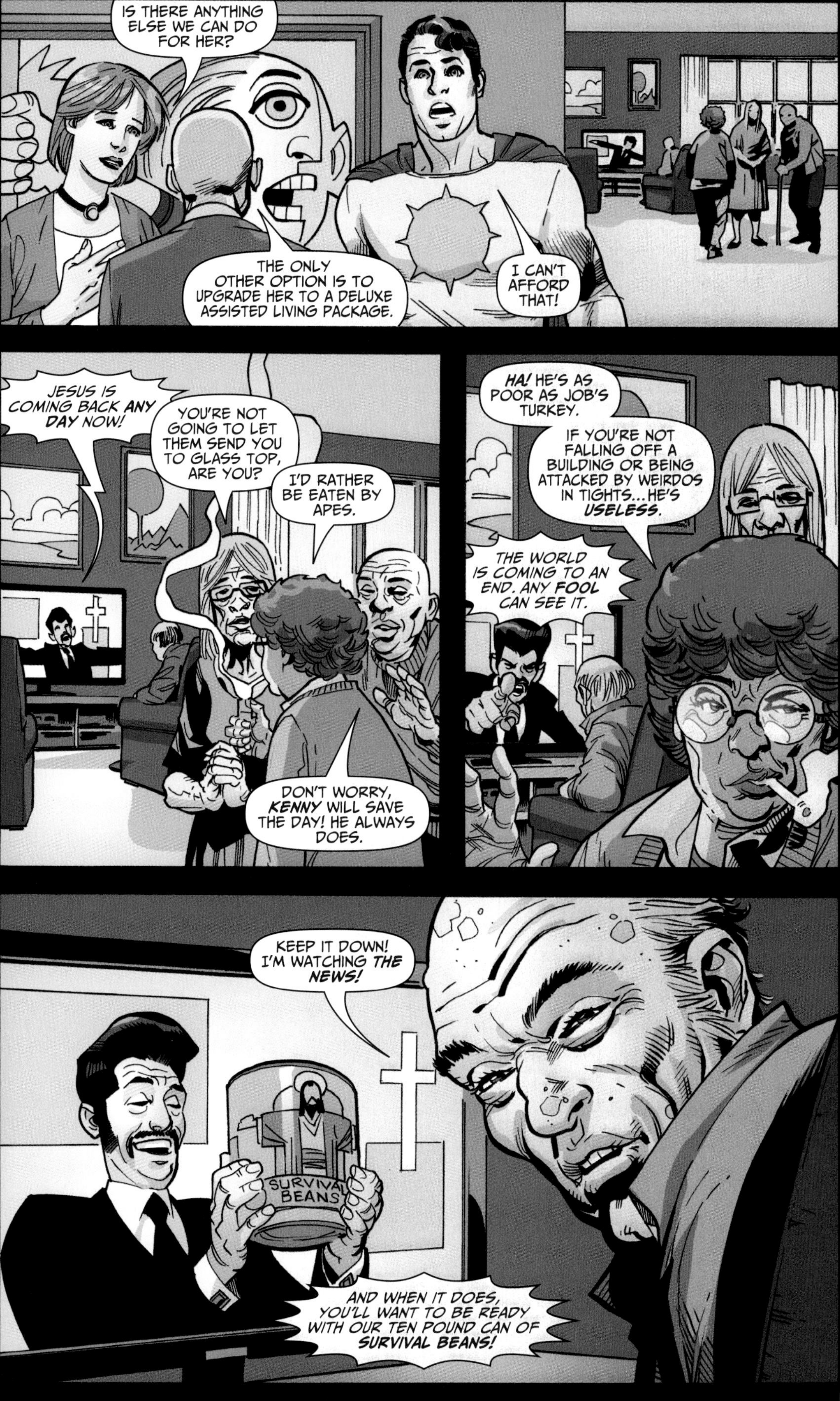
IS THERE ANYTHING ELSE WE CAN DO FOR HER?
THE ONLY OTHER OPTION IS TO UPGRADE HER TO A DELUXE ASSISTED LIVING PACKAGE.
I CAN'T AFFORD THAT!
JESUS IS COMING BACK ANY DAY NOW!
YOU'RE NOT GOING TO LET THEM SEND YOU TO GLASS TOP, ARE YOU?
I'D RATHER BE EATEN BY APES.
DON'T WORRY, KENNY WILL SAVE THE DAY! HE ALWAYS DOES.
HA! HE'S AS POOR AS JOB'S TURKEY.
IF YOU'RE NOT FALLING OFF A BUILDING OR BEING ATTACKED BY WEIRDOS IN TIGHTS... HE'S USELESS.
THE WORLD IS COMING TO AN END. ANY FOOL CAN SEE IT.
KEEP IT DOWN! I'M WATCHING THE NEWS!
SURVIVAL BEANS
AND WHEN IT DOES, YOU'LL WANT TO BE READY WITH OUR TEN POUND CAN OF SURVIVAL BEANS!

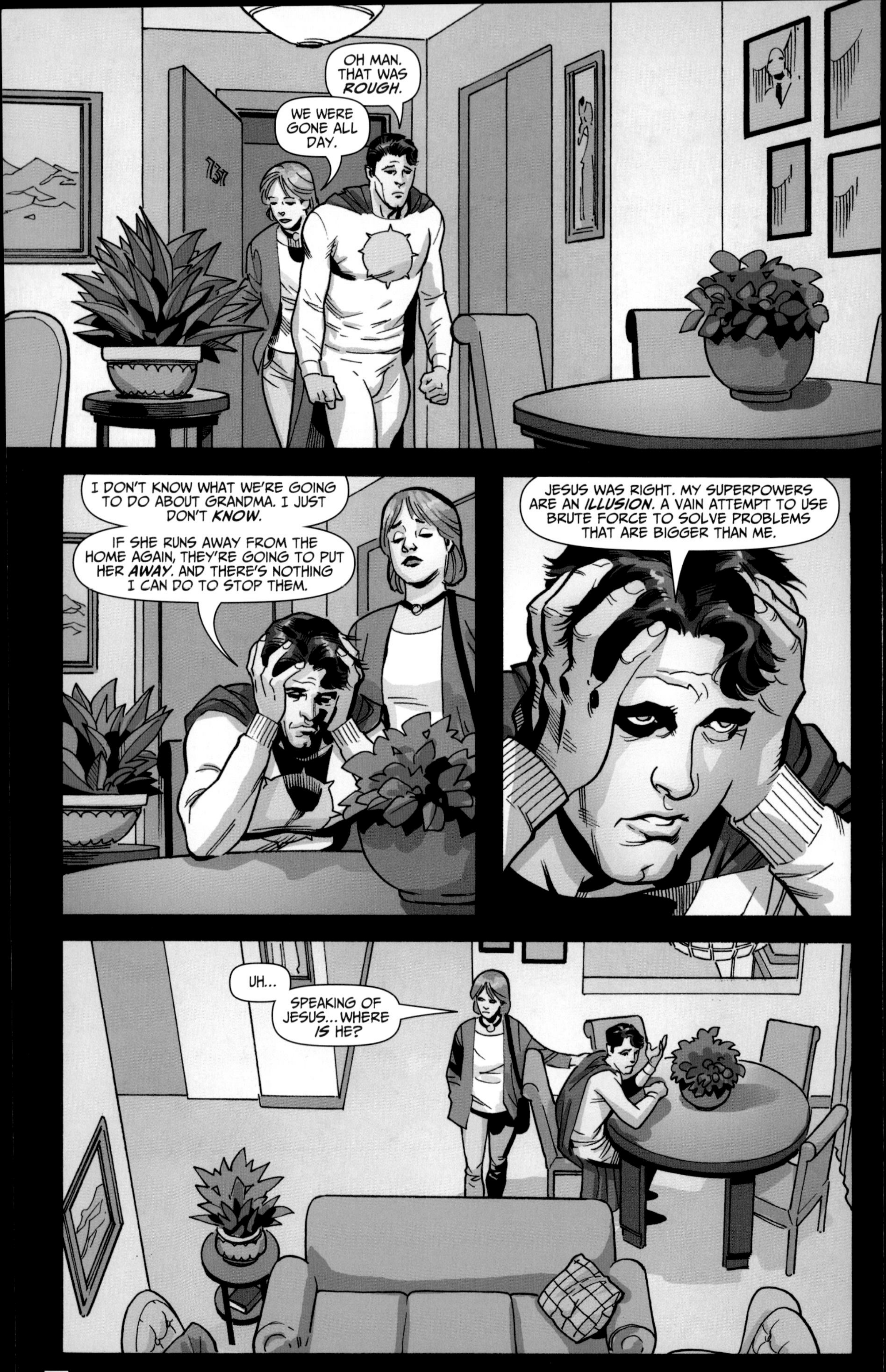
OH MAN. THAT WAS *ROUGH*.
WE WERE GONE ALL DAY.
I DON'T KNOW WHAT WE'RE GOING TO DO ABOUT GRANDMA. I JUST DON'T *KNOW*.
IF SHE RUNS AWAY FROM THE HOME AGAIN, THEY'RE GOING TO PUT HER *AWAY*. AND THERE'S NOTHING I CAN DO TO STOP THEM.
JESUS WAS RIGHT. MY SUPERPOWERS ARE AN *ILLUSION*. A VAIN ATTEMPT TO USE BRUTE FORCE TO SOLVE PROBLEMS THAT ARE BIGGER THAN ME.
UH...
SPEAKING OF JESUS... WHERE *IS* HE?

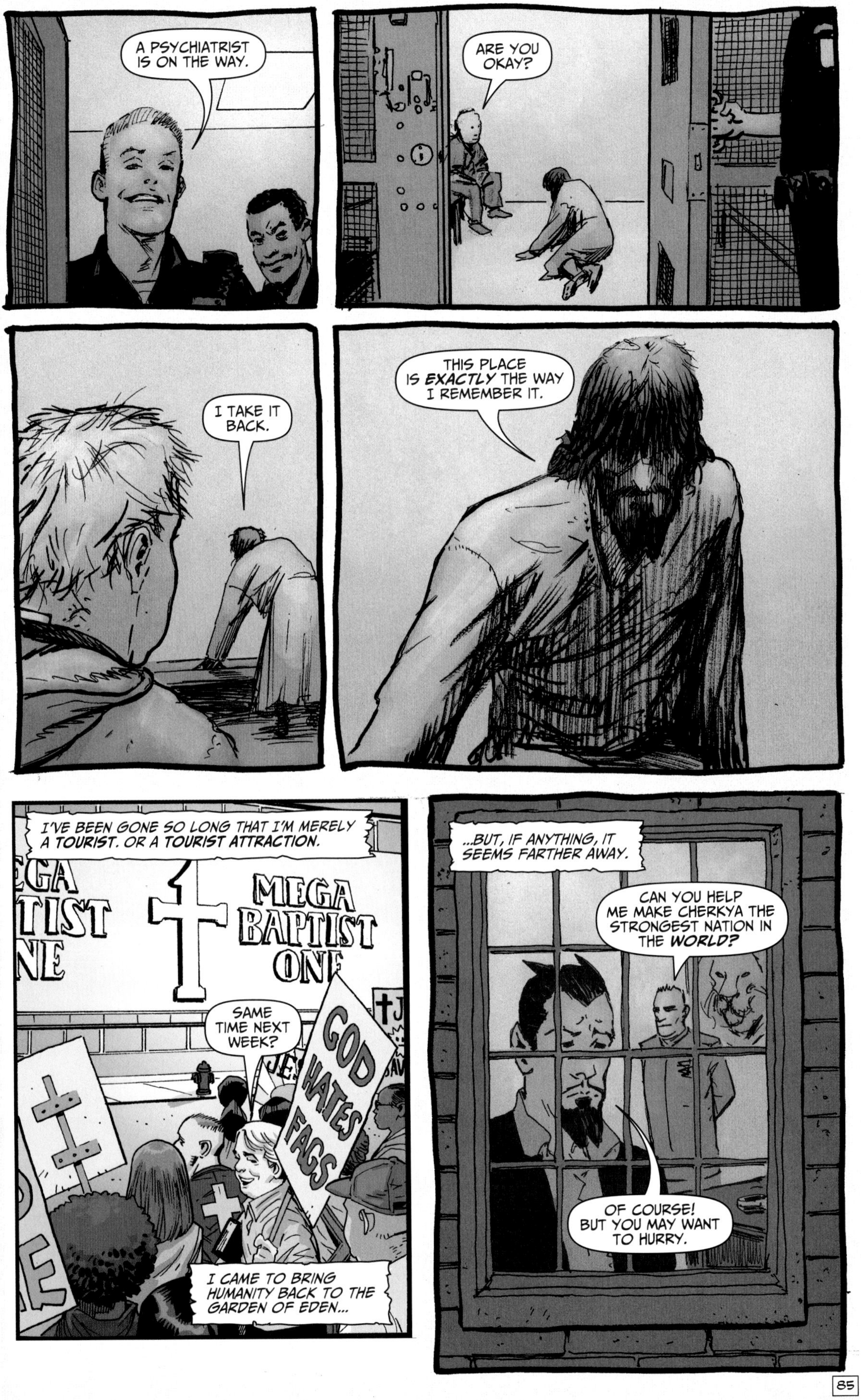

A PSYCHIATRIST IS ON THE WAY.
ARE YOU OKAY?
I TAKE IT BACK.
THIS PLACE IS *EXACTLY* THE WAY I REMEMBER IT.
*I'VE BEEN GONE SO LONG THAT I'M MERELY A **TOURIST**. OR A **TOURIST ATTRACTION**.*
MEGA BAPTIST ONE
SAME TIME NEXT WEEK?
GOD HATES FAGS
I CAME TO BRING HUMANITY BACK TO THE GARDEN OF EDEN...
...BUT, IF ANYTHING, IT SEEMS FARTHER AWAY.
CAN YOU HELP ME MAKE CHERKYA THE STRONGEST NATION IN THE ***WORLD?***
OF COURSE! BUT YOU MAY WANT TO HURRY.

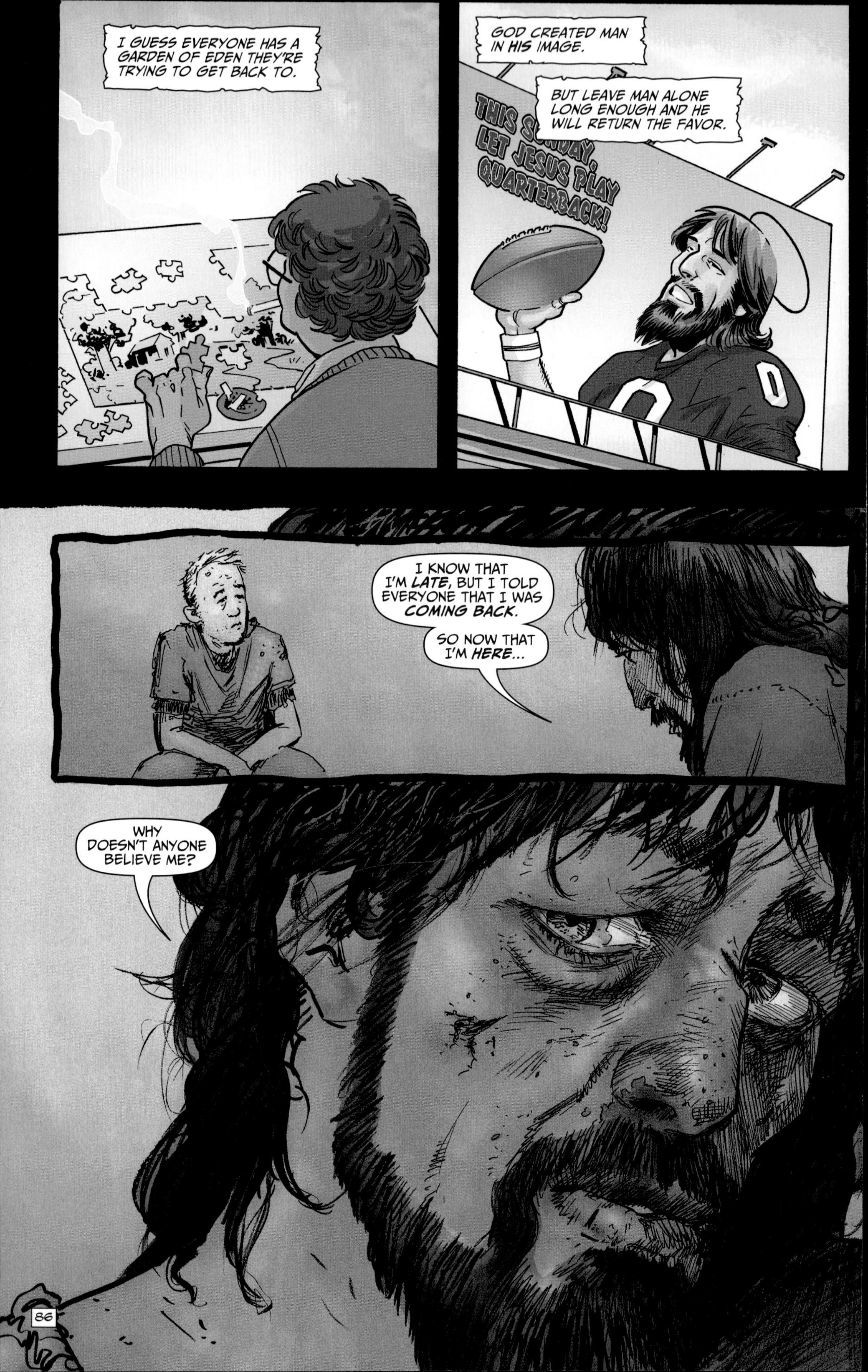
I GUESS EVERYONE HAS A GARDEN OF EDEN THEY'RE TRYING TO GET BACK TO.
GOD CREATED MAN IN HIS IMAGE.
BUT LEAVE MAN ALONE LONG ENOUGH AND HE WILL RETURN THE FAVOR.
THIS SUNDAY, LET JESUS PLAY QUARTERBACK!
I KNOW THAT I'M LATE, BUT I TOLD EVERYONE THAT I WAS COMING BACK.
SO NOW THAT I'M HERE...
WHY DOESN'T ANYONE BELIEVE ME?

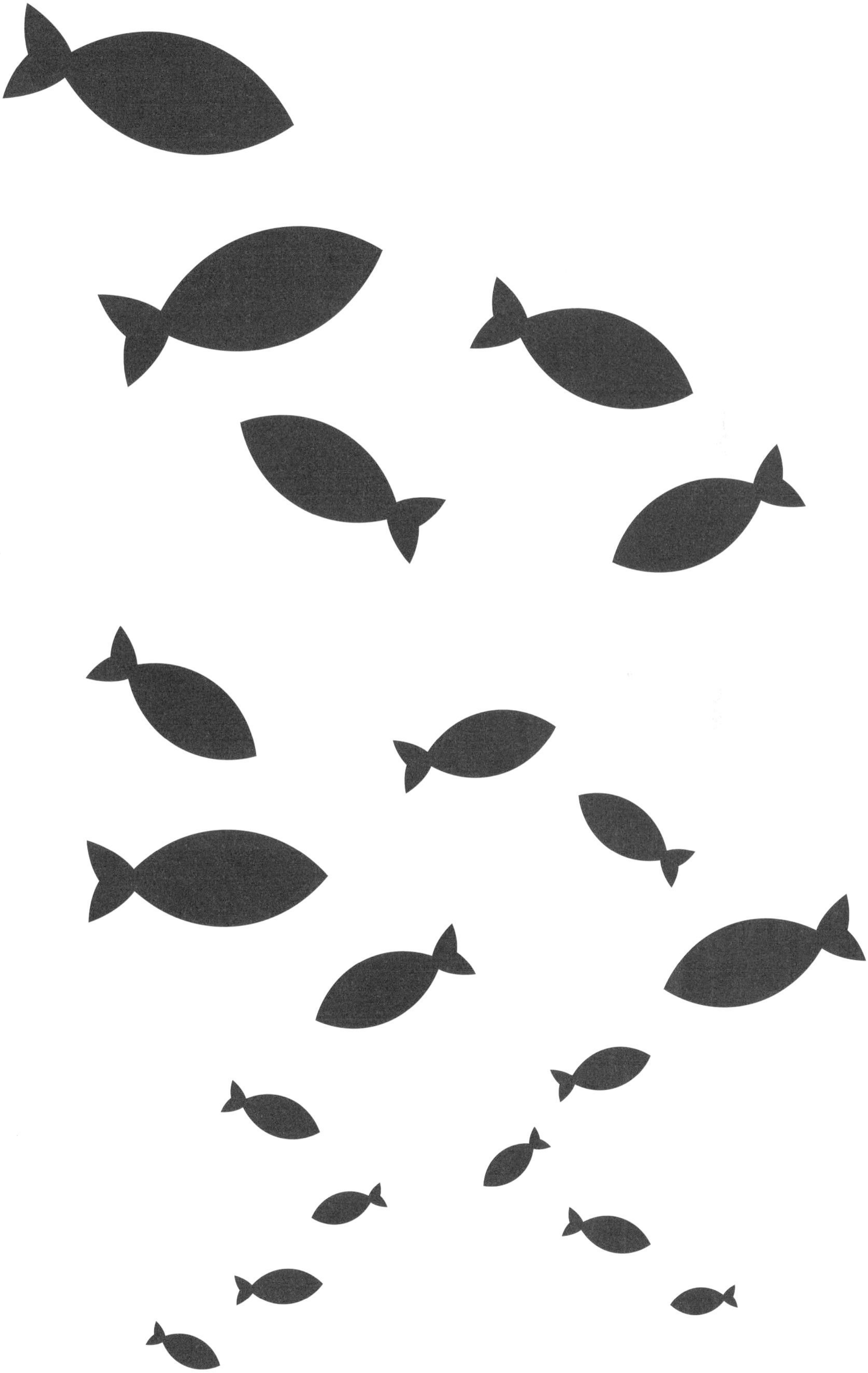

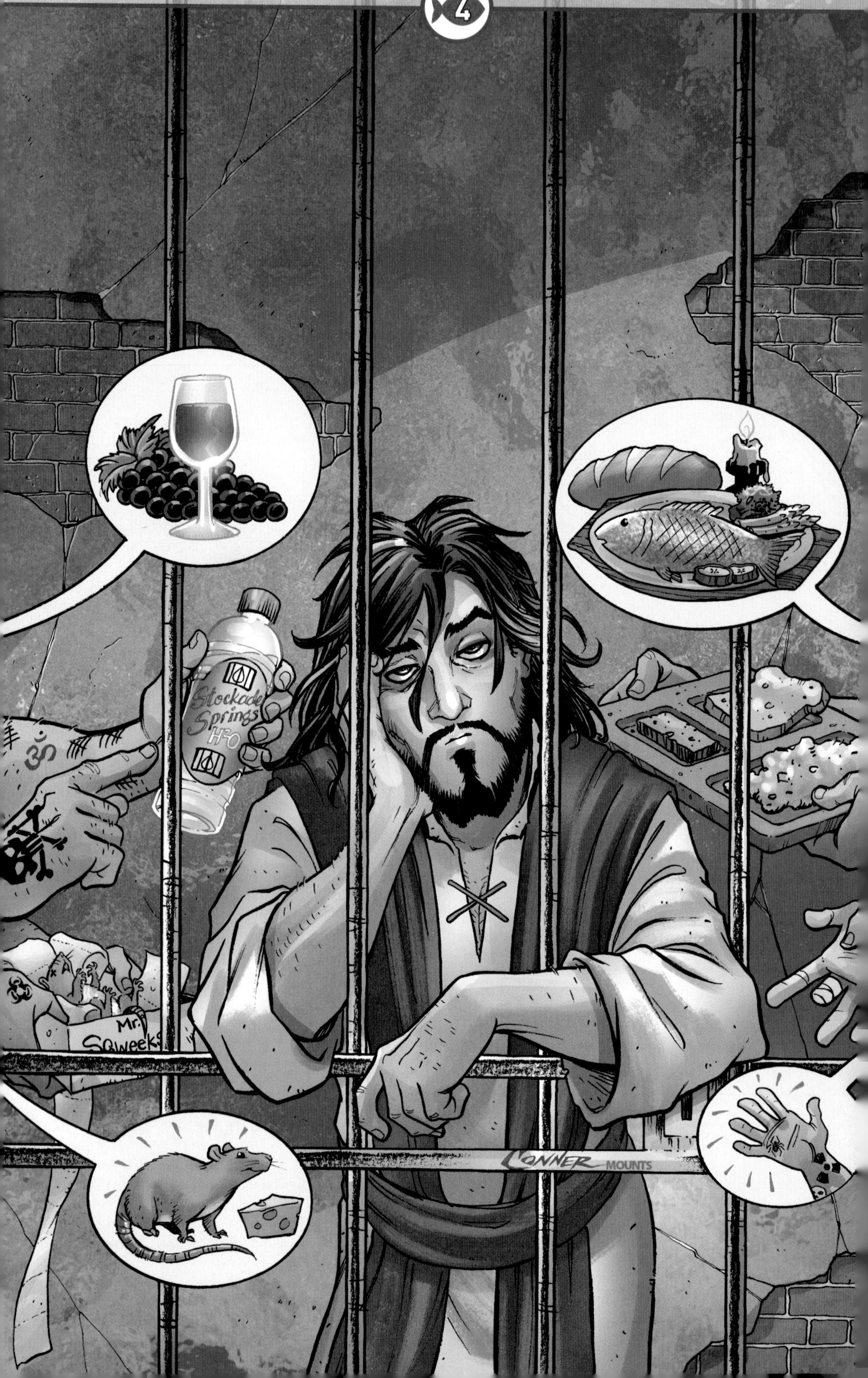
Stockade Springs H2O
Mr. SQweeks
CONNER MOUNTS

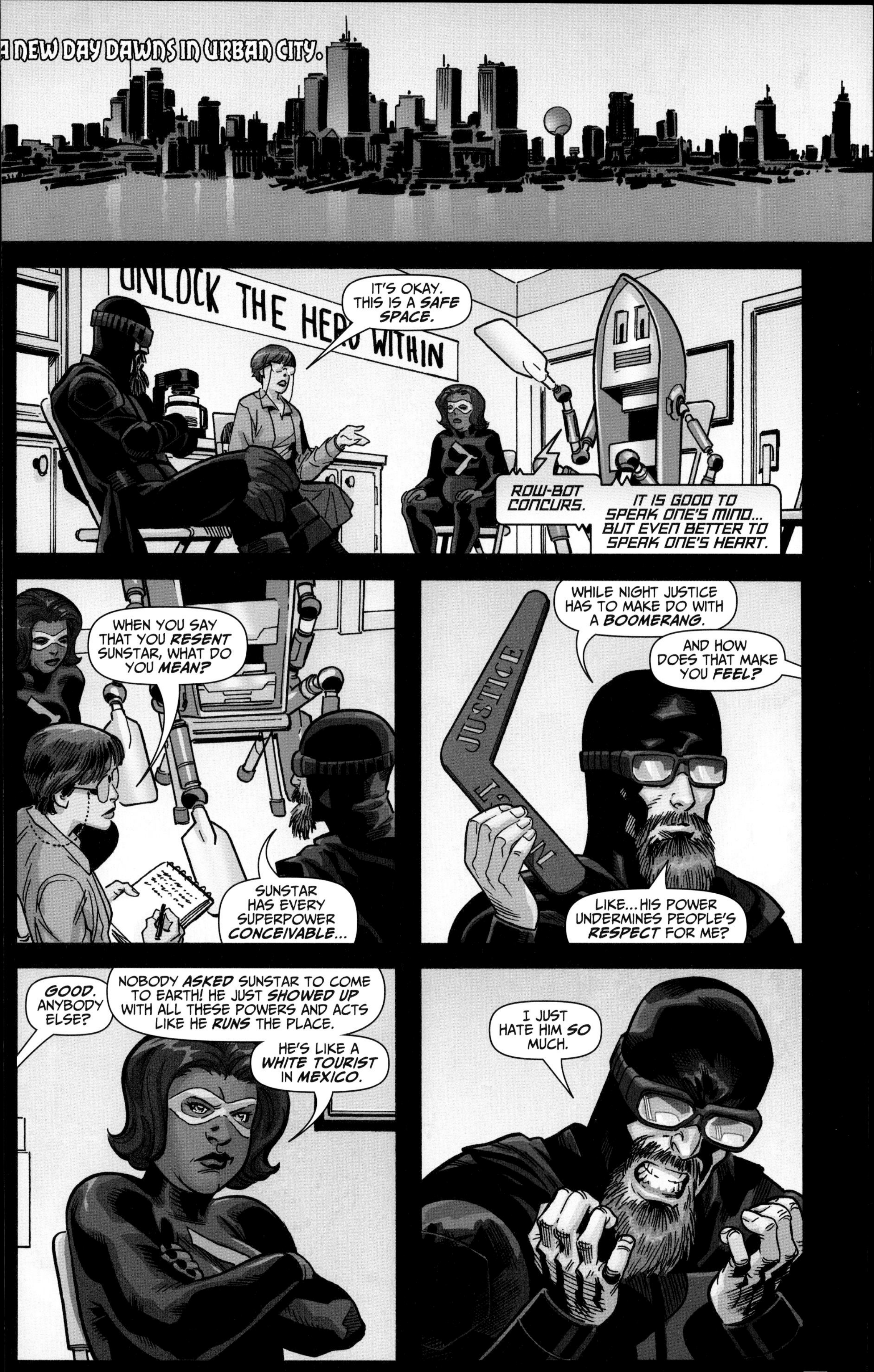
A NEW DAY DAWNS IN URBAN CITY.
UNLOCK THE HERO WITHIN
IT'S OKAY. THIS IS A SAFE SPACE.
ROW-BOT CONCURS.
IT IS GOOD TO SPEAK ONE'S MIND... BUT EVEN BETTER TO SPEAK ONE'S HEART.
WHEN YOU SAY THAT YOU RESENT SUNSTAR, WHAT DO YOU MEAN?
SUNSTAR HAS EVERY SUPERPOWER CONCEIVABLE...
WHILE NIGHT JUSTICE HAS TO MAKE DO WITH A BOOMERANG.
JUSTICE
AND HOW DOES THAT MAKE YOU FEEL?
LIKE... HIS POWER UNDERMINES PEOPLE'S RESPECT FOR ME?
GOOD. ANYBODY ELSE?
NOBODY ASKED SUNSTAR TO COME TO EARTH! HE JUST SHOWED UP WITH ALL THESE POWERS AND ACTS LIKE HE RUNS THE PLACE.
HE'S LIKE A WHITE TOURIST IN MEXICO.
I JUST HATE HIM SO MUCH.

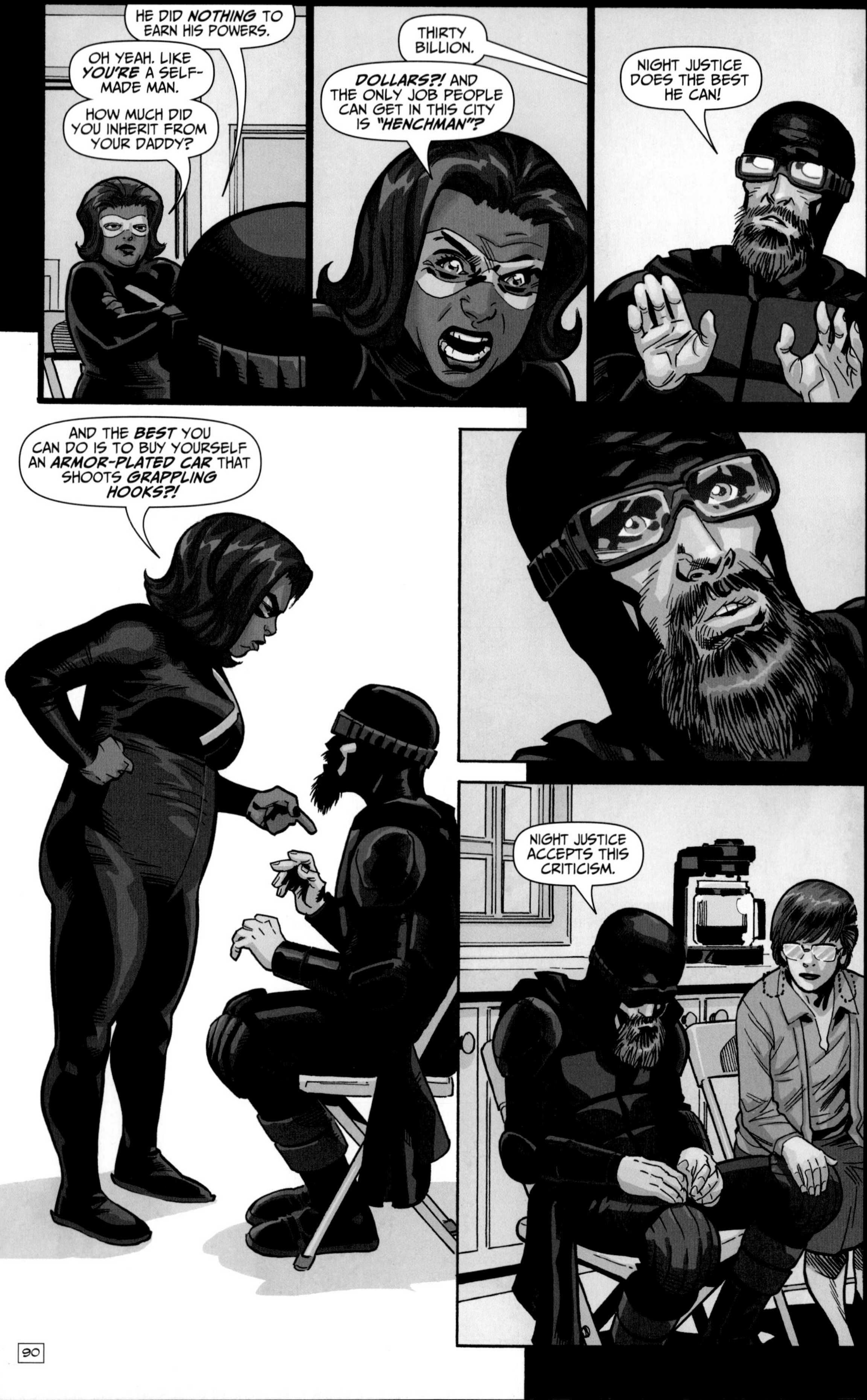
HE DID NOTHING TO EARN HIS POWERS.
OH YEAH. LIKE YOU'RE A SELF-MADE MAN.
HOW MUCH DID YOU INHERIT FROM YOUR DADDY?
THIRTY BILLION.
DOLLARS?! AND THE ONLY JOB PEOPLE CAN GET IN THIS CITY IS "HENCHMAN"?
NIGHT JUSTICE DOES THE BEST HE CAN!
AND THE BEST YOU CAN DO IS TO BUY YOURSELF AN ARMOR-PLATED CAR THAT SHOOTS GRAPPLING HOOKS?!
NIGHT JUSTICE ACCEPTS THIS CRITICISM.

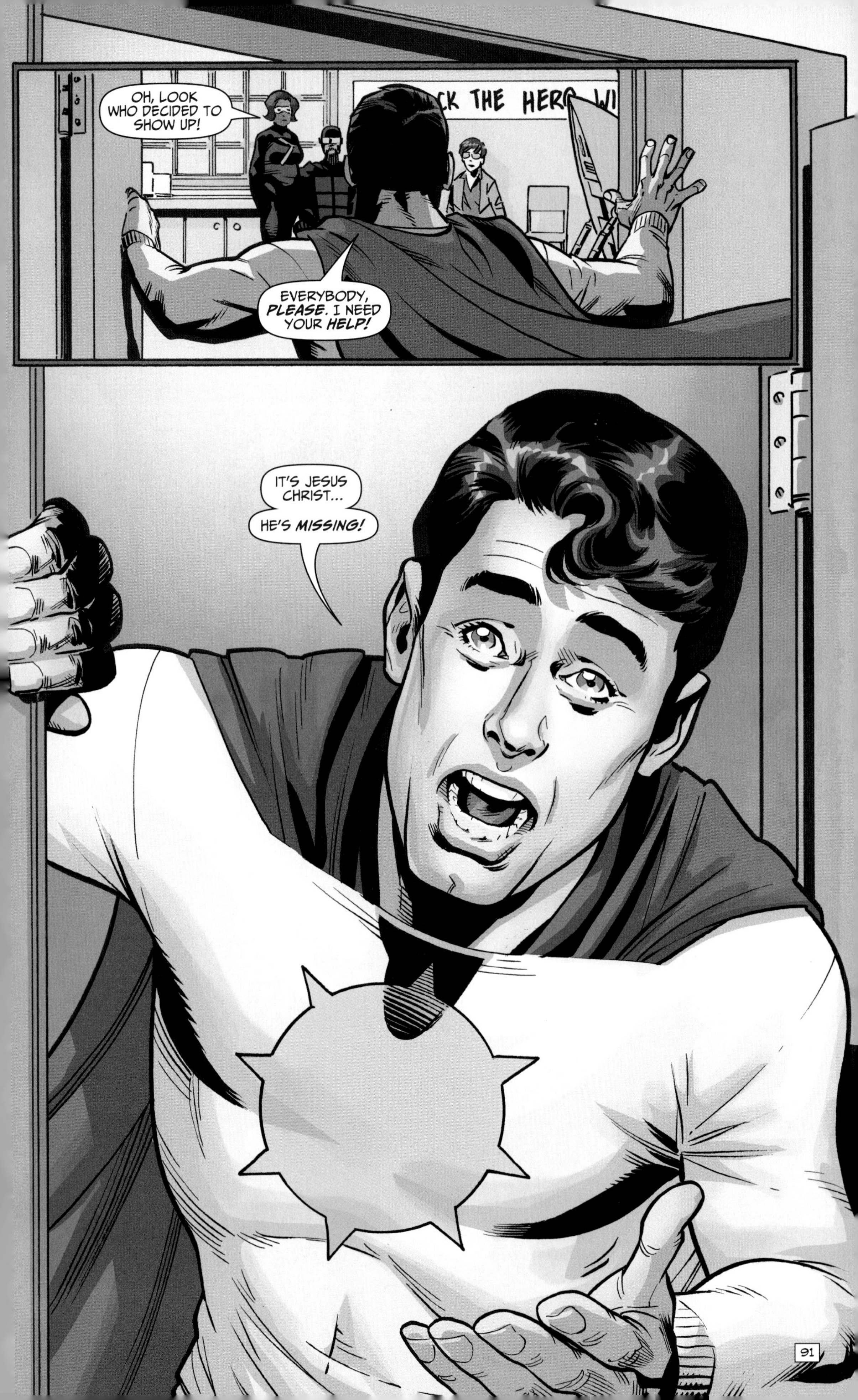
OH, LOOK WHO DECIDED TO SHOW UP!
EVERYBODY, PLEASE. I NEED YOUR HELP!
IT'S JESUS CHRIST...
HE'S MISSING!

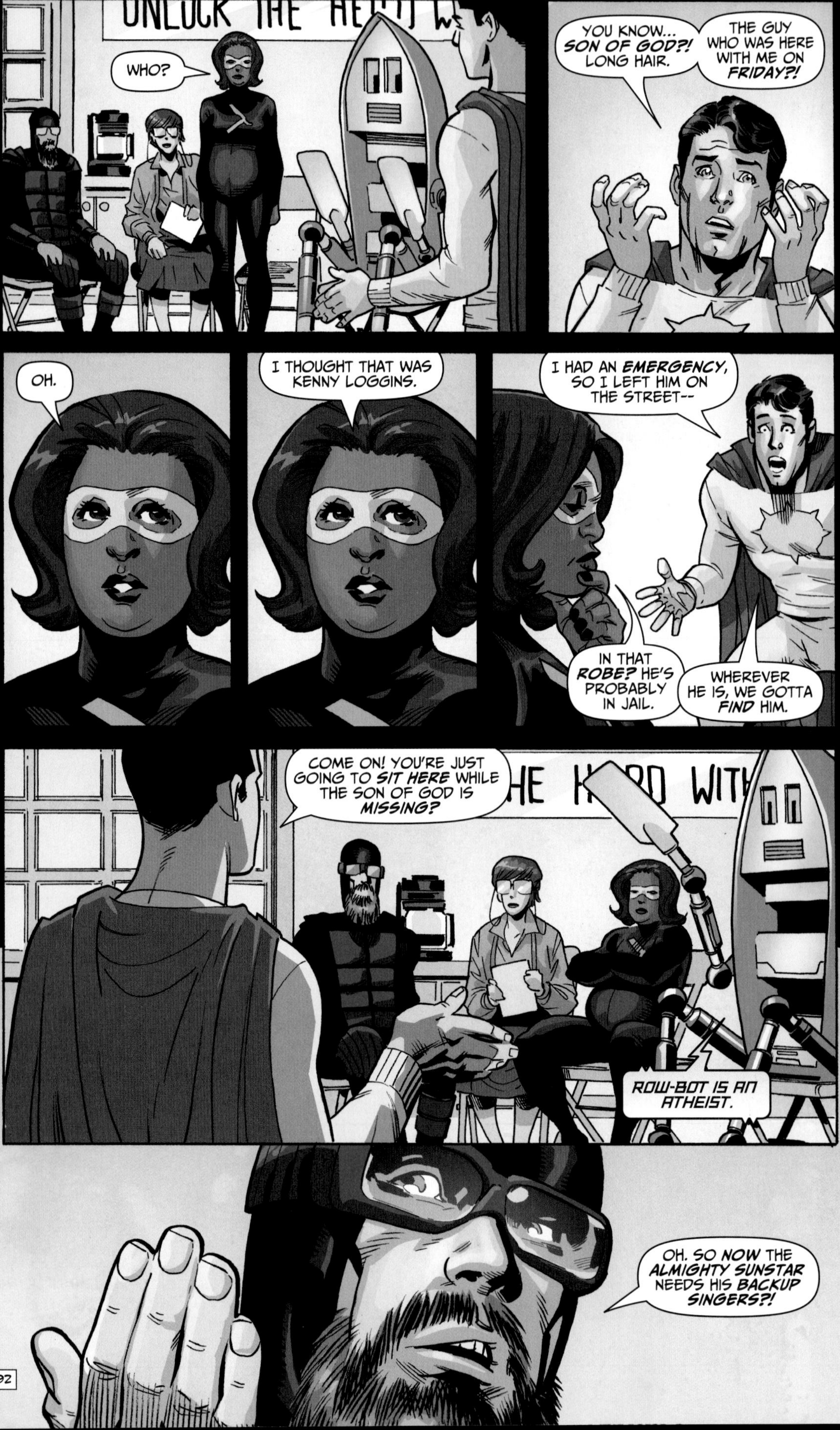
WHO?
YOU KNOW... SON OF GOD?! LONG HAIR.
THE GUY WHO WAS HERE WITH ME ON FRIDAY?!
OH.
I THOUGHT THAT WAS KENNY LOGGINS.
I HAD AN EMERGENCY, SO I LEFT HIM ON THE STREET--
IN THAT ROBE? HE'S PROBABLY IN JAIL.
WHEREVER HE IS, WE GOTTA FIND HIM.
COME ON! YOU'RE JUST GOING TO SIT HERE WHILE THE SON OF GOD IS MISSING?
ROW-BOT IS AN ATHEIST.
OH. SO NOW THE ALMIGHTY SUNSTAR NEEDS HIS BACKUP SINGERS?!

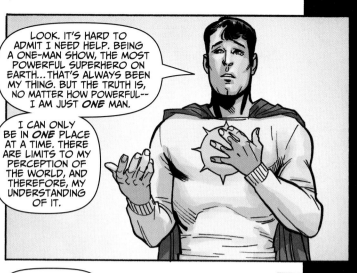

LOOK. IT'S HARD TO ADMIT I NEED HELP. BEING A ONE-MAN SHOW, THE MOST POWERFUL SUPERHERO ON EARTH... THAT'S ALWAYS BEEN MY THING. BUT THE TRUTH IS, NO MATTER HOW POWERFUL-- I AM JUST *ONE* MAN.

I CAN ONLY BE IN *ONE* PLACE AT A TIME. THERE ARE LIMITS TO MY PERCEPTION OF THE WORLD, AND THEREFORE, MY UNDERSTANDING OF IT.

SO, *YES.* I *NEED* YOU.

NIGHT JUSTICE IS WITH YOU... *MY BROTHER.*

YEAH, OKAY. WHATEVER. LET'S JUST *GO.*

HEY! WE WERE MAKING SOME REAL *BREAKTHROUGHS* HERE!

WITH UTMOST RESPECT, NOBODY GIVES A *SHIT.*

ROW-BOT OUTTA HERE.

SO ARE YOU GOING TO *HELP?*

WE STILL HAVE *FLUTE THERAPY!*

YEAH, I'M COMIN'.

ALL RIGHT, EVERYBODY! LET'S FIND *JESUS!*

LITERALLY SPEAKING, I MEAN.

REFRESH MY MEMORY... IS HE A *WHITE GUY?*

I DON'T KNOW. NOT REALLY.

OH, THEN THEY *DEFINITELY* THREW HIS ASS IN JAIL.

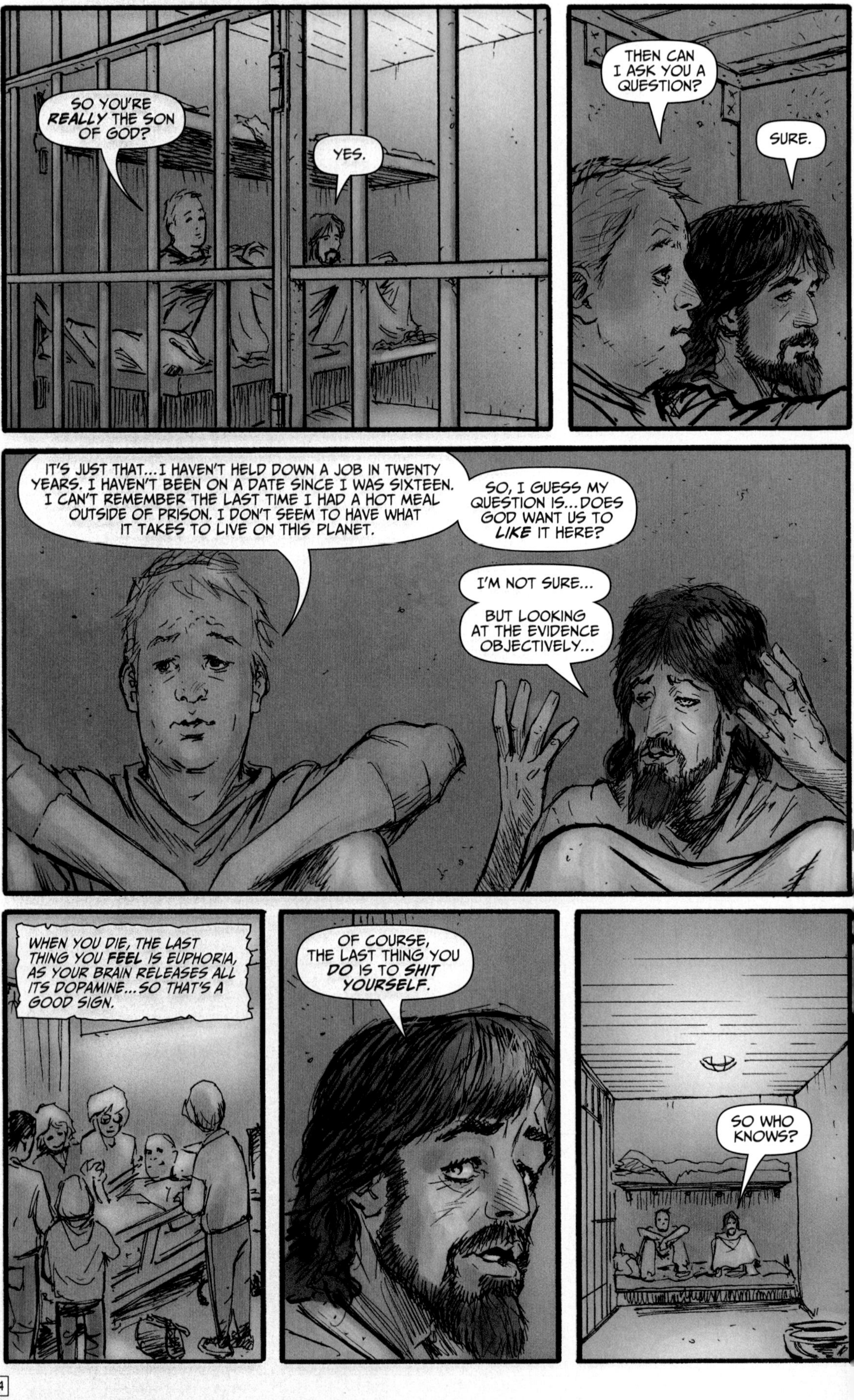
SO YOU'RE *REALLY* THE SON OF GOD?
YES.
THEN CAN I ASK YOU A QUESTION?
SURE.
IT'S JUST THAT... I HAVEN'T HELD DOWN A JOB IN TWENTY YEARS. I HAVEN'T BEEN ON A DATE SINCE I WAS SIXTEEN. I CAN'T REMEMBER THE LAST TIME I HAD A HOT MEAL OUTSIDE OF PRISON. I DON'T SEEM TO HAVE WHAT IT TAKES TO LIVE ON THIS PLANET.
SO, I GUESS MY QUESTION IS... DOES GOD WANT US TO *LIKE* IT HERE?
I'M NOT SURE...
BUT LOOKING AT THE EVIDENCE OBJECTIVELY...
WHEN YOU DIE, THE LAST THING YOU **FEEL** IS EUPHORIA, AS YOUR BRAIN RELEASES ALL ITS DOPAMINE... SO THAT'S A GOOD SIGN.
OF COURSE, THE LAST THING YOU *DO* IS TO ***SHIT YOURSELF***.
SO WHO KNOWS?

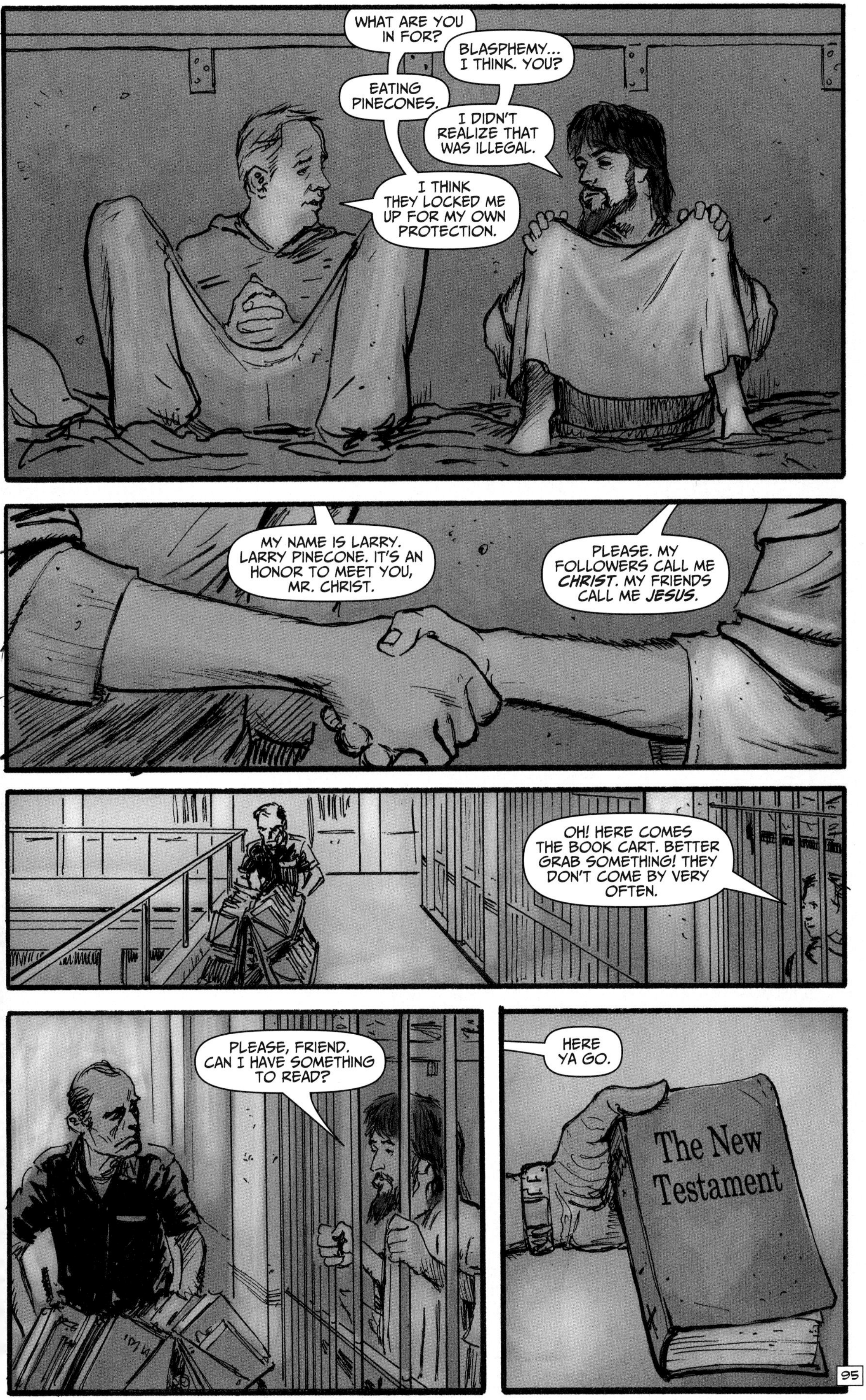
WHAT ARE YOU IN FOR?
BLASPHEMY... I THINK. YOU?
EATING PINECONES.
I DIDN'T REALIZE THAT WAS ILLEGAL.
I THINK THEY LOCKED ME UP FOR MY OWN PROTECTION.
MY NAME IS LARRY. LARRY PINECONE. IT'S AN HONOR TO MEET YOU, MR. CHRIST.
PLEASE. MY FOLLOWERS CALL ME CHRIST. MY FRIENDS CALL ME JESUS.
OH! HERE COMES THE BOOK CART. BETTER GRAB SOMETHING! THEY DON'T COME BY VERY OFTEN.
PLEASE, FRIEND. CAN I HAVE SOMETHING TO READ?
HERE YA GO.
The New Testament

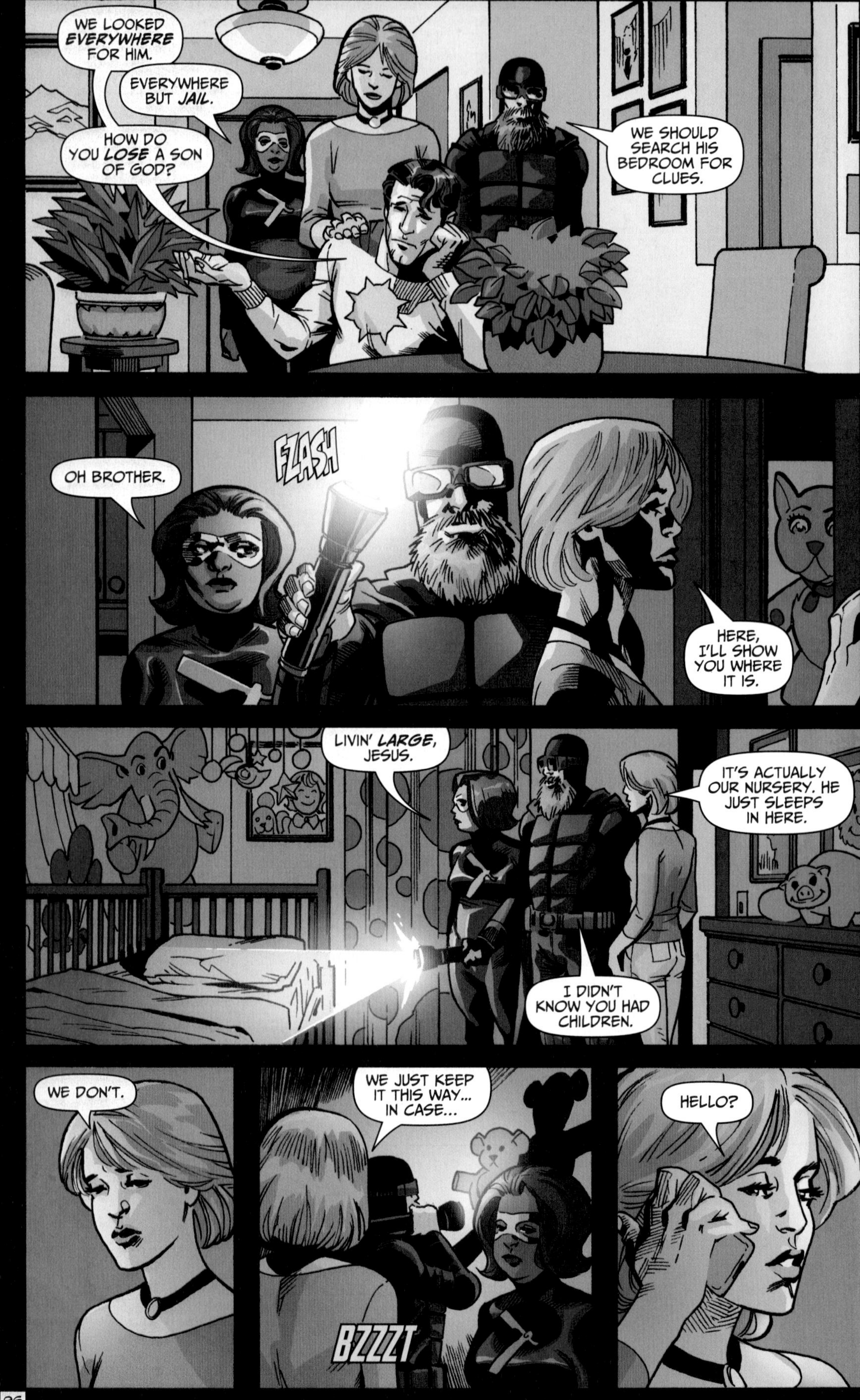
WE LOOKED EVERYWHERE FOR HIM.
EVERYWHERE BUT JAIL.
HOW DO YOU LOSE A SON OF GOD?
WE SHOULD SEARCH HIS BEDROOM FOR CLUES.
OH BROTHER.
FLASH
HERE, I'LL SHOW YOU WHERE IT IS.
LIVIN' LARGE, JESUS.
IT'S ACTUALLY OUR NURSERY. HE JUST SLEEPS IN HERE.
I DIDN'T KNOW YOU HAD CHILDREN.
WE DON'T.
WE JUST KEEP IT THIS WAY... IN CASE...
BZZZT
HELLO?

I THINK I FOUND YOUR BOY.

THE POLICE SENT A JOHN DOE TO JAIL FOR A PSYCH EVALUATION.

GAYLORD BLACK

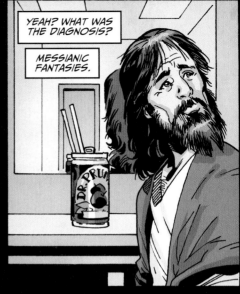

YEAH? WHAT WAS THE DIAGNOSIS?

MESSIANIC FANTASIES.

WITH DELUSIONS OF GRANDEUR AND A PERSECUTION COMPLEX.

THAT'S HIM!

THEY FOUND HIM! HE'S LOCKED UP IN THE DOWNTOWN JAIL!

TOLD YA.

WE'LL TAKE MY CAR. TO THE WHEELS OF JUSTICE!

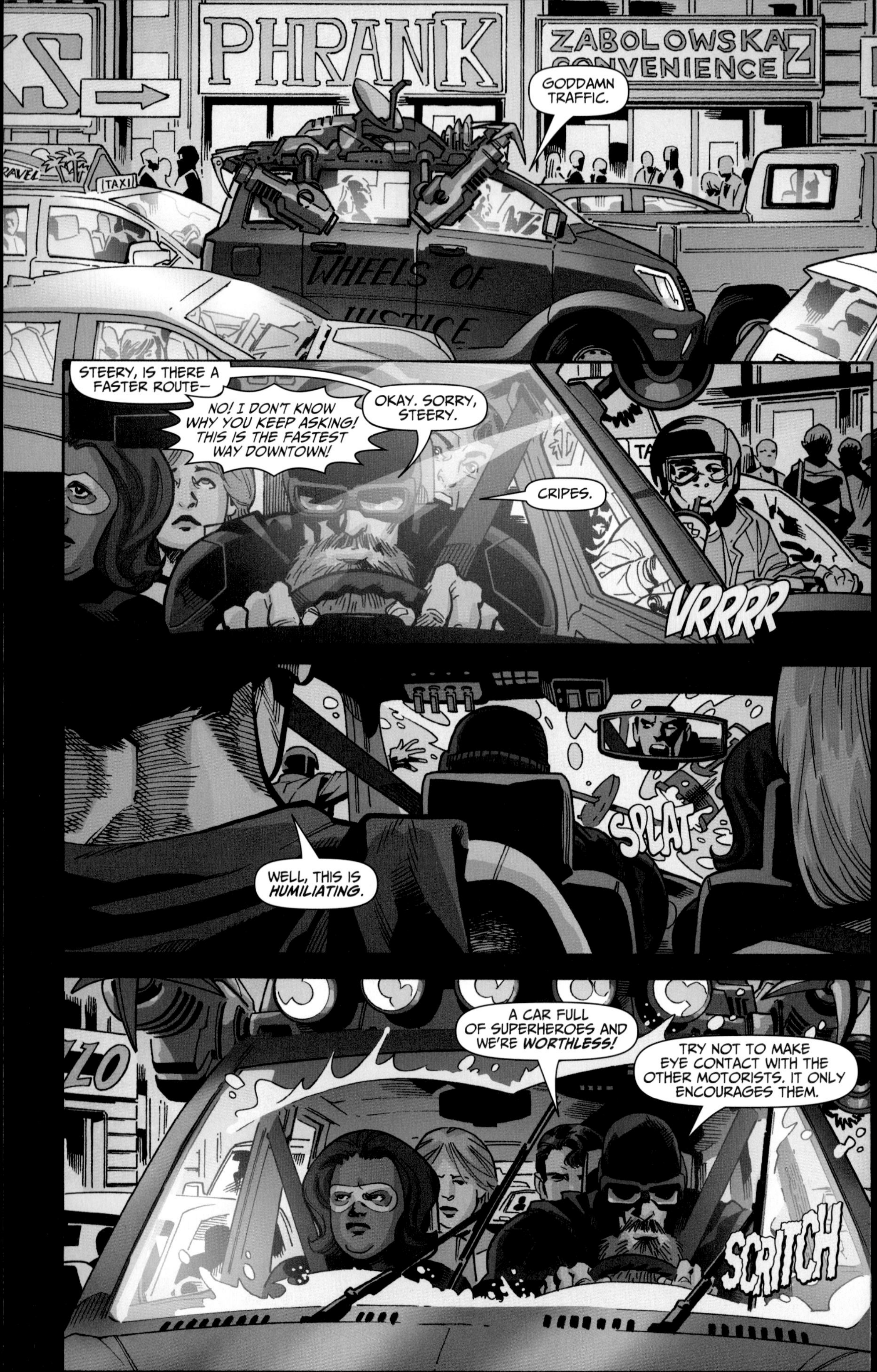
PHRANK
ZABOLOWSKA CONVENIENCE
TAXI
WHEELS OF JUSTICE
GODDAMN TRAFFIC.
STEERY, IS THERE A FASTER ROUTE—
NO! I DON'T KNOW WHY YOU KEEP ASKING! THIS IS THE FASTEST WAY DOWNTOWN!
OKAY. SORRY, STEERY.
CRIPES.
VRRRR
SPLAT
WELL, THIS IS *HUMILIATING*.
A CAR FULL OF SUPERHEROES AND WE'RE *WORTHLESS!*
TRY NOT TO MAKE EYE CONTACT WITH THE OTHER MOTORISTS. IT ONLY ENCOURAGES THEM.
SCRITCH

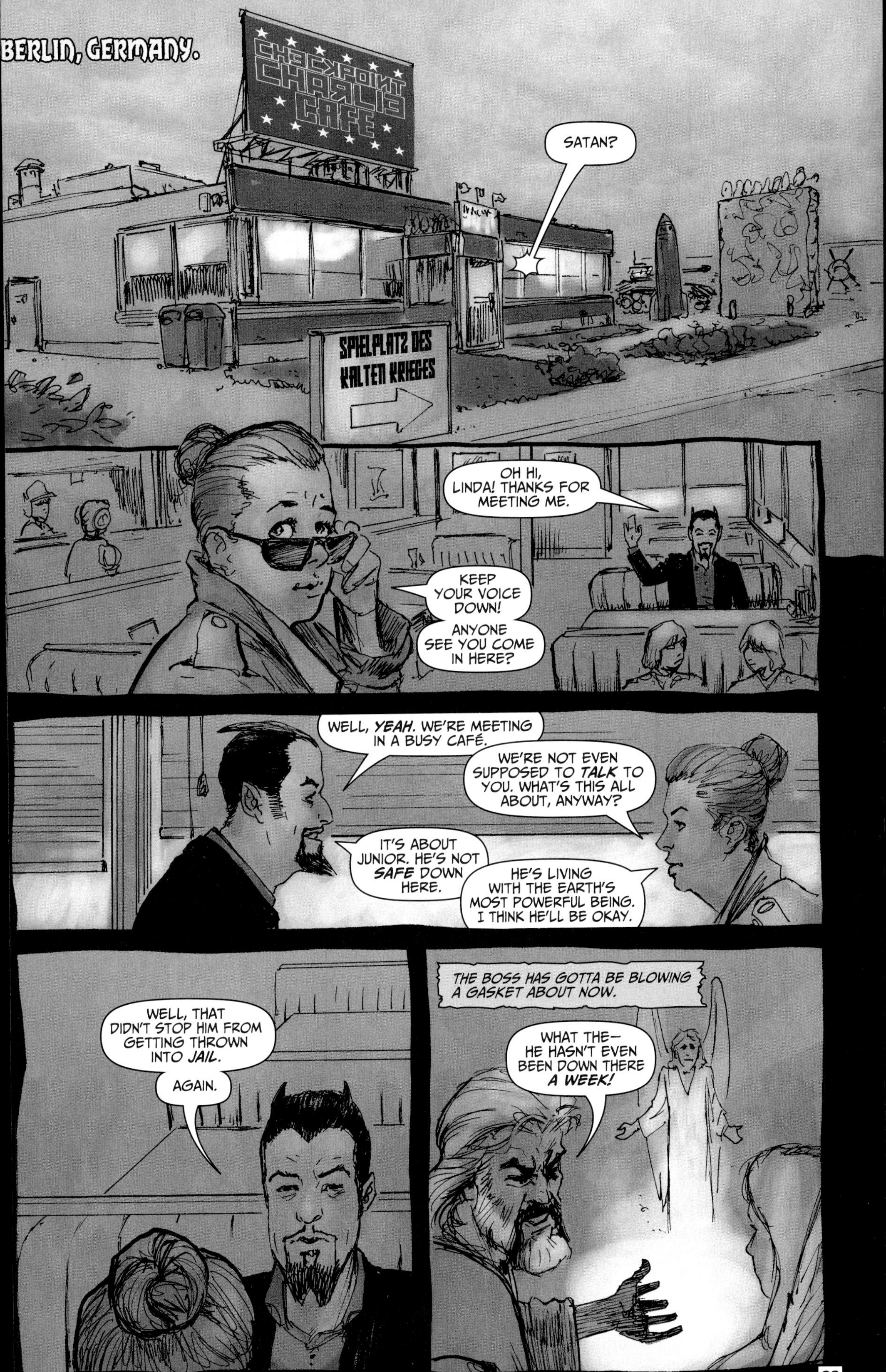
BERLIN, GERMANY.
CHECKPOINT CHARLIE CAFE
SATAN?
SPIELPLATZ DES KALTEN KRIEGES
OH HI, LINDA! THANKS FOR MEETING ME.
KEEP YOUR VOICE DOWN!
ANYONE SEE YOU COME IN HERE?
WELL, *YEAH*. WE'RE MEETING IN A BUSY CAFÉ.
WE'RE NOT EVEN SUPPOSED TO *TALK* TO YOU. WHAT'S THIS ALL ABOUT, ANYWAY?
IT'S ABOUT JUNIOR. HE'S NOT *SAFE* DOWN HERE.
HE'S LIVING WITH THE EARTH'S MOST POWERFUL BEING. I THINK HE'LL BE OKAY.
WELL, THAT DIDN'T STOP HIM FROM GETTING THROWN INTO *JAIL*.
AGAIN.
THE BOSS HAS GOTTA BE BLOWING A GASKET ABOUT NOW.
WHAT THE— HE HASN'T EVEN BEEN DOWN THERE ***A WEEK!***

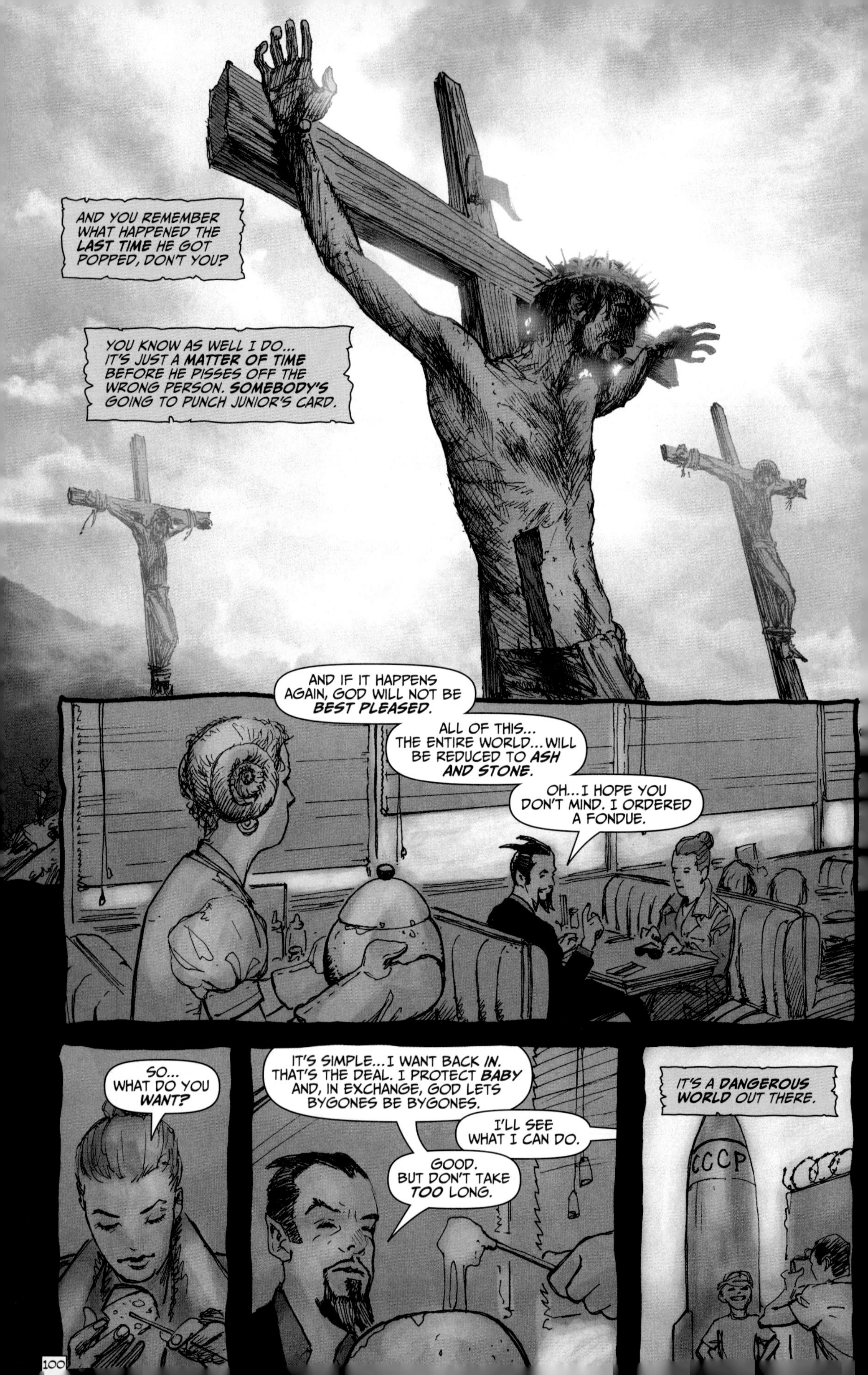
AND YOU REMEMBER WHAT HAPPENED THE LAST TIME HE GOT POPPED, DON'T YOU?
YOU KNOW AS WELL I DO... IT'S JUST A MATTER OF TIME BEFORE HE PISSES OFF THE WRONG PERSON. SOMEBODY'S GOING TO PUNCH JUNIOR'S CARD.
AND IF IT HAPPENS AGAIN, GOD WILL NOT BE BEST PLEASED.
ALL OF THIS... THE ENTIRE WORLD... WILL BE REDUCED TO ASH AND STONE.
OH... I HOPE YOU DON'T MIND. I ORDERED A FONDUE.
SO... WHAT DO YOU WANT?
IT'S SIMPLE... I WANT BACK IN. THAT'S THE DEAL. I PROTECT BABY AND, IN EXCHANGE, GOD LETS BYGONES BE BYGONES.
I'LL SEE WHAT I CAN DO.
GOOD. BUT DON'T TAKE TOO LONG.
IT'S A DANGEROUS WORLD OUT THERE.
CCCP

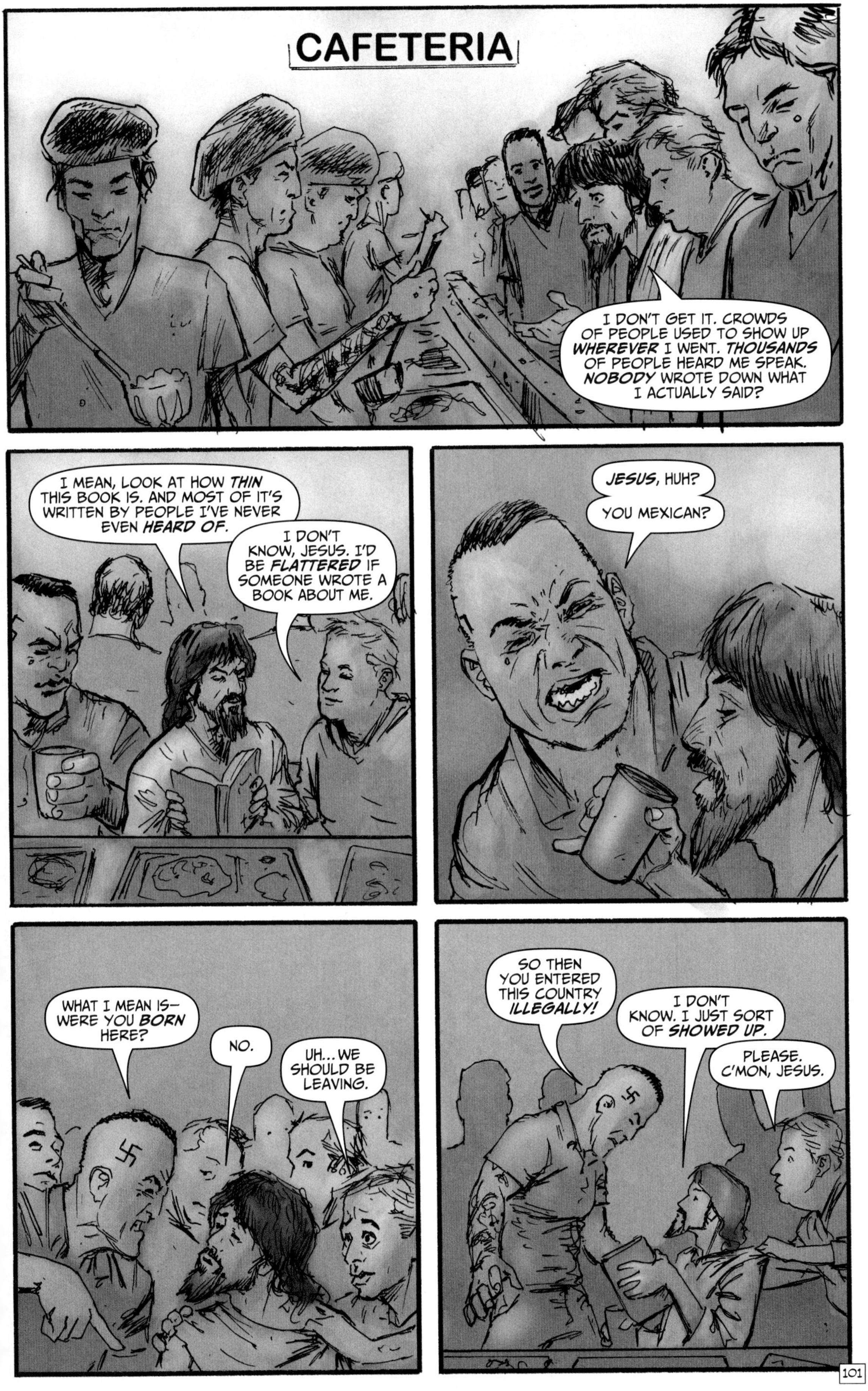
CAFETERIA
I DON'T GET IT. CROWDS OF PEOPLE USED TO SHOW UP WHEREVER I WENT. THOUSANDS OF PEOPLE HEARD ME SPEAK. NOBODY WROTE DOWN WHAT I ACTUALLY SAID?
I MEAN, LOOK AT HOW THIN THIS BOOK IS. AND MOST OF IT'S WRITTEN BY PEOPLE I'VE NEVER EVEN HEARD OF.
I DON'T KNOW, JESUS. I'D BE FLATTERED IF SOMEONE WROTE A BOOK ABOUT ME.
JESUS, HUH?
YOU MEXICAN?
WHAT I MEAN IS— WERE YOU BORN HERE?
NO.
UH...WE SHOULD BE LEAVING.
SO THEN YOU ENTERED THIS COUNTRY ILLEGALLY!
I DON'T KNOW. I JUST SORT OF SHOWED UP.
PLEASE. C'MON, JESUS.

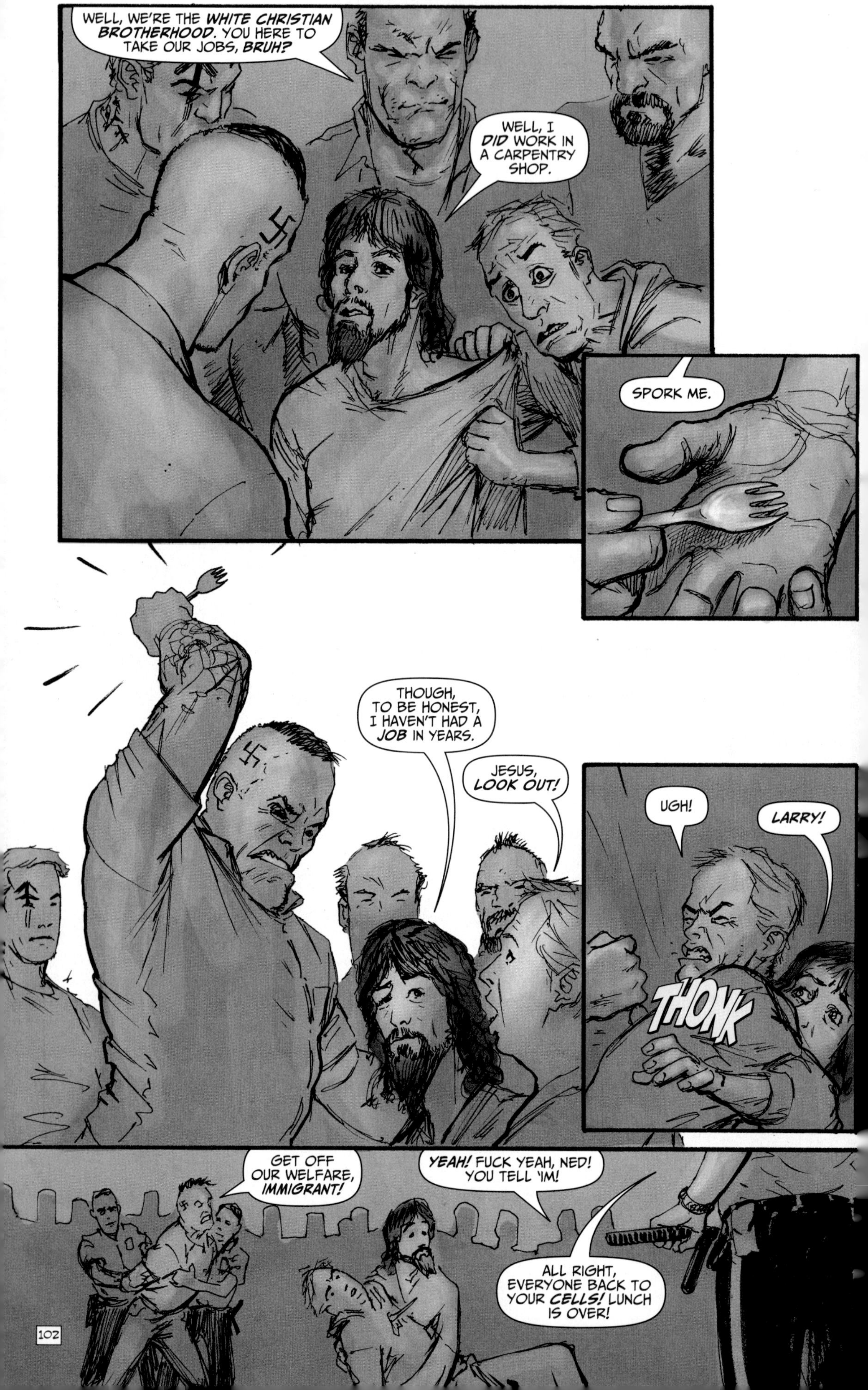
WELL, WE'RE THE WHITE CHRISTIAN BROTHERHOOD. YOU HERE TO TAKE OUR JOBS, BRUH?
WELL, I DID WORK IN A CARPENTRY SHOP.
SPORK ME.
THOUGH, TO BE HONEST, I HAVEN'T HAD A JOB IN YEARS.
JESUS, LOOK OUT!
UGH!
LARRY!
THONK
GET OFF OUR WELFARE, IMMIGRANT!
YEAH! FUCK YEAH, NED! YOU TELL 'IM!
ALL RIGHT, EVERYONE BACK TO YOUR CELLS! LUNCH IS OVER!

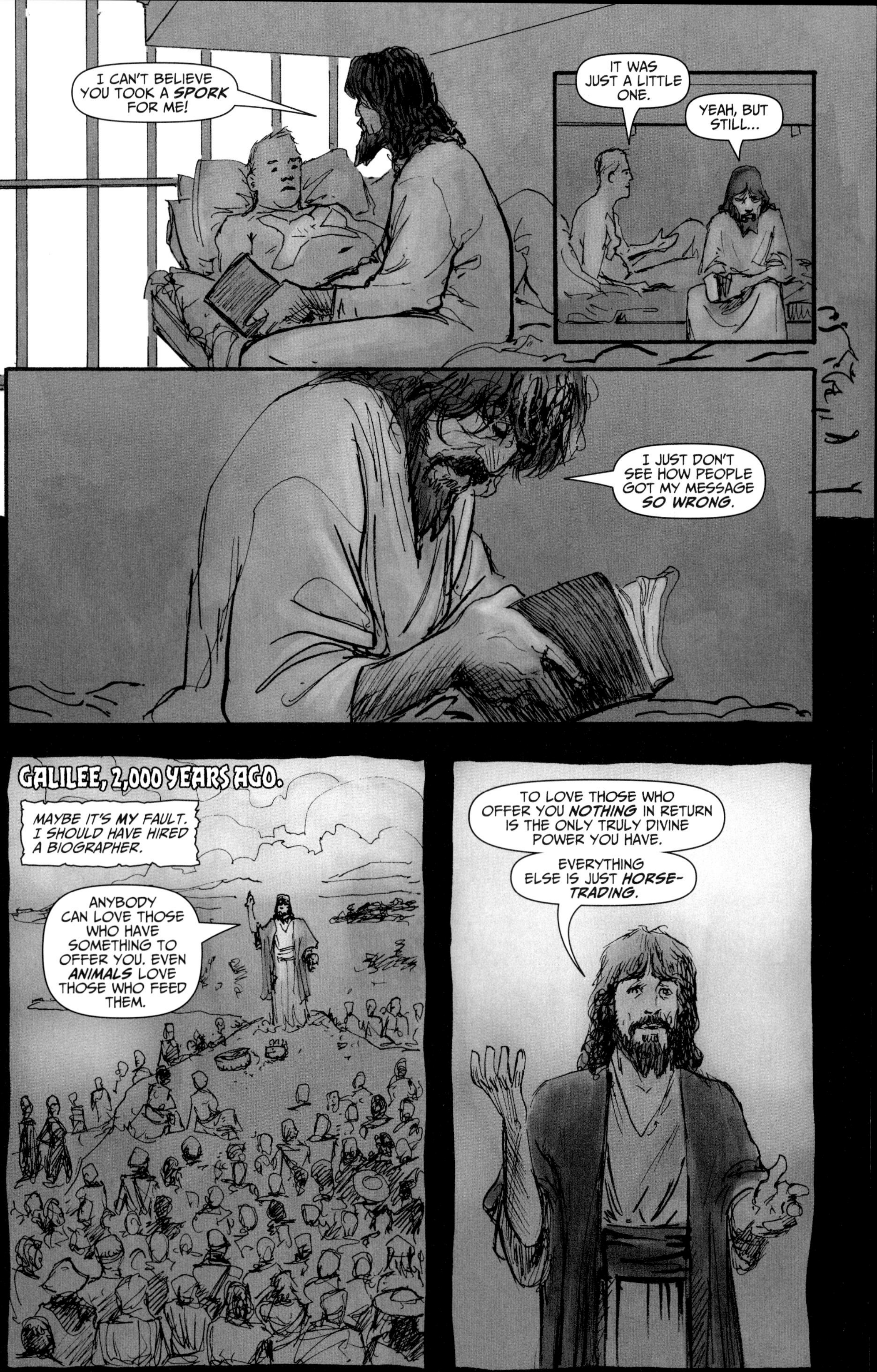
I CAN'T BELIEVE YOU TOOK A SPORK FOR ME!
IT WAS JUST A LITTLE ONE.
YEAH, BUT STILL...
I JUST DON'T SEE HOW PEOPLE GOT MY MESSAGE SO WRONG.
GALILEE, 2,000 YEARS AGO.
MAYBE IT'S MY FAULT. I SHOULD HAVE HIRED A BIOGRAPHER.
ANYBODY CAN LOVE THOSE WHO HAVE SOMETHING TO OFFER YOU. EVEN ANIMALS LOVE THOSE WHO FEED THEM.
TO LOVE THOSE WHO OFFER YOU NOTHING IN RETURN IS THE ONLY TRULY DIVINE POWER YOU HAVE.
EVERYTHING ELSE IS JUST HORSE-TRADING.

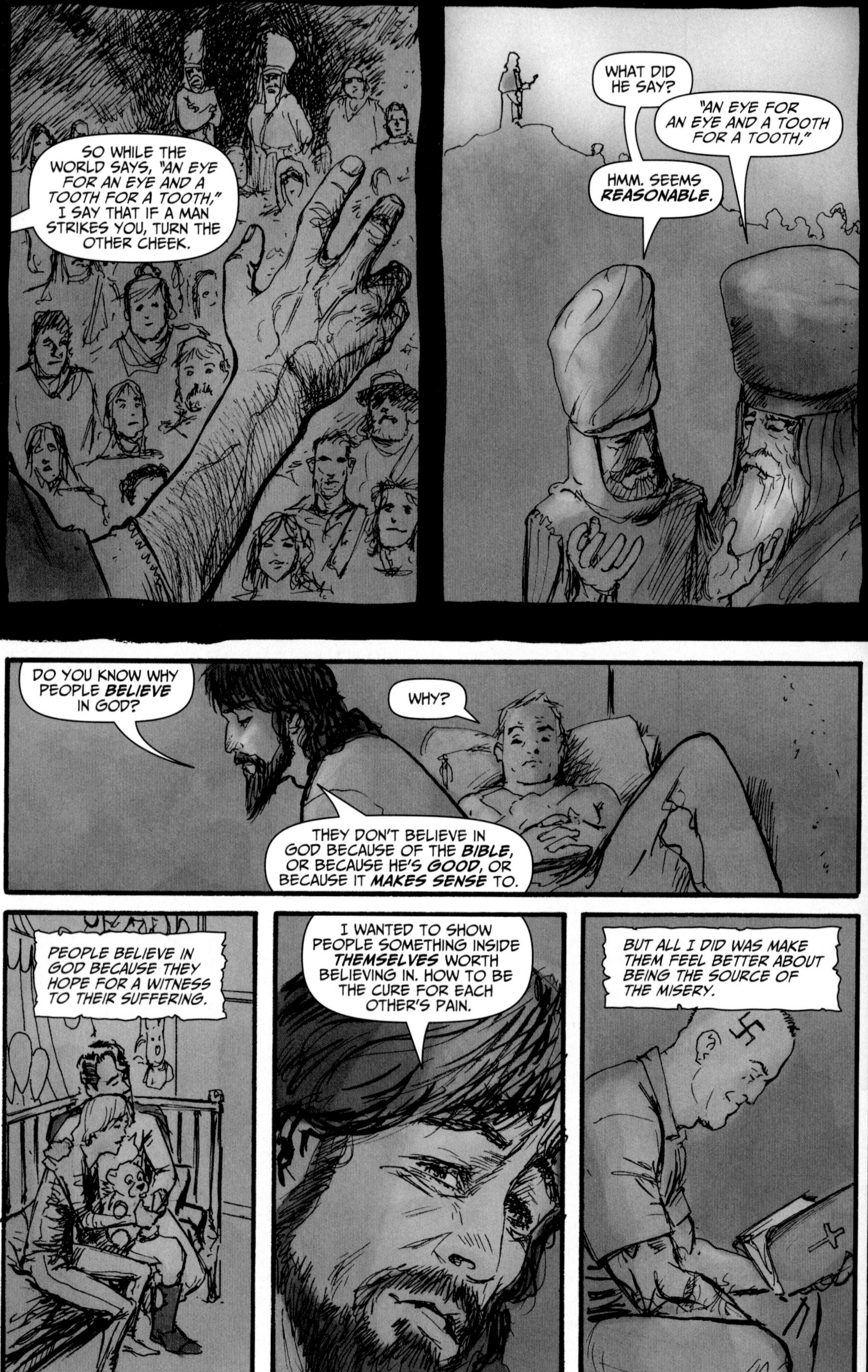
SO WHILE THE WORLD SAYS, *"AN EYE FOR AN EYE AND A TOOTH FOR A TOOTH,"* I SAY THAT IF A MAN STRIKES YOU, TURN THE OTHER CHEEK.
WHAT DID HE SAY?
"AN EYE FOR AN EYE AND A TOOTH FOR A TOOTH,"
HMM. SEEMS ***REASONABLE.***
DO YOU KNOW WHY PEOPLE ***BELIEVE*** IN GOD?
WHY?
THEY DON'T BELIEVE IN GOD BECAUSE OF THE ***BIBLE***, OR BECAUSE HE'S ***GOOD***, OR BECAUSE IT ***MAKES SENSE*** TO.
PEOPLE BELIEVE IN GOD BECAUSE THEY HOPE FOR A WITNESS TO THEIR SUFFERING.
I WANTED TO SHOW PEOPLE SOMETHING INSIDE ***THEMSELVES*** WORTH BELIEVING IN. HOW TO BE THE CURE FOR EACH OTHER'S PAIN.
BUT ALL I DID WAS MAKE THEM FEEL BETTER ABOUT BEING THE SOURCE OF THE MISERY.

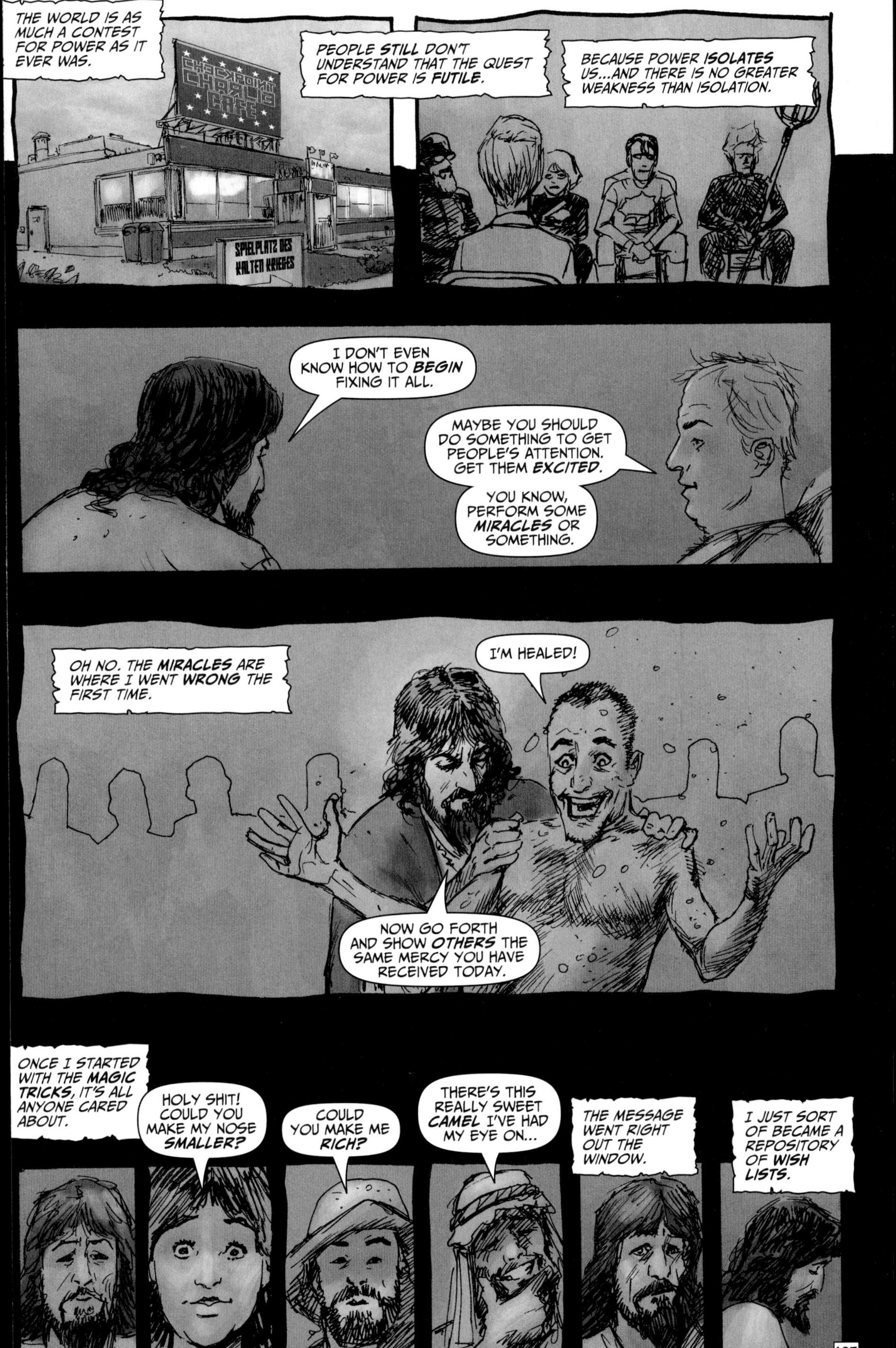
THE WORLD IS AS MUCH A CONTEST FOR POWER AS IT EVER WAS.
SPIELPLATZ DES KALTEN KRIEGES
PEOPLE STILL DON'T UNDERSTAND THAT THE QUEST FOR POWER IS FUTILE.
BECAUSE POWER ISOLATES US...AND THERE IS NO GREATER WEAKNESS THAN ISOLATION.
I DON'T EVEN KNOW HOW TO BEGIN FIXING IT ALL.
MAYBE YOU SHOULD DO SOMETHING TO GET PEOPLE'S ATTENTION. GET THEM EXCITED.
YOU KNOW, PERFORM SOME MIRACLES OR SOMETHING.
OH NO. THE MIRACLES ARE WHERE I WENT WRONG THE FIRST TIME.
I'M HEALED!
NOW GO FORTH AND SHOW OTHERS THE SAME MERCY YOU HAVE RECEIVED TODAY.
ONCE I STARTED WITH THE MAGIC TRICKS, IT'S ALL ANYONE CARED ABOUT.
HOLY SHIT! COULD YOU MAKE MY NOSE SMALLER?
COULD YOU MAKE ME RICH?
THERE'S THIS REALLY SWEET CAMEL I'VE HAD MY EYE ON...
THE MESSAGE WENT RIGHT OUT THE WINDOW.
I JUST SORT OF BECAME A REPOSITORY OF WISH LISTS.

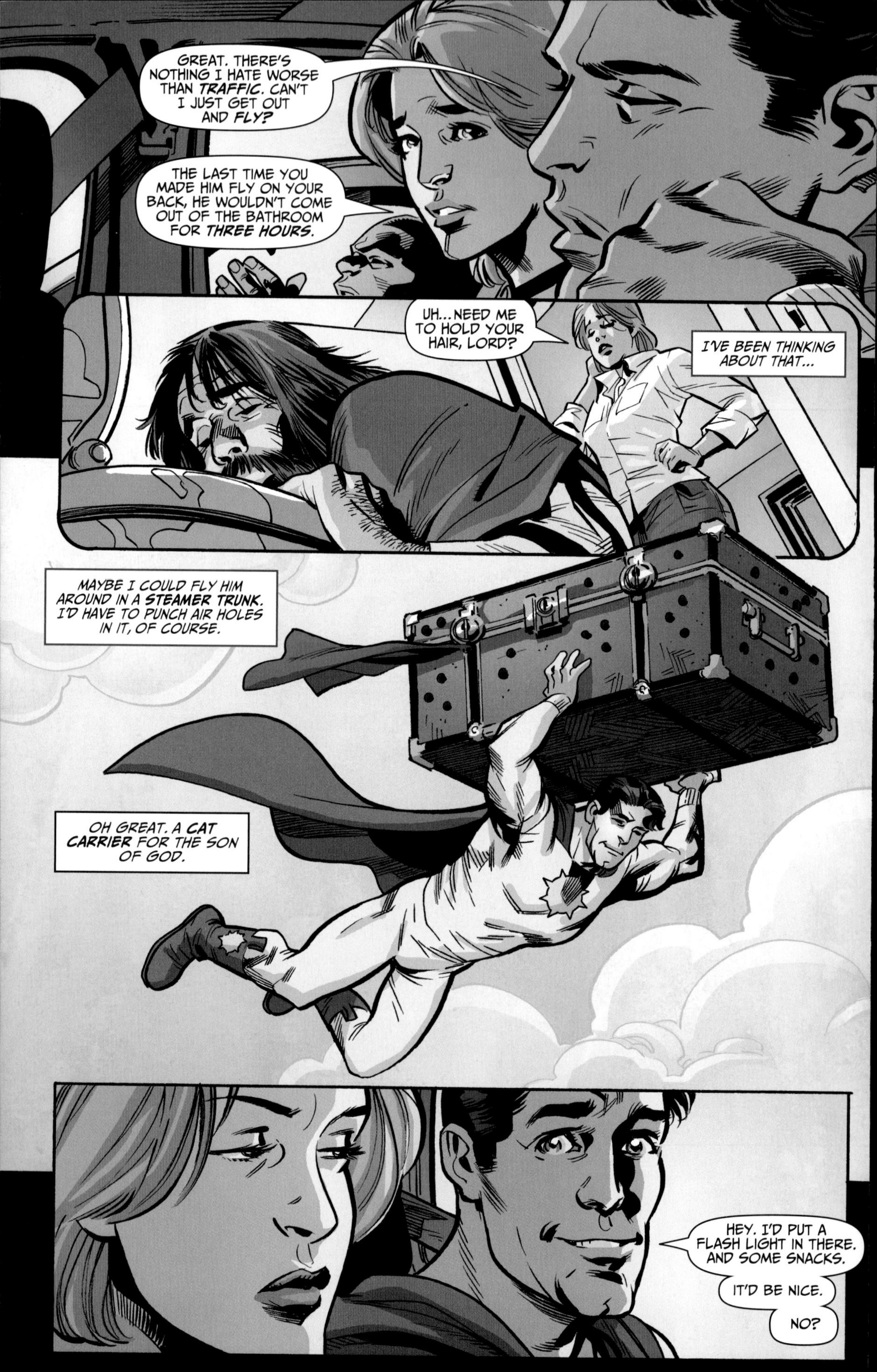
GREAT. THERE'S NOTHING I HATE WORSE THAN TRAFFIC. CAN'T I JUST GET OUT AND FLY?
THE LAST TIME YOU MADE HIM FLY ON YOUR BACK, HE WOULDN'T COME OUT OF THE BATHROOM FOR THREE HOURS.
UH...NEED ME TO HOLD YOUR HAIR, LORD?
I'VE BEEN THINKING ABOUT THAT...
MAYBE I COULD FLY HIM AROUND IN A STEAMER TRUNK. I'D HAVE TO PUNCH AIR HOLES IN IT, OF COURSE.
OH GREAT. A CAT CARRIER FOR THE SON OF GOD.
HEY. I'D PUT A FLASH LIGHT IN THERE. AND SOME SNACKS.
IT'D BE NICE.
NO?

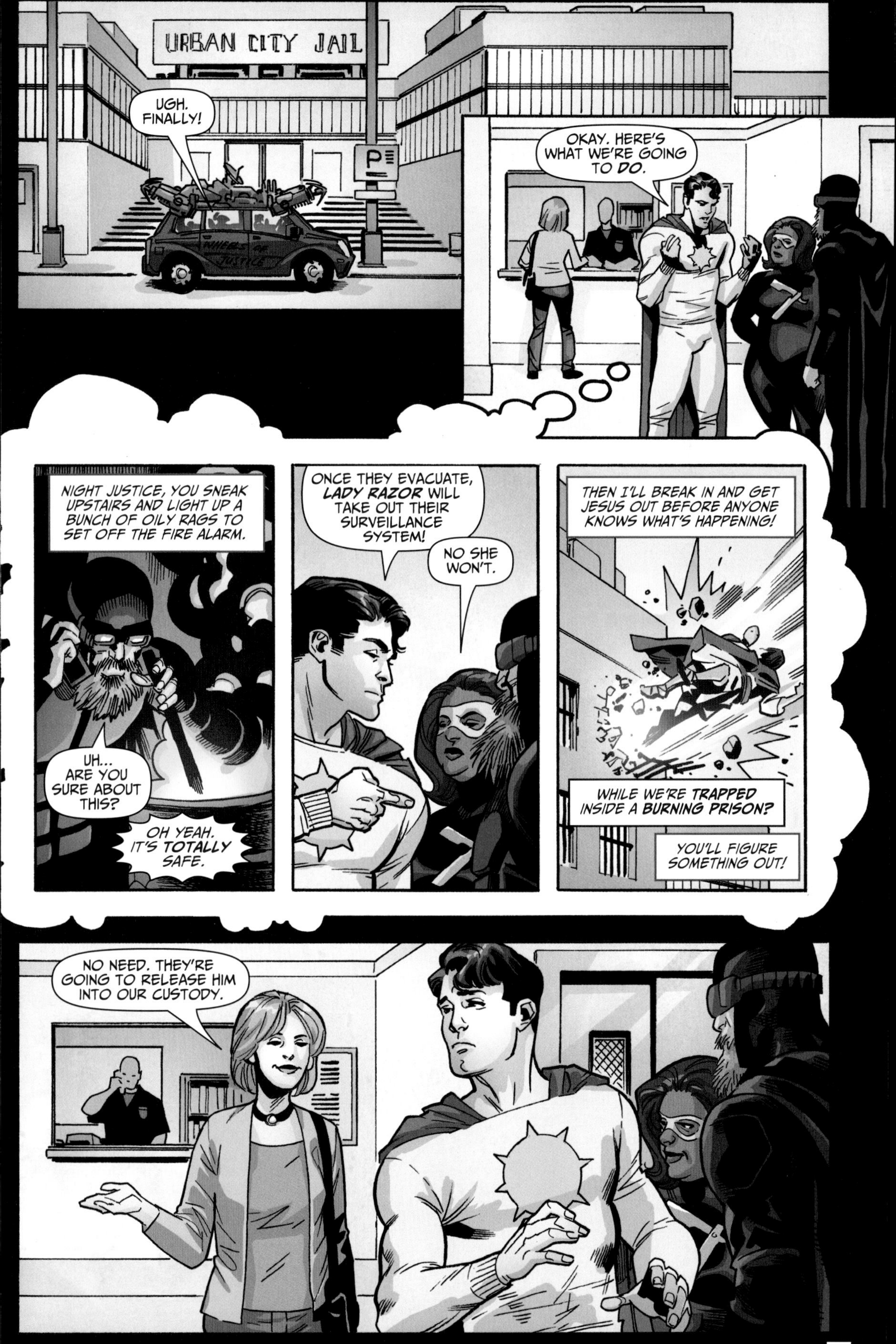
URBAN CITY JAIL
UGH. FINALLY!
P
WHEELS OF JUSTICE
OKAY. HERE'S WHAT WE'RE GOING TO DO.
NIGHT JUSTICE, YOU SNEAK UPSTAIRS AND LIGHT UP A BUNCH OF OILY RAGS TO SET OFF THE FIRE ALARM.
UH... ARE YOU SURE ABOUT THIS?
OH YEAH. IT'S TOTALLY SAFE.
ONCE THEY EVACUATE, LADY RAZOR WILL TAKE OUT THEIR SURVEILLANCE SYSTEM!
NO SHE WON'T.
THEN I'LL BREAK IN AND GET JESUS OUT BEFORE ANYONE KNOWS WHAT'S HAPPENING!
WHILE WE'RE TRAPPED INSIDE A BURNING PRISON?
YOU'LL FIGURE SOMETHING OUT!
NO NEED. THEY'RE GOING TO RELEASE HIM INTO OUR CUSTODY.

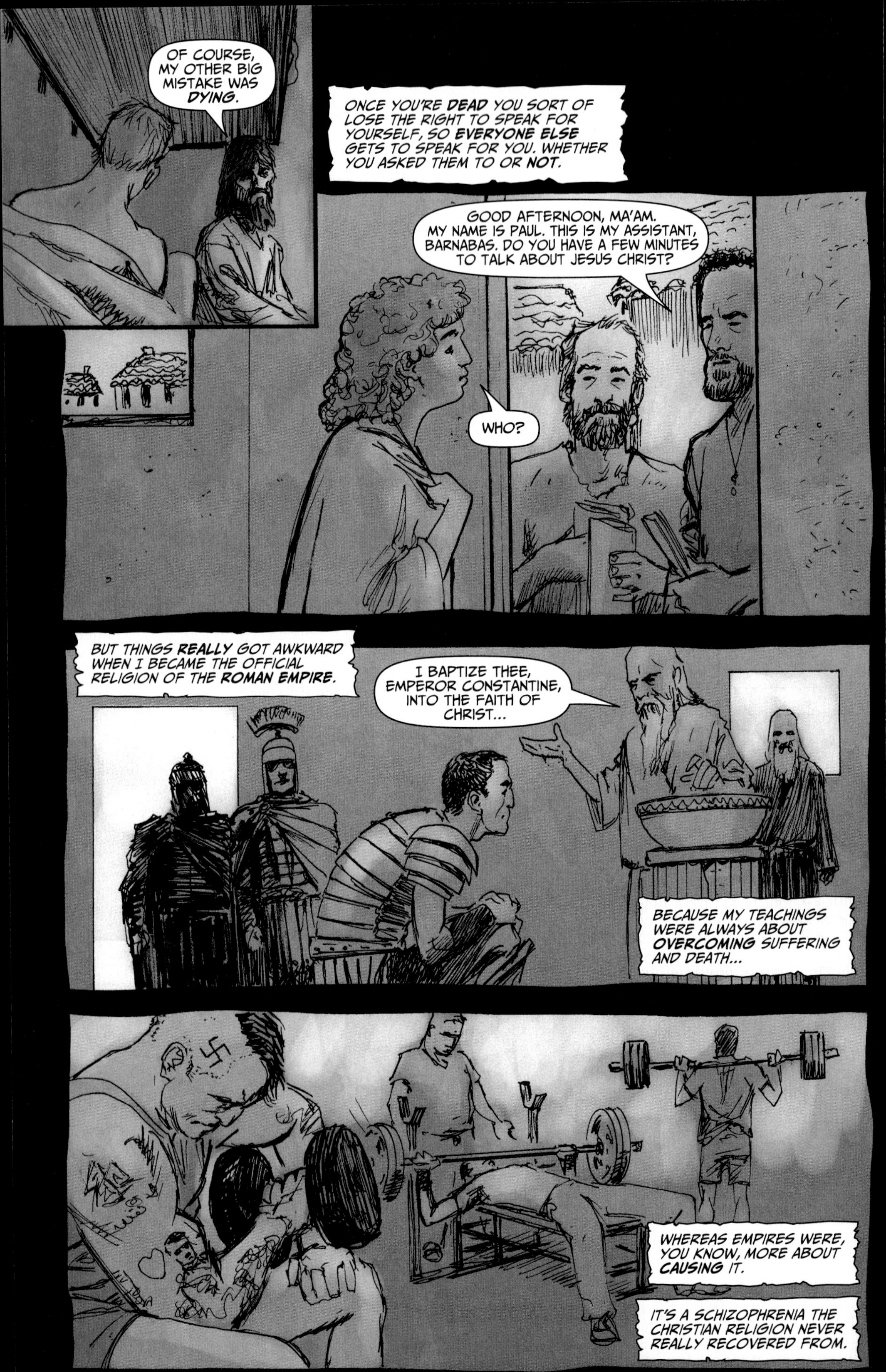
OF COURSE, MY OTHER BIG MISTAKE WAS **DYING**.
*ONCE YOU'RE **DEAD** YOU SORT OF LOSE THE RIGHT TO SPEAK FOR YOURSELF, SO **EVERYONE ELSE** GETS TO SPEAK FOR YOU. WHETHER YOU ASKED THEM TO OR **NOT**.*
GOOD AFTERNOON, MA'AM. MY NAME IS PAUL. THIS IS MY ASSISTANT, BARNABAS. DO YOU HAVE A FEW MINUTES TO TALK ABOUT JESUS CHRIST?
WHO?
*BUT THINGS **REALLY** GOT AWKWARD WHEN I BECAME THE OFFICIAL RELIGION OF THE **ROMAN EMPIRE**.*
I BAPTIZE THEE, EMPEROR CONSTANTINE, INTO THE FAITH OF CHRIST...
*BECAUSE MY TEACHINGS WERE ALWAYS ABOUT **OVERCOMING** SUFFERING AND DEATH...*
*WHEREAS EMPIRES WERE, YOU KNOW, MORE ABOUT **CAUSING** IT.*
IT'S A SCHIZOPHRENIA THE CHRISTIAN RELIGION NEVER REALLY RECOVERED FROM.

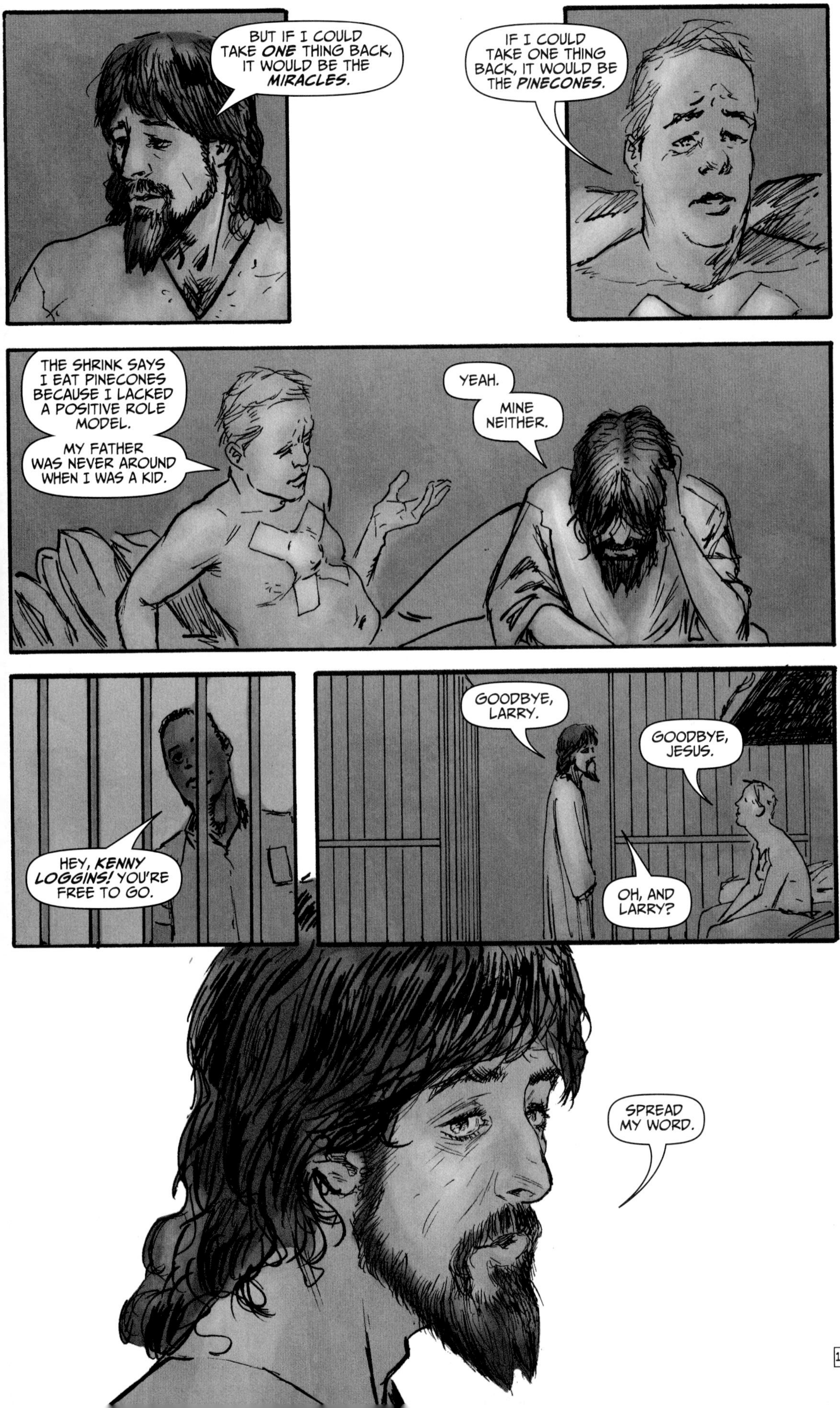
BUT IF I COULD TAKE ONE THING BACK, IT WOULD BE THE MIRACLES.
IF I COULD TAKE ONE THING BACK, IT WOULD BE THE PINECONES.
THE SHRINK SAYS I EAT PINECONES BECAUSE I LACKED A POSITIVE ROLE MODEL.
MY FATHER WAS NEVER AROUND WHEN I WAS A KID.
YEAH.
MINE NEITHER.
HEY, KENNY LOGGINS! YOU'RE FREE TO GO.
GOODBYE, LARRY.
GOODBYE, JESUS.
OH, AND LARRY?
SPREAD MY WORD.

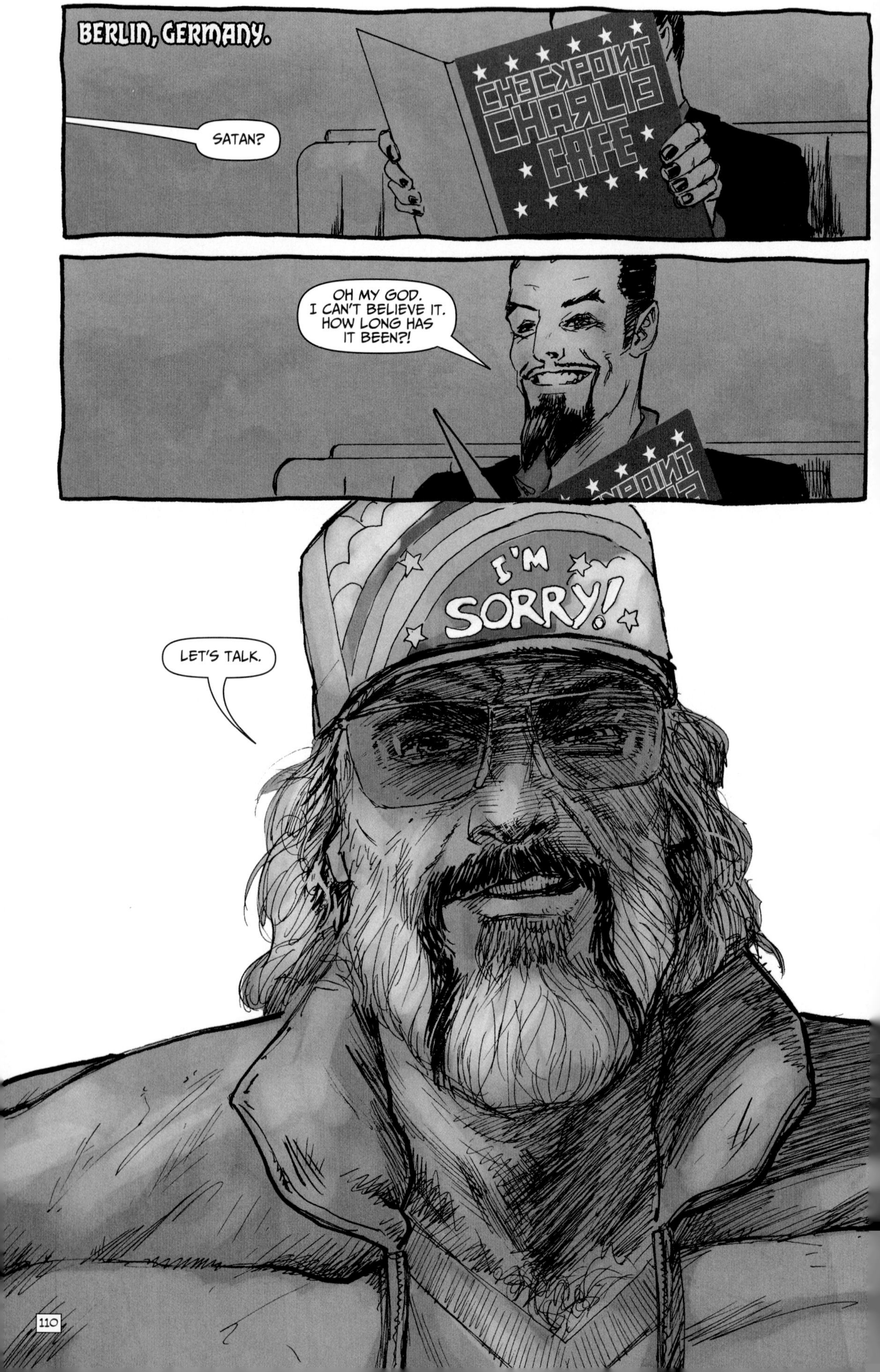
BERLIN, GERMANY.
SATAN?
CHECKPOINT CHARLIE CAFE
OH MY GOD. I CAN'T BELIEVE IT. HOW LONG HAS IT BEEN?!
I'M SORRY!
LET'S TALK.

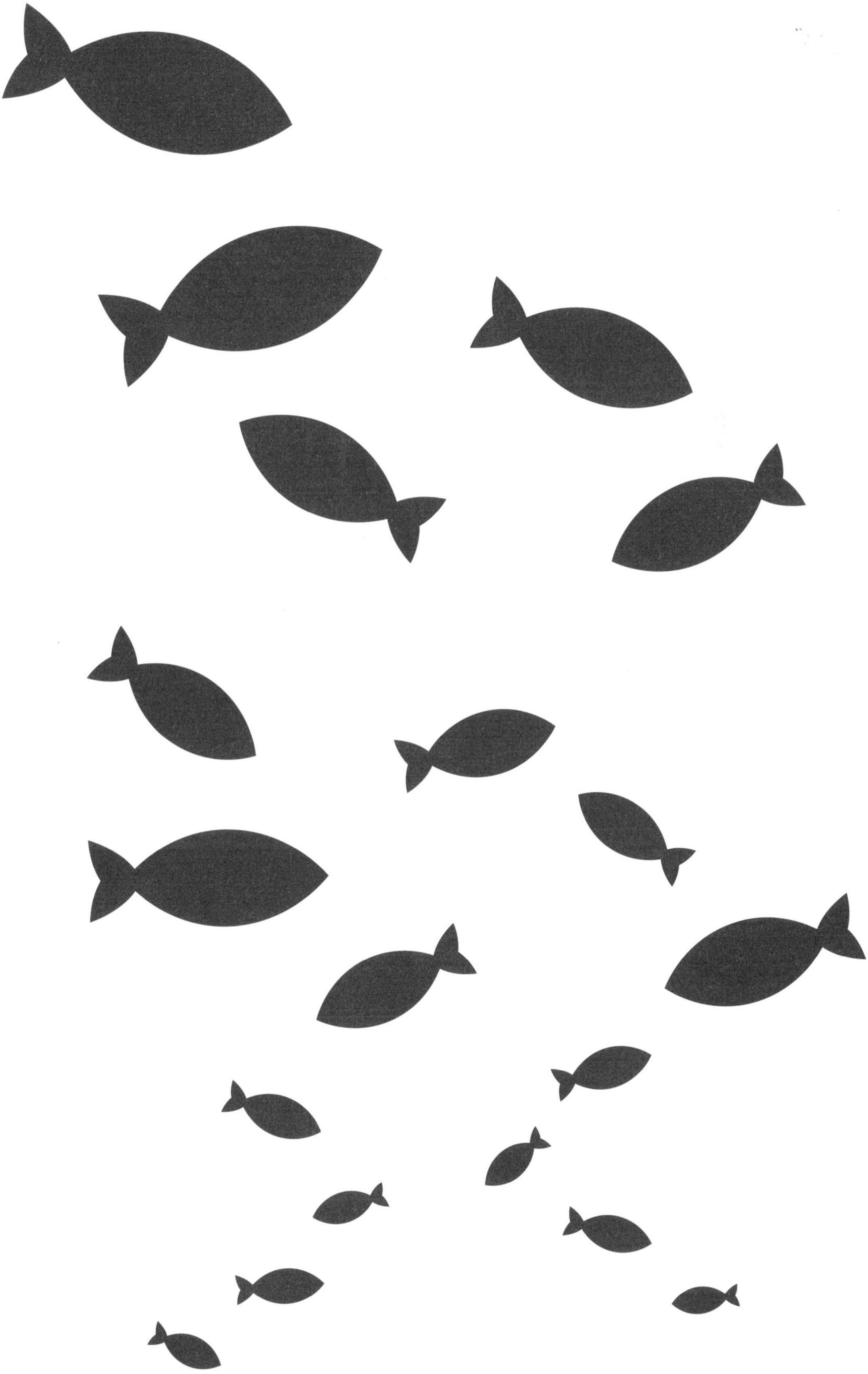

5

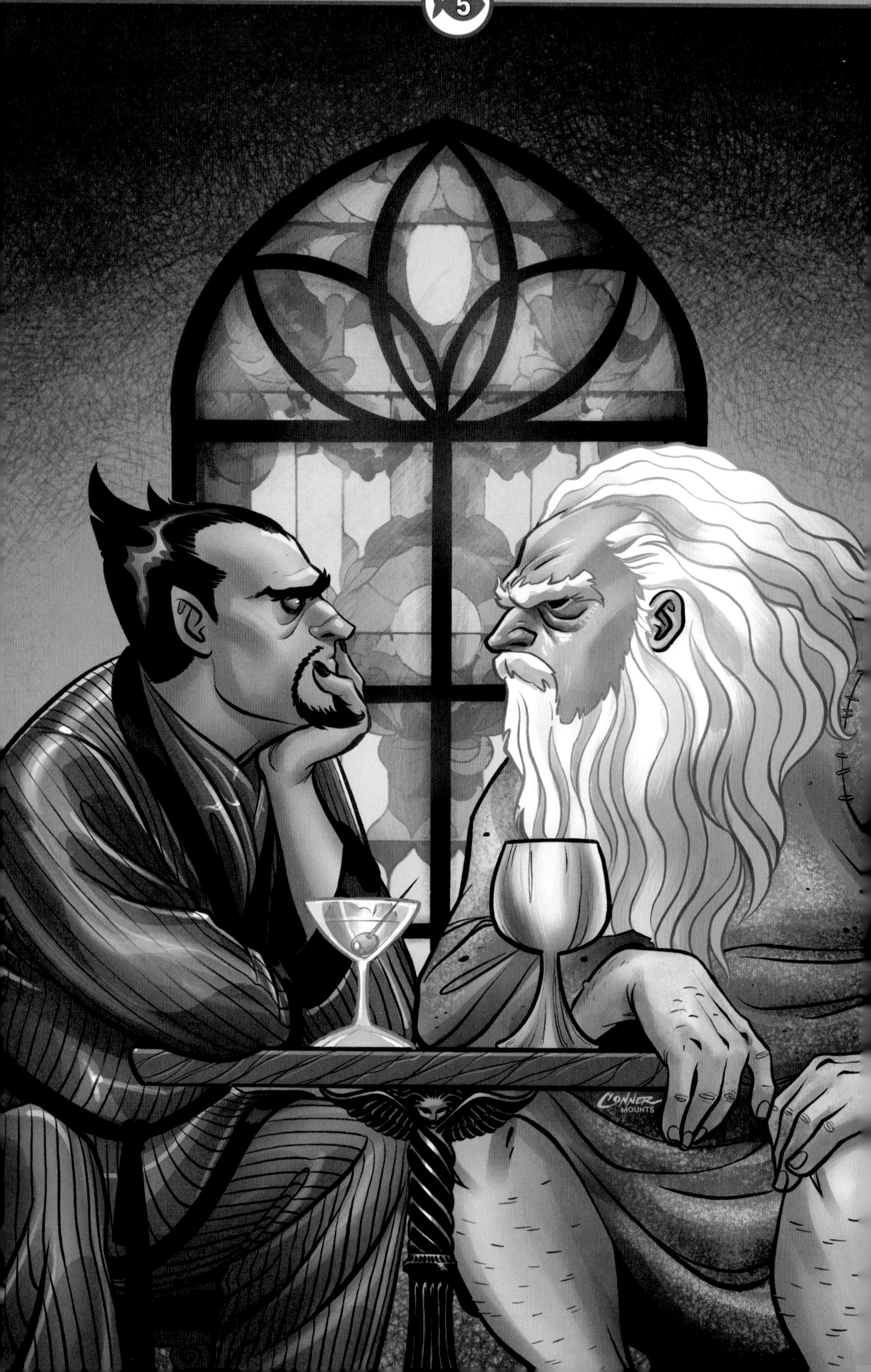
CONNER
MOUNTS

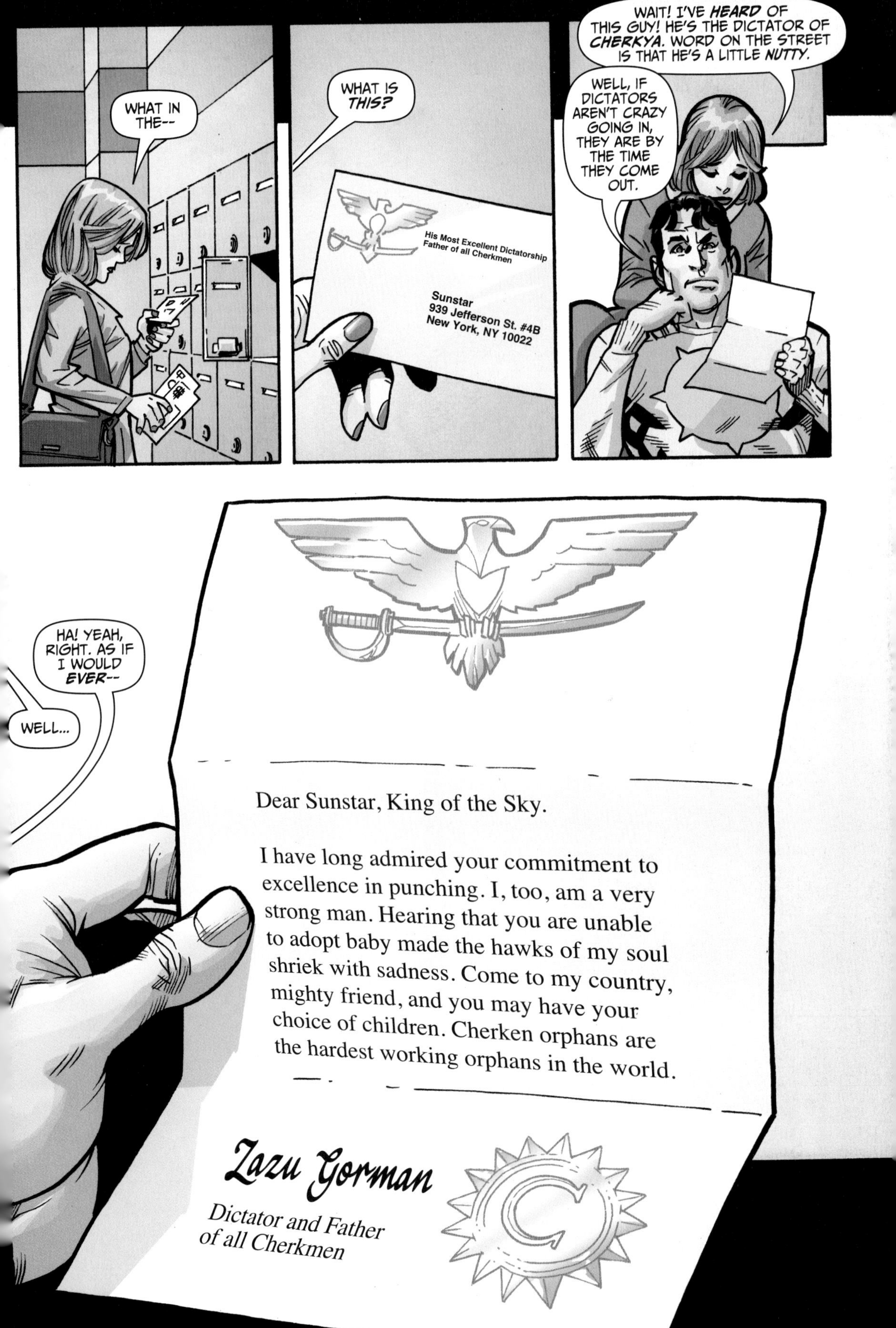
WHAT IN THE--
WHAT IS THIS?
His Most Excellent Dictatorship Father of all Cherkmen
Sunstar
939 Jefferson St. #4B
New York, NY 10022
WAIT! I'VE HEARD OF THIS GUY! HE'S THE DICTATOR OF CHERKYA. WORD ON THE STREET IS THAT HE'S A LITTLE NUTTY.
WELL, IF DICTATORS AREN'T CRAZY GOING IN, THEY ARE BY THE TIME THEY COME OUT.
HA! YEAH, RIGHT. AS IF I WOULD EVER--
WELL...
Dear Sunstar, King of the Sky.
I have long admired your commitment to excellence in punching. I, too, am a very strong man. Hearing that you are unable to adopt baby made the hawks of my soul shriek with sadness. Come to my country, mighty friend, and you may have your choice of children. Cherken orphans are the hardest working orphans in the world.
Zazu Gorman
Dictator and Father of all Cherkmen

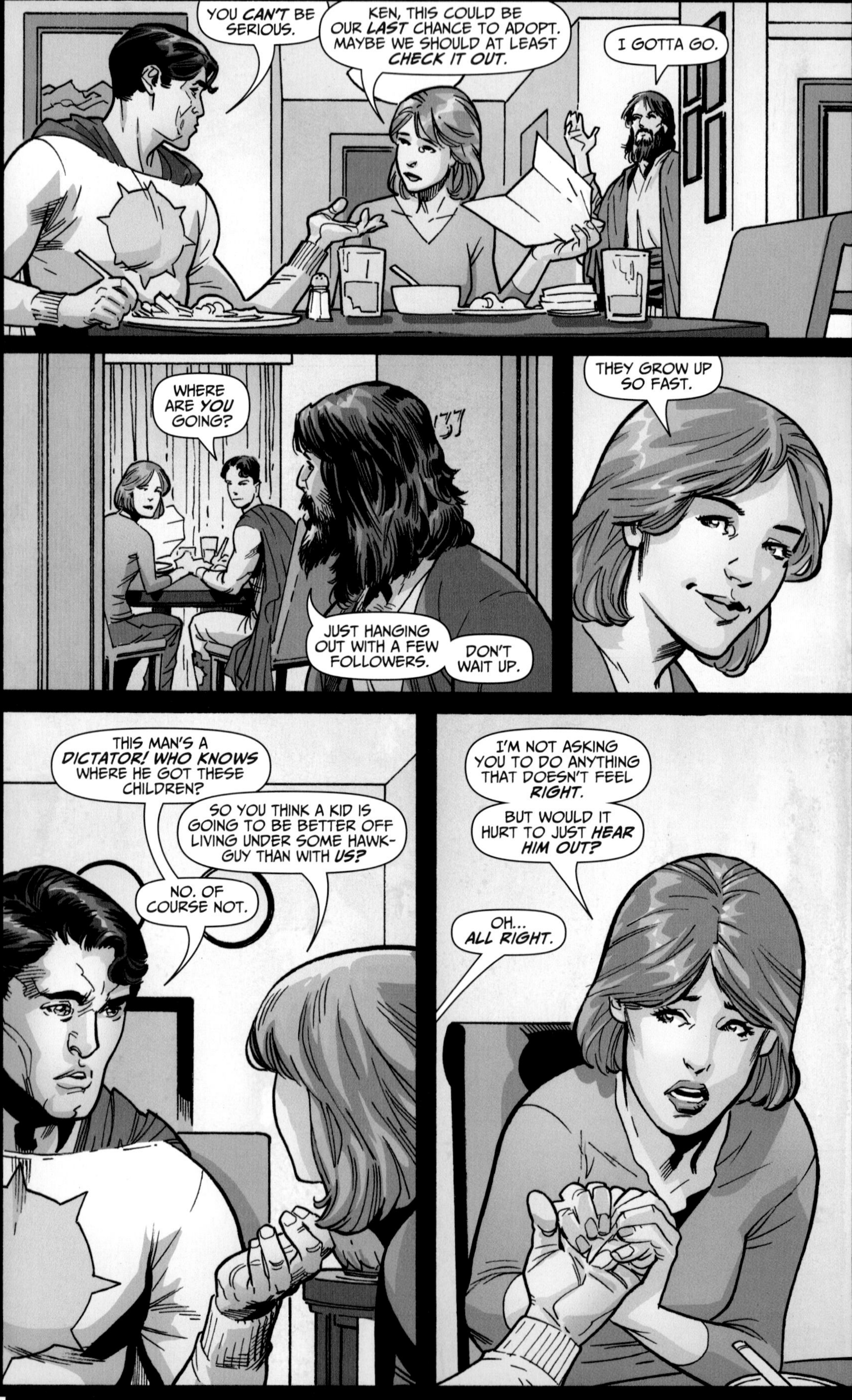
YOU CAN'T BE SERIOUS.
KEN, THIS COULD BE OUR LAST CHANCE TO ADOPT. MAYBE WE SHOULD AT LEAST CHECK IT OUT.
I GOTTA GO.
WHERE ARE YOU GOING?
JUST HANGING OUT WITH A FEW FOLLOWERS.
DON'T WAIT UP.
THEY GROW UP SO FAST.
THIS MAN'S A DICTATOR! WHO KNOWS WHERE HE GOT THESE CHILDREN?
SO YOU THINK A KID IS GOING TO BE BETTER OFF LIVING UNDER SOME HAWK-GUY THAN WITH US?
NO. OF COURSE NOT.
I'M NOT ASKING YOU TO DO ANYTHING THAT DOESN'T FEEL RIGHT.
BUT WOULD IT HURT TO JUST HEAR HIM OUT?
OH... ALL RIGHT.

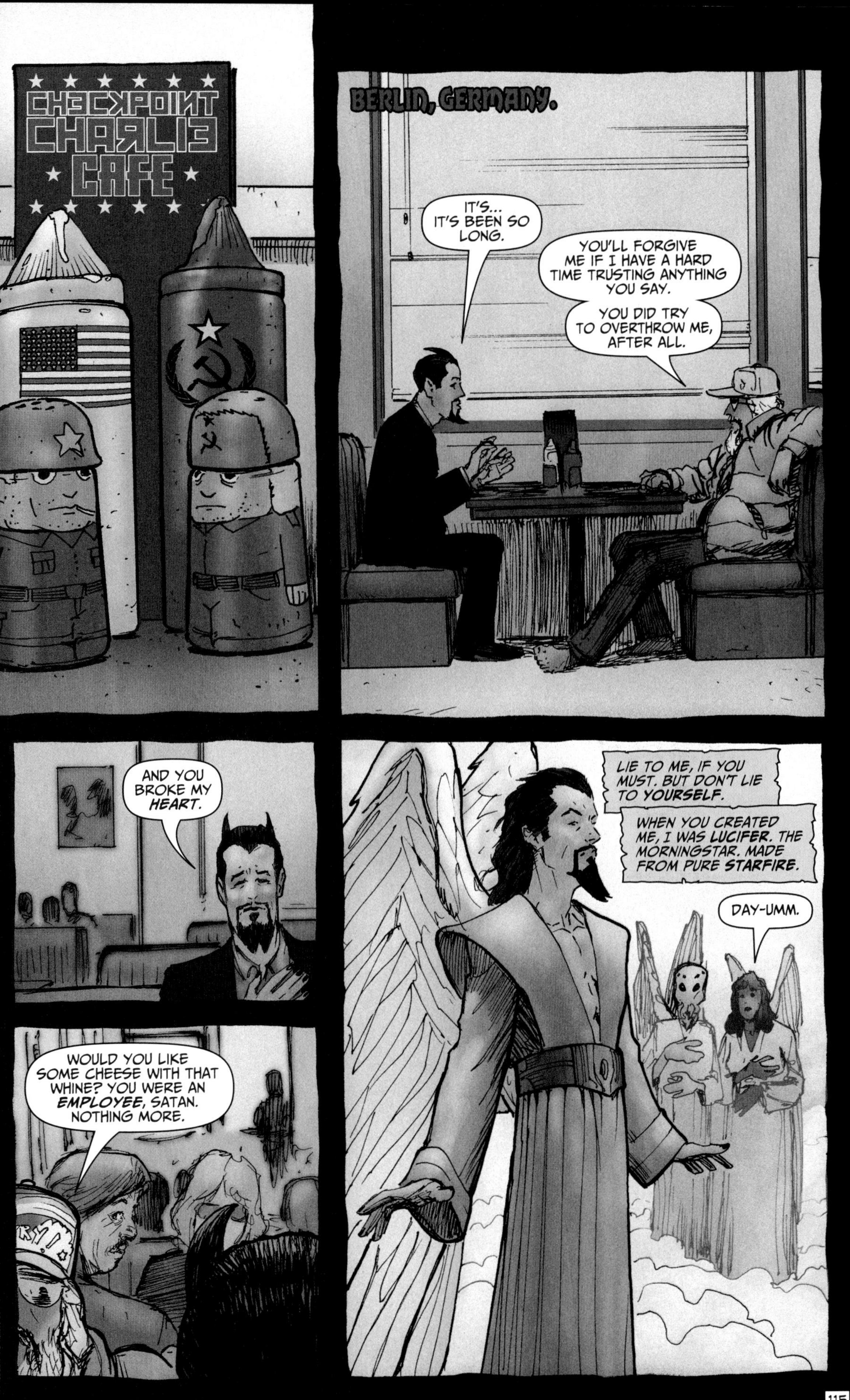
CHECKPOINT CHARLIE CAFE
BERLIN, GERMANY.
IT'S... IT'S BEEN SO LONG.
YOU'LL FORGIVE ME IF I HAVE A HARD TIME TRUSTING ANYTHING YOU SAY.
YOU DID TRY TO OVERTHROW ME, AFTER ALL.
AND YOU BROKE MY HEART.
WOULD YOU LIKE SOME CHEESE WITH THAT WHINE? YOU WERE AN EMPLOYEE, SATAN. NOTHING MORE.
LIE TO ME, IF YOU MUST. BUT DON'T LIE TO YOURSELF.
WHEN YOU CREATED ME, I WAS LUCIFER. THE MORNINGSTAR. MADE FROM PURE STARFIRE.
DAY-UMM.

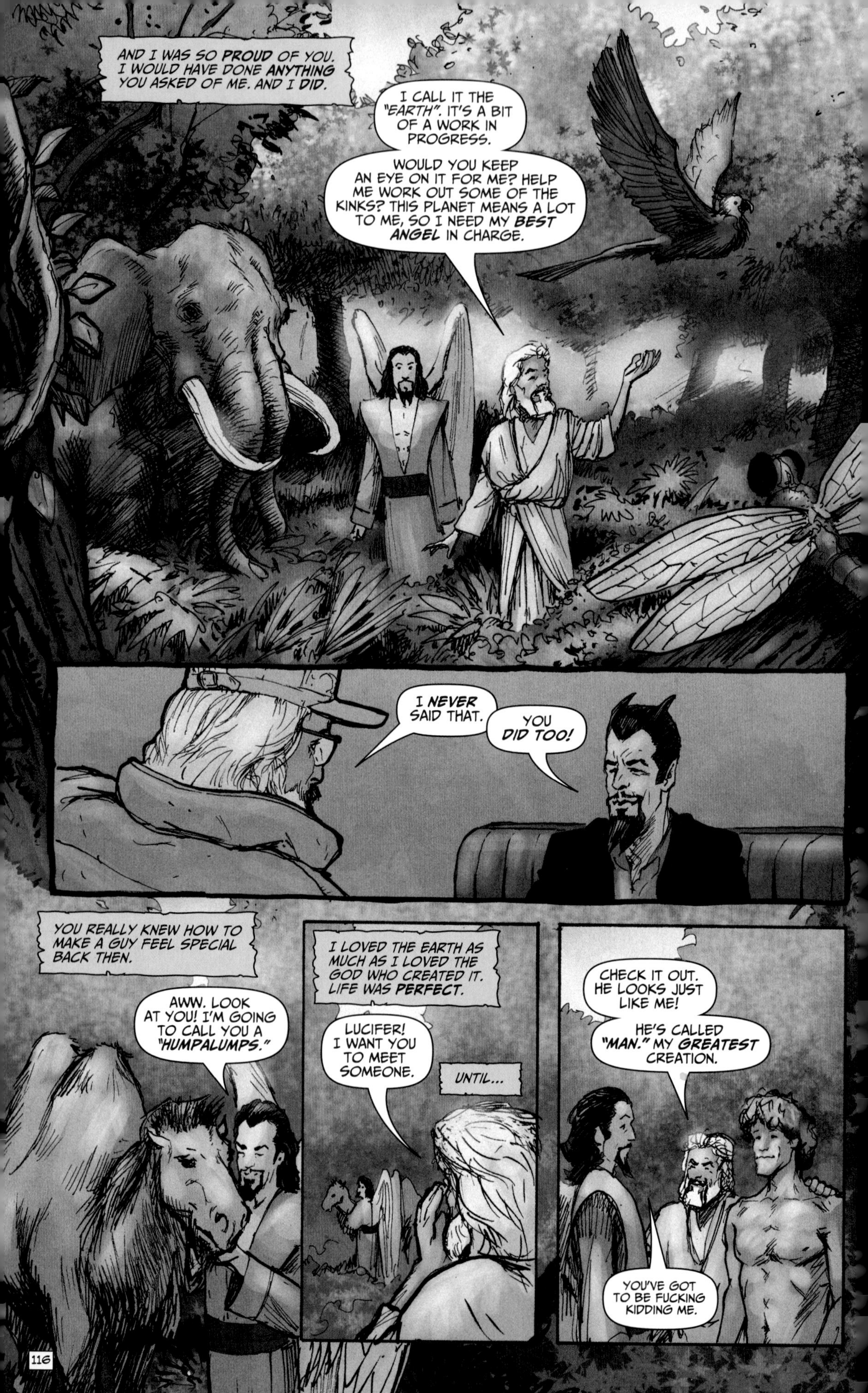

AND I WAS SO PROUD OF YOU. I WOULD HAVE DONE ANYTHING YOU ASKED OF ME. AND I DID.
I CALL IT THE "EARTH". IT'S A BIT OF A WORK IN PROGRESS.
WOULD YOU KEEP AN EYE ON IT FOR ME? HELP ME WORK OUT SOME OF THE KINKS? THIS PLANET MEANS A LOT TO ME, SO I NEED MY BEST ANGEL IN CHARGE.
I NEVER SAID THAT.
YOU DID TOO!
YOU REALLY KNEW HOW TO MAKE A GUY FEEL SPECIAL BACK THEN.
AWW. LOOK AT YOU! I'M GOING TO CALL YOU A "HUMPALUMPS."
I LOVED THE EARTH AS MUCH AS I LOVED THE GOD WHO CREATED IT. LIFE WAS PERFECT.
LUCIFER! I WANT YOU TO MEET SOMEONE.
UNTIL...
CHECK IT OUT. HE LOOKS JUST LIKE ME!
HE'S CALLED "MAN." MY GREATEST CREATION.
YOU'VE GOT TO BE FUCKING KIDDING ME.

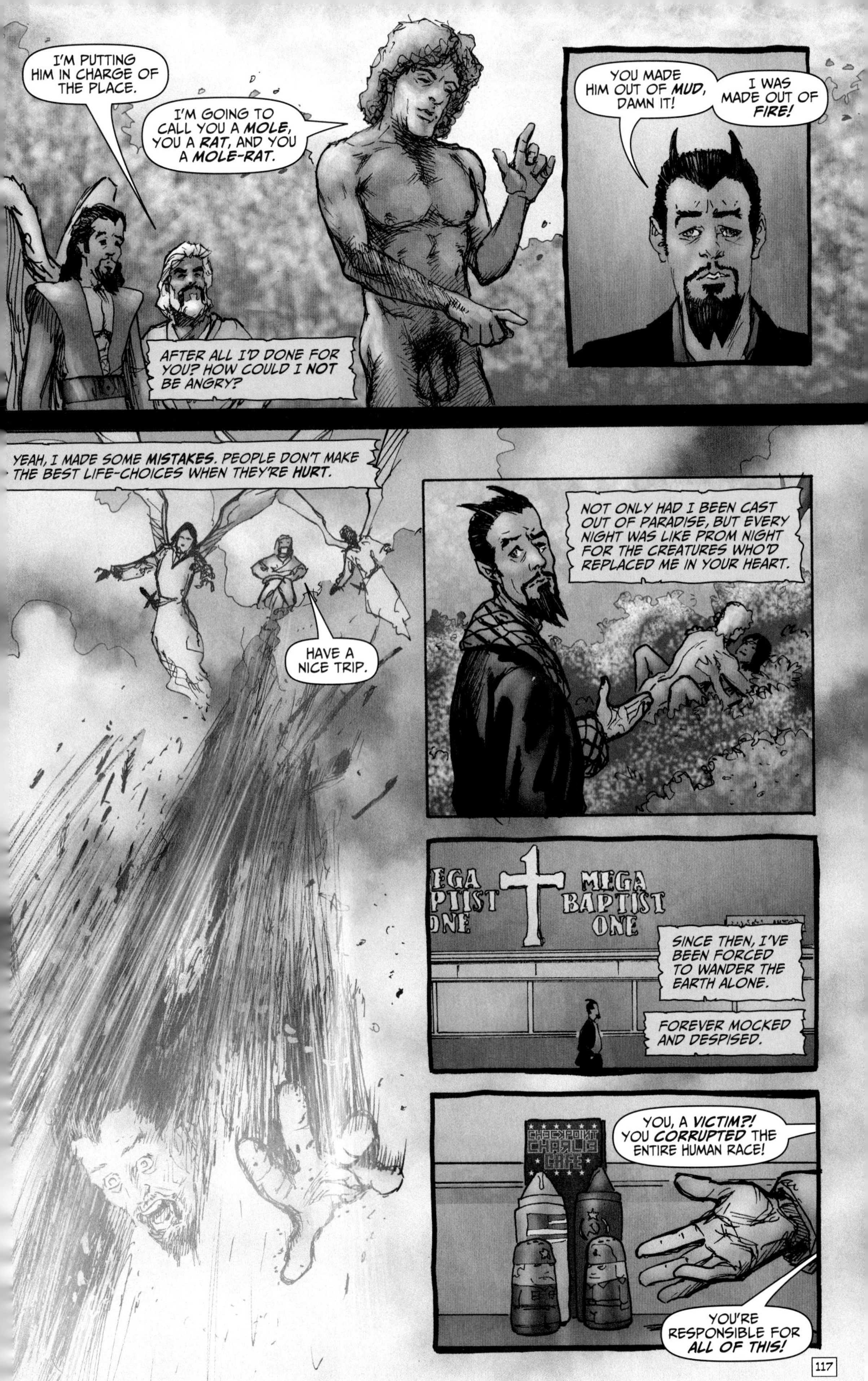
I'M PUTTING HIM IN CHARGE OF THE PLACE.
I'M GOING TO CALL YOU A MOLE, YOU A RAT, AND YOU A MOLE-RAT.
AFTER ALL I'D DONE FOR YOU? HOW COULD I NOT BE ANGRY?
YOU MADE HIM OUT OF MUD, DAMN IT!
I WAS MADE OUT OF FIRE!
YEAH, I MADE SOME MISTAKES. PEOPLE DON'T MAKE THE BEST LIFE-CHOICES WHEN THEY'RE HURT.
HAVE A NICE TRIP.
NOT ONLY HAD I BEEN CAST OUT OF PARADISE, BUT EVERY NIGHT WAS LIKE PROM NIGHT FOR THE CREATURES WHO'D REPLACED ME IN YOUR HEART.
MEGA BAPTIST ONE
SINCE THEN, I'VE BEEN FORCED TO WANDER THE EARTH ALONE.
FOREVER MOCKED AND DESPISED.
YOU, A VICTIM?! YOU CORRUPTED THE ENTIRE HUMAN RACE!
YOU'RE RESPONSIBLE FOR ALL OF THIS!

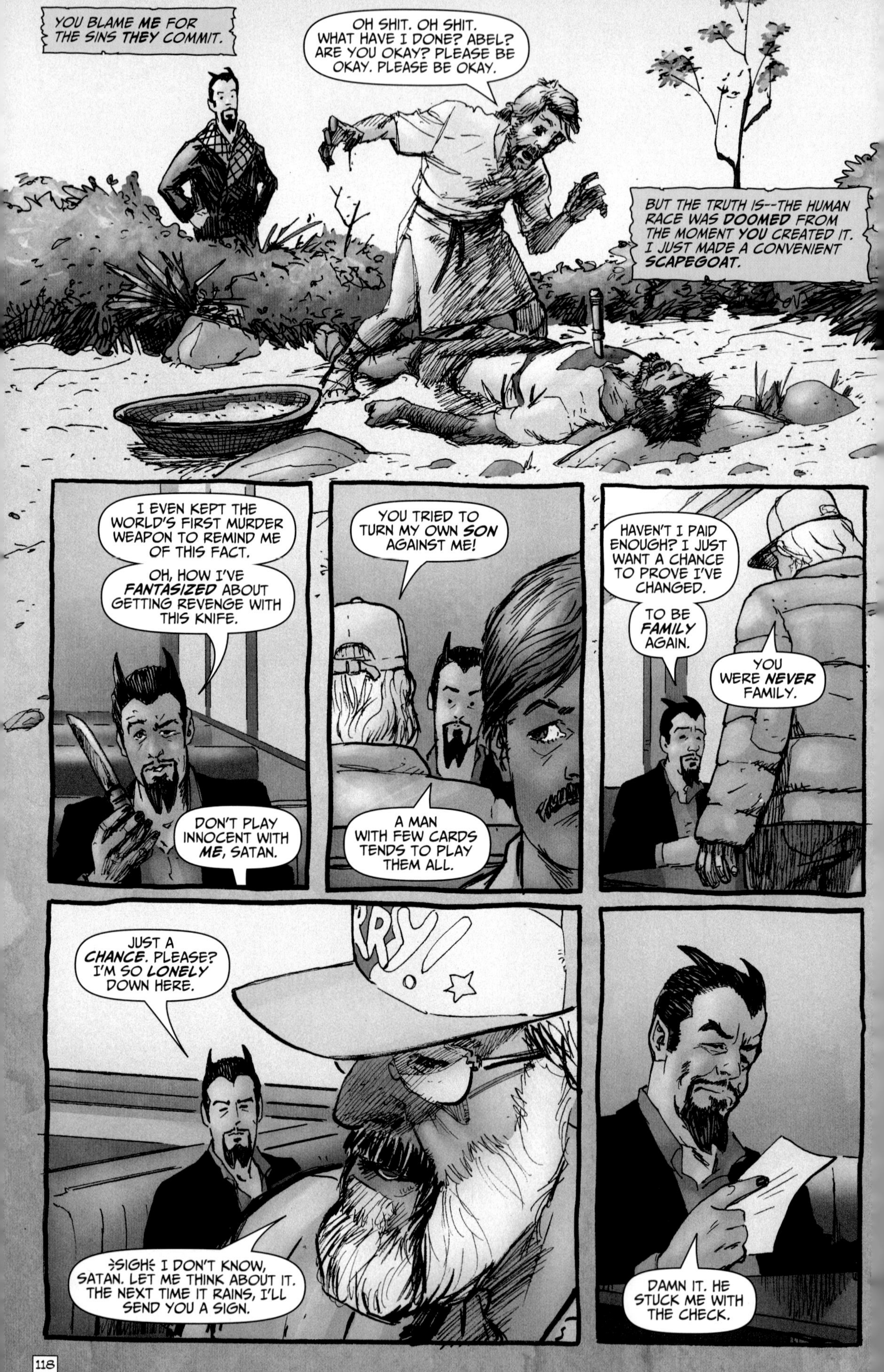
YOU BLAME **ME** FOR THE SINS **THEY** COMMIT.
OH SHIT. OH SHIT. WHAT HAVE I DONE? ABEL? ARE YOU OKAY? PLEASE BE OKAY. PLEASE BE OKAY.
BUT THE TRUTH IS--THE HUMAN RACE WAS **DOOMED** FROM THE MOMENT **YOU** CREATED IT. I JUST MADE A CONVENIENT **SCAPEGOAT.**
I EVEN KEPT THE WORLD'S FIRST MURDER WEAPON TO REMIND ME OF THIS FACT.
OH, HOW I'VE ***FANTASIZED*** ABOUT GETTING REVENGE WITH THIS KNIFE.
DON'T PLAY INNOCENT WITH ***ME***, SATAN.
YOU TRIED TO TURN MY OWN ***SON*** AGAINST ME!
A MAN WITH FEW CARDS TENDS TO PLAY THEM ALL.
HAVEN'T I PAID ENOUGH? I JUST WANT A CHANCE TO PROVE I'VE CHANGED.
TO BE ***FAMILY*** AGAIN.
YOU WERE ***NEVER*** FAMILY.
JUST A ***CHANCE***. PLEASE? I'M SO ***LONELY*** DOWN HERE.
SIGH I DON'T KNOW, SATAN. LET ME THINK ABOUT IT. THE NEXT TIME IT RAINS, I'LL SEND YOU A SIGN.
DAMN IT. HE STUCK ME WITH THE CHECK.

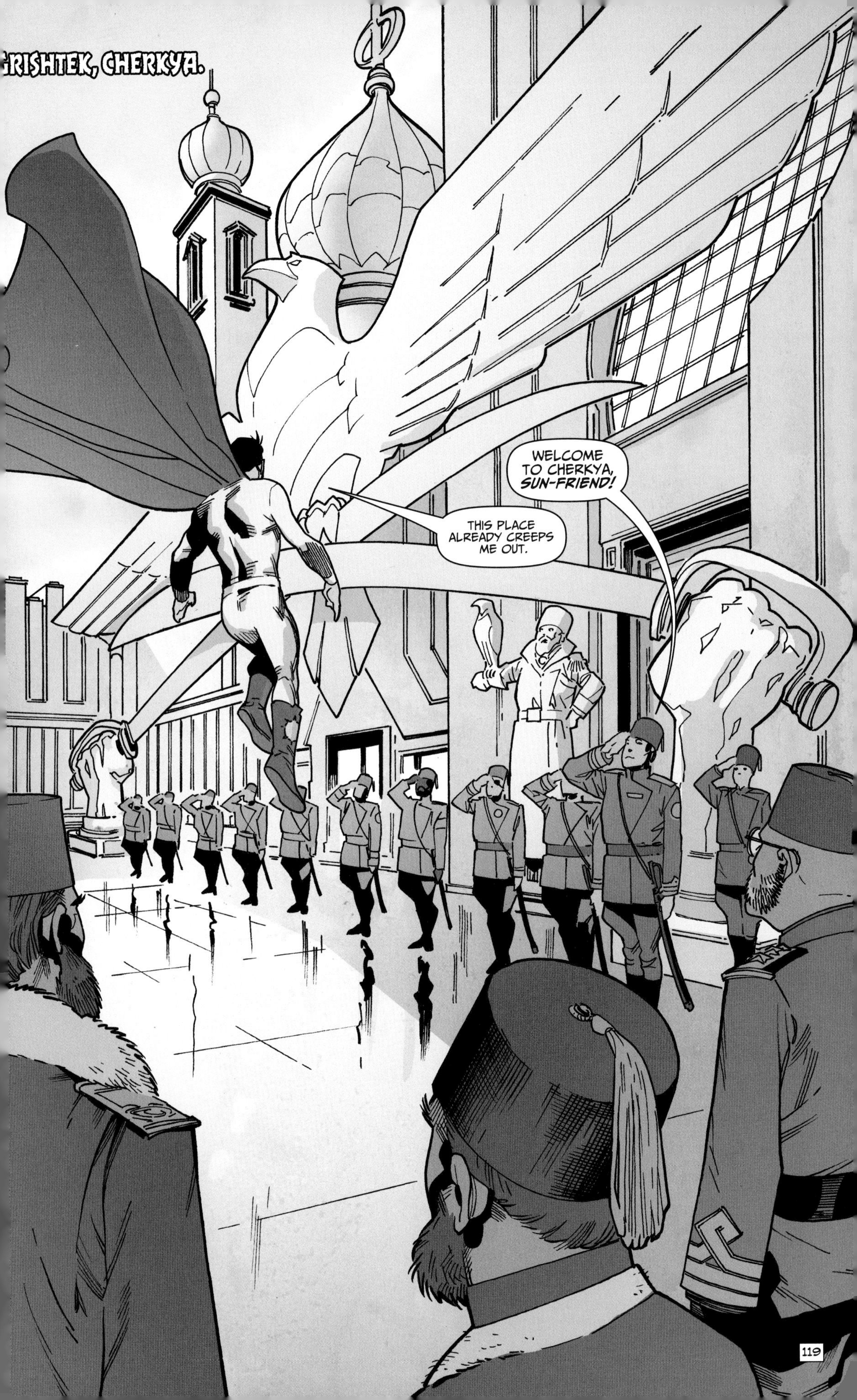
GRISHTEK, CHERKYA.
WELCOME TO CHERKYA, SUN-FRIEND!
THIS PLACE ALREADY CREEPS ME OUT.

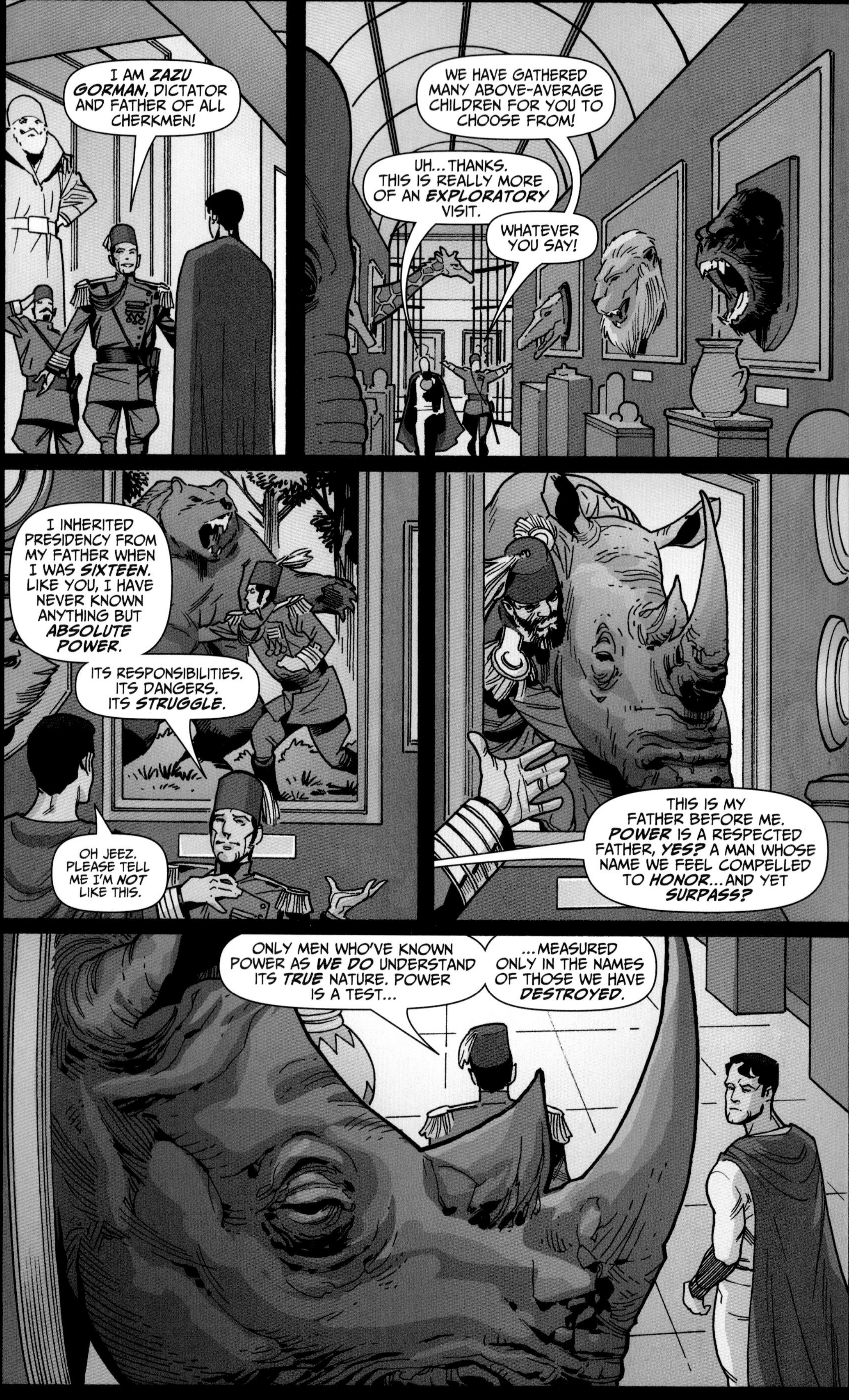
I AM ZAZU GORMAN, DICTATOR AND FATHER OF ALL CHERKMEN!
WE HAVE GATHERED MANY ABOVE-AVERAGE CHILDREN FOR YOU TO CHOOSE FROM!
UH... THANKS. THIS IS REALLY MORE OF AN EXPLORATORY VISIT.
WHATEVER YOU SAY!
I INHERITED PRESIDENCY FROM MY FATHER WHEN I WAS SIXTEEN. LIKE YOU, I HAVE NEVER KNOWN ANYTHING BUT ABSOLUTE POWER.
ITS RESPONSIBILITIES. ITS DANGERS. ITS STRUGGLE.
OH JEEZ. PLEASE TELL ME I'M NOT LIKE THIS.
THIS IS MY FATHER BEFORE ME. POWER IS A RESPECTED FATHER, YES? A MAN WHOSE NAME WE FEEL COMPELLED TO HONOR...AND YET SURPASS?
ONLY MEN WHO'VE KNOWN POWER AS WE DO UNDERSTAND ITS TRUE NATURE. POWER IS A TEST...
...MEASURED ONLY IN THE NAMES OF THOSE WE HAVE DESTROYED.

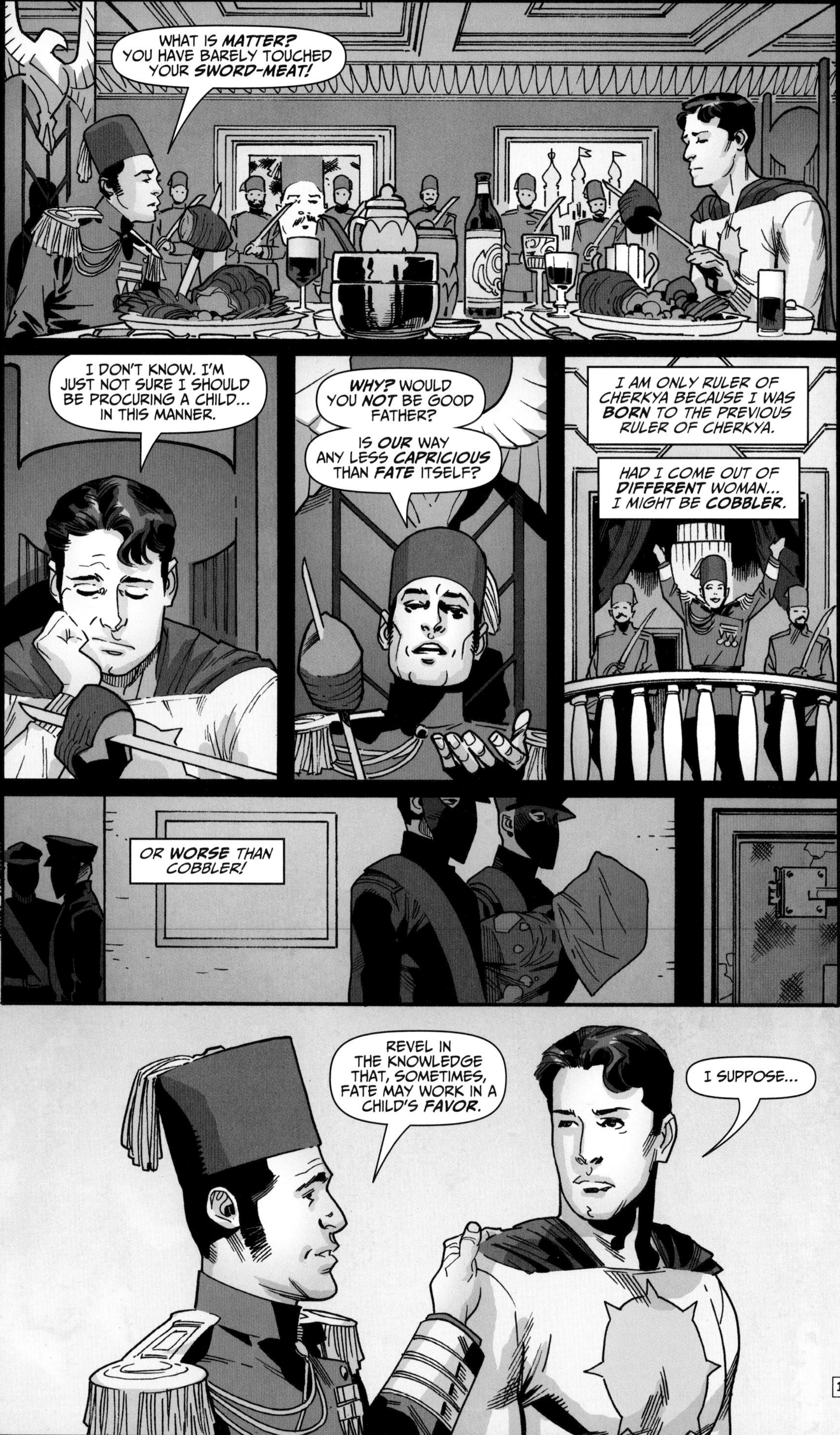
WHAT IS MATTER? YOU HAVE BARELY TOUCHED YOUR SWORD-MEAT!
I DON'T KNOW. I'M JUST NOT SURE I SHOULD BE PROCURING A CHILD... IN THIS MANNER.
WHY? WOULD YOU NOT BE GOOD FATHER?
IS OUR WAY ANY LESS CAPRICIOUS THAN FATE ITSELF?
I AM ONLY RULER OF CHERKYA BECAUSE I WAS BORN TO THE PREVIOUS RULER OF CHERKYA.
HAD I COME OUT OF DIFFERENT WOMAN... I MIGHT BE COBBLER.
OR WORSE THAN COBBLER!
REVEL IN THE KNOWLEDGE THAT, SOMETIMES, FATE MAY WORK IN A CHILD'S FAVOR.
I SUPPOSE...

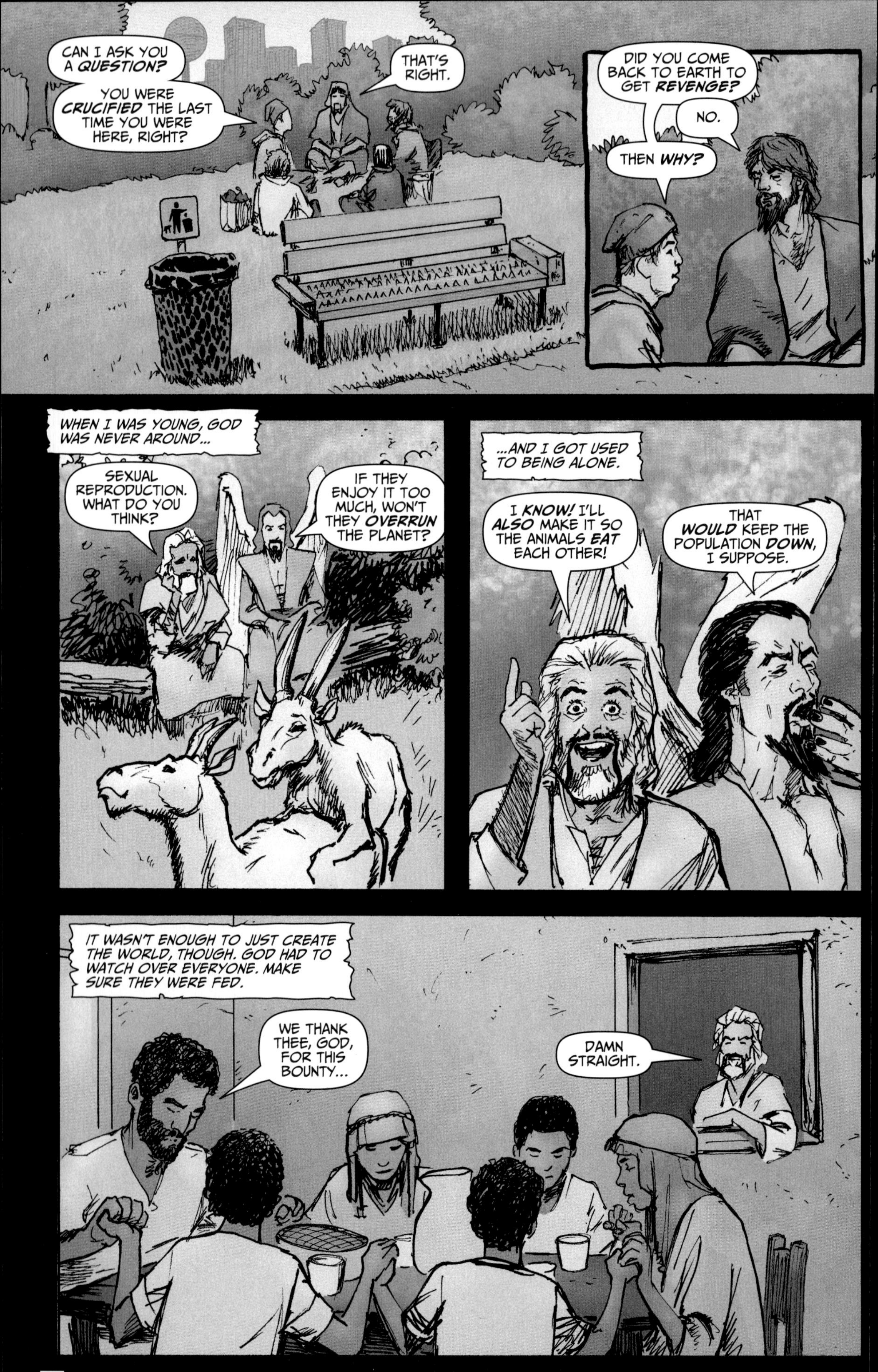
CAN I ASK YOU A QUESTION?
YOU WERE CRUCIFIED THE LAST TIME YOU WERE HERE, RIGHT?
THAT'S RIGHT.
DID YOU COME BACK TO EARTH TO GET REVENGE?
NO.
THEN WHY?
WHEN I WAS YOUNG, GOD WAS NEVER AROUND...
SEXUAL REPRODUCTION. WHAT DO YOU THINK?
IF THEY ENJOY IT TOO MUCH, WON'T THEY OVERRUN THE PLANET?
...AND I GOT USED TO BEING ALONE.
I KNOW! I'LL ALSO MAKE IT SO THE ANIMALS EAT EACH OTHER!
THAT WOULD KEEP THE POPULATION DOWN, I SUPPOSE.
IT WASN'T ENOUGH TO JUST CREATE THE WORLD, THOUGH. GOD HAD TO WATCH OVER EVERYONE. MAKE SURE THEY WERE FED.
WE THANK THEE, GOD, FOR THIS BOUNTY...
DAMN STRAIGHT.

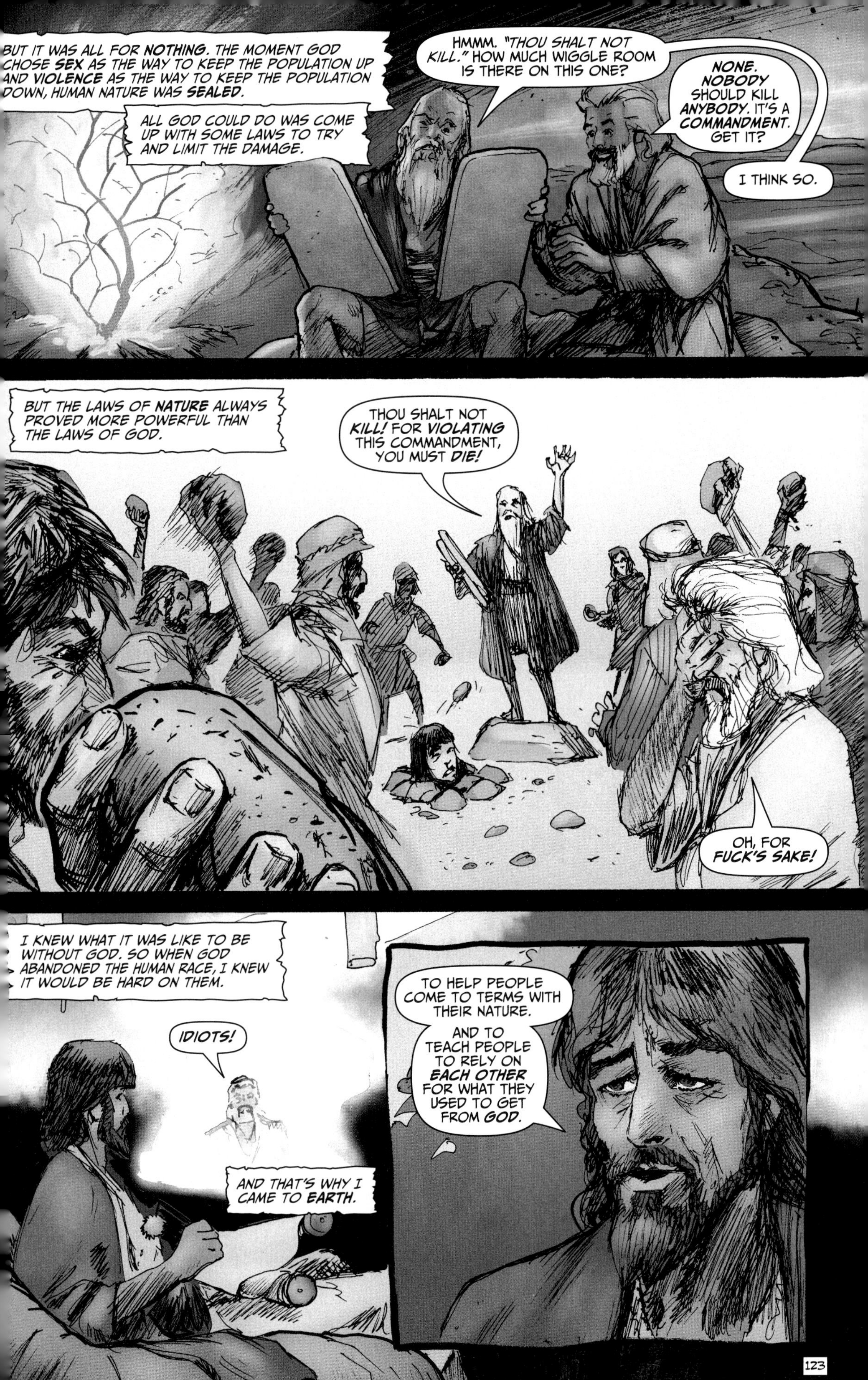

BUT IT WAS ALL FOR NOTHING. THE MOMENT GOD CHOSE SEX AS THE WAY TO KEEP THE POPULATION UP AND VIOLENCE AS THE WAY TO KEEP THE POPULATION DOWN, HUMAN NATURE WAS SEALED.
ALL GOD COULD DO WAS COME UP WITH SOME LAWS TO TRY AND LIMIT THE DAMAGE.
HMMM. "THOU SHALT NOT KILL." HOW MUCH WIGGLE ROOM IS THERE ON THIS ONE?
NONE. NOBODY SHOULD KILL ANYBODY. IT'S A COMMANDMENT. GET IT?
I THINK SO.
BUT THE LAWS OF NATURE ALWAYS PROVED MORE POWERFUL THAN THE LAWS OF GOD.
THOU SHALT NOT KILL! FOR VIOLATING THIS COMMANDMENT, YOU MUST DIE!
OH, FOR FUCK'S SAKE!
I KNEW WHAT IT WAS LIKE TO BE WITHOUT GOD. SO WHEN GOD ABANDONED THE HUMAN RACE, I KNEW IT WOULD BE HARD ON THEM.
IDIOTS!
AND THAT'S WHY I CAME TO EARTH.
TO HELP PEOPLE COME TO TERMS WITH THEIR NATURE.
AND TO TEACH PEOPLE TO RELY ON EACH OTHER FOR WHAT THEY USED TO GET FROM GOD.

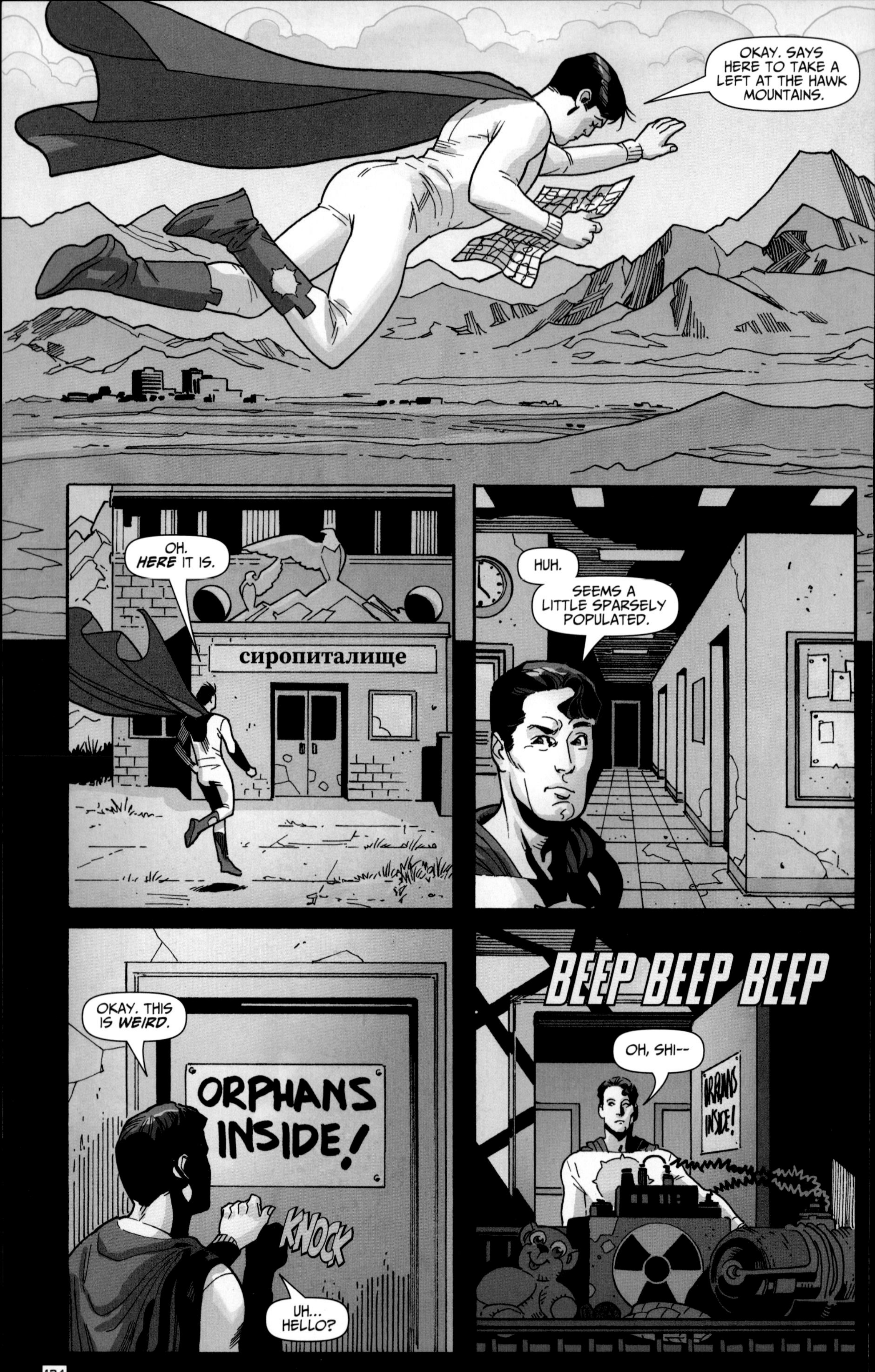
OKAY. SAYS HERE TO TAKE A LEFT AT THE HAWK MOUNTAINS.
OH. *HERE* IT IS.
сиропиталище
HUH.
SEEMS A LITTLE SPARSELY POPULATED.
OKAY. THIS IS *WEIRD*.
ORPHANS INSIDE!
KNOCK
UH... HELLO?
BEEP BEEP BEEP
OH, SHI--
ORPHANS INSIDE!

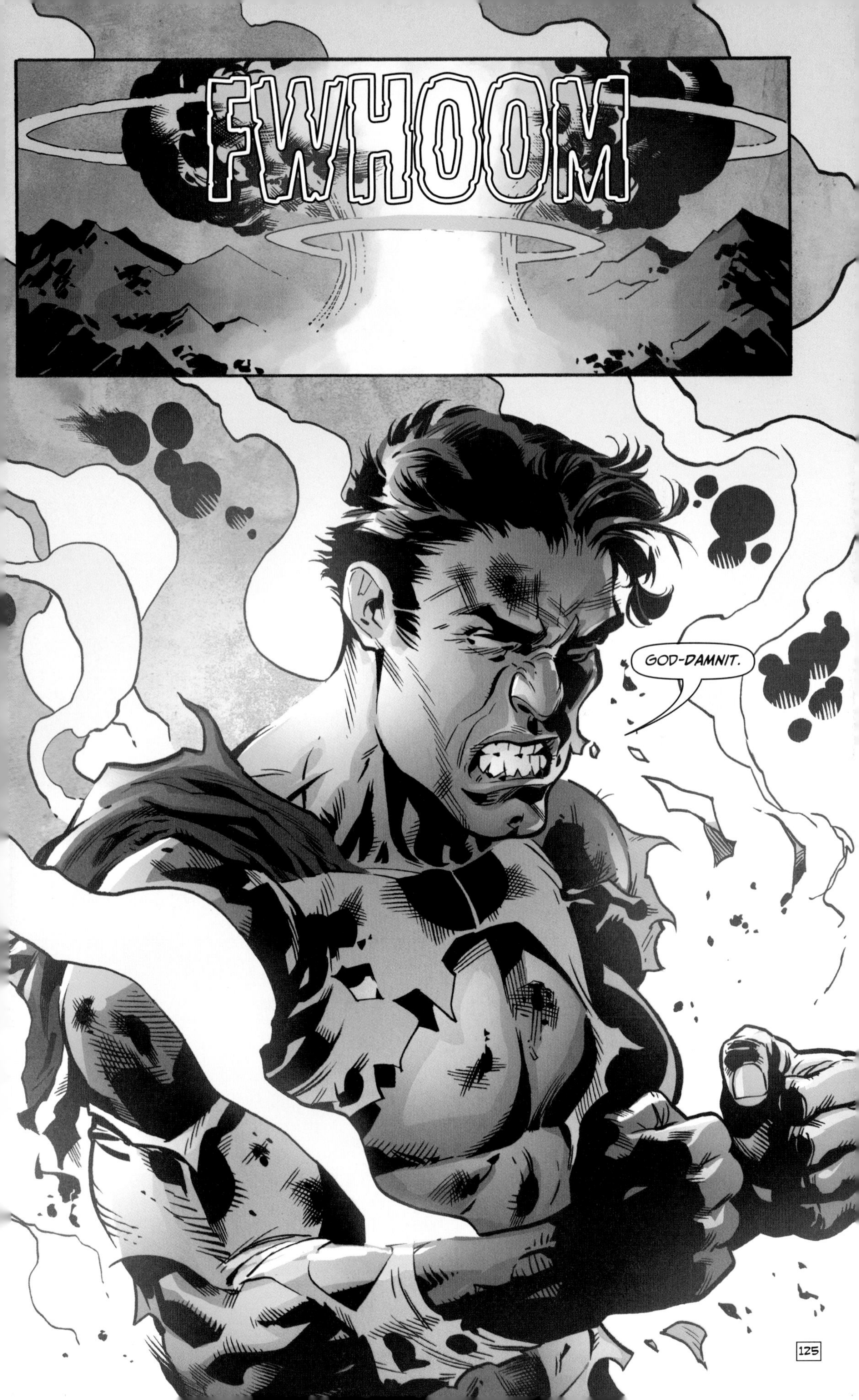
FWHOOM
GOD-DAMNIT.

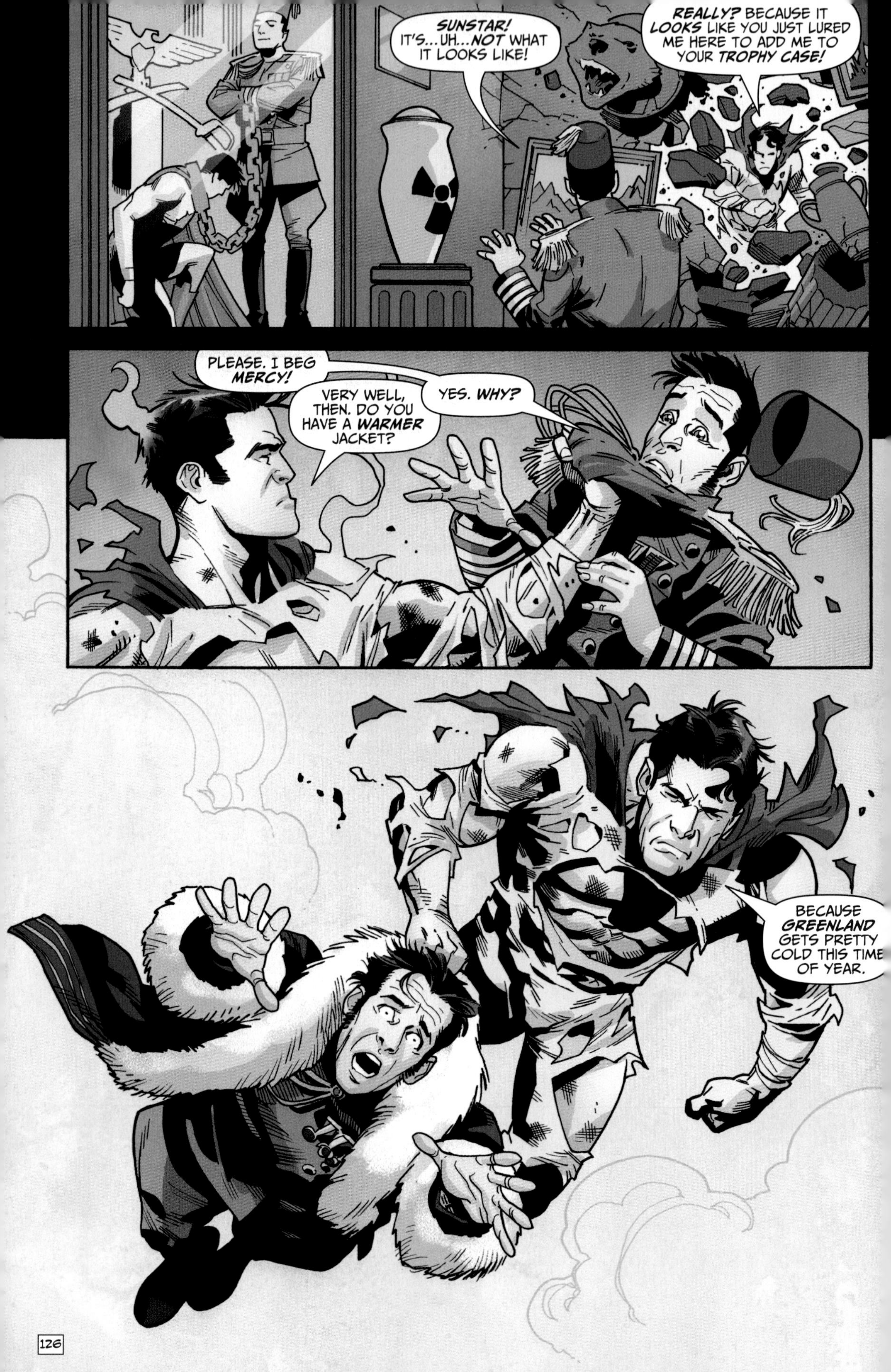
SUNSTAR! IT'S...UH...NOT WHAT IT LOOKS LIKE!
REALLY? BECAUSE IT LOOKS LIKE YOU JUST LURED ME HERE TO ADD ME TO YOUR TROPHY CASE!
PLEASE. I BEG MERCY!
VERY WELL, THEN. DO YOU HAVE A WARMER JACKET?
YES. WHY?
BECAUSE GREENLAND GETS PRETTY COLD THIS TIME OF YEAR.

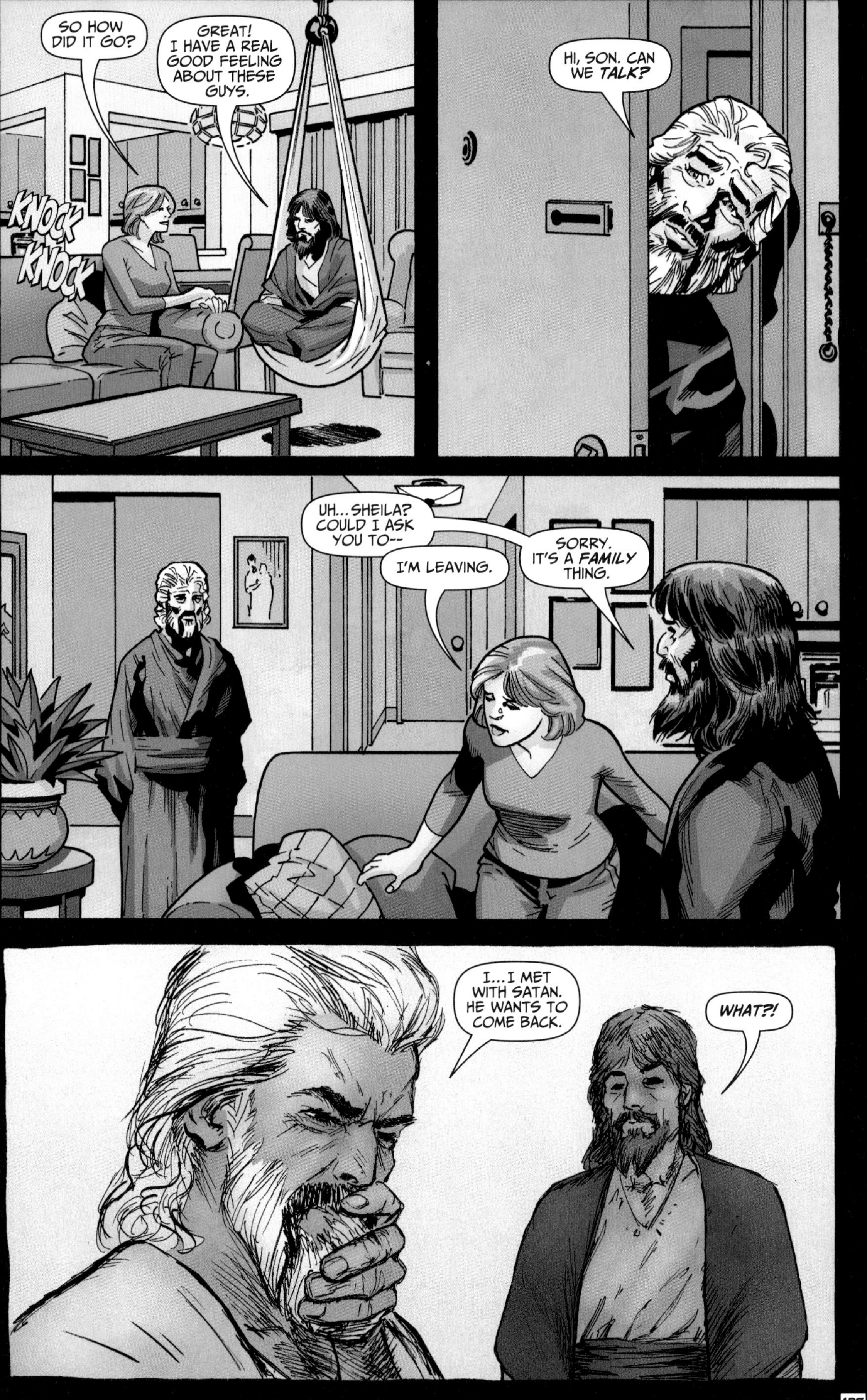
SO HOW DID IT GO?
GREAT! I HAVE A REAL GOOD FEELING ABOUT THESE GUYS.
KNOCK KNOCK
HI, SON. CAN WE TALK?
UH...SHEILA? COULD I ASK YOU TO--
SORRY. IT'S A FAMILY THING.
I'M LEAVING.
I...I MET WITH SATAN. HE WANTS TO COME BACK.
WHAT?!

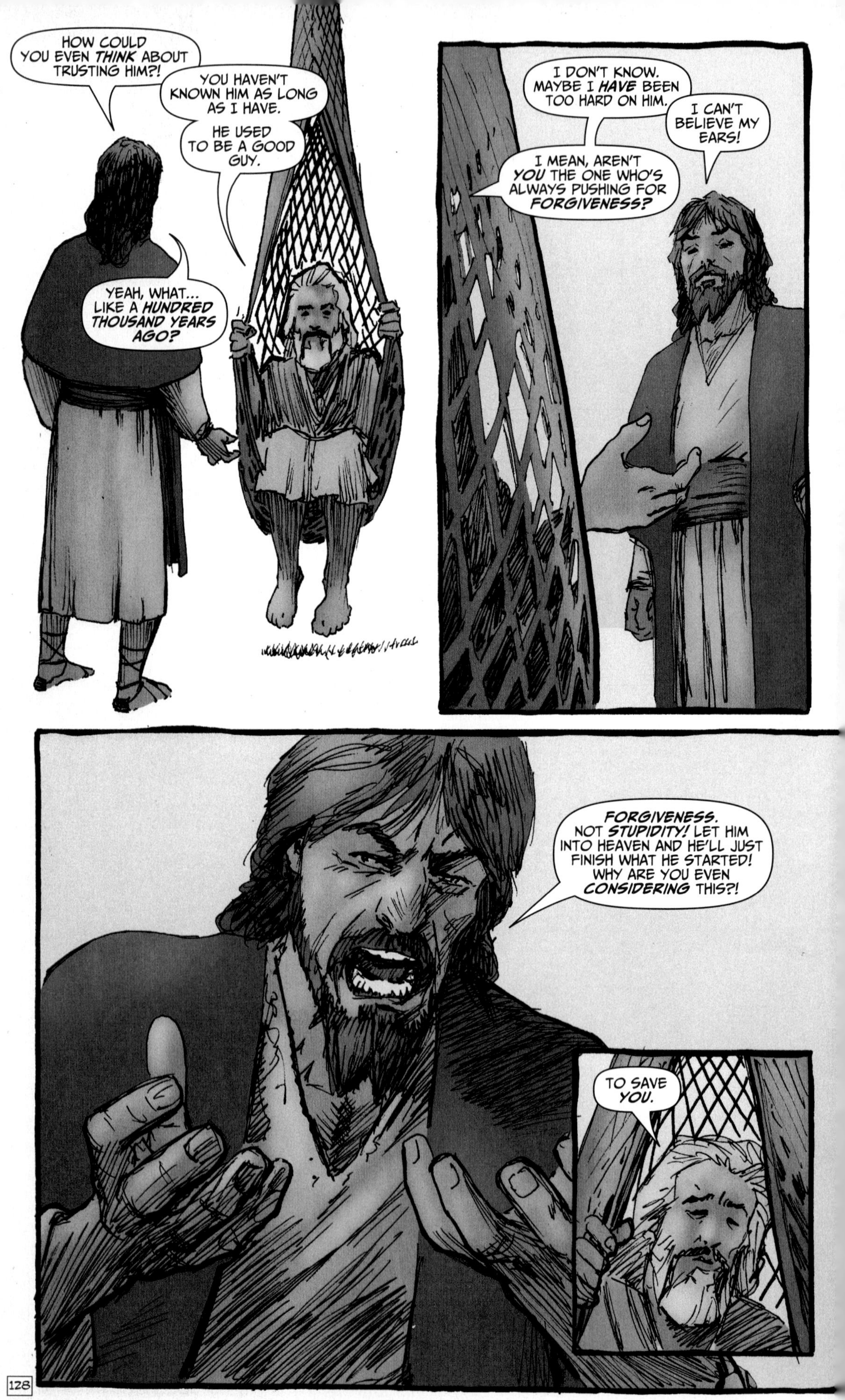
HOW COULD YOU EVEN THINK ABOUT TRUSTING HIM?!
YOU HAVEN'T KNOWN HIM AS LONG AS I HAVE.
HE USED TO BE A GOOD GUY.
YEAH, WHAT... LIKE A HUNDRED THOUSAND YEARS AGO?
I DON'T KNOW. MAYBE I HAVE BEEN TOO HARD ON HIM.
I MEAN, AREN'T YOU THE ONE WHO'S ALWAYS PUSHING FOR FORGIVENESS?
I CAN'T BELIEVE MY EARS!
FORGIVENESS. NOT STUPIDITY! LET HIM INTO HEAVEN AND HE'LL JUST FINISH WHAT HE STARTED! WHY ARE YOU EVEN CONSIDERING THIS?!
TO SAVE YOU.

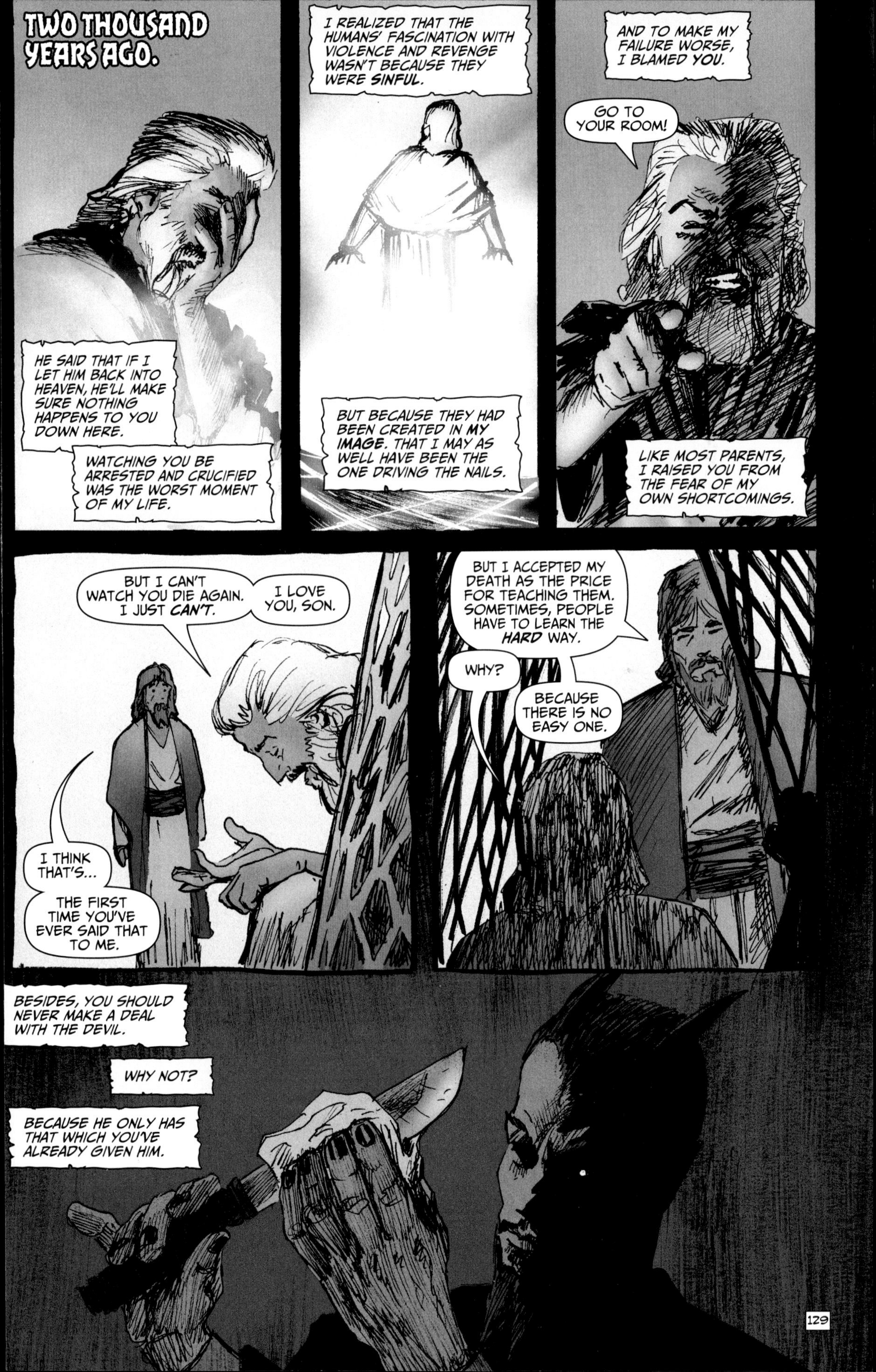

TWO THOUSAND YEARS AGO.
HE SAID THAT IF I LET HIM BACK INTO HEAVEN, HE'LL MAKE SURE NOTHING HAPPENS TO YOU DOWN HERE.
WATCHING YOU BE ARRESTED AND CRUCIFIED WAS THE WORST MOMENT OF MY LIFE.
I REALIZED THAT THE HUMANS' FASCINATION WITH VIOLENCE AND REVENGE WASN'T BECAUSE THEY WERE SINFUL.
BUT BECAUSE THEY HAD BEEN CREATED IN MY IMAGE. THAT I MAY AS WELL HAVE BEEN THE ONE DRIVING THE NAILS.
AND TO MAKE MY FAILURE WORSE, I BLAMED YOU.
GO TO YOUR ROOM!
LIKE MOST PARENTS, I RAISED YOU FROM THE FEAR OF MY OWN SHORTCOMINGS.
BUT I CAN'T WATCH YOU DIE AGAIN. I JUST CAN'T.
I LOVE YOU, SON.
I THINK THAT'S...
THE FIRST TIME YOU'VE EVER SAID THAT TO ME.
BUT I ACCEPTED MY DEATH AS THE PRICE FOR TEACHING THEM. SOMETIMES, PEOPLE HAVE TO LEARN THE HARD WAY.
WHY?
BECAUSE THERE IS NO EASY ONE.
BESIDES, YOU SHOULD NEVER MAKE A DEAL WITH THE DEVIL.
WHY NOT?
BECAUSE HE ONLY HAS THAT WHICH YOU'VE ALREADY GIVEN HIM.

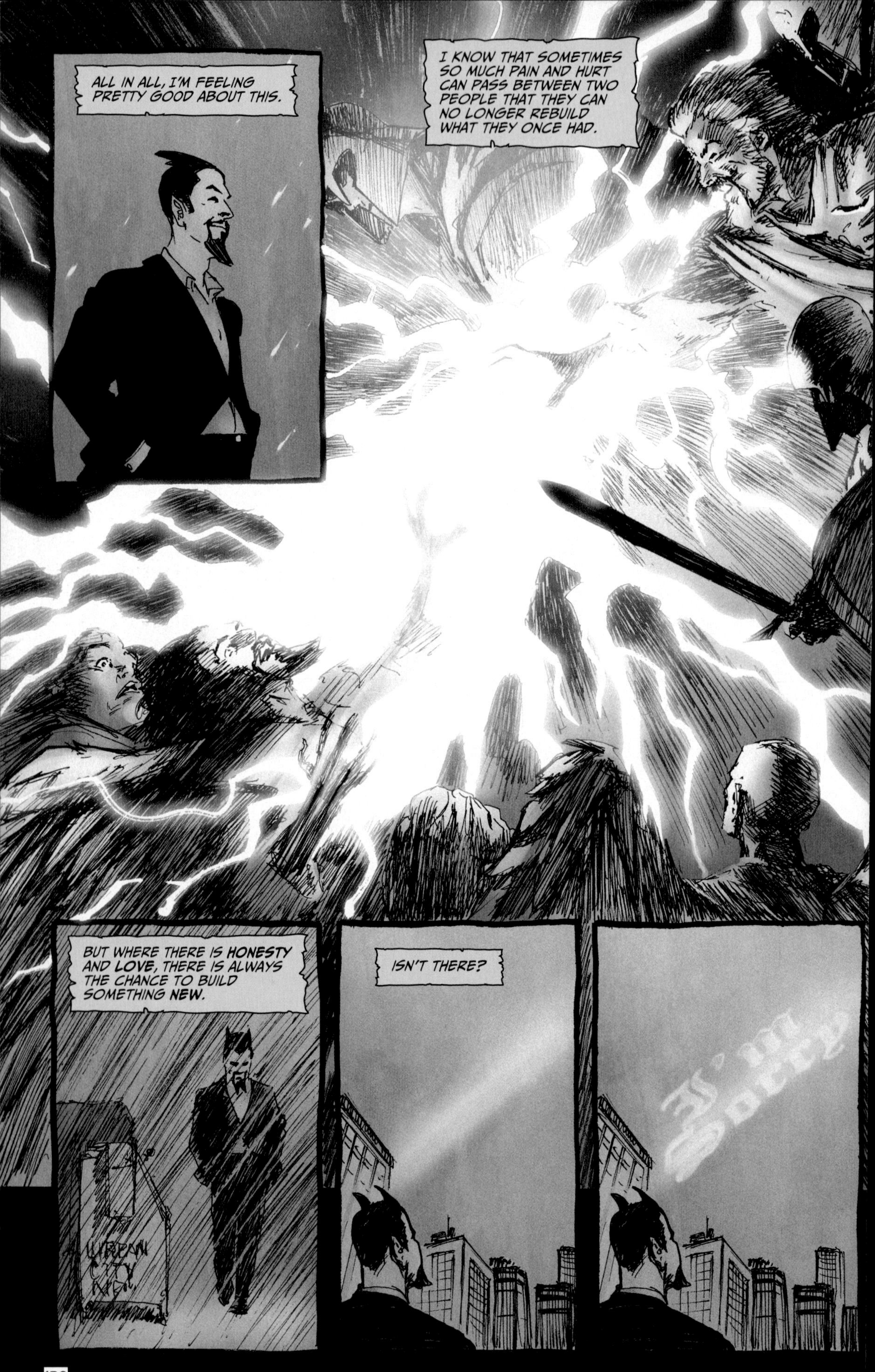
ALL IN ALL, I'M FEELING PRETTY GOOD ABOUT THIS.
I KNOW THAT SOMETIMES SO MUCH PAIN AND HURT CAN PASS BETWEEN TWO PEOPLE THAT THEY CAN NO LONGER REBUILD WHAT THEY ONCE HAD.
BUT WHERE THERE IS **HONESTY** AND **LOVE**, THERE IS ALWAYS THE CHANCE TO BUILD SOMETHING **NEW**.
ISN'T THERE?
I'm Sorry

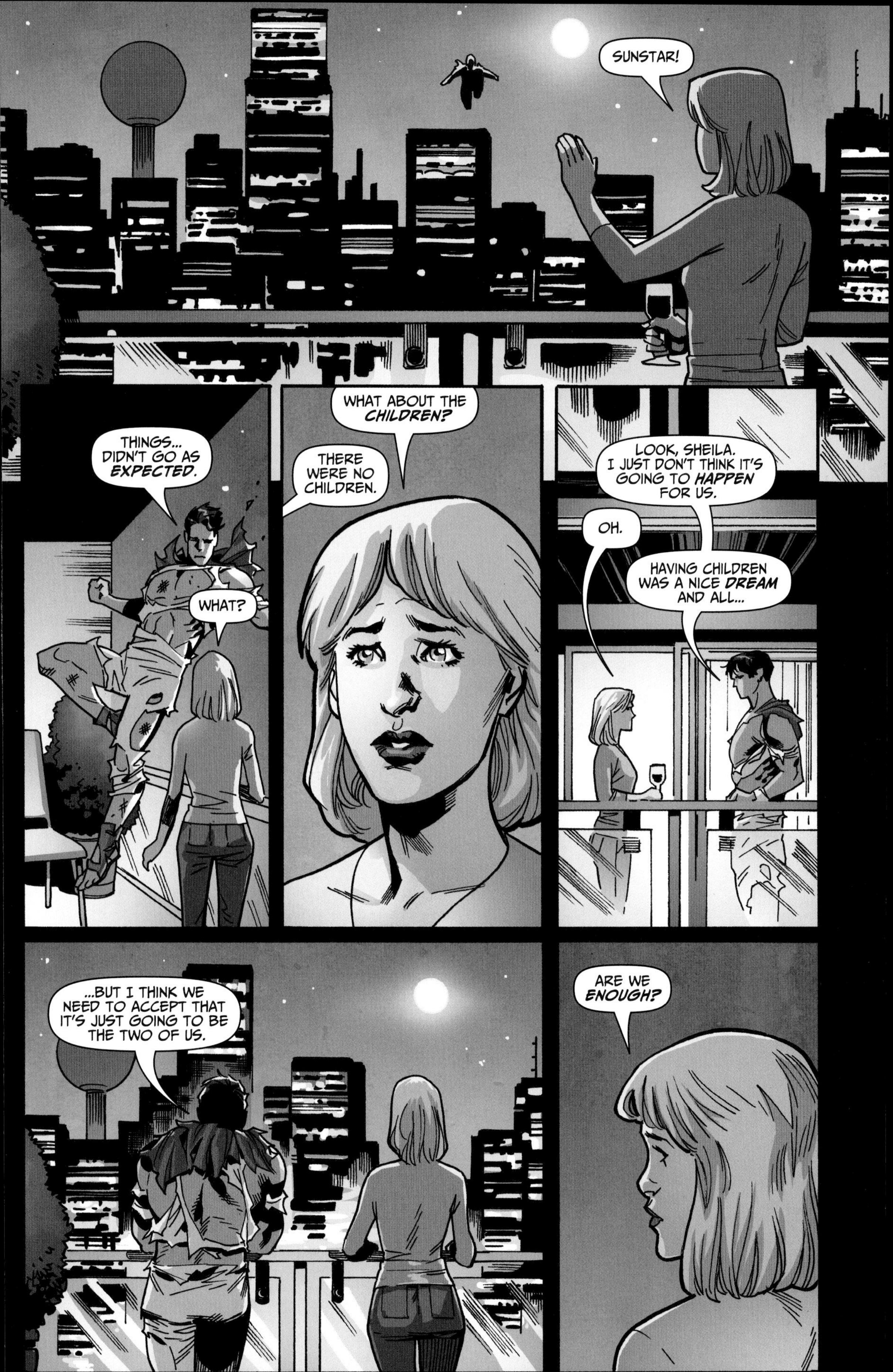
SUNSTAR!
THINGS... DIDN'T GO AS EXPECTED.
WHAT?
WHAT ABOUT THE CHILDREN?
THERE WERE NO CHILDREN.
LOOK, SHEILA. I JUST DON'T THINK IT'S GOING TO HAPPEN FOR US.
OH.
HAVING CHILDREN WAS A NICE DREAM AND ALL...
...BUT I THINK WE NEED TO ACCEPT THAT IT'S JUST GOING TO BE THE TWO OF US.
ARE WE ENOUGH?

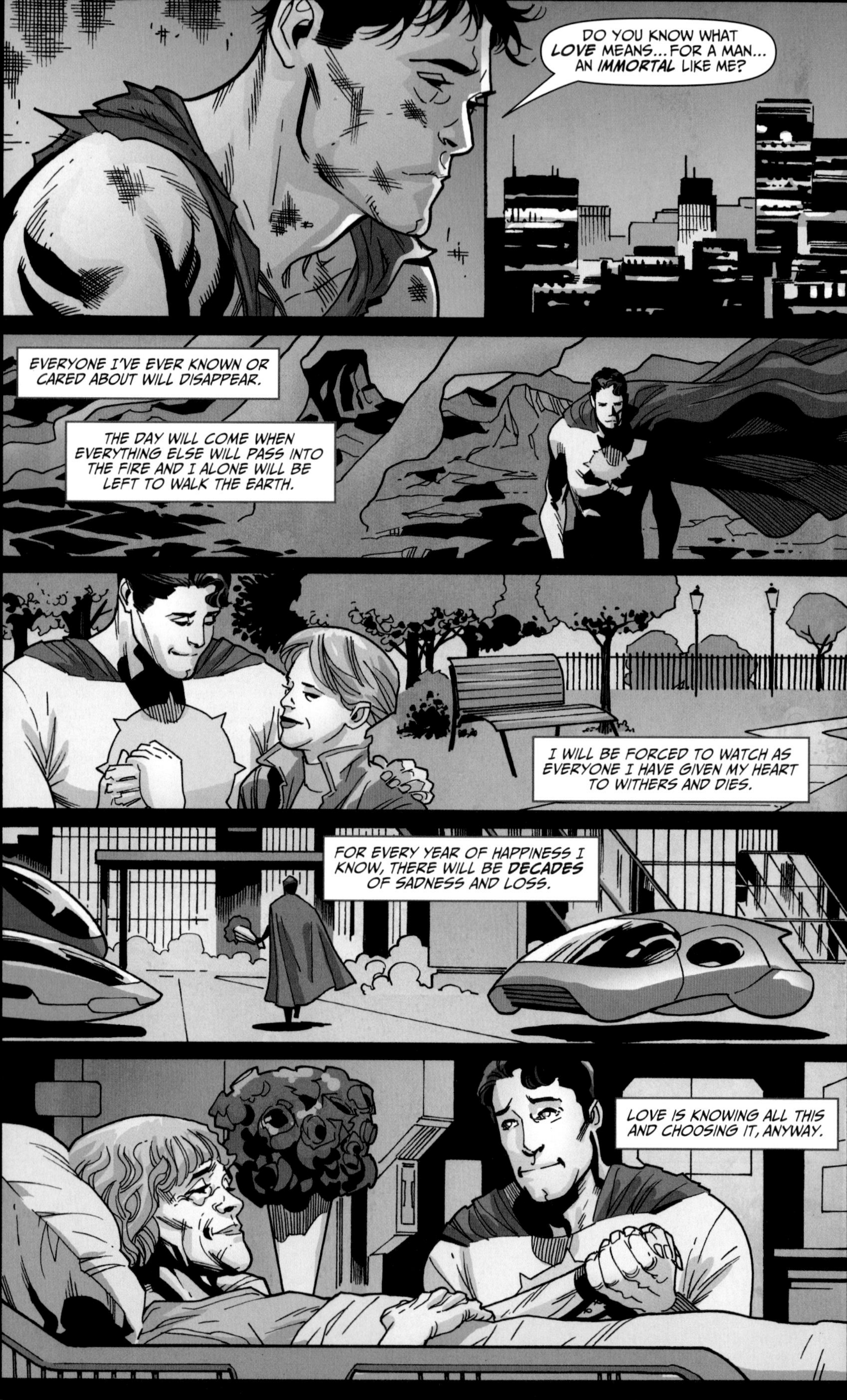
DO YOU KNOW WHAT LOVE MEANS... FOR A MAN... AN IMMORTAL LIKE ME?
EVERYONE I'VE EVER KNOWN OR CARED ABOUT WILL DISAPPEAR.
THE DAY WILL COME WHEN EVERYTHING ELSE WILL PASS INTO THE FIRE AND I ALONE WILL BE LEFT TO WALK THE EARTH.
I WILL BE FORCED TO WATCH AS EVERYONE I HAVE GIVEN MY HEART TO WITHERS AND DIES.
FOR EVERY YEAR OF HAPPINESS I KNOW, THERE WILL BE DECADES OF SADNESS AND LOSS.
LOVE IS KNOWING ALL THIS AND CHOOSING IT, ANYWAY.

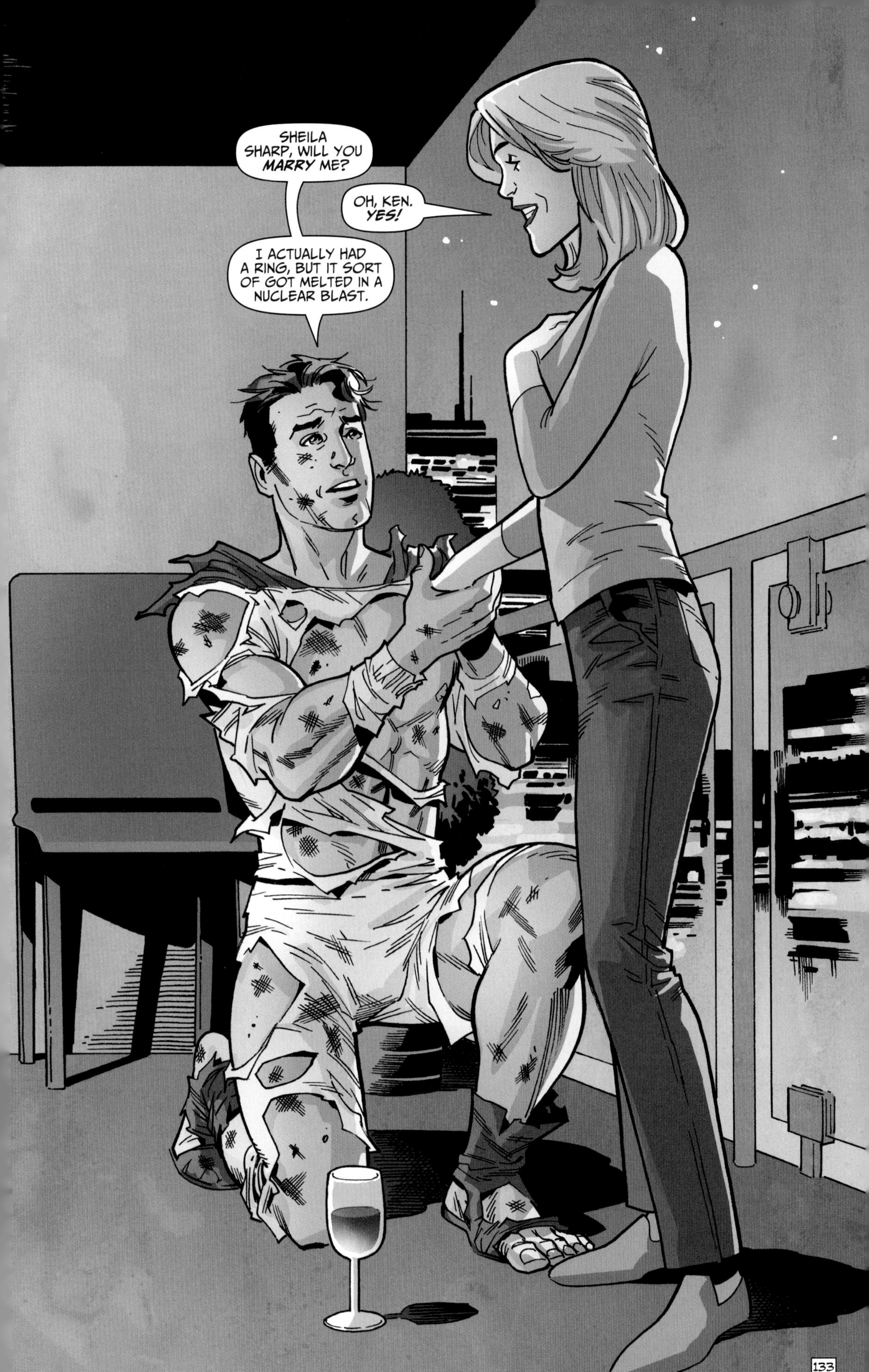
SHEILA SHARP, WILL YOU MARRY ME?
I ACTUALLY HAD A RING, BUT IT SORT OF GOT MELTED IN A NUCLEAR BLAST.
OH, KEN. YES!

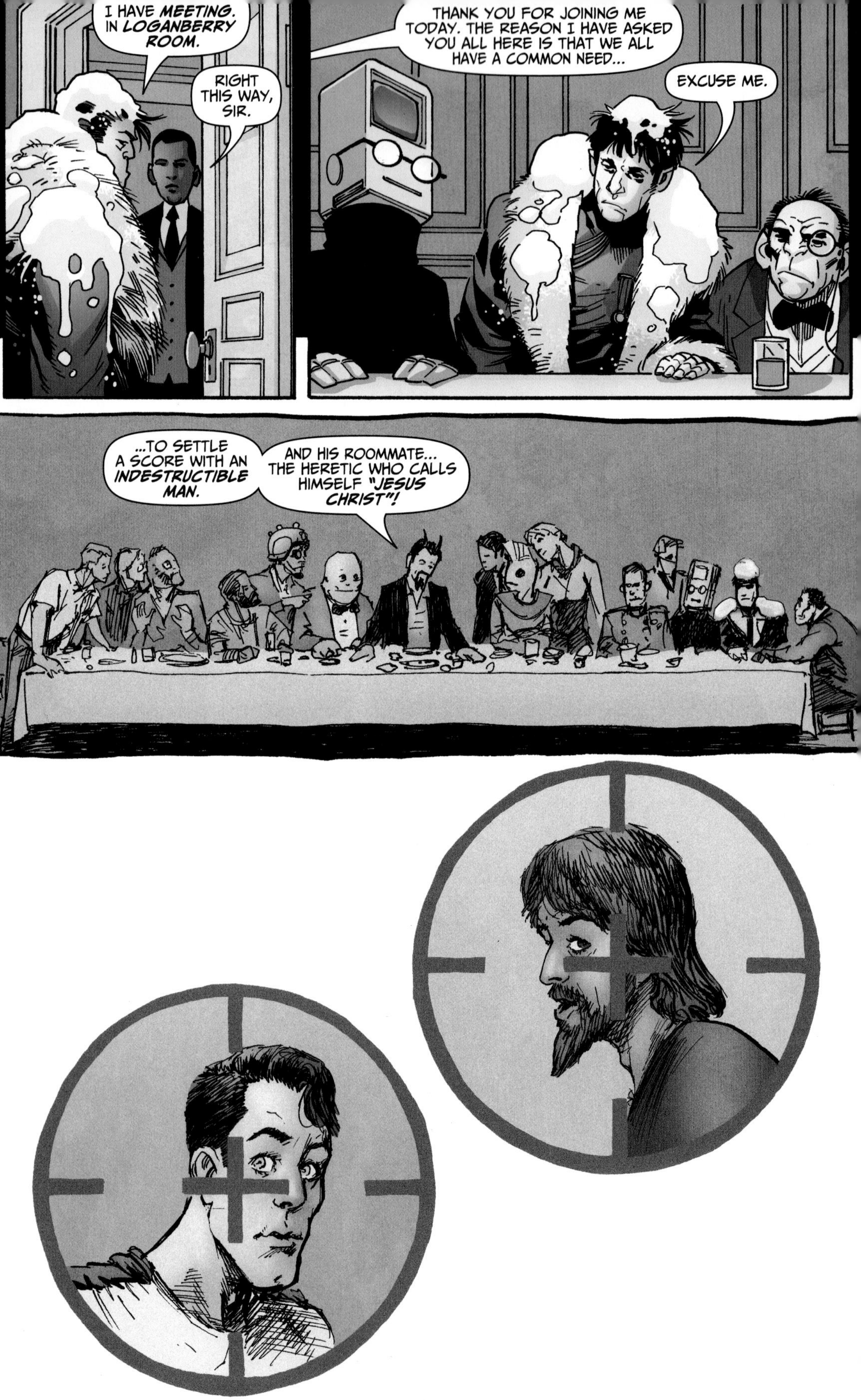
I HAVE *MEETING*. IN *LOGANBERRY ROOM*.
RIGHT THIS WAY, SIR.
THANK YOU FOR JOINING ME TODAY. THE REASON I HAVE ASKED YOU ALL HERE IS THAT WE ALL HAVE A COMMON NEED...
EXCUSE ME.
...TO SETTLE A SCORE WITH AN *INDESTRUCTIBLE MAN*.
AND HIS ROOMMATE... THE HERETIC WHO CALLS HIMSELF *"JESUS CHRIST"*!

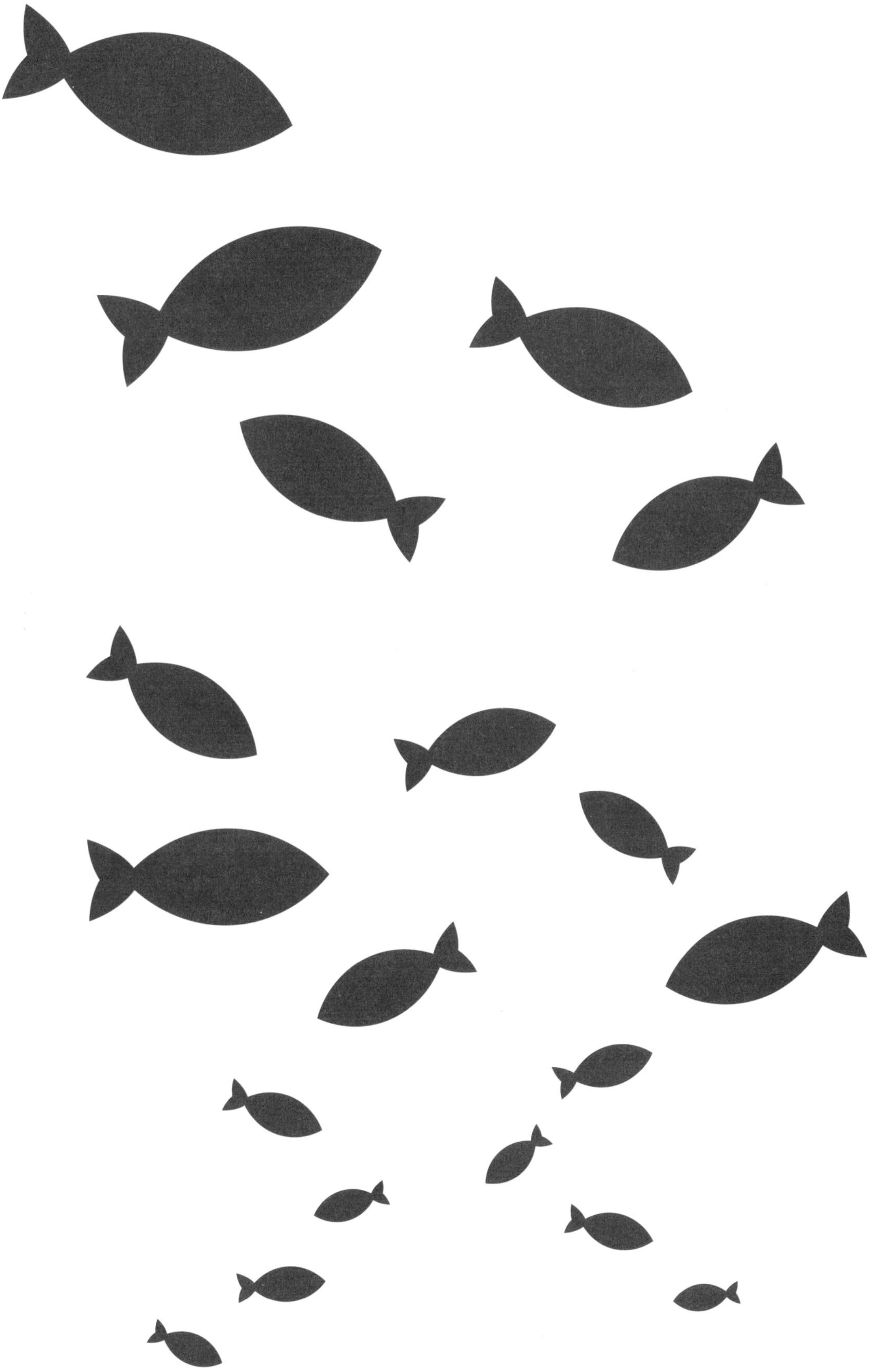

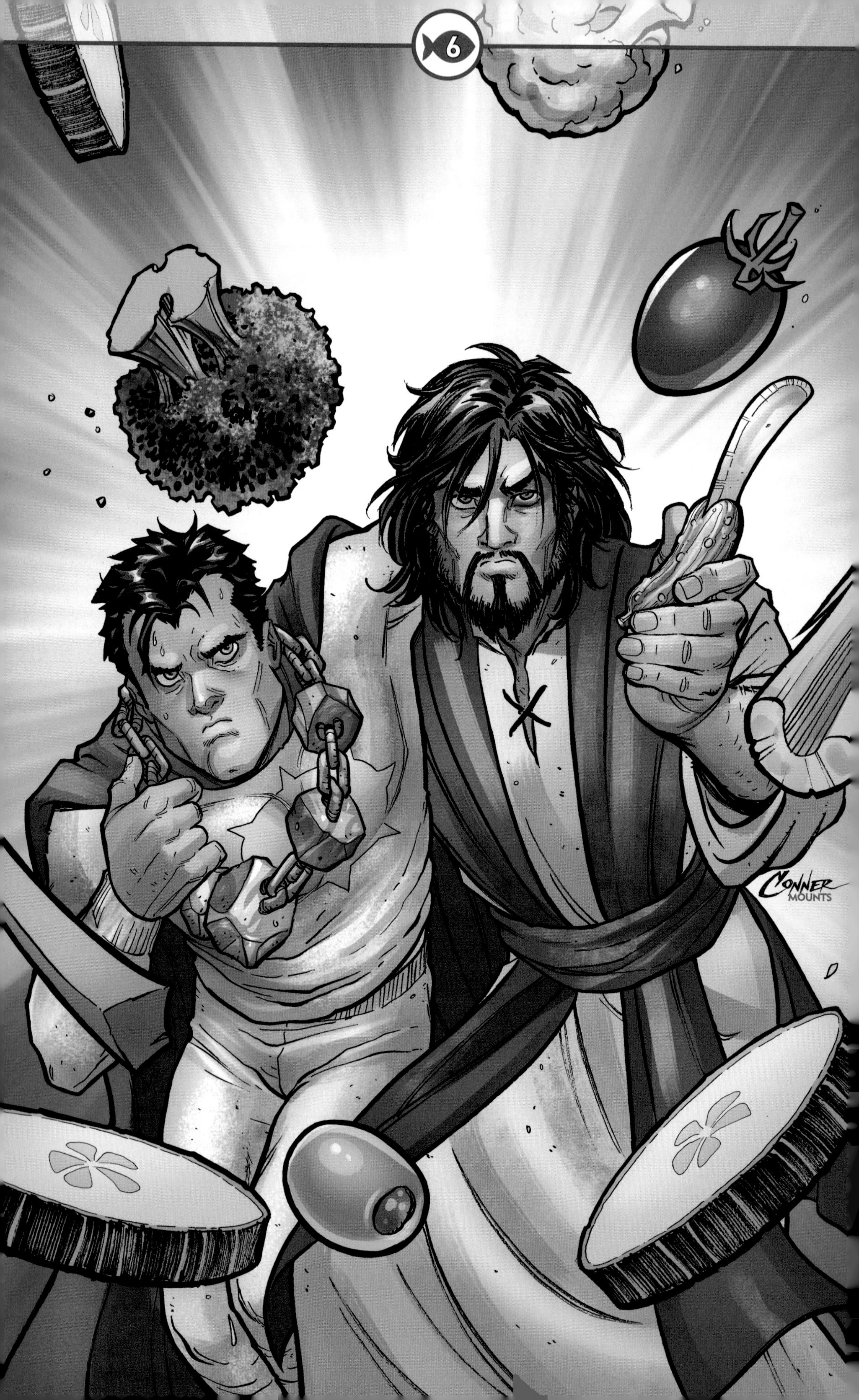
CONNER
MOUNTS

UNLOCK THE HERO WITHIN

GROUP THERAPY.

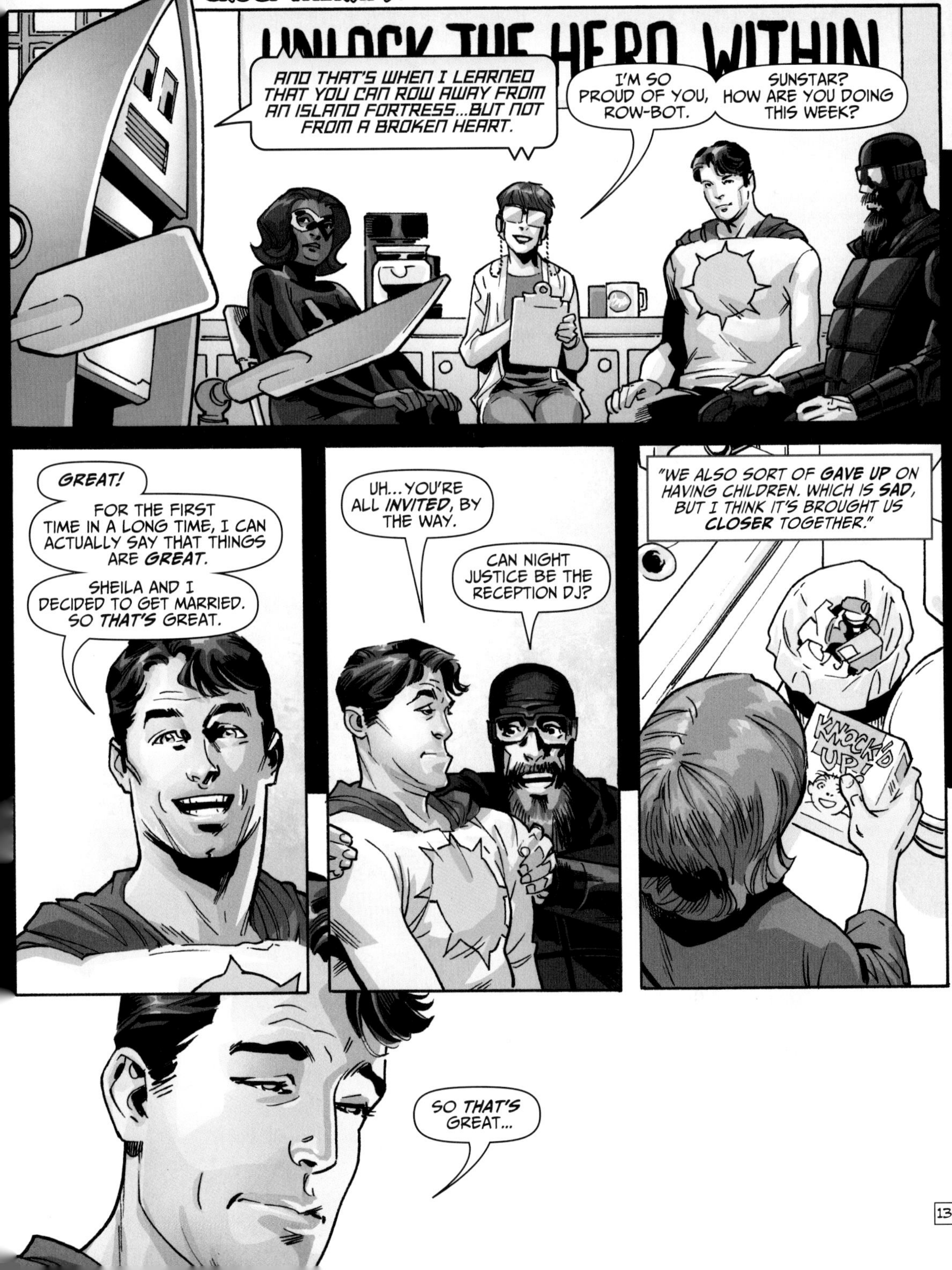
AND THAT'S WHEN I LEARNED THAT YOU CAN ROW AWAY FROM AN ISLAND FORTRESS...BUT NOT FROM A BROKEN HEART.
I'M SO PROUD OF YOU, ROW-BOT.
SUNSTAR? HOW ARE YOU DOING THIS WEEK?
GREAT!
FOR THE FIRST TIME IN A LONG TIME, I CAN ACTUALLY SAY THAT THINGS ARE GREAT.
SHEILA AND I DECIDED TO GET MARRIED. SO THAT'S GREAT.
UH... YOU'RE ALL INVITED, BY THE WAY.
CAN NIGHT JUSTICE BE THE RECEPTION DJ?
"WE ALSO SORT OF GAVE UP ON HAVING CHILDREN. WHICH IS SAD, BUT I THINK IT'S BROUGHT US CLOSER TOGETHER."
KNOCK'D UP!
SO THAT'S GREAT...

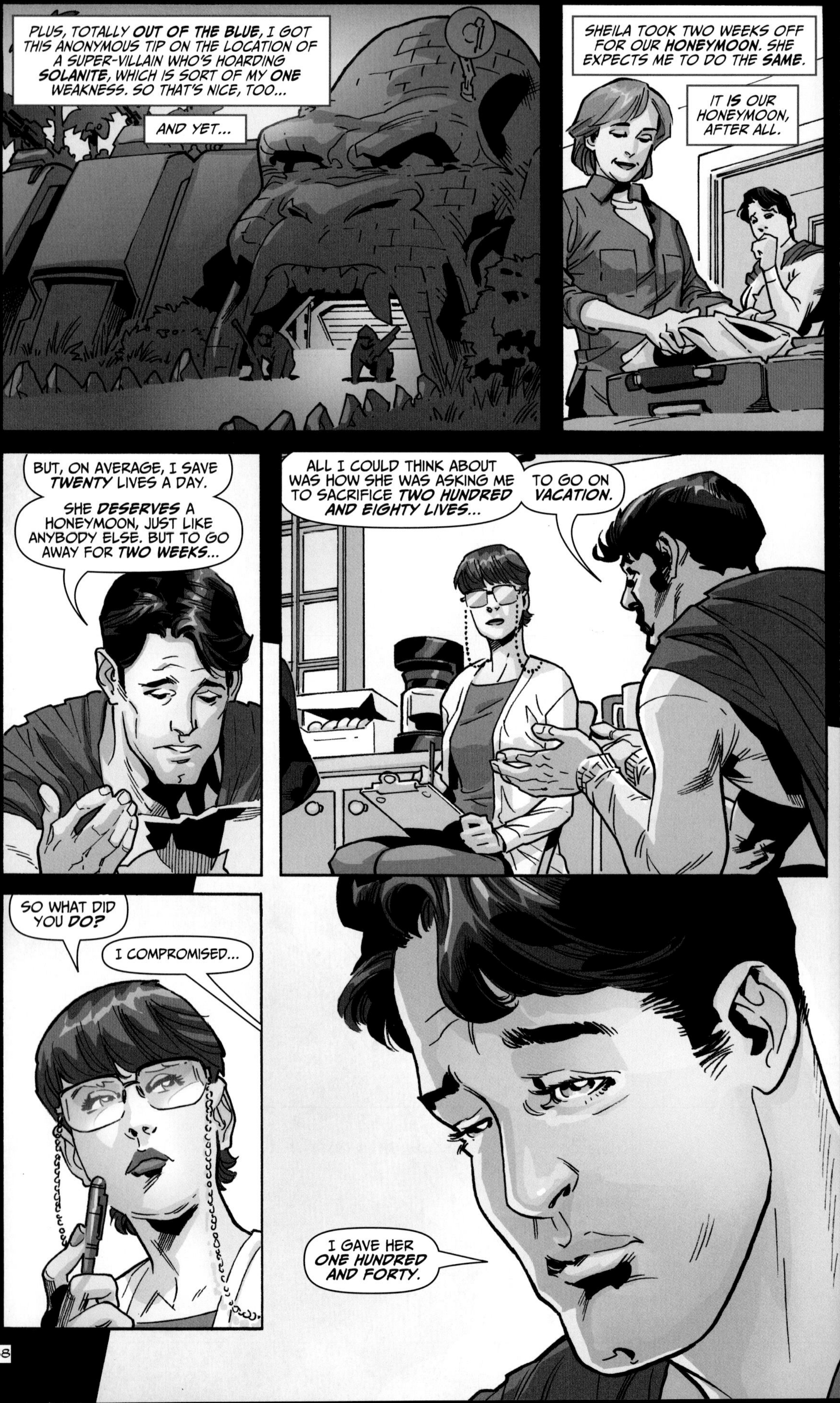

PLUS, TOTALLY **OUT OF THE BLUE**, I GOT THIS ANONYMOUS TIP ON THE LOCATION OF A SUPER-VILLAIN WHO'S HOARDING **SOLANITE**, WHICH IS SORT OF MY **ONE** WEAKNESS. SO THAT'S NICE, TOO...
AND YET...
SHEILA TOOK TWO WEEKS OFF FOR OUR **HONEYMOON**. SHE EXPECTS ME TO DO THE **SAME**.
IT **IS** OUR HONEYMOON, AFTER ALL.
BUT, ON AVERAGE, I SAVE ***TWENTY*** LIVES A DAY.
SHE ***DESERVES*** A HONEYMOON, JUST LIKE ANYBODY ELSE. BUT TO GO AWAY FOR ***TWO WEEKS***...
ALL I COULD THINK ABOUT WAS HOW SHE WAS ASKING ME TO SACRIFICE ***TWO HUNDRED AND EIGHTY LIVES***...
TO GO ON ***VACATION***.
SO WHAT DID YOU ***DO?***
I COMPROMISED...
I GAVE HER ***ONE HUNDRED AND FORTY***.

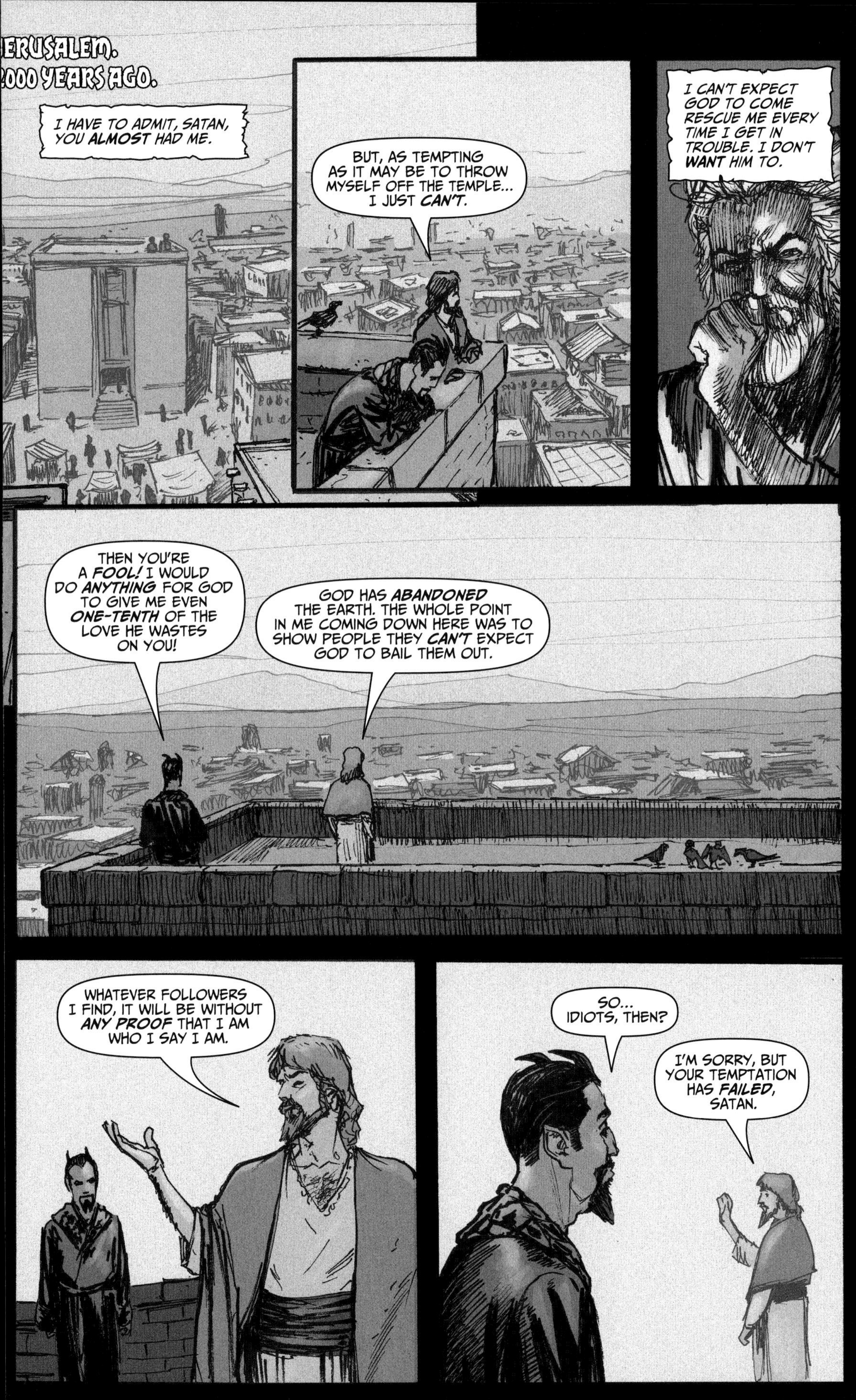

ERUSALEM.
2000 YEARS AGO.
I HAVE TO ADMIT, SATAN, YOU ALMOST HAD ME.
BUT, AS TEMPTING AS IT MAY BE TO THROW MYSELF OFF THE TEMPLE... I JUST CAN'T.
I CAN'T EXPECT GOD TO COME RESCUE ME EVERY TIME I GET IN TROUBLE. I DON'T WANT HIM TO.
THEN YOU'RE A FOOL! I WOULD DO ANYTHING FOR GOD TO GIVE ME EVEN ONE-TENTH OF THE LOVE HE WASTES ON YOU!
GOD HAS ABANDONED THE EARTH. THE WHOLE POINT IN ME COMING DOWN HERE WAS TO SHOW PEOPLE THEY CAN'T EXPECT GOD TO BAIL THEM OUT.
WHATEVER FOLLOWERS I FIND, IT WILL BE WITHOUT ANY PROOF THAT I AM WHO I SAY I AM.
SO... IDIOTS, THEN?
I'M SORRY, BUT YOUR TEMPTATION HAS FAILED, SATAN.

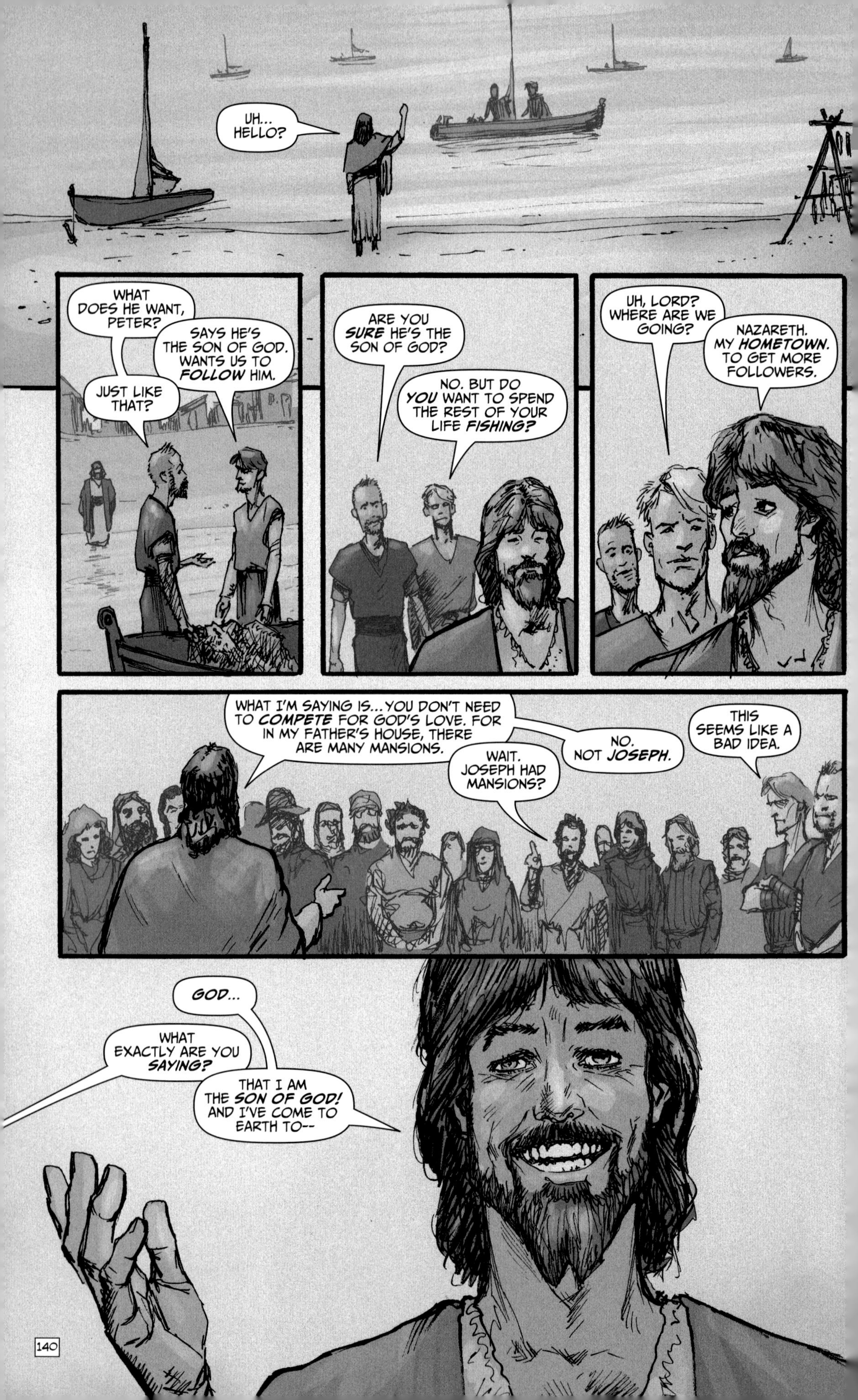
UH... HELLO?
WHAT DOES HE WANT, PETER?
SAYS HE'S THE SON OF GOD. WANTS US TO FOLLOW HIM.
JUST LIKE THAT?
ARE YOU SURE HE'S THE SON OF GOD?
NO. BUT DO YOU WANT TO SPEND THE REST OF YOUR LIFE FISHING?
UH, LORD? WHERE ARE WE GOING?
NAZARETH. MY HOMETOWN. TO GET MORE FOLLOWERS.
WHAT I'M SAYING IS...YOU DON'T NEED TO COMPETE FOR GOD'S LOVE. FOR IN MY FATHER'S HOUSE, THERE ARE MANY MANSIONS.
WAIT. JOSEPH HAD MANSIONS?
NO. NOT JOSEPH.
THIS SEEMS LIKE A BAD IDEA.
GOD...
WHAT EXACTLY ARE YOU SAYING?
THAT I AM THE SON OF GOD! AND I'VE COME TO EARTH TO--

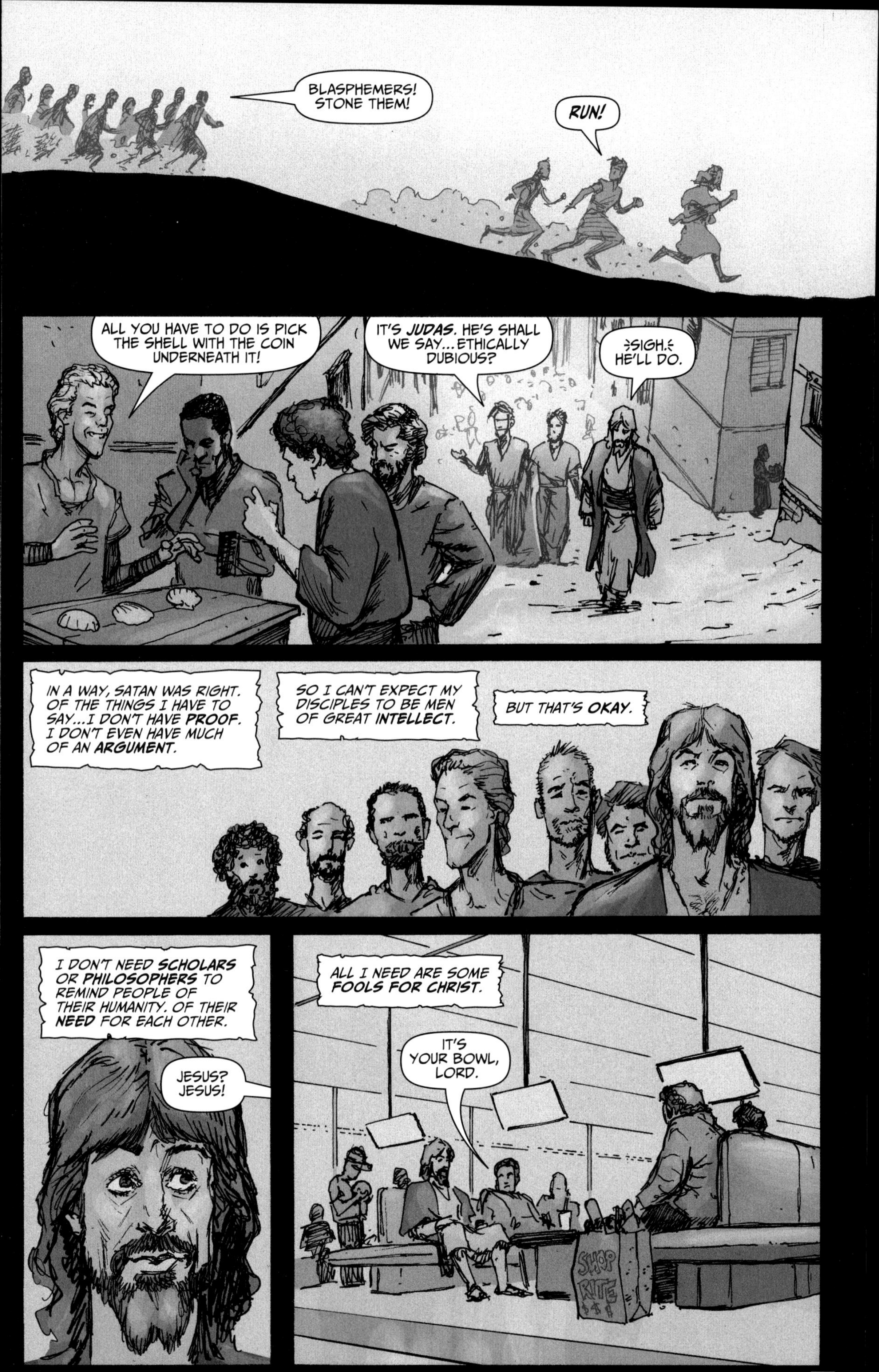
BLASPHEMERS! STONE THEM!
RUN!
ALL YOU HAVE TO DO IS PICK THE SHELL WITH THE COIN UNDERNEATH IT!
IT'S JUDAS. HE'S SHALL WE SAY...ETHICALLY DUBIOUS?
SIGH. HE'LL DO.
IN A WAY, SATAN WAS RIGHT. OF THE THINGS I HAVE TO SAY...I DON'T HAVE PROOF. I DON'T EVEN HAVE MUCH OF AN ARGUMENT.
SO I CAN'T EXPECT MY DISCIPLES TO BE MEN OF GREAT INTELLECT.
BUT THAT'S OKAY.
I DON'T NEED SCHOLARS OR PHILOSOPHERS TO REMIND PEOPLE OF THEIR HUMANITY. OF THEIR NEED FOR EACH OTHER.
JESUS? JESUS!
ALL I NEED ARE SOME FOOLS FOR CHRIST.
IT'S YOUR BOWL, LORD.
SHOP RITE

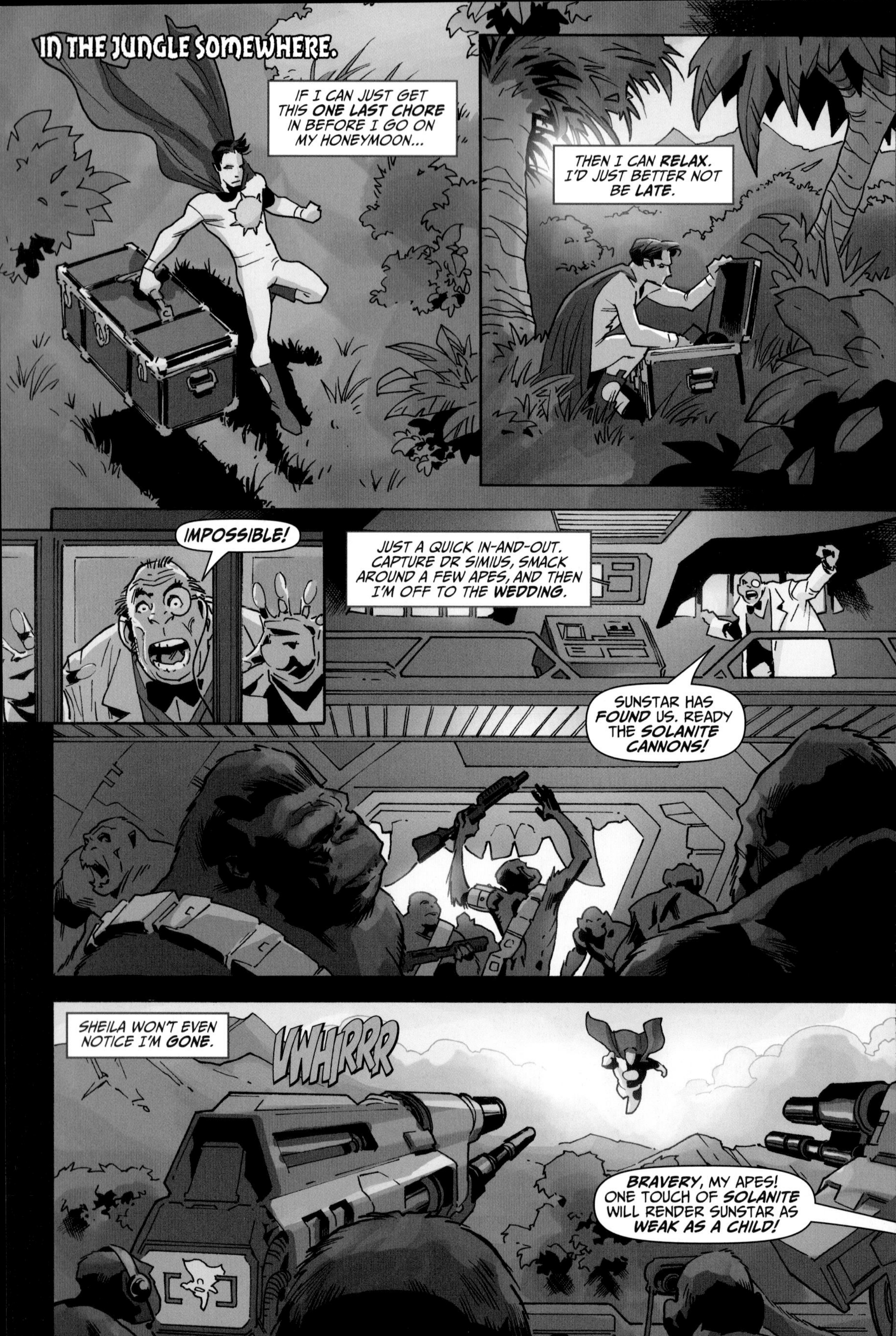
IN THE JUNGLE SOMEWHERE.
IF I CAN JUST GET THIS ONE LAST CHORE IN BEFORE I GO ON MY HONEYMOON...
THEN I CAN RELAX. I'D JUST BETTER NOT BE LATE.
IMPOSSIBLE!
JUST A QUICK IN-AND-OUT. CAPTURE DR SIMIUS, SMACK AROUND A FEW APES, AND THEN I'M OFF TO THE WEDDING.
SUNSTAR HAS FOUND US. READY THE SOLANITE CANNONS!
SHEILA WON'T EVEN NOTICE I'M GONE.
VWHIRRR
BRAVERY, MY APES! ONE TOUCH OF SOLANITE WILL RENDER SUNSTAR AS WEAK AS A CHILD!

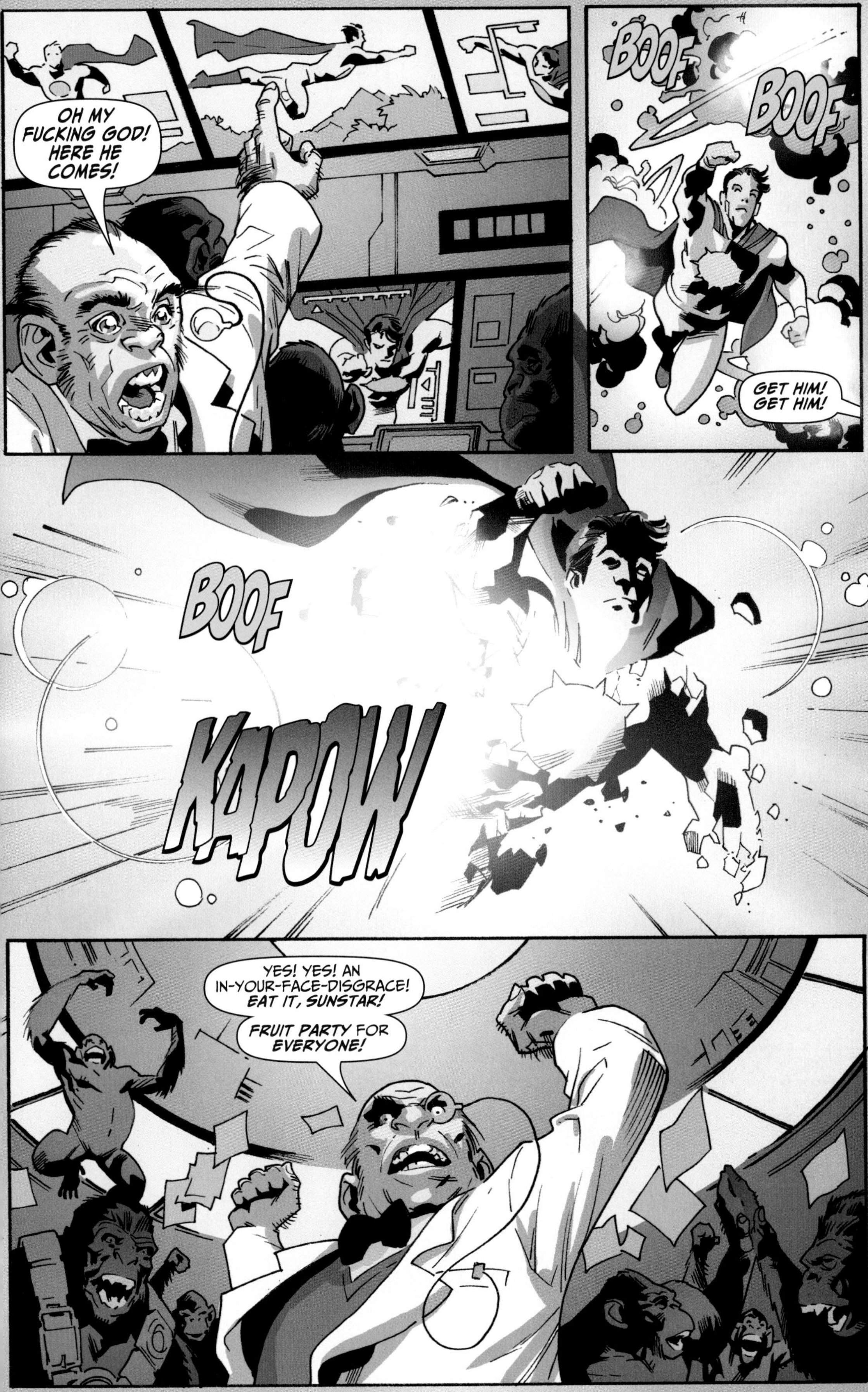
OH MY FUCKING GOD! HERE HE COMES!
BOOF
BOOF
GET HIM! GET HIM!
BOOF
KAPOW
YES! YES! AN IN-YOUR-FACE-DISGRACE! EAT IT, SUNSTAR!
FRUIT PARTY FOR EVERYONE!

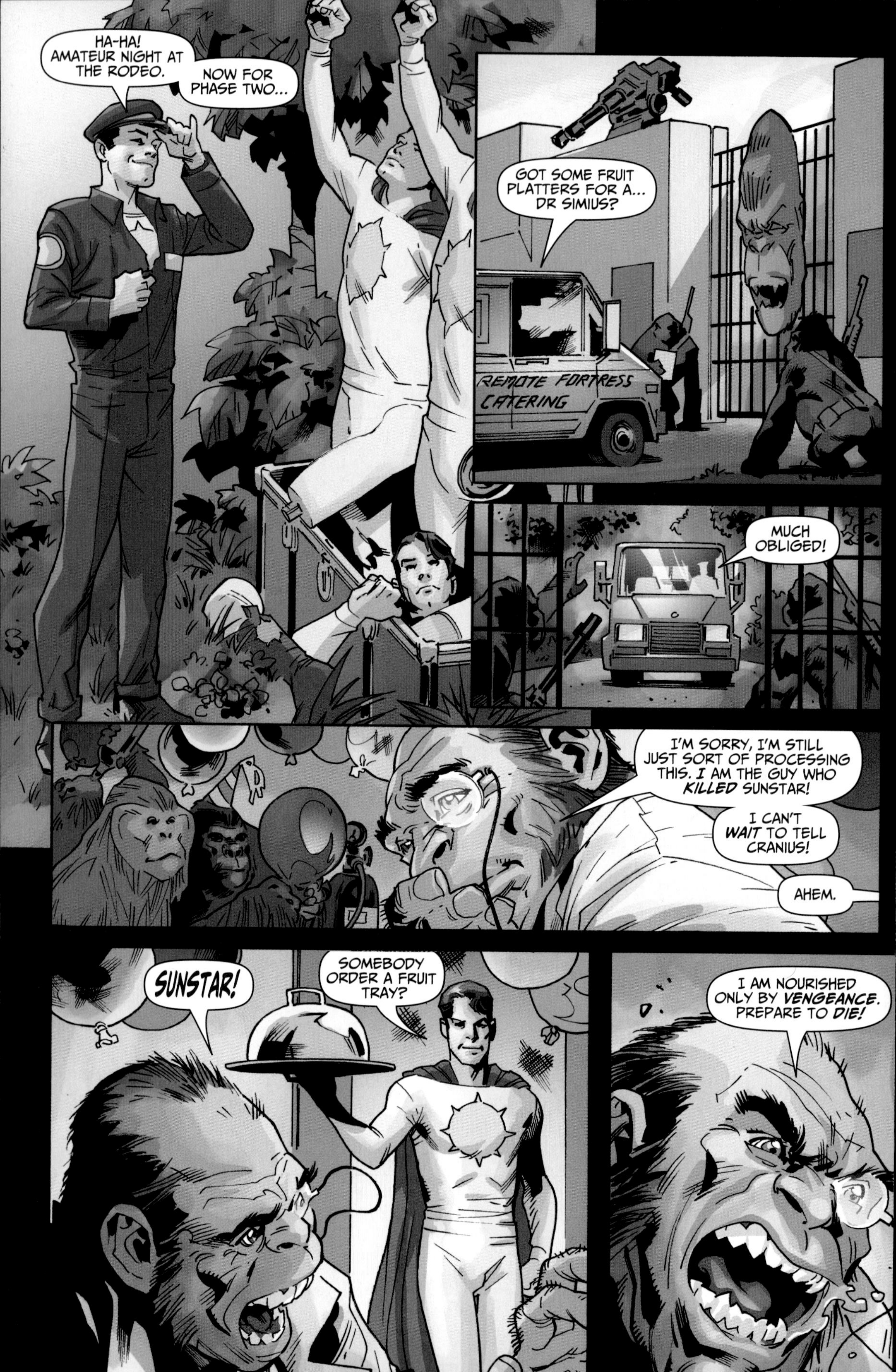
HA-HA! AMATEUR NIGHT AT THE RODEO.
NOW FOR PHASE TWO...
GOT SOME FRUIT PLATTERS FOR A... DR SIMIUS?
REMOTE FORTRESS CATERING
MUCH OBLIGED!
I'M SORRY, I'M STILL JUST SORT OF PROCESSING THIS. I AM THE GUY WHO KILLED SUNSTAR!
I CAN'T WAIT TO TELL CRANIUS!
AHEM.
SUNSTAR!
SOMEBODY ORDER A FRUIT TRAY?
I AM NOURISHED ONLY BY VENGEANCE. PREPARE TO DIE!

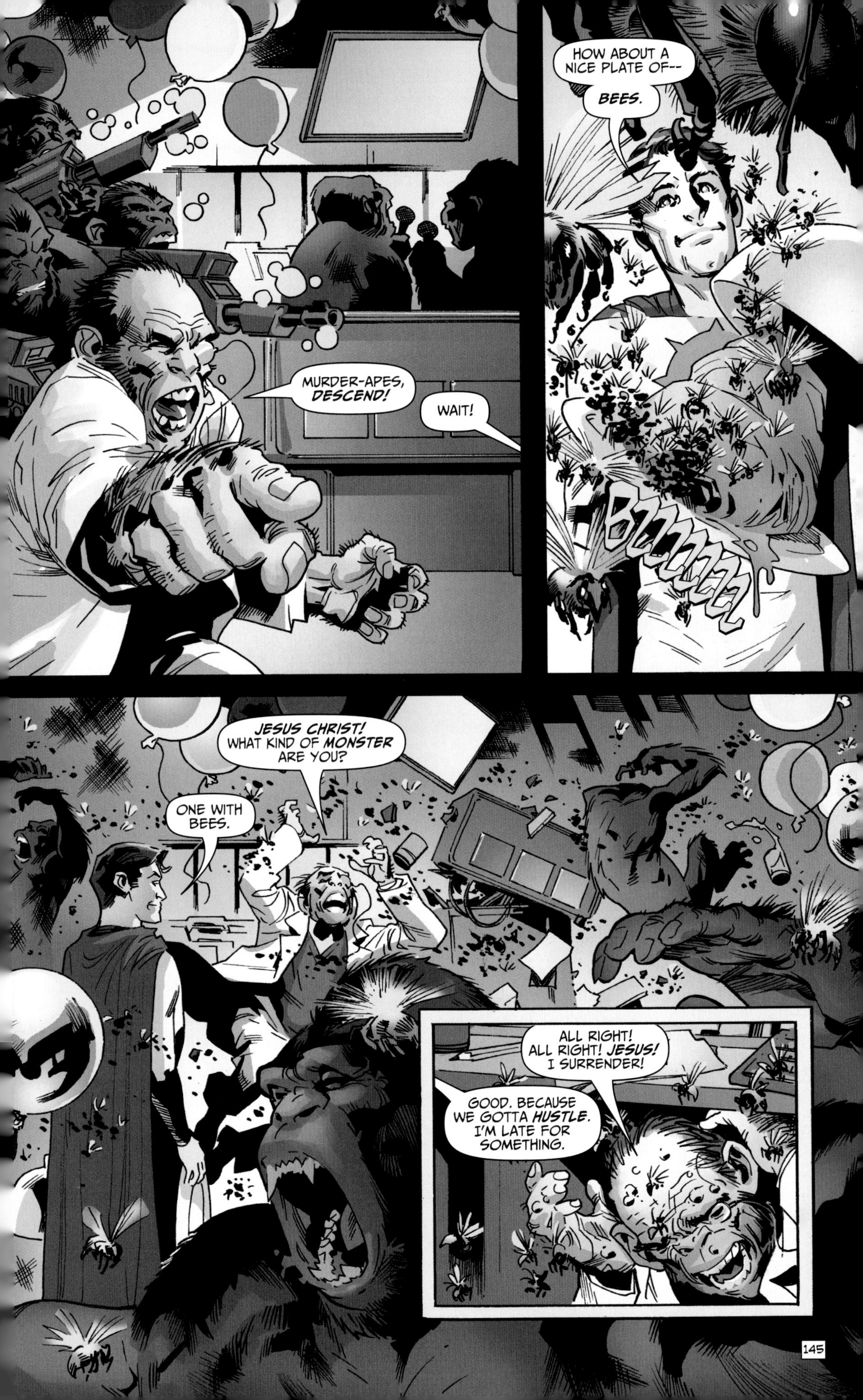
MURDER-APES, *DESCEND!*
WAIT!
HOW ABOUT A NICE PLATE OF--
BEES.
JESUS CHRIST! WHAT KIND OF *MONSTER* ARE YOU?
ONE WITH BEES.
ALL RIGHT! ALL RIGHT! *JESUS!* I SURRENDER!
GOOD. BECAUSE WE GOTTA *HUSTLE.* I'M LATE FOR SOMETHING.

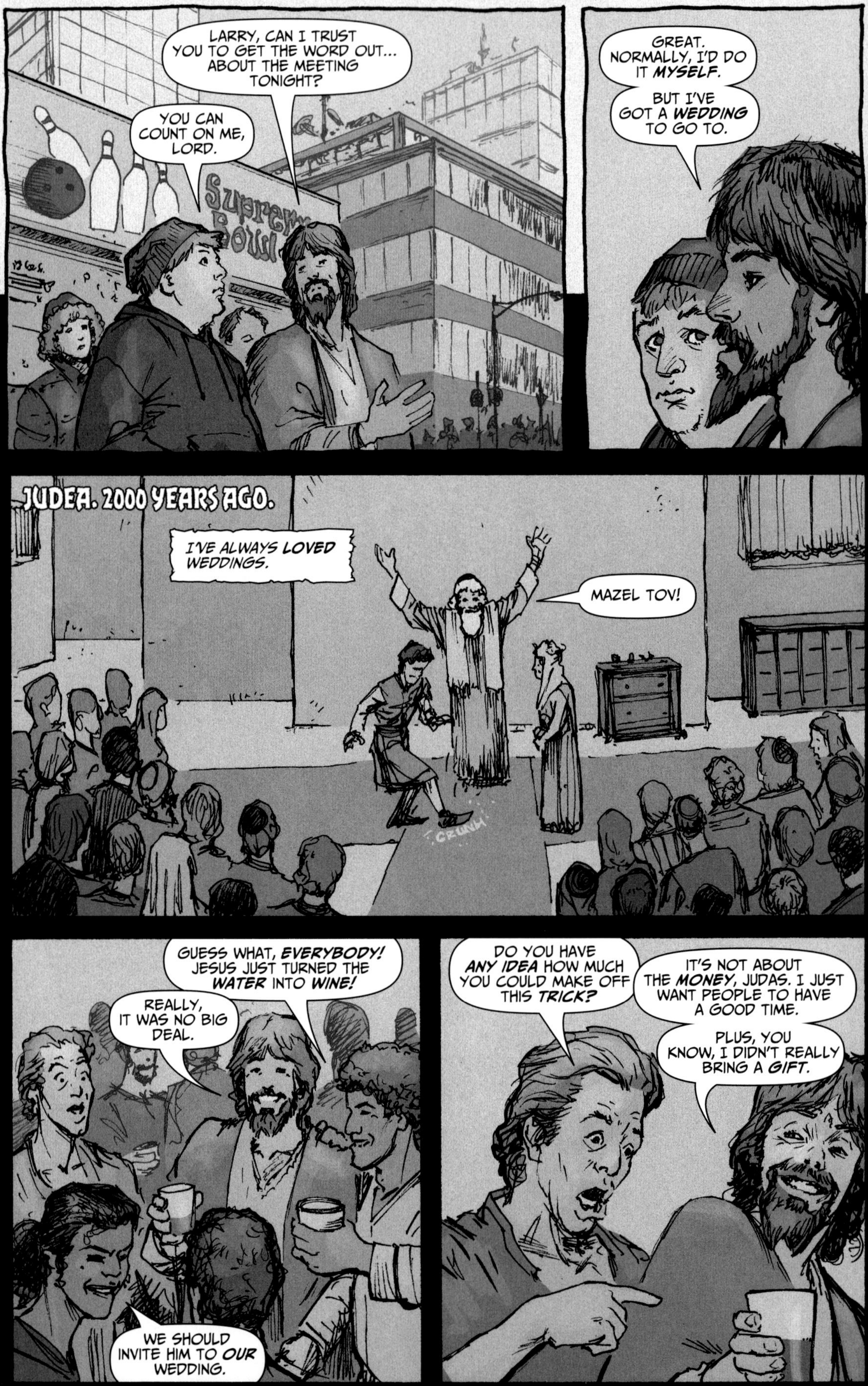
LARRY, CAN I TRUST YOU TO GET THE WORD OUT... ABOUT THE MEETING TONIGHT?
YOU CAN COUNT ON ME, LORD.
GREAT. NORMALLY, I'D DO IT *MYSELF*.
BUT I'VE GOT A *WEDDING* TO GO TO.
JUDEA. 2000 YEARS AGO.
*I'VE ALWAYS **LOVED** WEDDINGS.*
MAZEL TOV!
GUESS WHAT, ***EVERYBODY!*** JESUS JUST TURNED THE ***WATER*** INTO ***WINE!***
REALLY, IT WAS NO BIG DEAL.
WE SHOULD INVITE HIM TO ***OUR*** WEDDING.
DO YOU HAVE ***ANY IDEA*** HOW MUCH YOU COULD MAKE OFF THIS ***TRICK?***
IT'S NOT ABOUT THE ***MONEY***, JUDAS. I JUST WANT PEOPLE TO HAVE A GOOD TIME.
PLUS, YOU KNOW, I DIDN'T REALLY BRING A ***GIFT***.

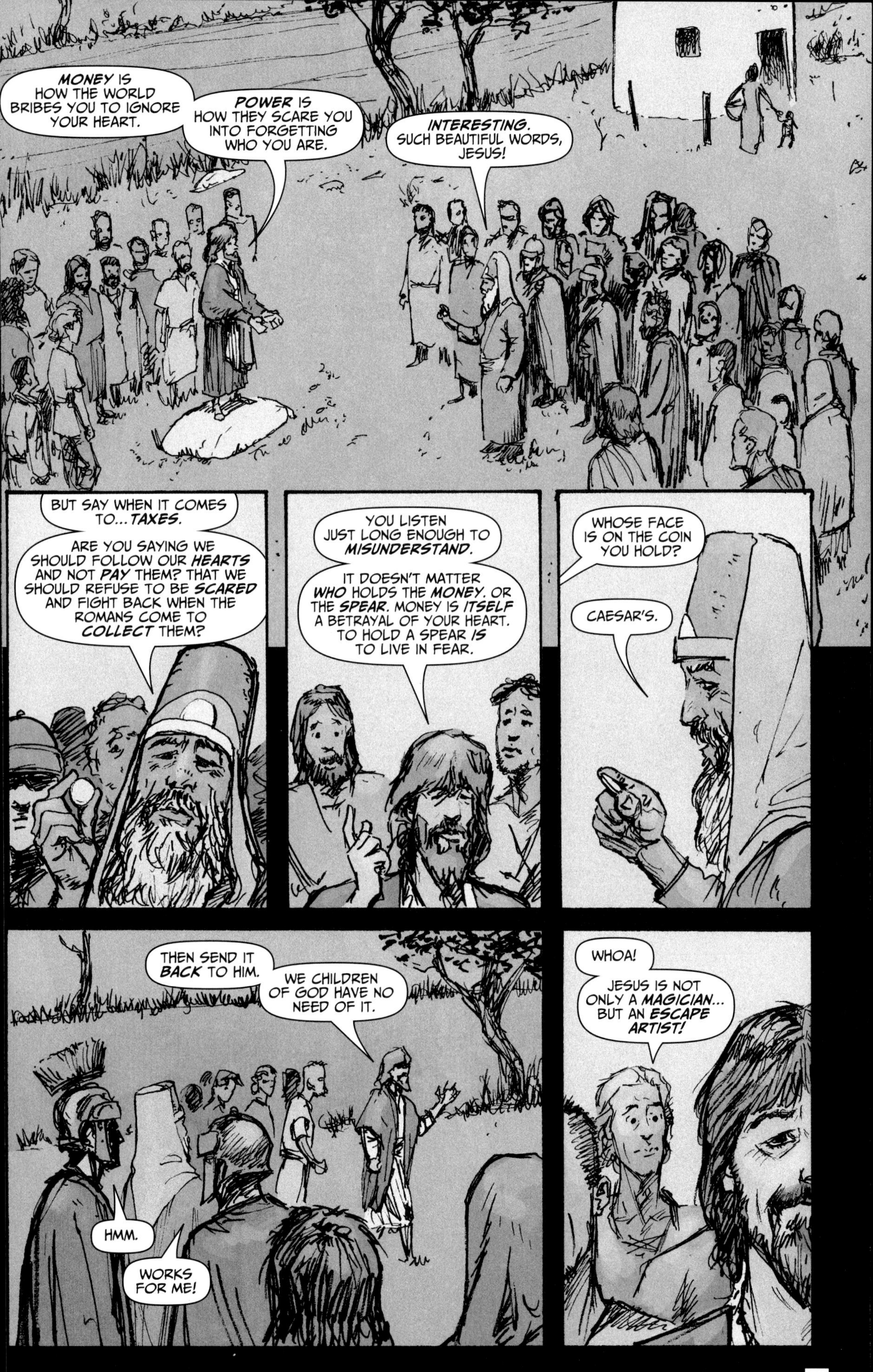
MONEY IS HOW THE WORLD BRIBES YOU TO IGNORE YOUR HEART.
POWER IS HOW THEY SCARE YOU INTO FORGETTING WHO YOU ARE.
INTERESTING. SUCH BEAUTIFUL WORDS, JESUS!
BUT SAY WHEN IT COMES TO... TAXES.
ARE YOU SAYING WE SHOULD FOLLOW OUR HEARTS AND NOT PAY THEM? THAT WE SHOULD REFUSE TO BE SCARED AND FIGHT BACK WHEN THE ROMANS COME TO COLLECT THEM?
YOU LISTEN JUST LONG ENOUGH TO MISUNDERSTAND.
IT DOESN'T MATTER WHO HOLDS THE MONEY. OR THE SPEAR. MONEY IS ITSELF A BETRAYAL OF YOUR HEART. TO HOLD A SPEAR IS TO LIVE IN FEAR.
WHOSE FACE IS ON THE COIN YOU HOLD?
CAESAR'S.
THEN SEND IT BACK TO HIM.
WE CHILDREN OF GOD HAVE NO NEED OF IT.
HMM.
WORKS FOR ME!
WHOA!
JESUS IS NOT ONLY A MAGICIAN... BUT AN ESCAPE ARTIST!

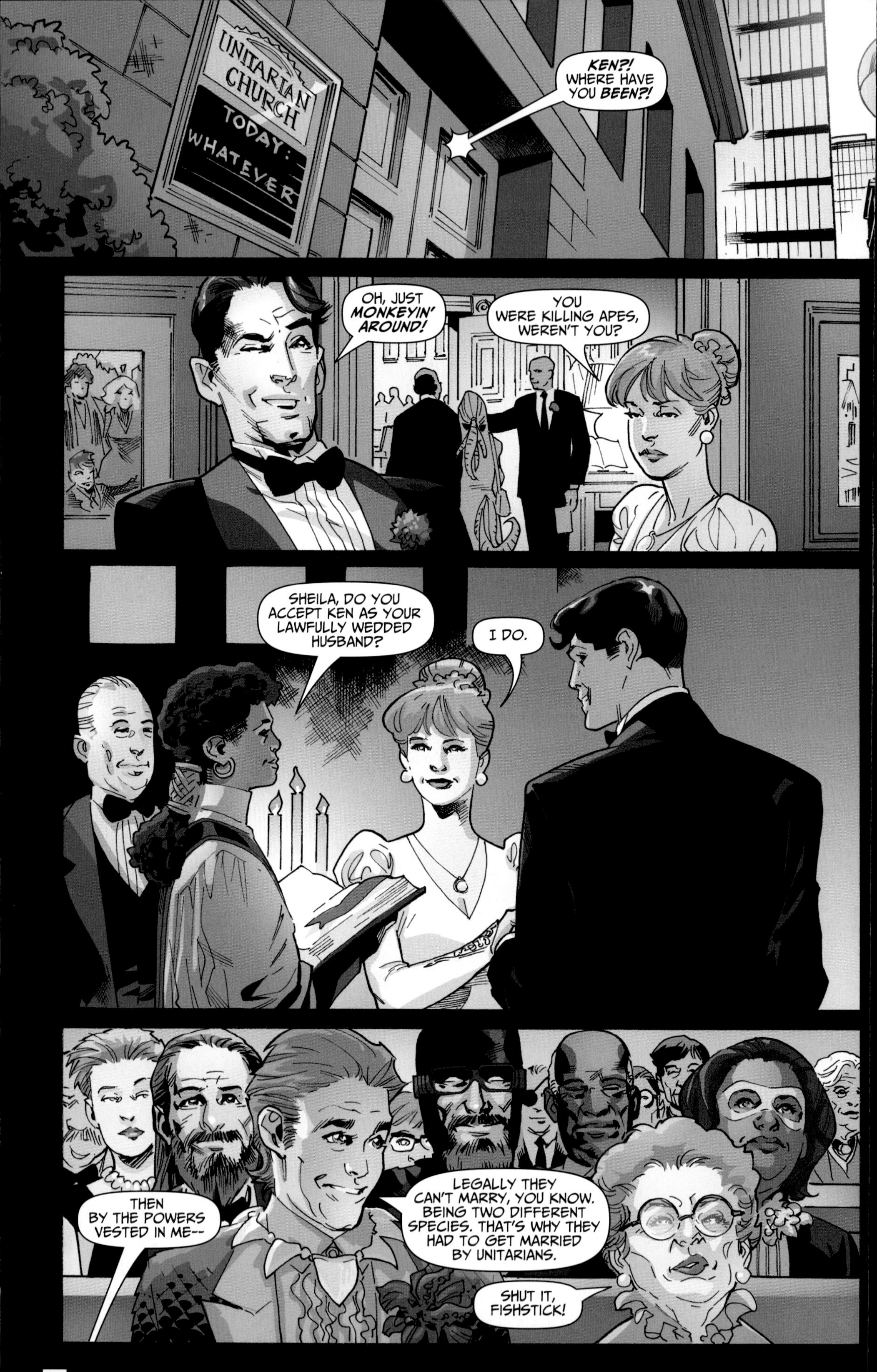
UNITARIAN CHURCH
TODAY: WHATEVER
KEN?! WHERE HAVE YOU BEEN?!
OH, JUST MONKEYIN' AROUND!
YOU WERE KILLING APES, WEREN'T YOU?
SHEILA, DO YOU ACCEPT KEN AS YOUR LAWFULLY WEDDED HUSBAND?
I DO.
THEN BY THE POWERS VESTED IN ME--
LEGALLY THEY CAN'T MARRY, YOU KNOW. BEING TWO DIFFERENT SPECIES. THAT'S WHY THEY HAD TO GET MARRIED BY UNITARIANS.
SHUT IT, FISHSTICK!

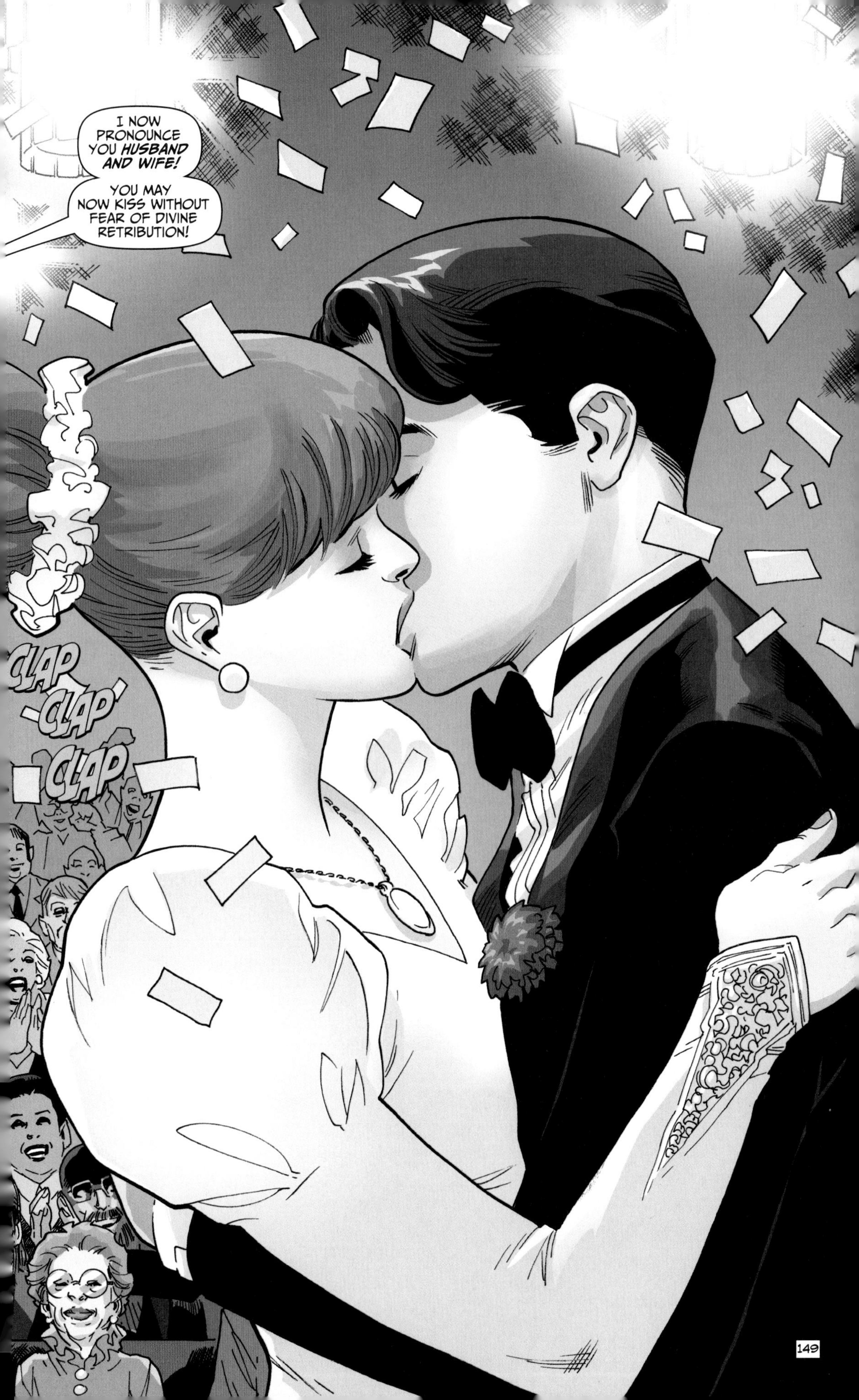
I NOW PRONOUNCE YOU HUSBAND AND WIFE!
YOU MAY NOW KISS WITHOUT FEAR OF DIVINE RETRIBUTION!
CLAP
CLAP
CLAP

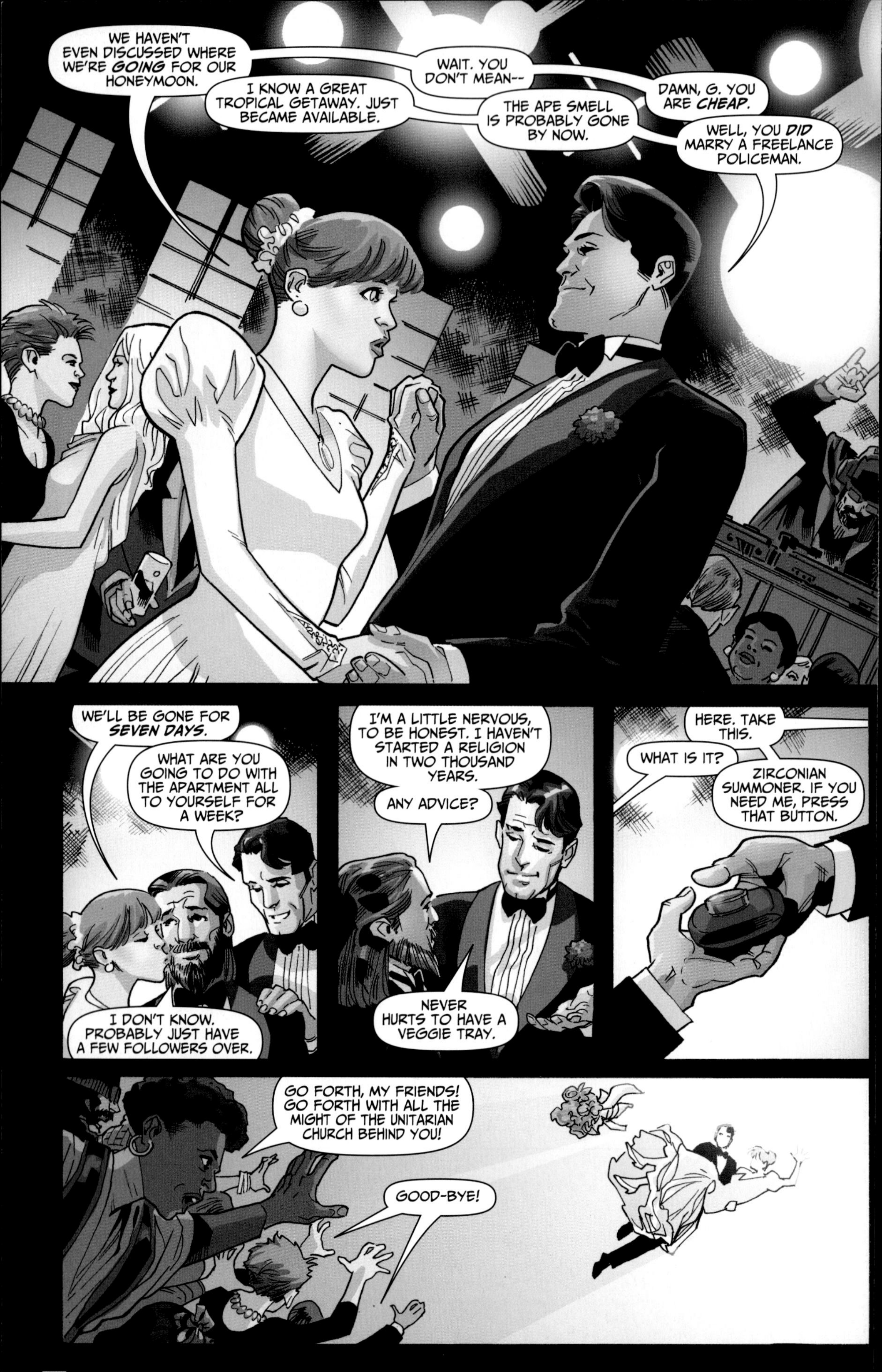
WE HAVEN'T EVEN DISCUSSED WHERE WE'RE GOING FOR OUR HONEYMOON.
I KNOW A GREAT TROPICAL GETAWAY. JUST BECAME AVAILABLE.
WAIT. YOU DON'T MEAN--
THE APE SMELL IS PROBABLY GONE BY NOW.
DAMN, G. YOU ARE CHEAP.
WELL, YOU DID MARRY A FREELANCE POLICEMAN.
WE'LL BE GONE FOR SEVEN DAYS.
WHAT ARE YOU GOING TO DO WITH THE APARTMENT ALL TO YOURSELF FOR A WEEK?
I DON'T KNOW. PROBABLY JUST HAVE A FEW FOLLOWERS OVER.
I'M A LITTLE NERVOUS, TO BE HONEST. I HAVEN'T STARTED A RELIGION IN TWO THOUSAND YEARS.
ANY ADVICE?
NEVER HURTS TO HAVE A VEGGIE TRAY.
HERE. TAKE THIS.
WHAT IS IT?
ZIRCONIAN SUMMONER. IF YOU NEED ME, PRESS THAT BUTTON.
GO FORTH, MY FRIENDS! GO FORTH WITH ALL THE MIGHT OF THE UNITARIAN CHURCH BEHIND YOU!
GOOD-BYE!

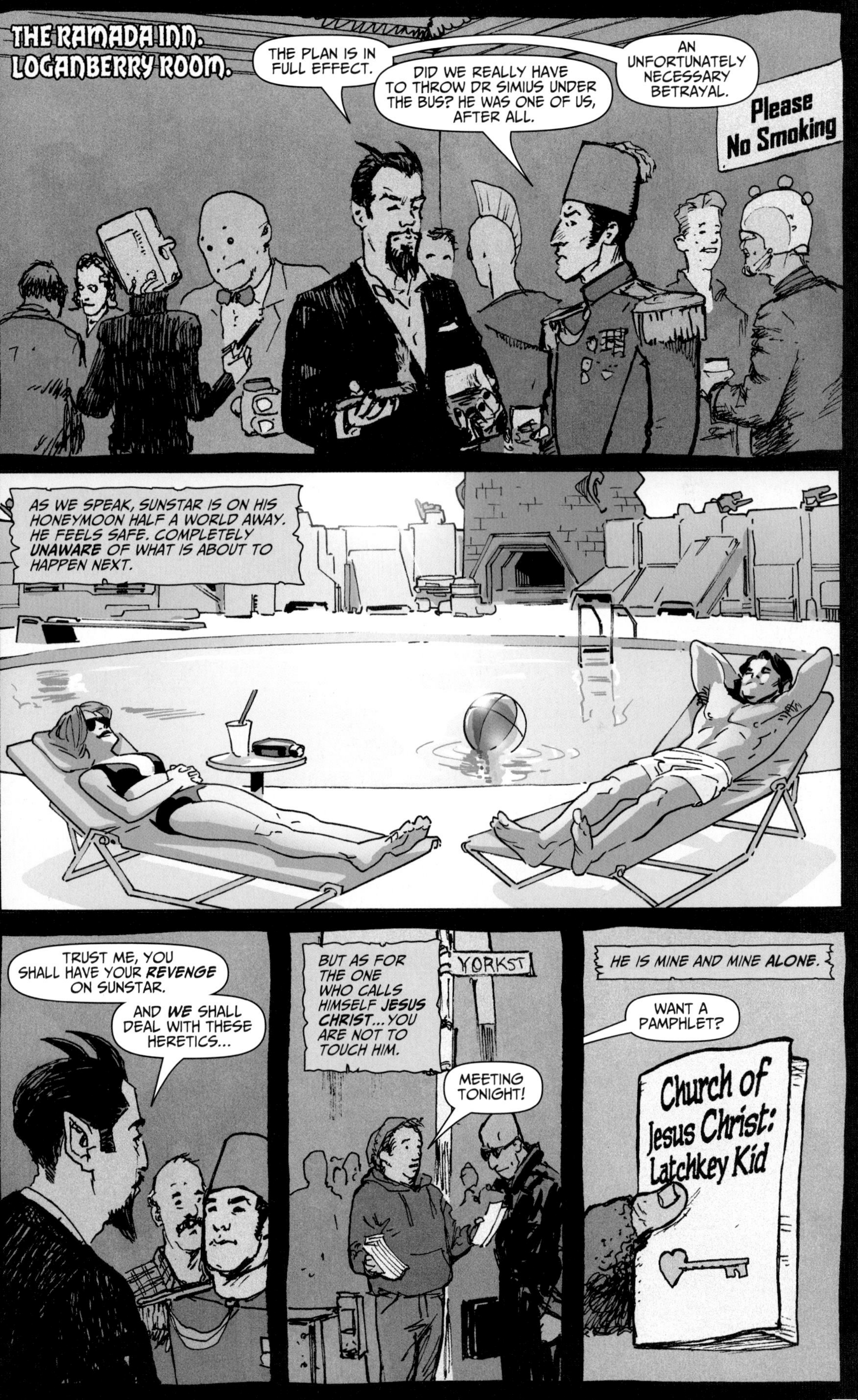
THE RAMADA INN. LOGANBERRY ROOM.
THE PLAN IS IN FULL EFFECT.
DID WE REALLY HAVE TO THROW DR SIMIUS UNDER THE BUS? HE WAS ONE OF US, AFTER ALL.
AN UNFORTUNATELY NECESSARY BETRAYAL.
Please No Smoking
AS WE SPEAK, SUNSTAR IS ON HIS HONEYMOON HALF A WORLD AWAY. HE FEELS SAFE. COMPLETELY UNAWARE OF WHAT IS ABOUT TO HAPPEN NEXT.
TRUST ME, YOU SHALL HAVE YOUR REVENGE ON SUNSTAR.
AND WE SHALL DEAL WITH THESE HERETICS...
BUT AS FOR THE ONE WHO CALLS HIMSELF JESUS CHRIST... YOU ARE NOT TO TOUCH HIM.
YORK ST
MEETING TONIGHT!
HE IS MINE AND MINE ALONE.
WANT A PAMPHLET?
Church of Jesus Christ: Latchkey Kid

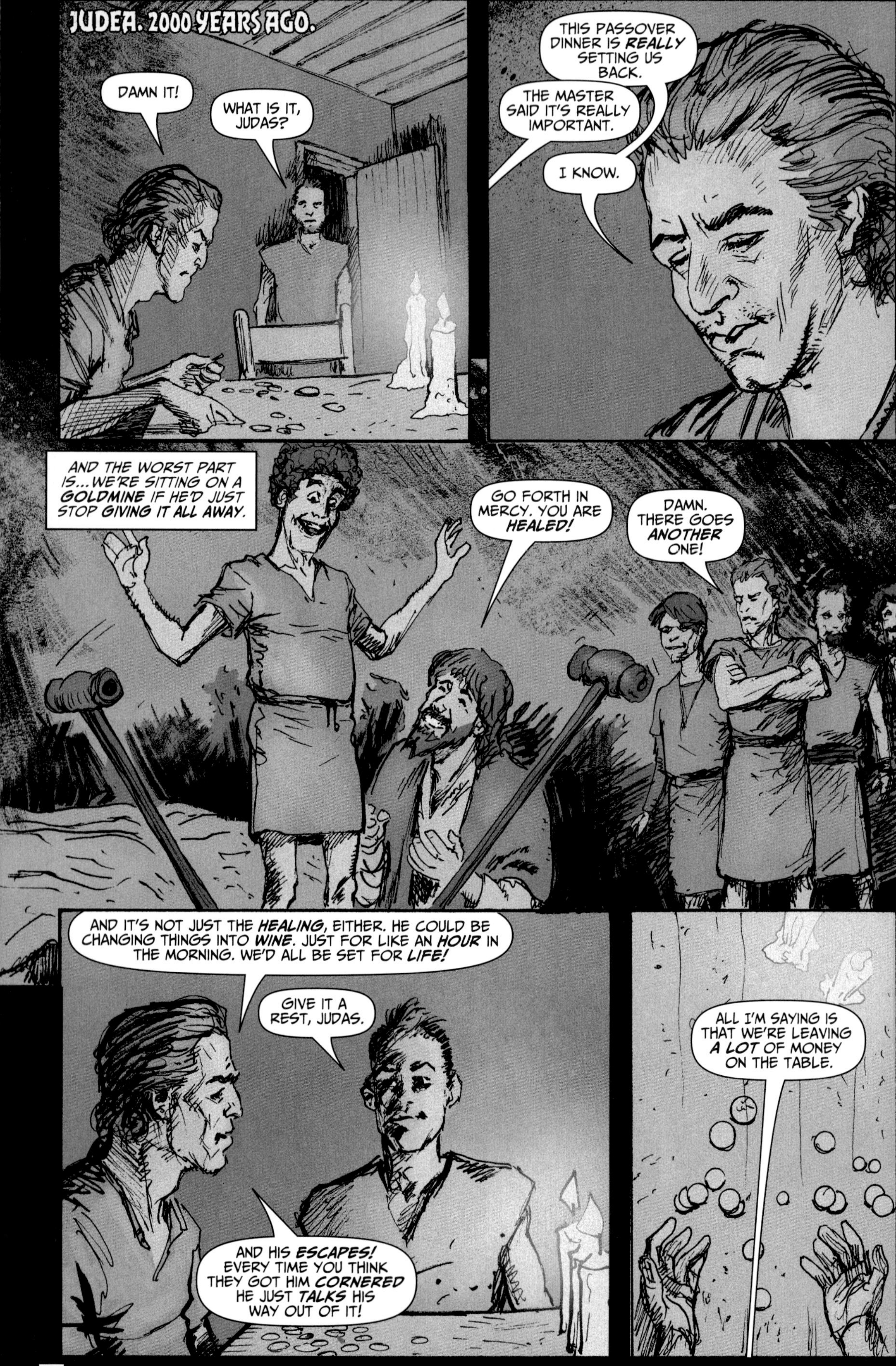
JUDEA. 2000 YEARS AGO.
DAMN IT!
WHAT IS IT, JUDAS?
THIS PASSOVER DINNER IS *REALLY* SETTING US BACK.
THE MASTER SAID IT'S REALLY IMPORTANT.
I KNOW.
AND THE WORST PART IS...WE'RE SITTING ON A *GOLDMINE* IF HE'D JUST STOP *GIVING IT ALL AWAY*.
GO FORTH IN MERCY. YOU ARE *HEALED!*
DAMN. THERE GOES *ANOTHER* ONE!
AND IT'S NOT JUST THE *HEALING*, EITHER. HE COULD BE CHANGING THINGS INTO *WINE*. JUST FOR LIKE AN *HOUR* IN THE MORNING. WE'D ALL BE SET FOR *LIFE!*
GIVE IT A REST, JUDAS.
AND HIS *ESCAPES!* EVERY TIME YOU THINK THEY GOT HIM *CORNERED* HE JUST *TALKS* HIS WAY OUT OF IT!
ALL I'M SAYING IS THAT WE'RE LEAVING *A LOT* OF MONEY ON THE TABLE.

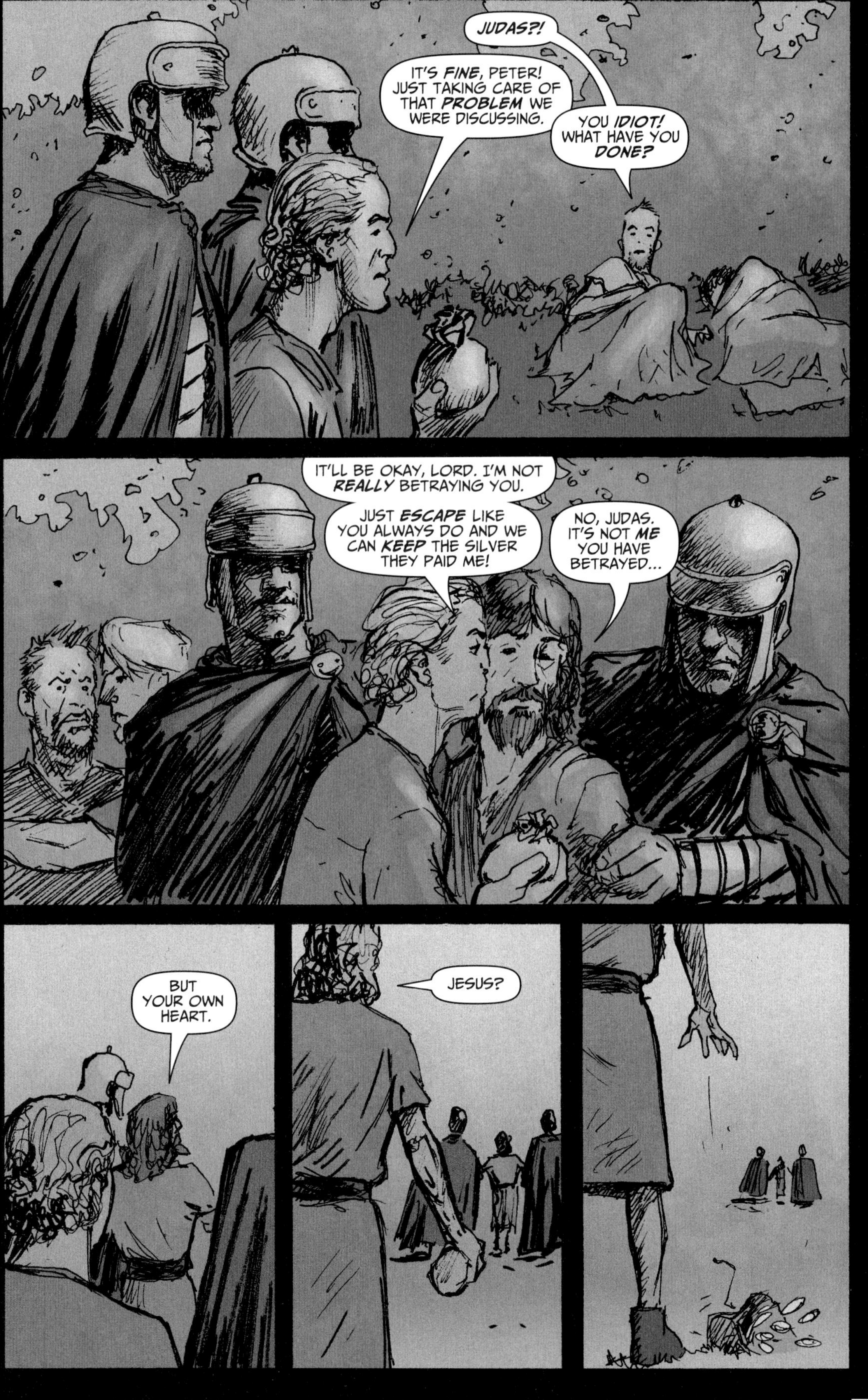
JUDAS?!
IT'S FINE, PETER! JUST TAKING CARE OF THAT PROBLEM WE WERE DISCUSSING.
YOU IDIOT! WHAT HAVE YOU DONE?
IT'LL BE OKAY, LORD. I'M NOT REALLY BETRAYING YOU.
JUST ESCAPE LIKE YOU ALWAYS DO AND WE CAN KEEP THE SILVER THEY PAID ME!
NO, JUDAS. IT'S NOT ME YOU HAVE BETRAYED...
BUT YOUR OWN HEART.
JESUS?

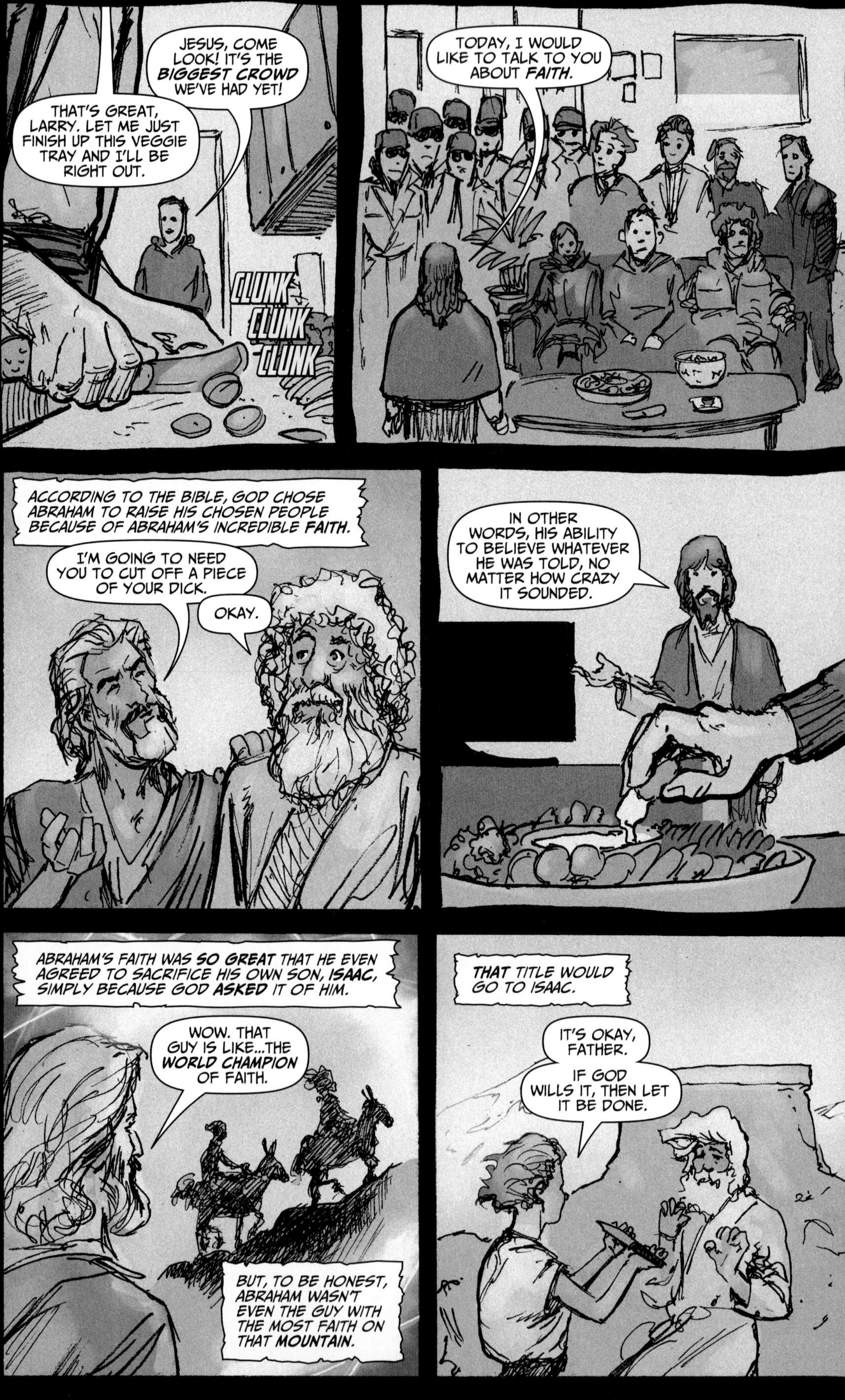

JESUS, COME LOOK! IT'S THE **BIGGEST CROWD** WE'VE HAD YET!
THAT'S GREAT, LARRY. LET ME JUST FINISH UP THIS VEGGIE TRAY AND I'LL BE RIGHT OUT.
CLUNK CLUNK CLUNK
TODAY, I WOULD LIKE TO TALK TO YOU ABOUT **FAITH.**
ACCORDING TO THE BIBLE, GOD CHOSE ABRAHAM TO RAISE HIS CHOSEN PEOPLE BECAUSE OF ABRAHAM'S INCREDIBLE **FAITH.**
I'M GOING TO NEED YOU TO CUT OFF A PIECE OF YOUR DICK.
OKAY.
IN OTHER WORDS, HIS ABILITY TO BELIEVE WHATEVER HE WAS TOLD, NO MATTER HOW CRAZY IT SOUNDED.
ABRAHAM'S FAITH WAS **SO GREAT** THAT HE EVEN AGREED TO SACRIFICE HIS OWN SON, **ISAAC,** SIMPLY BECAUSE GOD **ASKED** IT OF HIM.
WOW. THAT GUY IS LIKE...THE **WORLD CHAMPION** OF FAITH.
BUT, TO BE HONEST, ABRAHAM WASN'T EVEN THE GUY WITH THE MOST FAITH ON THAT **MOUNTAIN.**
THAT TITLE WOULD GO TO ISAAC.
IT'S OKAY, FATHER.
IF GOD WILLS IT, THEN LET IT BE DONE.

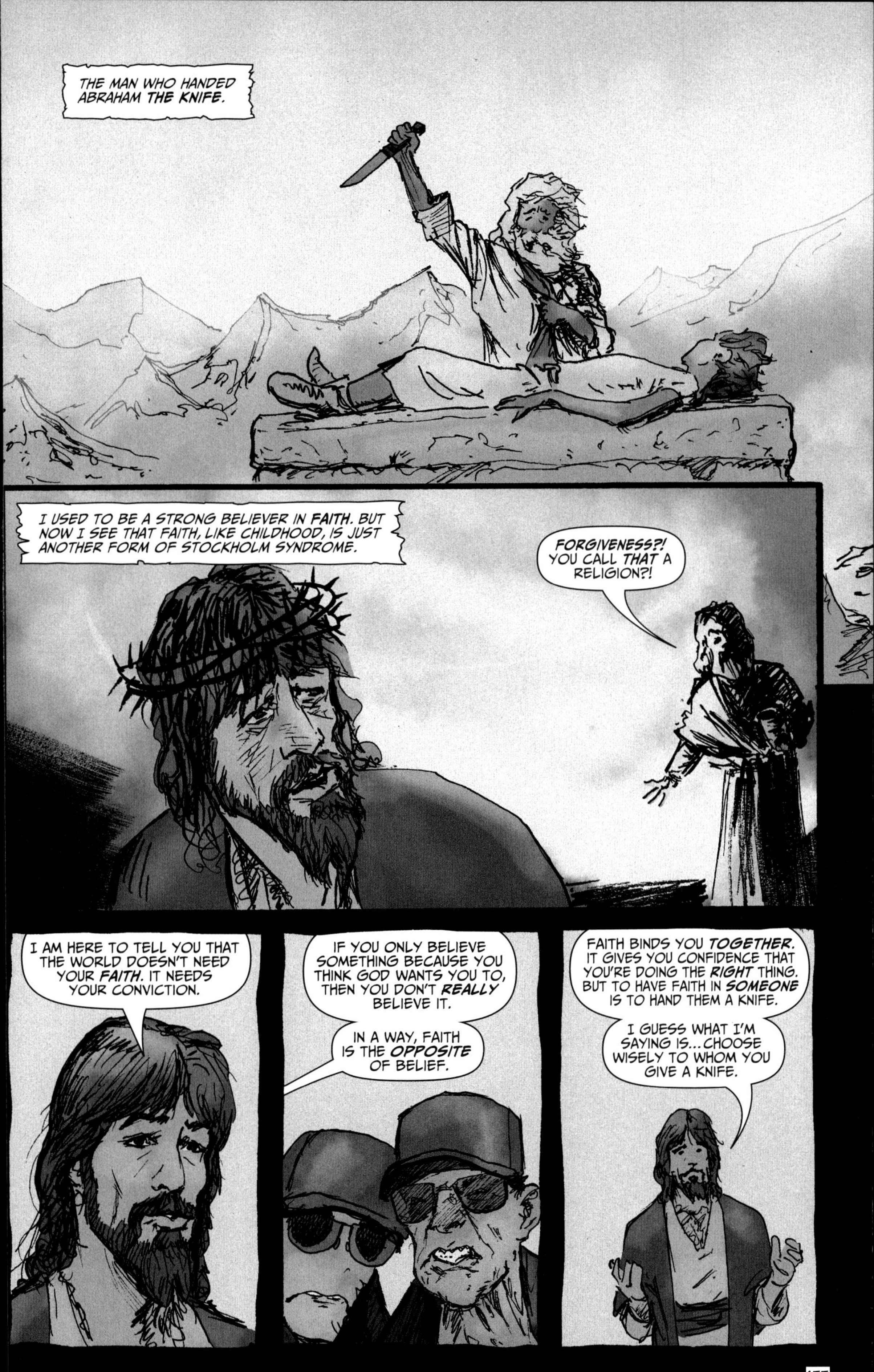
THE MAN WHO HANDED ABRAHAM THE KNIFE.
I USED TO BE A STRONG BELIEVER IN FAITH. BUT NOW I SEE THAT FAITH, LIKE CHILDHOOD, IS JUST ANOTHER FORM OF STOCKHOLM SYNDROME.
FORGIVENESS?! YOU CALL THAT A RELIGION?!
I AM HERE TO TELL YOU THAT THE WORLD DOESN'T NEED YOUR FAITH. IT NEEDS YOUR CONVICTION.
IF YOU ONLY BELIEVE SOMETHING BECAUSE YOU THINK GOD WANTS YOU TO, THEN YOU DON'T REALLY BELIEVE IT.
IN A WAY, FAITH IS THE OPPOSITE OF BELIEF.
FAITH BINDS YOU TOGETHER. IT GIVES YOU CONFIDENCE THAT YOU'RE DOING THE RIGHT THING. BUT TO HAVE FAITH IN SOMEONE IS TO HAND THEM A KNIFE.
I GUESS WHAT I'M SAYING IS...CHOOSE WISELY TO WHOM YOU GIVE A KNIFE.

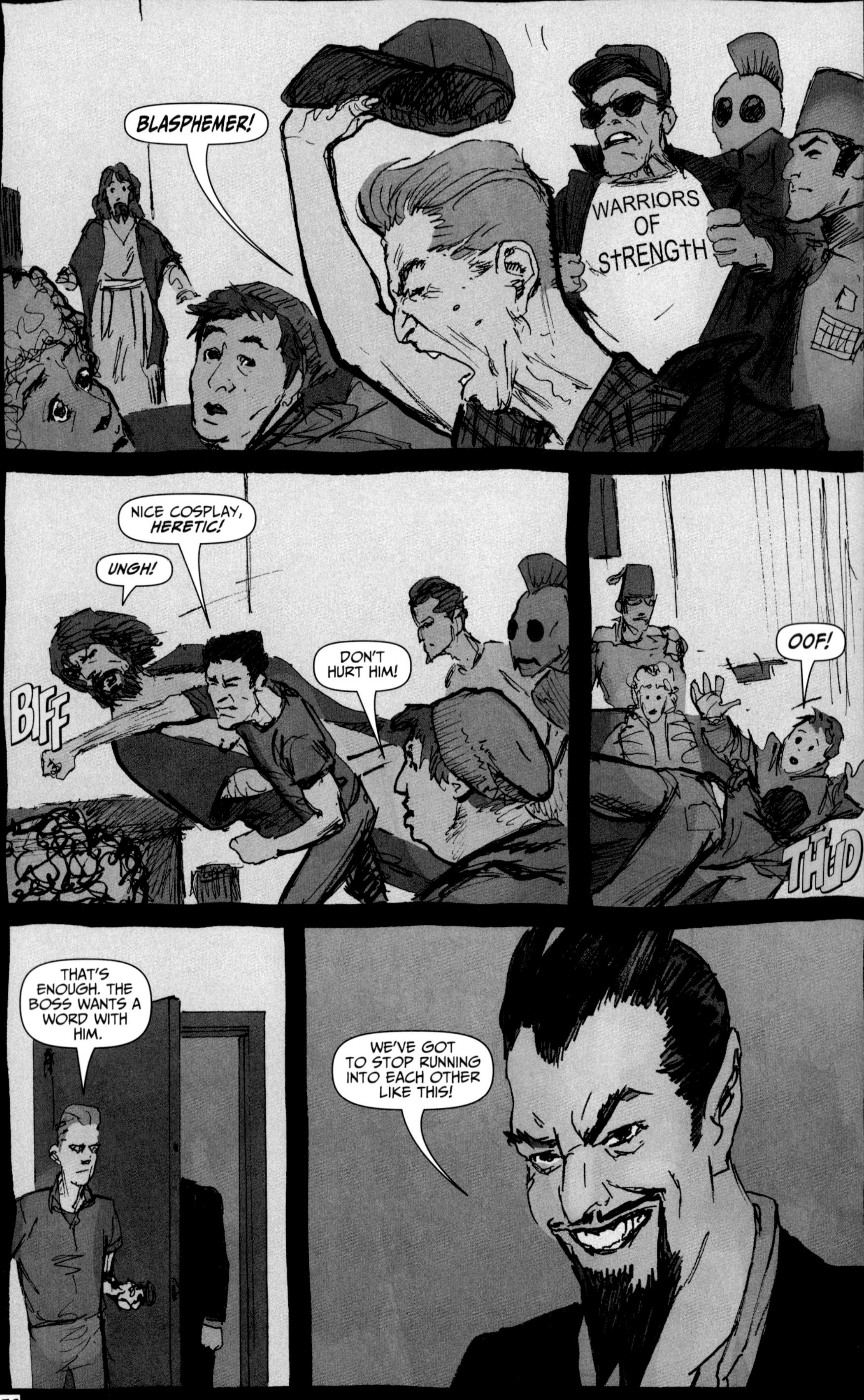
BLASPHEMER!
WARRIORS OF StRENGtH
NICE COSPLAY, HERETIC!
UNGH!
BIFF
DON'T HURT HIM!
OOF!
THUD
THAT'S ENOUGH. THE BOSS WANTS A WORD WITH HIM.
WE'VE GOT TO STOP RUNNING INTO EACH OTHER LIKE THIS!

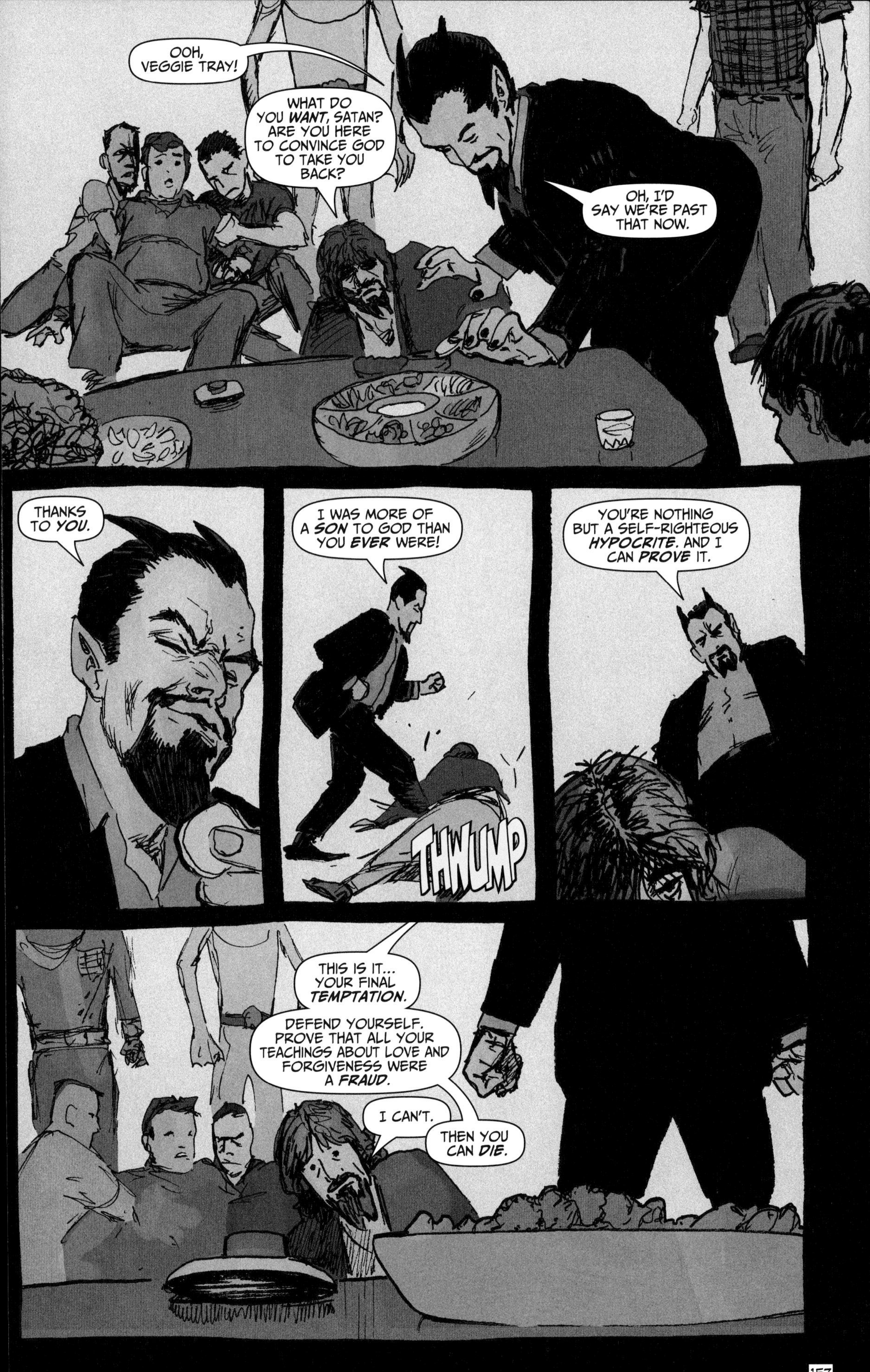
OOH, VEGGIE TRAY!
WHAT DO YOU *WANT*, SATAN? ARE YOU HERE TO CONVINCE GOD TO TAKE YOU BACK?
OH, I'D SAY WE'RE PAST THAT NOW.
THANKS TO *YOU*.
I WAS MORE OF A *SON* TO GOD THAN YOU *EVER* WERE!
THWUMP
YOU'RE NOTHING BUT A SELF-RIGHTEOUS *HYPOCRITE*. AND I CAN *PROVE* IT.
THIS IS IT... YOUR FINAL *TEMPTATION*.
DEFEND YOURSELF. PROVE THAT ALL YOUR TEACHINGS ABOUT LOVE AND FORGIVENESS WERE A *FRAUD*.
I CAN'T.
THEN YOU CAN *DIE*.

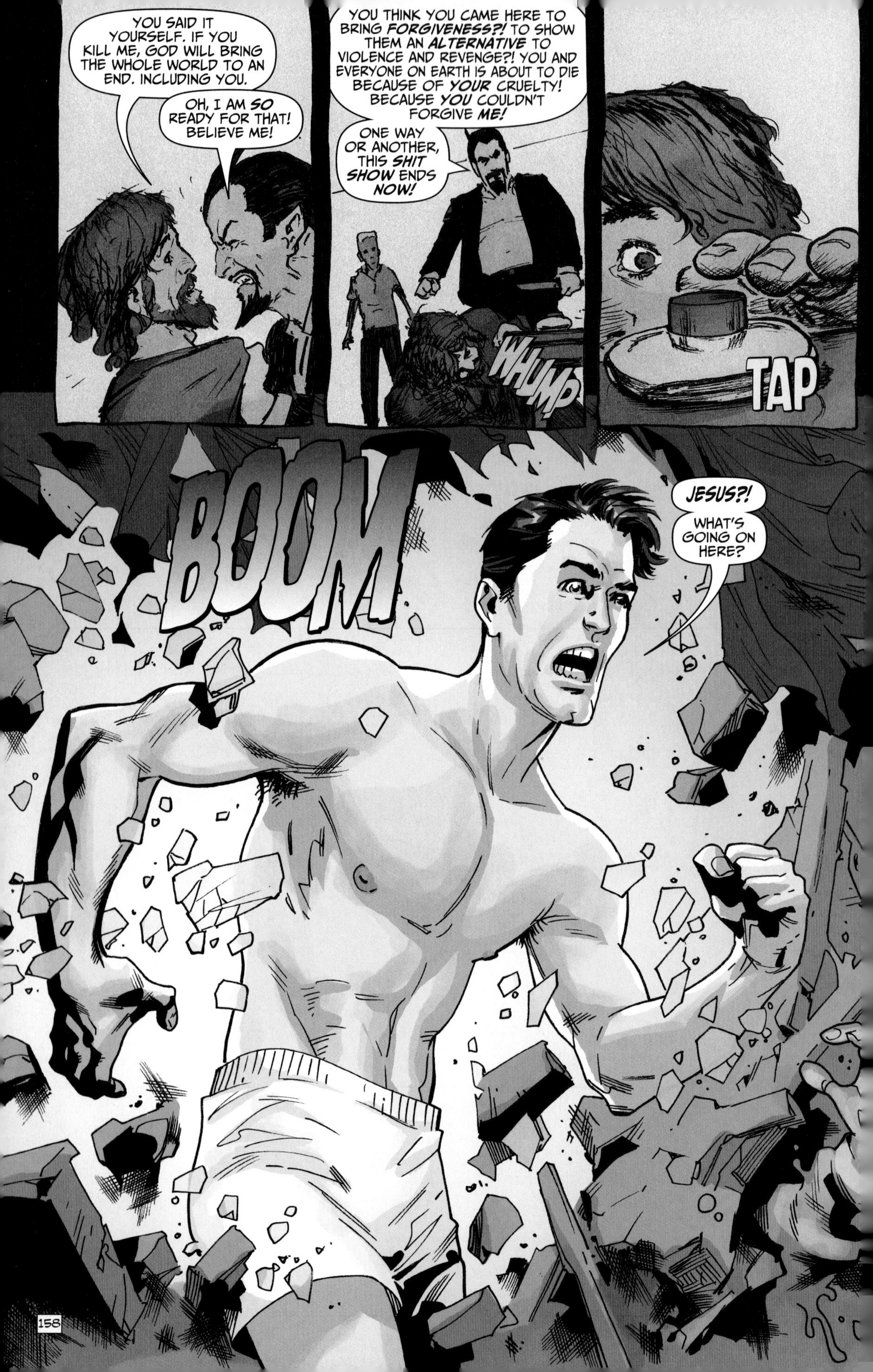
YOU SAID IT YOURSELF. IF YOU KILL ME, GOD WILL BRING THE WHOLE WORLD TO AN END. INCLUDING YOU.
OH, I AM SO READY FOR THAT! BELIEVE ME!
YOU THINK YOU CAME HERE TO BRING FORGIVENESS?! TO SHOW THEM AN ALTERNATIVE TO VIOLENCE AND REVENGE?! YOU AND EVERYONE ON EARTH IS ABOUT TO DIE BECAUSE OF YOUR CRUELTY! BECAUSE YOU COULDN'T FORGIVE ME!
ONE WAY OR ANOTHER, THIS SHIT SHOW ENDS NOW!
WHUMP
TAP
BOOM
JESUS?!
WHAT'S GOING ON HERE?

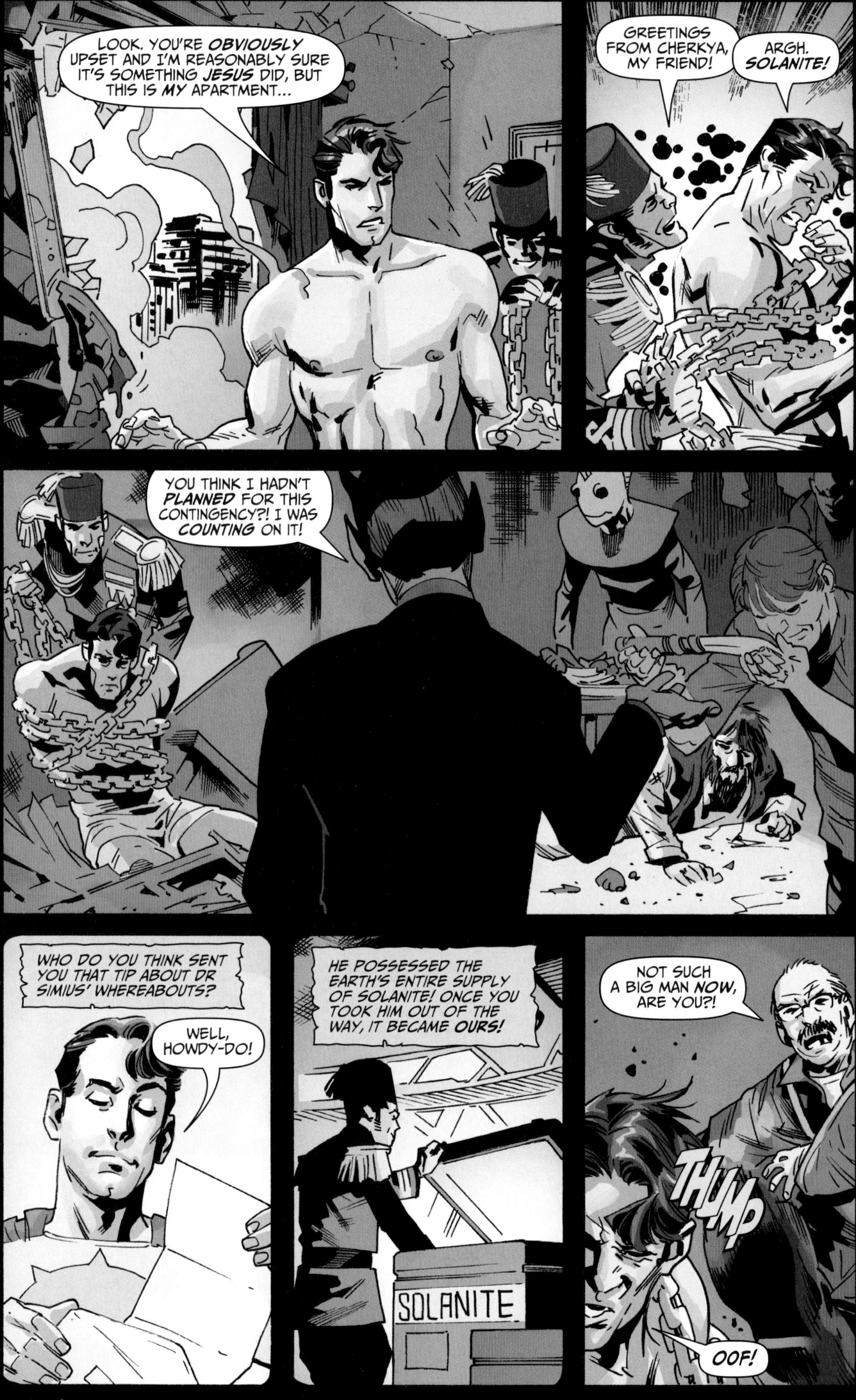
LOOK. YOU'RE OBVIOUSLY UPSET AND I'M REASONABLY SURE IT'S SOMETHING JESUS DID, BUT THIS IS MY APARTMENT...
GREETINGS FROM CHERKYA, MY FRIEND!
ARGH. SOLANITE!
YOU THINK I HADN'T PLANNED FOR THIS CONTINGENCY?! I WAS COUNTING ON IT!
WHO DO YOU THINK SENT YOU THAT TIP ABOUT DR SIMIUS' WHEREABOUTS?
WELL, HOWDY-DO!
HE POSSESSED THE EARTH'S ENTIRE SUPPLY OF SOLANITE! ONCE YOU TOOK HIM OUT OF THE WAY, IT BECAME OURS!
SOLANITE
NOT SUCH A BIG MAN NOW, ARE YOU?!
THUMP
OOF!

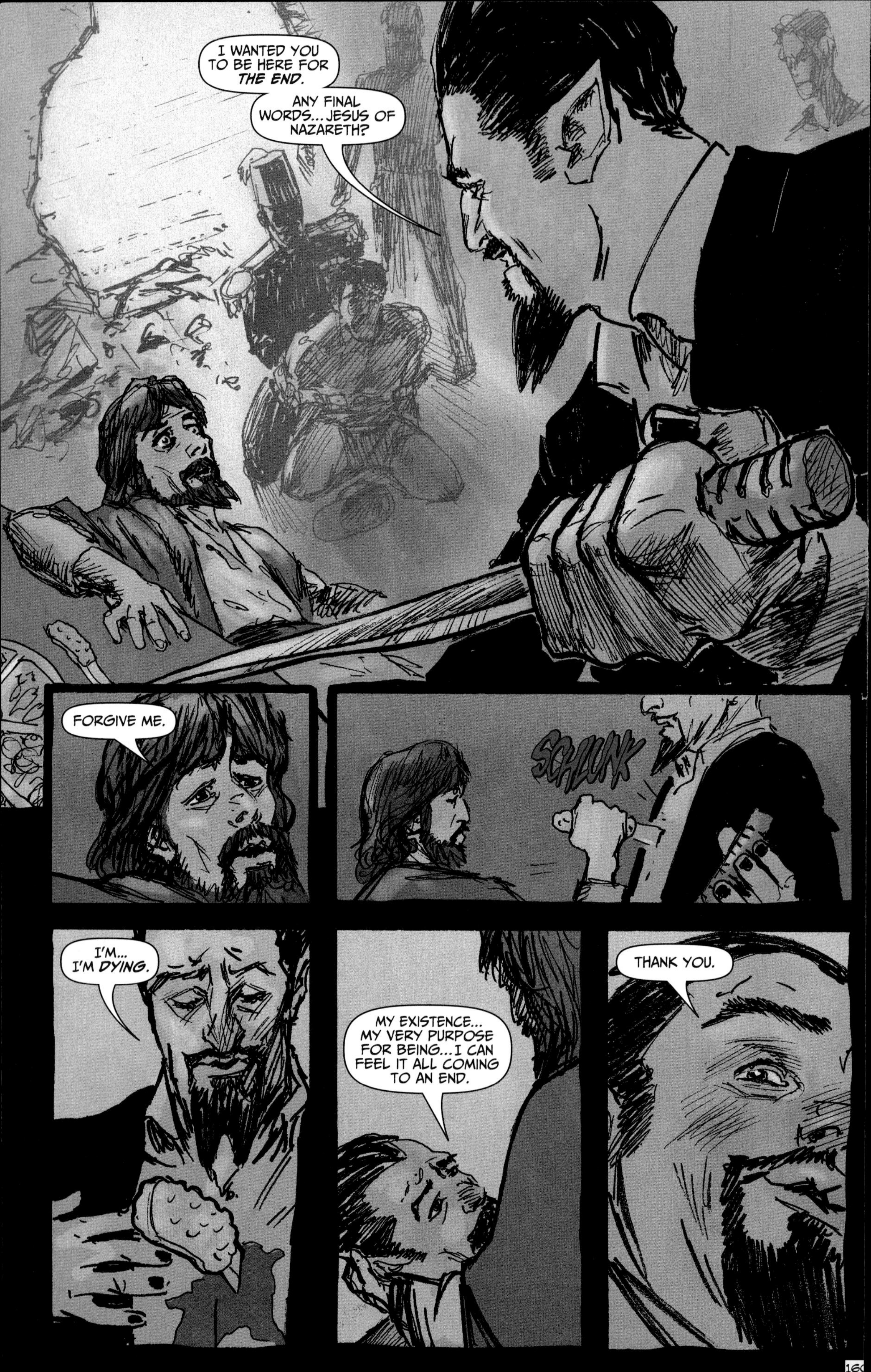
I WANTED YOU TO BE HERE FOR THE END.
ANY FINAL WORDS... JESUS OF NAZARETH?
FORGIVE ME.
SCHLUNK
I'M... I'M DYING.
MY EXISTENCE... MY VERY PURPOSE FOR BEING... I CAN FEEL IT ALL COMING TO AN END.
THANK YOU.

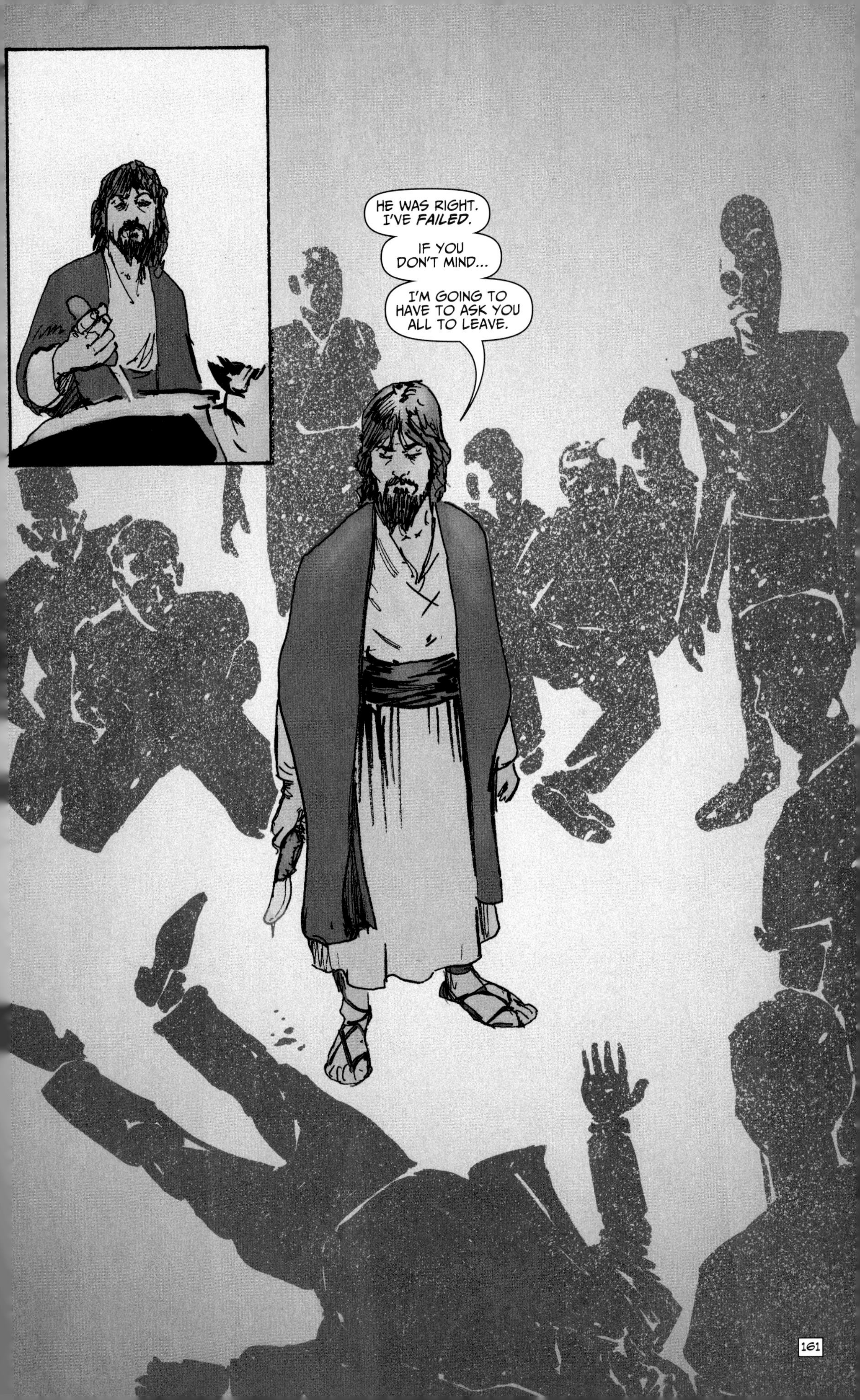
HE WAS RIGHT. I'VE *FAILED.*
IF YOU DON'T MIND...
I'M GOING TO HAVE TO ASK YOU ALL TO LEAVE.

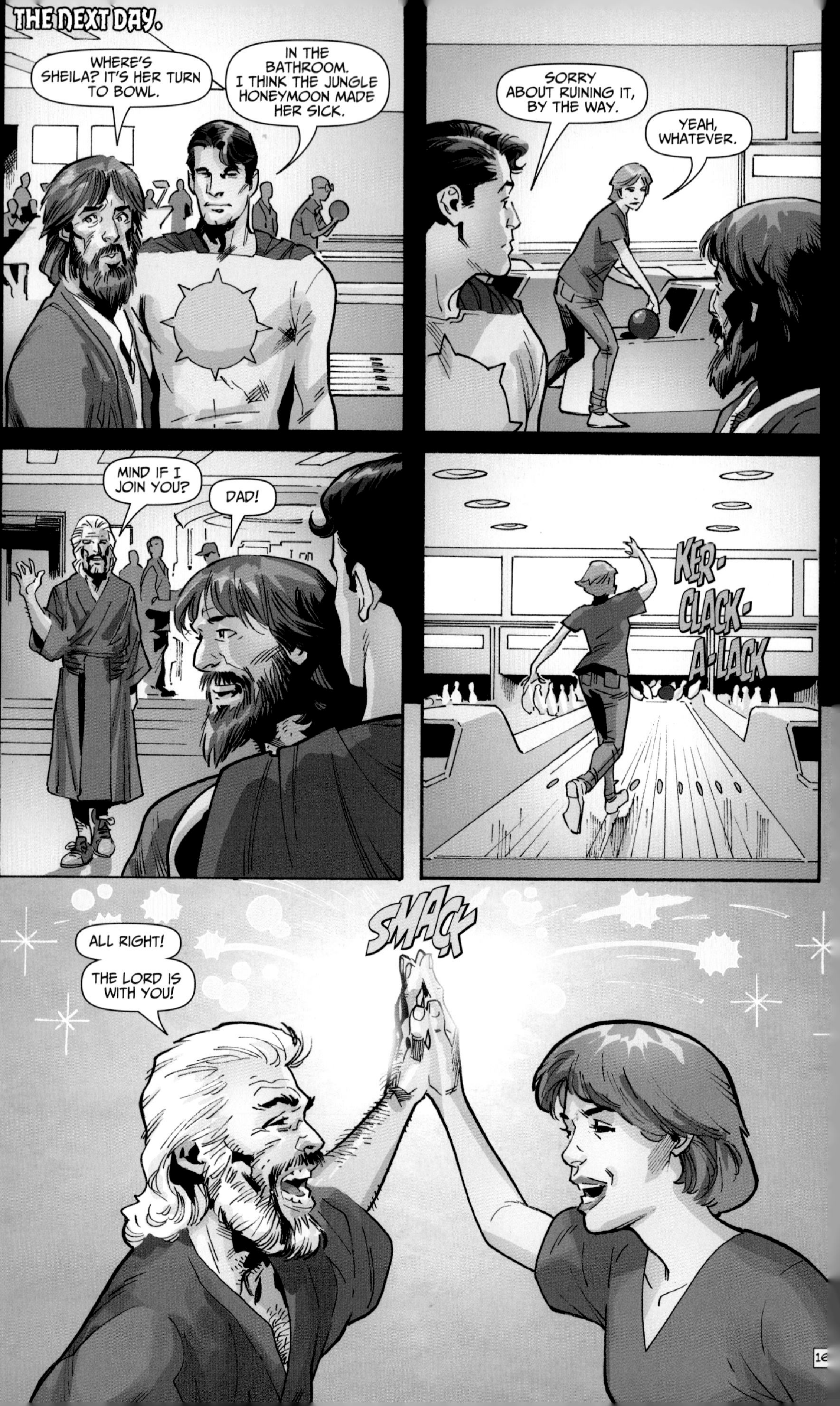
THE NEXT DAY.
WHERE'S SHEILA? IT'S HER TURN TO BOWL.
IN THE BATHROOM. I THINK THE JUNGLE HONEYMOON MADE HER SICK.
SORRY ABOUT RUINING IT, BY THE WAY.
YEAH, WHATEVER.
MIND IF I JOIN YOU?
DAD!
KER-CLACK-A-LACK
SMACK
ALL RIGHT!
THE LORD IS WITH YOU!

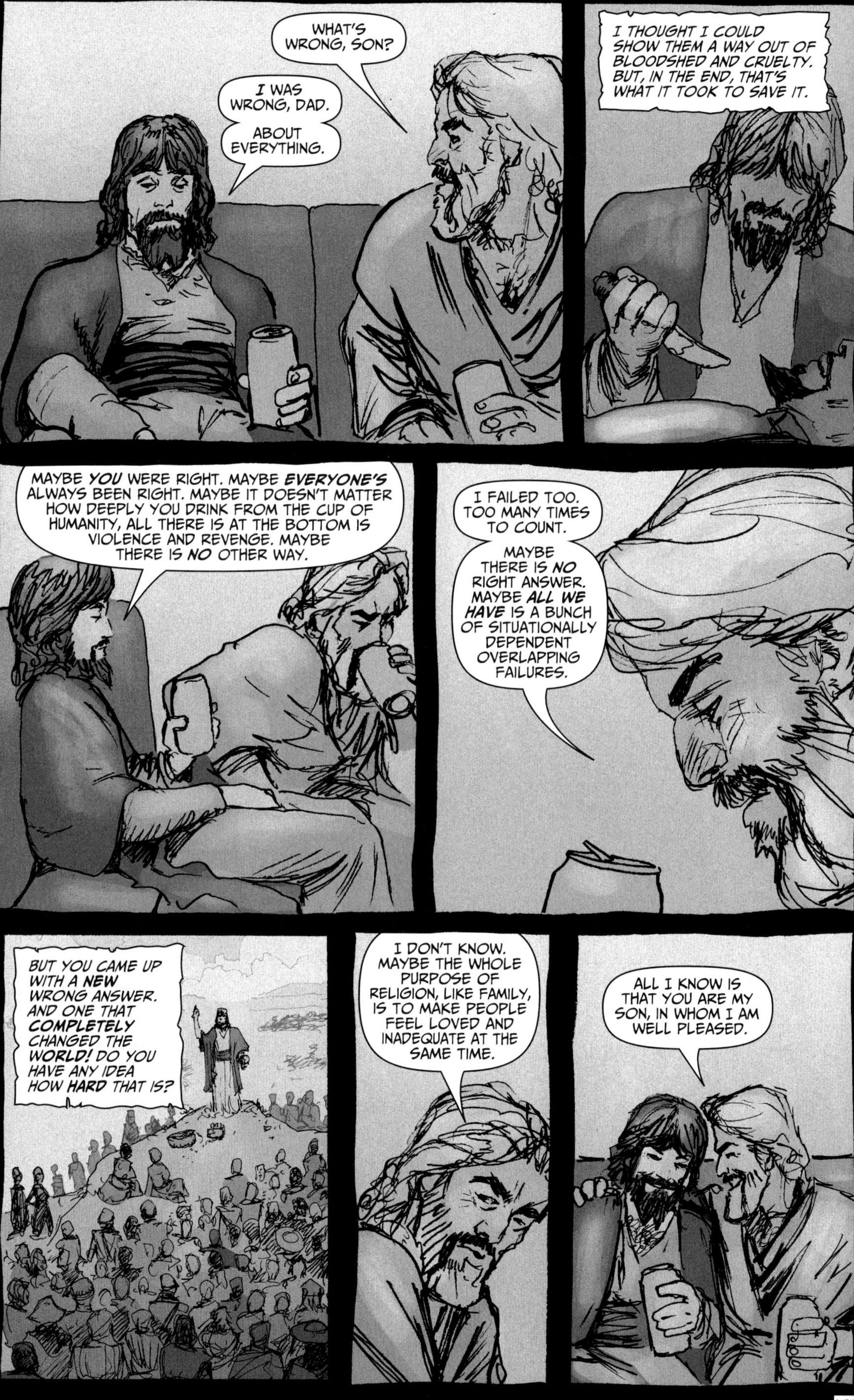
WHAT'S WRONG, SON?
I WAS WRONG, DAD.
ABOUT EVERYTHING.
I THOUGHT I COULD SHOW THEM A WAY OUT OF BLOODSHED AND CRUELTY. BUT, IN THE END, THAT'S WHAT IT TOOK TO SAVE IT.
MAYBE YOU WERE RIGHT. MAYBE EVERYONE'S ALWAYS BEEN RIGHT. MAYBE IT DOESN'T MATTER HOW DEEPLY YOU DRINK FROM THE CUP OF HUMANITY, ALL THERE IS AT THE BOTTOM IS VIOLENCE AND REVENGE. MAYBE THERE IS NO OTHER WAY.
I FAILED TOO. TOO MANY TIMES TO COUNT.
MAYBE THERE IS NO RIGHT ANSWER. MAYBE ALL WE HAVE IS A BUNCH OF SITUATIONALLY DEPENDENT OVERLAPPING FAILURES.
BUT YOU CAME UP WITH A NEW WRONG ANSWER. AND ONE THAT COMPLETELY CHANGED THE WORLD! DO YOU HAVE ANY IDEA HOW HARD THAT IS?
I DON'T KNOW. MAYBE THE WHOLE PURPOSE OF RELIGION, LIKE FAMILY, IS TO MAKE PEOPLE FEEL LOVED AND INADEQUATE AT THE SAME TIME.
ALL I KNOW IS THAT YOU ARE MY SON, IN WHOM I AM WELL PLEASED.

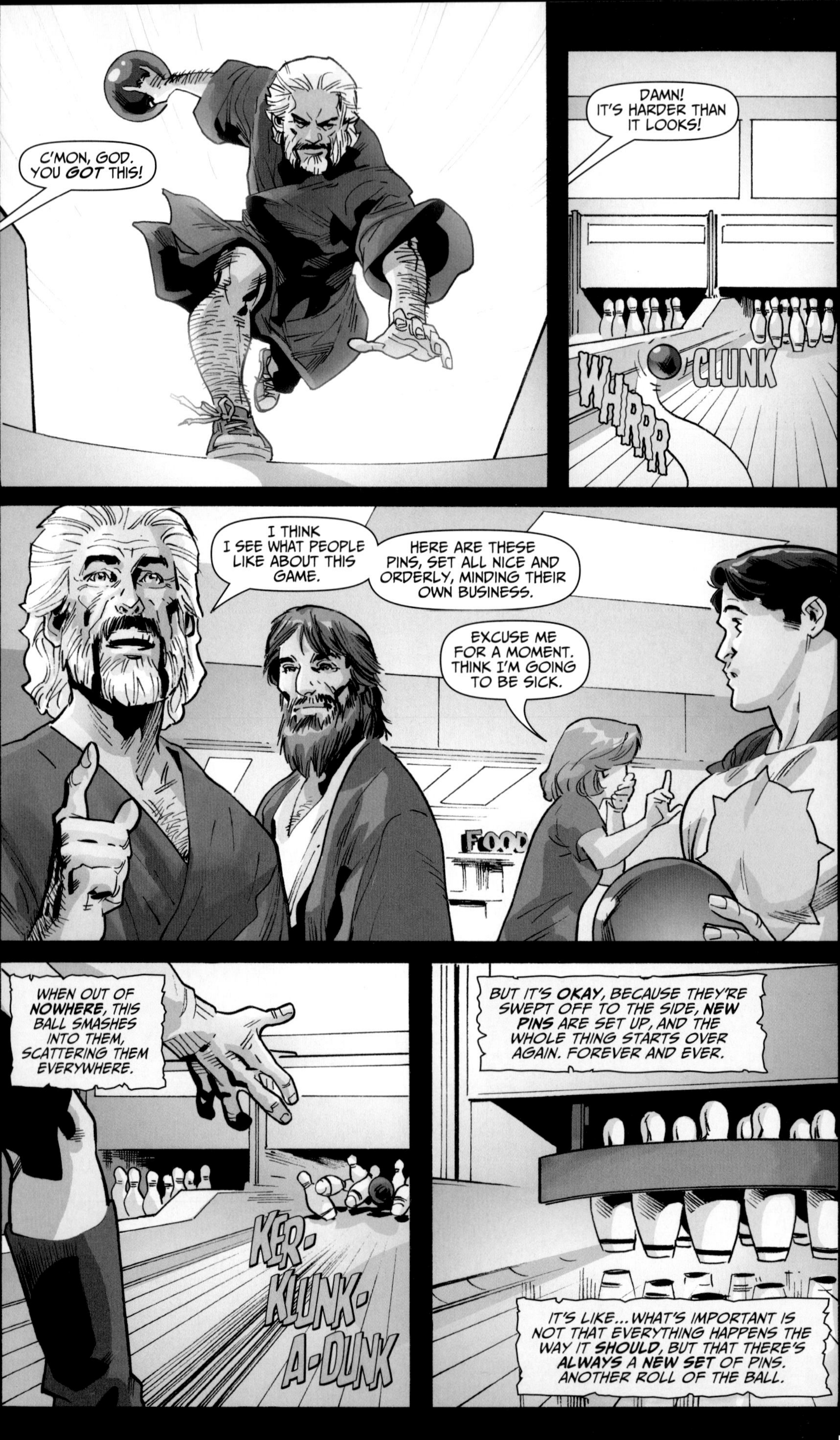
C'MON, GOD. YOU **GOT** THIS!
DAMN! IT'S HARDER THAN IT LOOKS!
WHRRR
CLUNK
I THINK I SEE WHAT PEOPLE LIKE ABOUT THIS GAME.
HERE ARE THESE PINS, SET ALL NICE AND ORDERLY, MINDING THEIR OWN BUSINESS.
EXCUSE ME FOR A MOMENT. THINK I'M GOING TO BE SICK.
FOOD
WHEN OUT OF **NOWHERE,** THIS BALL SMASHES INTO THEM, SCATTERING THEM EVERYWHERE.
KER-KLUNK-A-DUNK
BUT IT'S **OKAY,** BECAUSE THEY'RE SWEPT OFF TO THE SIDE, **NEW PINS** ARE SET UP, AND THE WHOLE THING STARTS OVER AGAIN. FOREVER AND EVER.
IT'S LIKE... WHAT'S IMPORTANT IS NOT THAT EVERYTHING HAPPENS THE WAY IT **SHOULD,** BUT THAT THERE'S **ALWAYS A NEW SET** OF PINS. ANOTHER ROLL OF THE BALL.

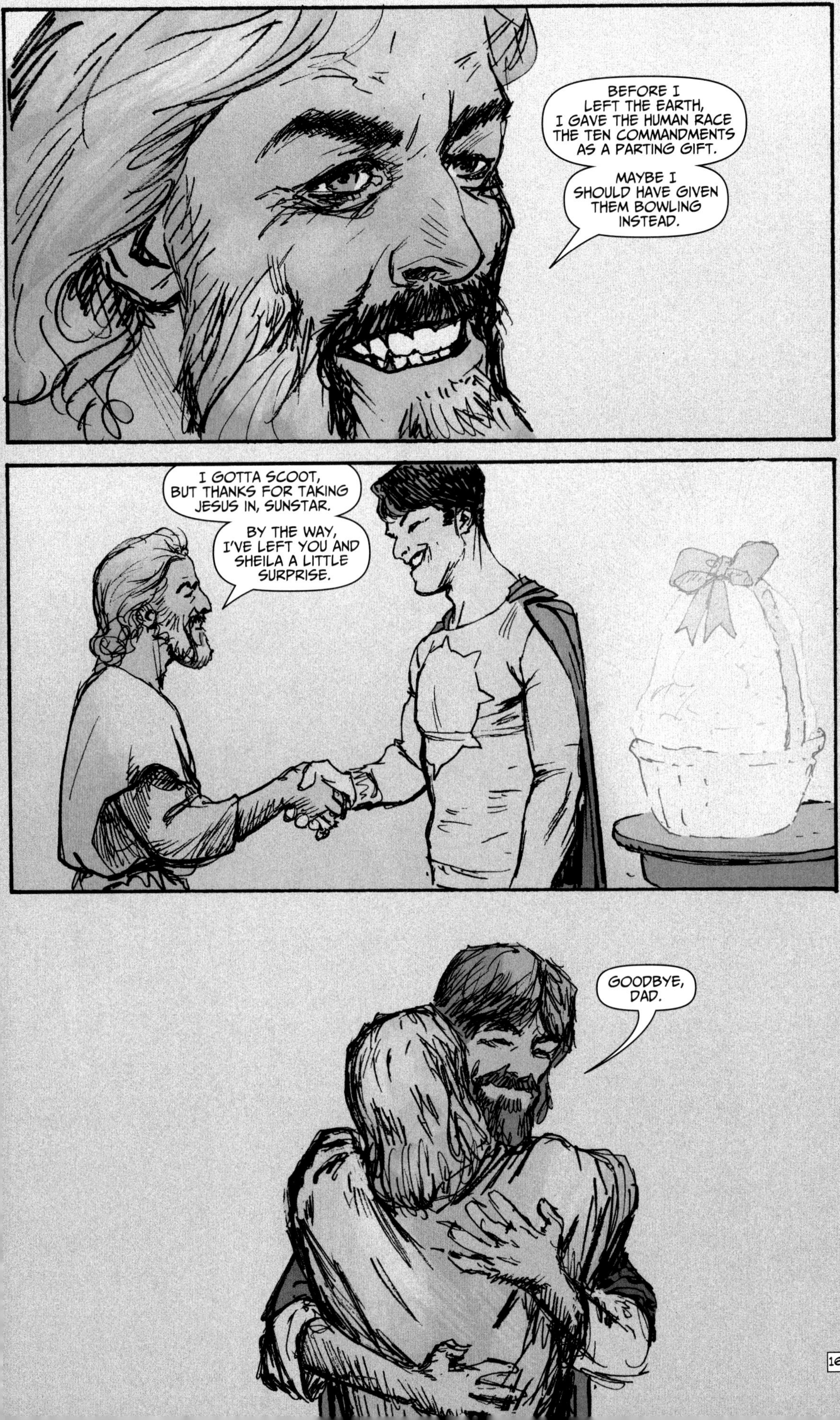
BEFORE I LEFT THE EARTH, I GAVE THE HUMAN RACE THE TEN COMMANDMENTS AS A PARTING GIFT.
MAYBE I SHOULD HAVE GIVEN THEM BOWLING INSTEAD.
I GOTTA SCOOT, BUT THANKS FOR TAKING JESUS IN, SUNSTAR.
BY THE WAY, I'VE LEFT YOU AND SHEILA A LITTLE SURPRISE.
GOODBYE, DAD.

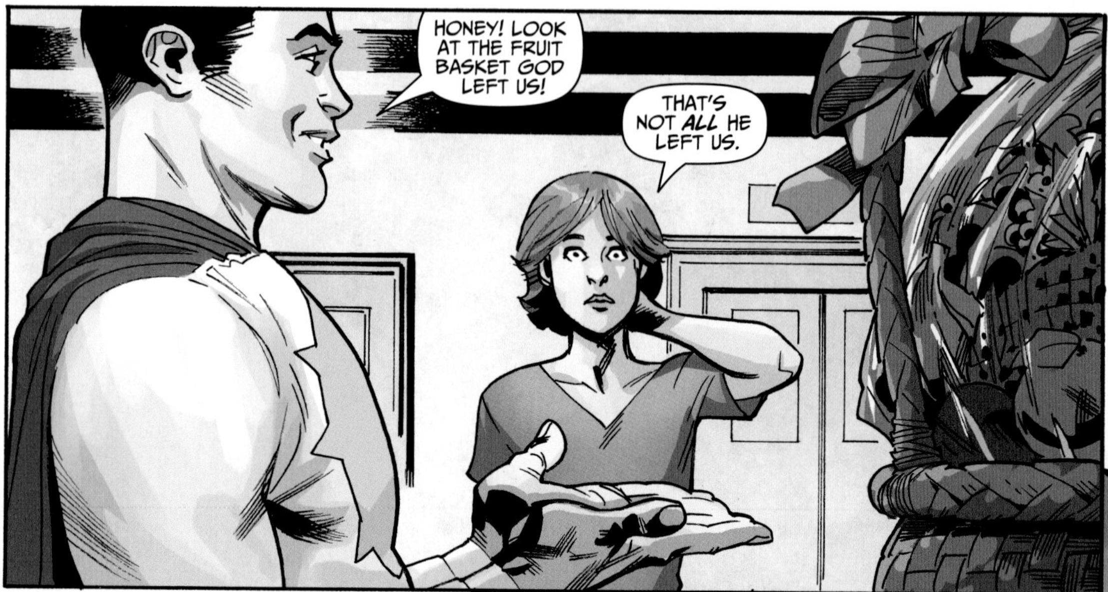
HONEY! LOOK AT THE FRUIT BASKET GOD LEFT US!
THAT'S NOT ALL HE LEFT US.

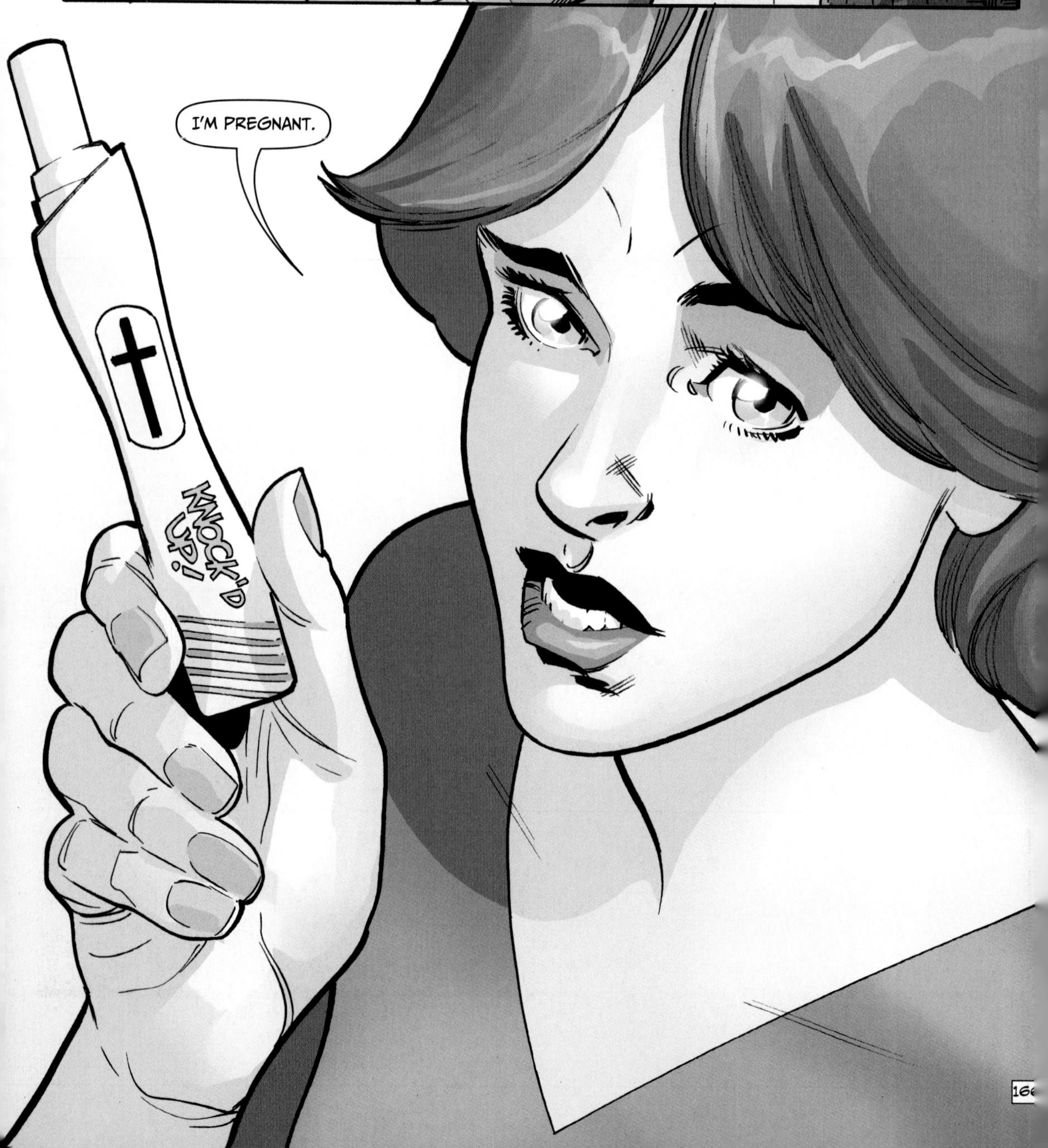
I'M PREGNANT.
KNOCK'D UP!

Dedicated to the Memory of Lucas McCain

1986-2016

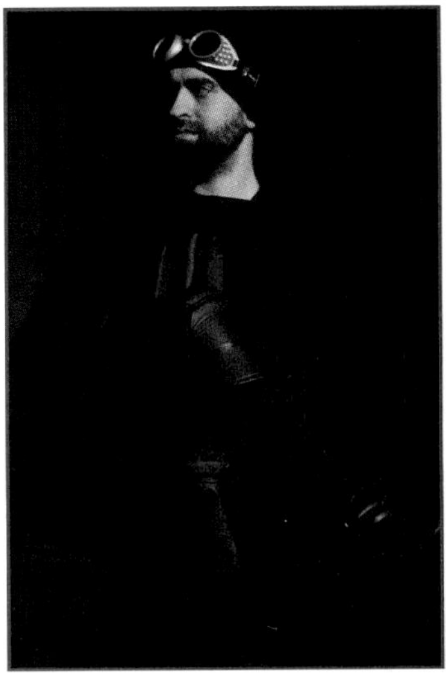

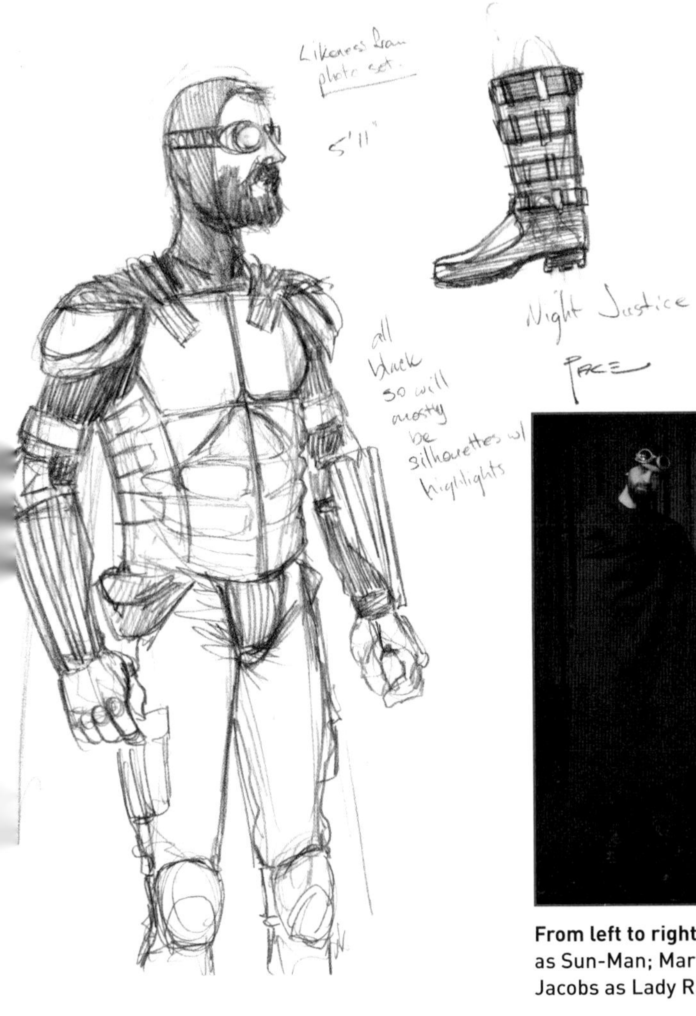
Likeness from photo set.
5'11"
Night Justice
all black so will mostly be silhouettes w/ highlights

The scenes of the group therapy sessions that appear in ***SECOND COMING*** are based on a short play I wrote called *Group Therapy*, in which my friend Lucas McCain played the character of Night Justice. He also served as the inspiration for Richard's designs of the Night Justice character in this series. Lucas passed away suddenly and far too young in 2016. We dedicate this book to him. Our best lives are those we live in the hearts of others.

– MARK RUSSELL

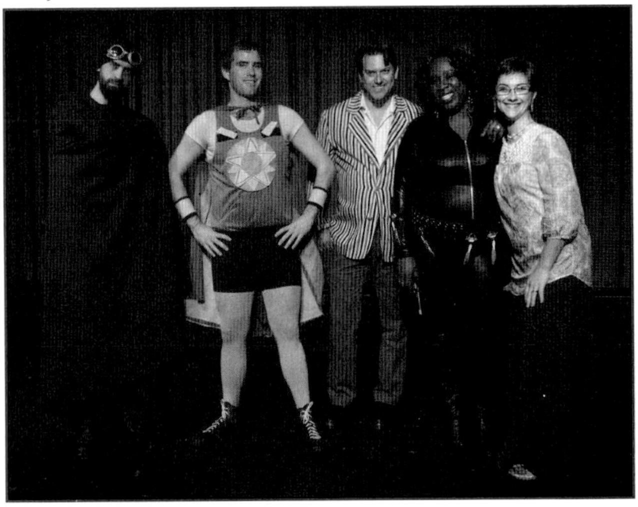

From left to right: Lucas McCain as Night Justice; Craig McCarthy as Sun-Man; Mark Russell, *Group Therapy* playwright; Shareen Jacobs as Lady Razor; and Gretchen Lively as the Therapist.

I wanted a more human looking, down-to-earth take on the S******* look. The goal was to get a Jon Hamm feel to him. An average, healthy body, handsome, but not perfect, and able to look worn out. The basic idea is his costume is essentially a faded sweatshirt, wrestler pants, a stitched-on symbol, and a large supply of red boots from a failed licensing deal with a show manufacturer.

– RICHARD PACE

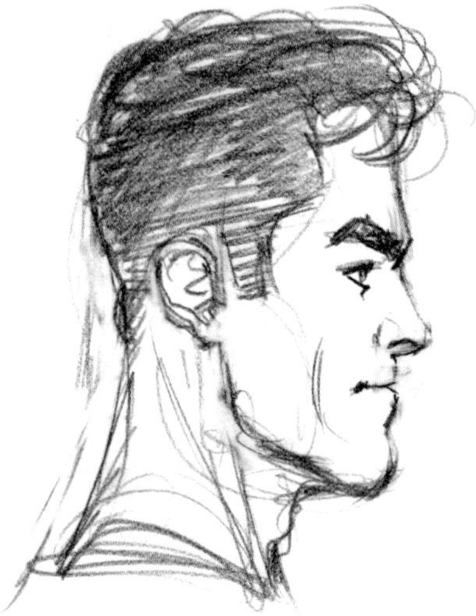

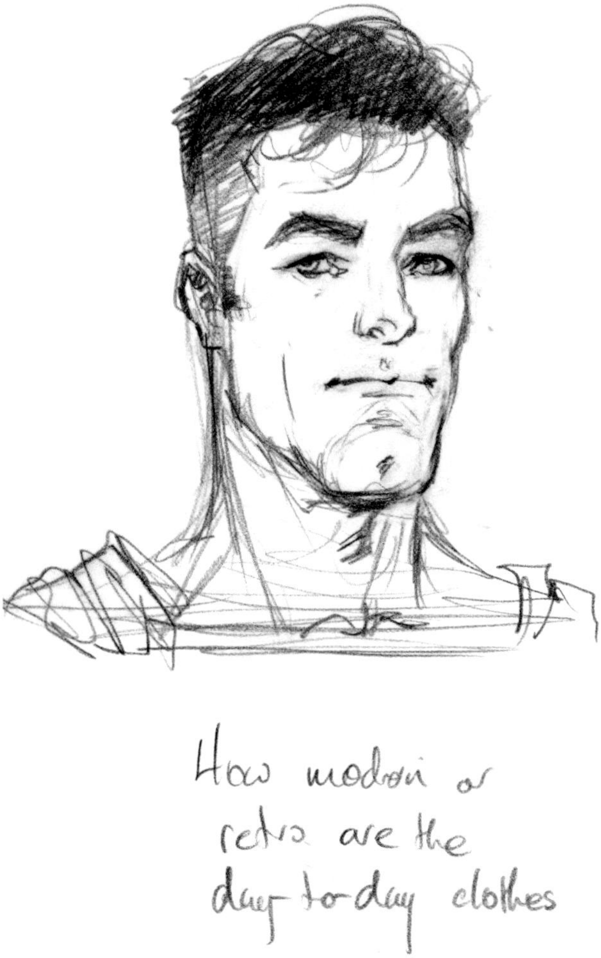
How modern or
retro are the
dary to-day clothes

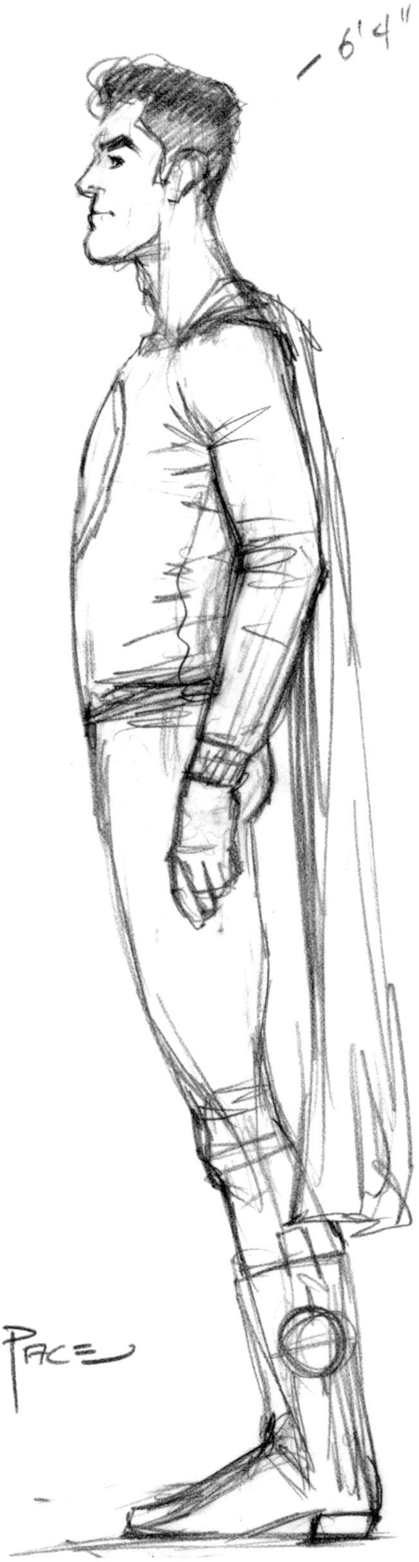
6'4"
PACE

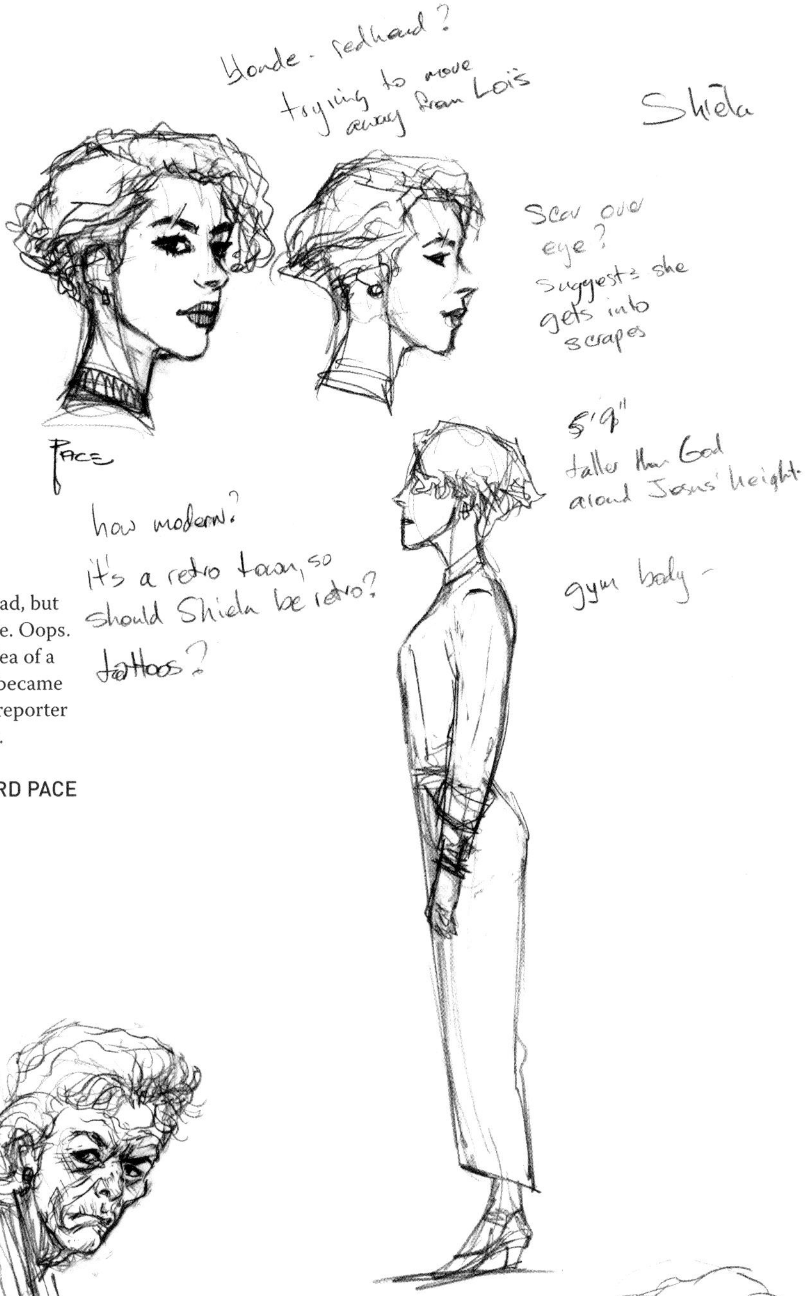
blonde - redhead?
trying to move away from Lois
Shiela
Scar over eye?
suggests she gets into scrapes
PACE
5'9"
taller than God
around Jesus' height
how modern?
it's a retro town, so should Shiela be retro?
tattoos?
gym body -

I wanted Sheila as a redhead, but she got colored as a blonde. Oops. I also opted to drop the idea of a scar over her eye when it became clear she was more a city reporter than a war correspondent.

– RICHARD PACE

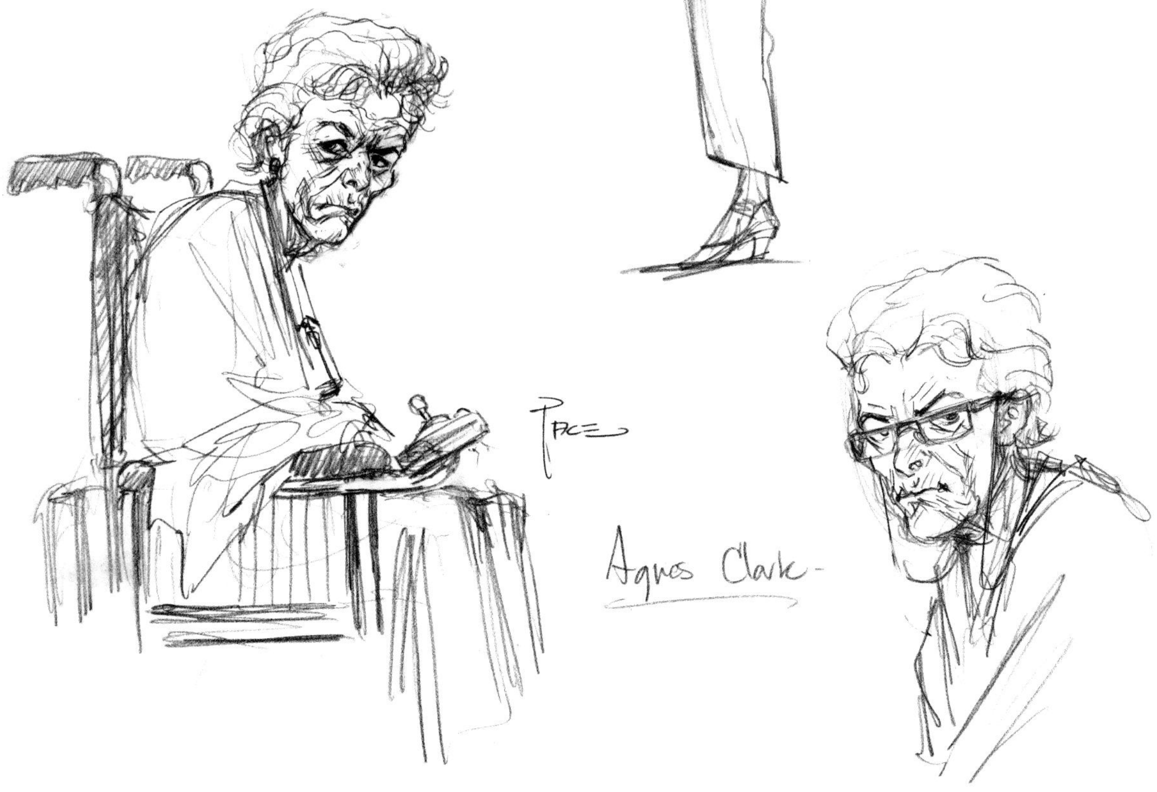
PACE
Agnes Clark -

With both Jesus and God, I felt we needed that universality of the historic appearances in Western culture so we don't have to explain who our characters are every issue.

God ended up inspired by Bryan Cox and Robert De Niro. I have a few rules when drawing him – barefoot (unless bowling) and his robe/toga thing is constantly changing how it's wrapped around him. A few people caught that, which is nice.

– RICHARD PACE

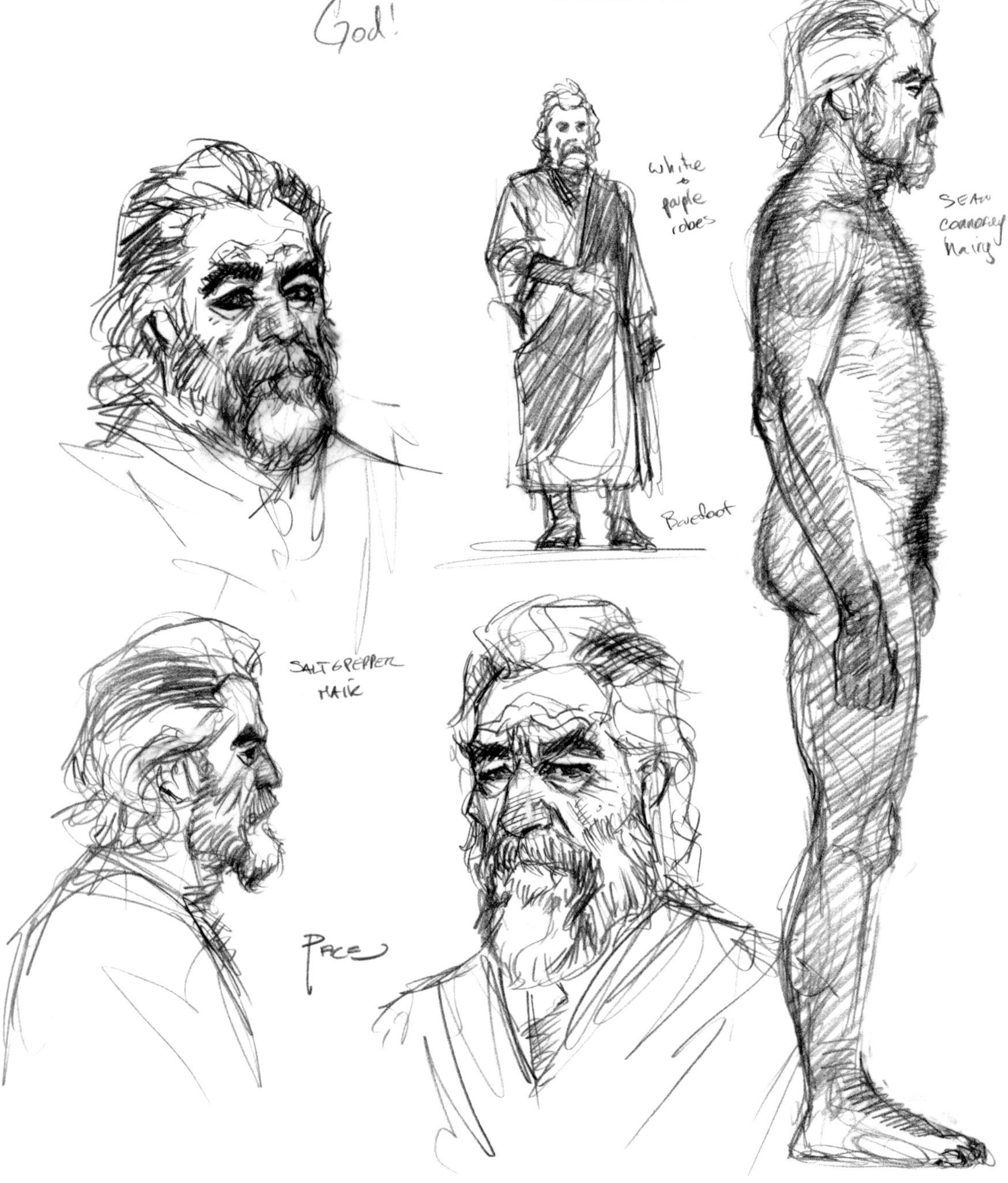
5'7"
God!
white + purple robes
SEAN connery hairy
Barefoot
SALT & PEPPER HAIR
PACE

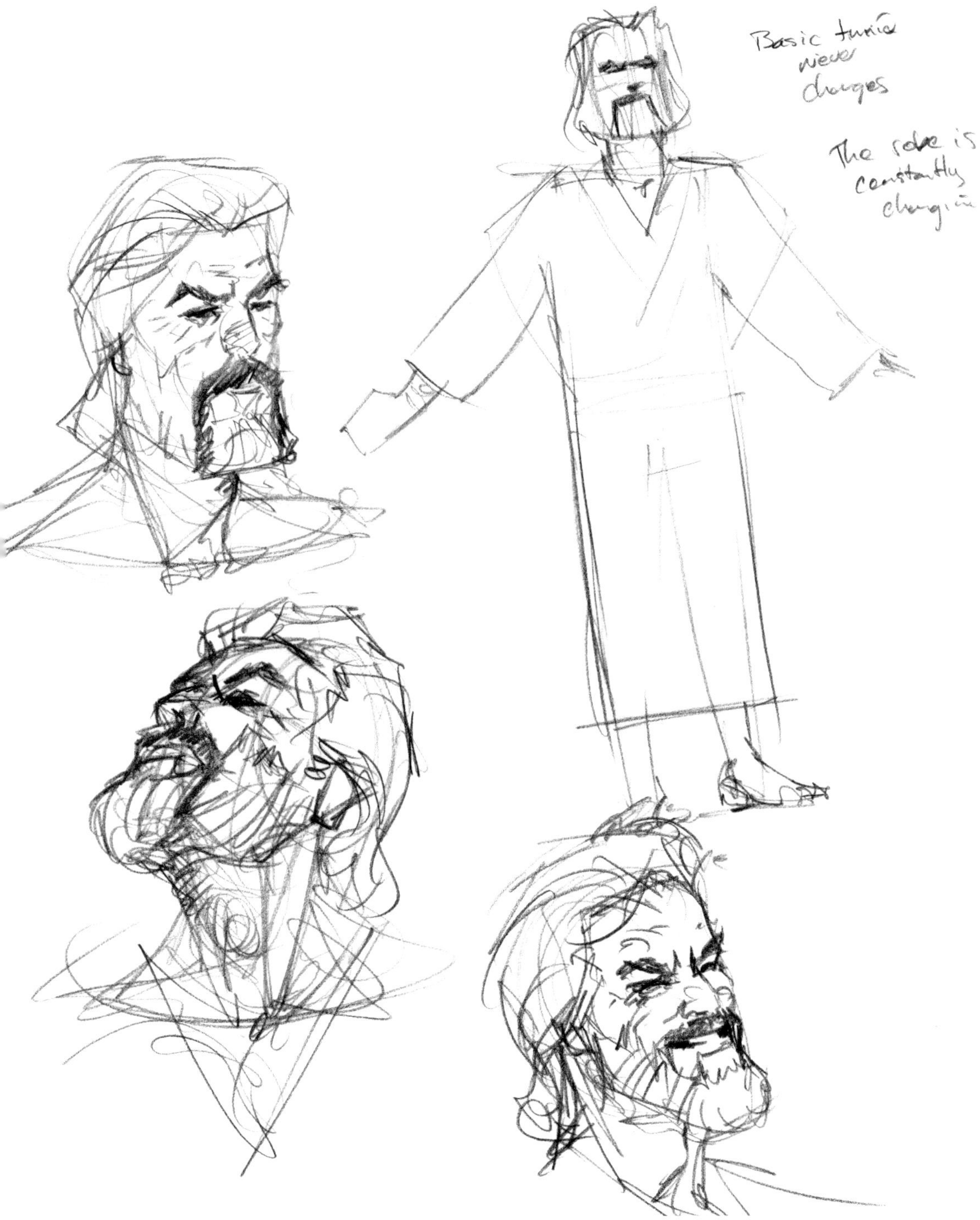
Basic tunic
never
changes
The robe is
constantly
changing

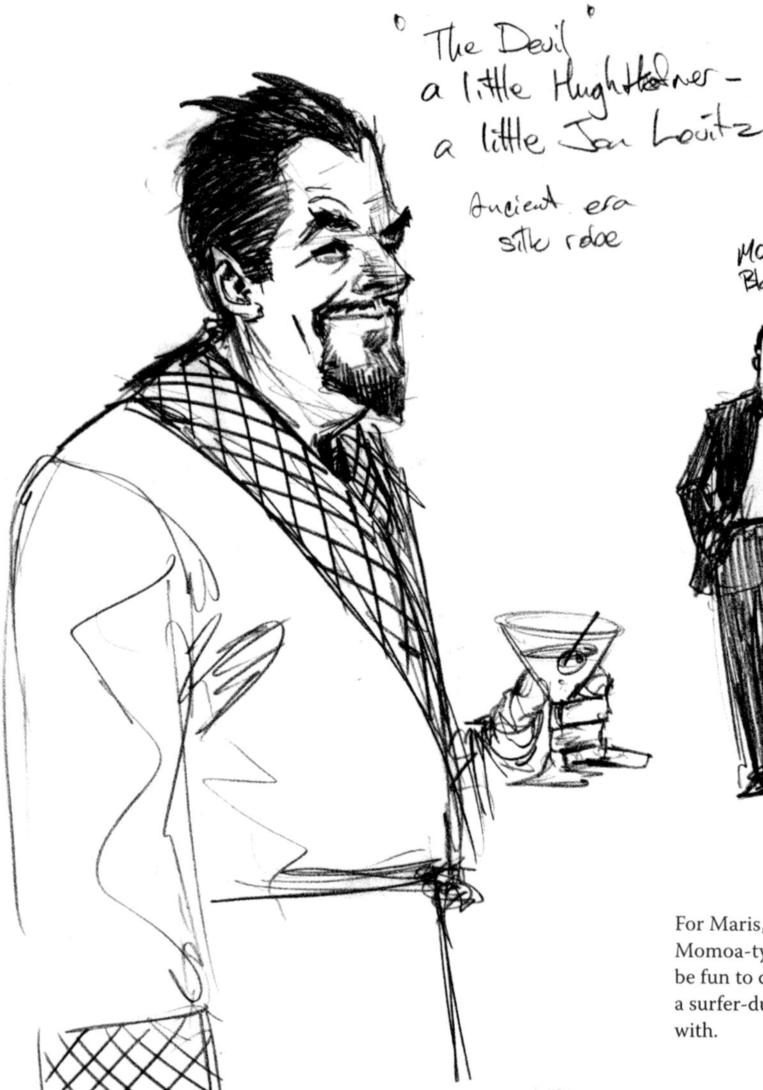
The Devil
a little Hugh Hefner -
a little Jon Lovitz
Ancient era
silk robe

The Devil is a cross between Hugh Hefner and Jon Lovitz's characters from back in his *SNL* heyday. The black fingernails became an addition when I was inking.

– RICHARD PAC

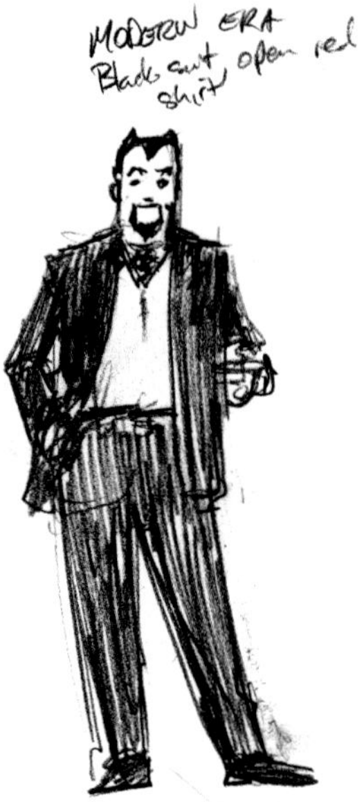
MODERN ERA
Black suit open red shirt

For Maris, it was a toss-up between a Jason Momoa-type (because, c'mon, Momoa would be fun to draw) or a fishier guy. Ended up with a surfer-dude in a scaly suit, which I'm happy with.

– RICHARD PACE

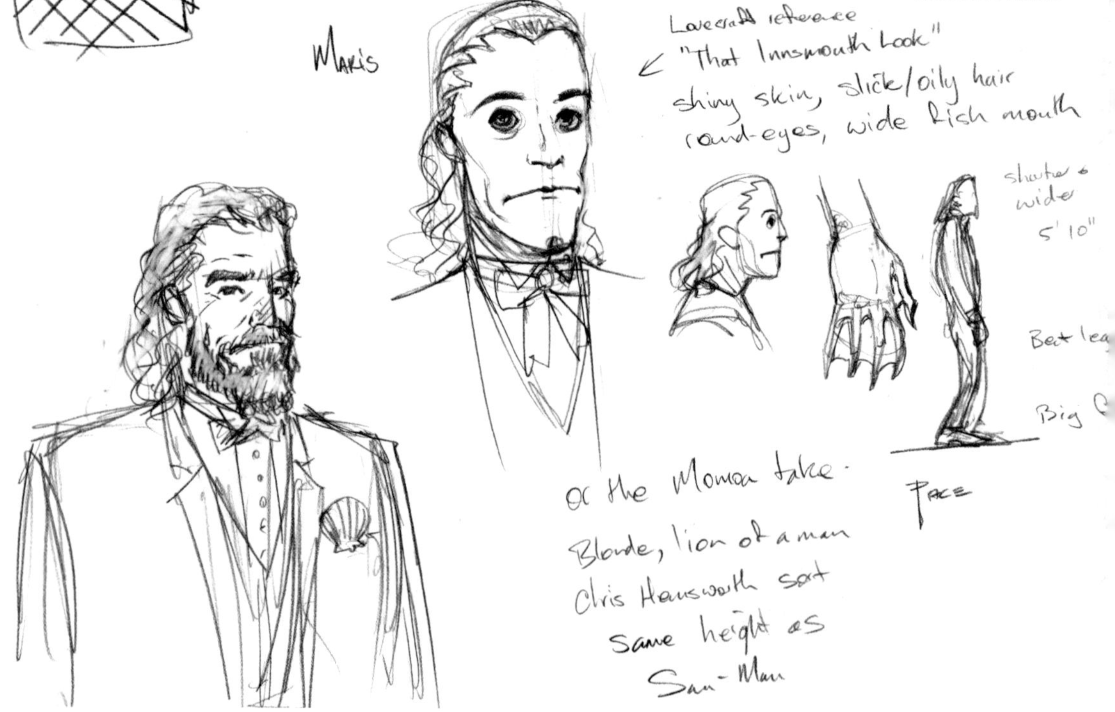
Maris
Lovecraft reference
"That Innsmouth Look"
shiny skin, slick/oily hair
round-eyes, wide fish mouth
shorter & wider
5'10"
Or the Momoa take.
Blonde, lion of a man
Chris Hemsworth sort
same height as
Sam-Man
PACE

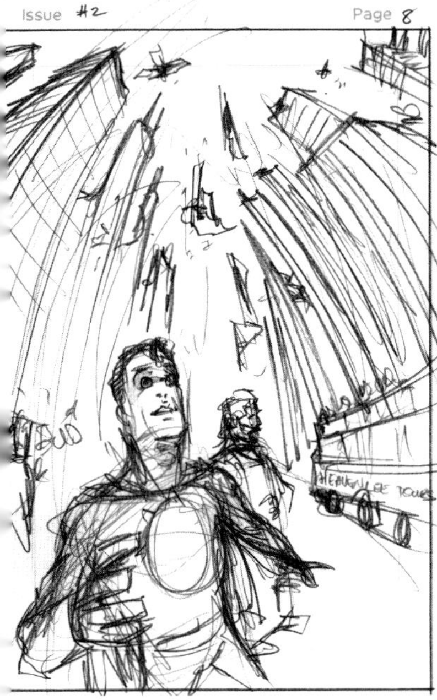
Issue #2
Page 8

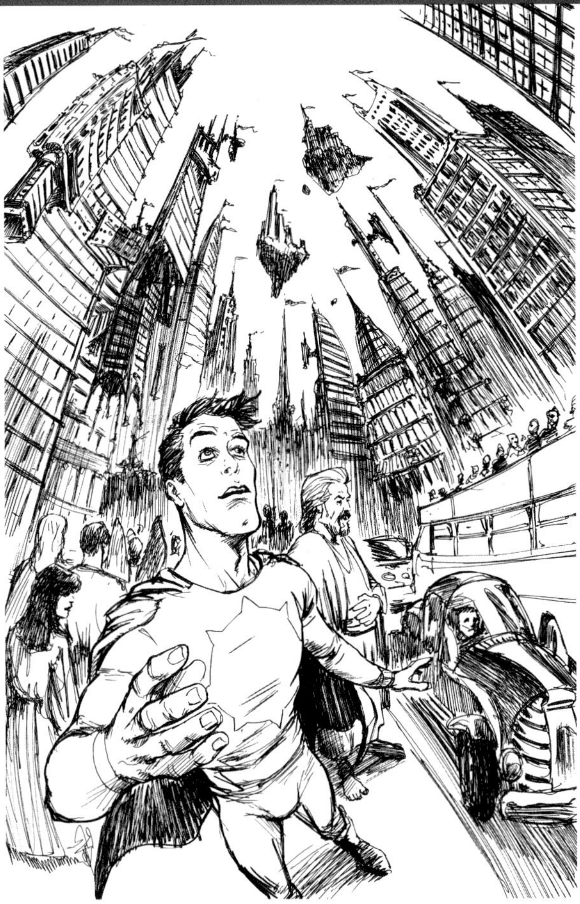

This is one of my favorite pages from *SECOND COMING*'s first season. Mark gave me carte-blanche to design heaven and I went for a fantasy city by way of a prog rock album cover. I felt pretty disappointed with my first pass on the page (top-right) and redrew it, adding more surprising denizens like flying whales, giant purple nosaurs, and the prankster aliens from the classic DeMatteis/ uth *Moonshadow* series.

lso, since some reviewers keep getting confused, I color all the ages I ink. Bringing Leonard and Andy on board allowed me to ally go off in my own direction to explore how to best bring the pernatural elements to the reader.

– RICHARD PACE

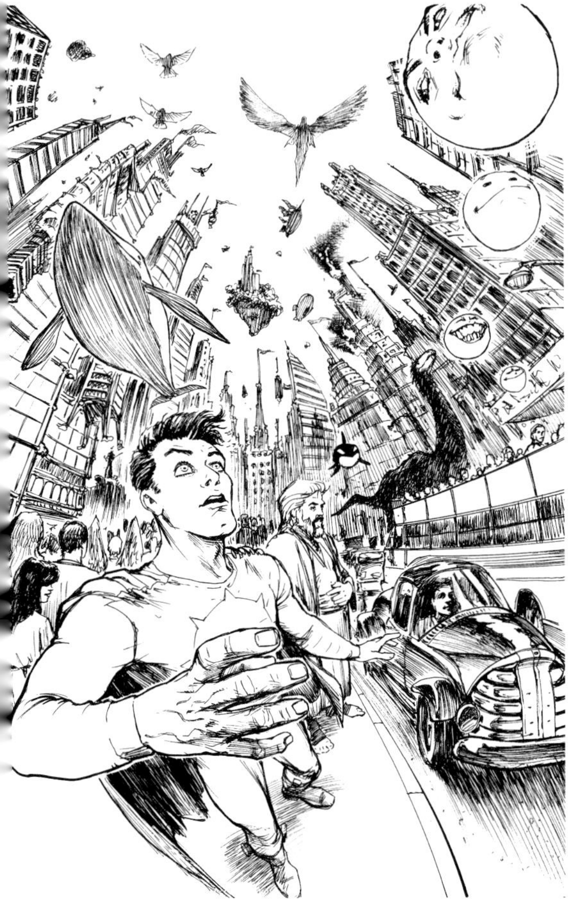

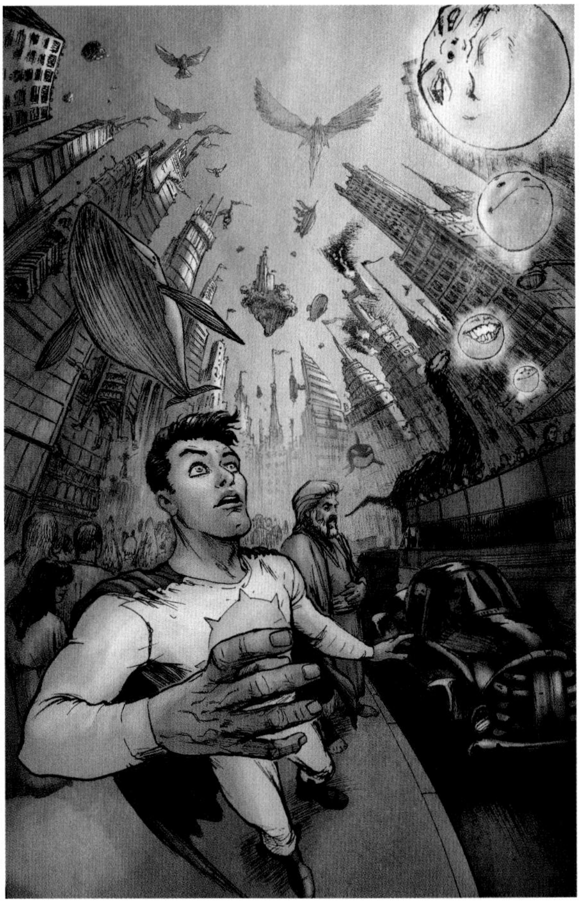

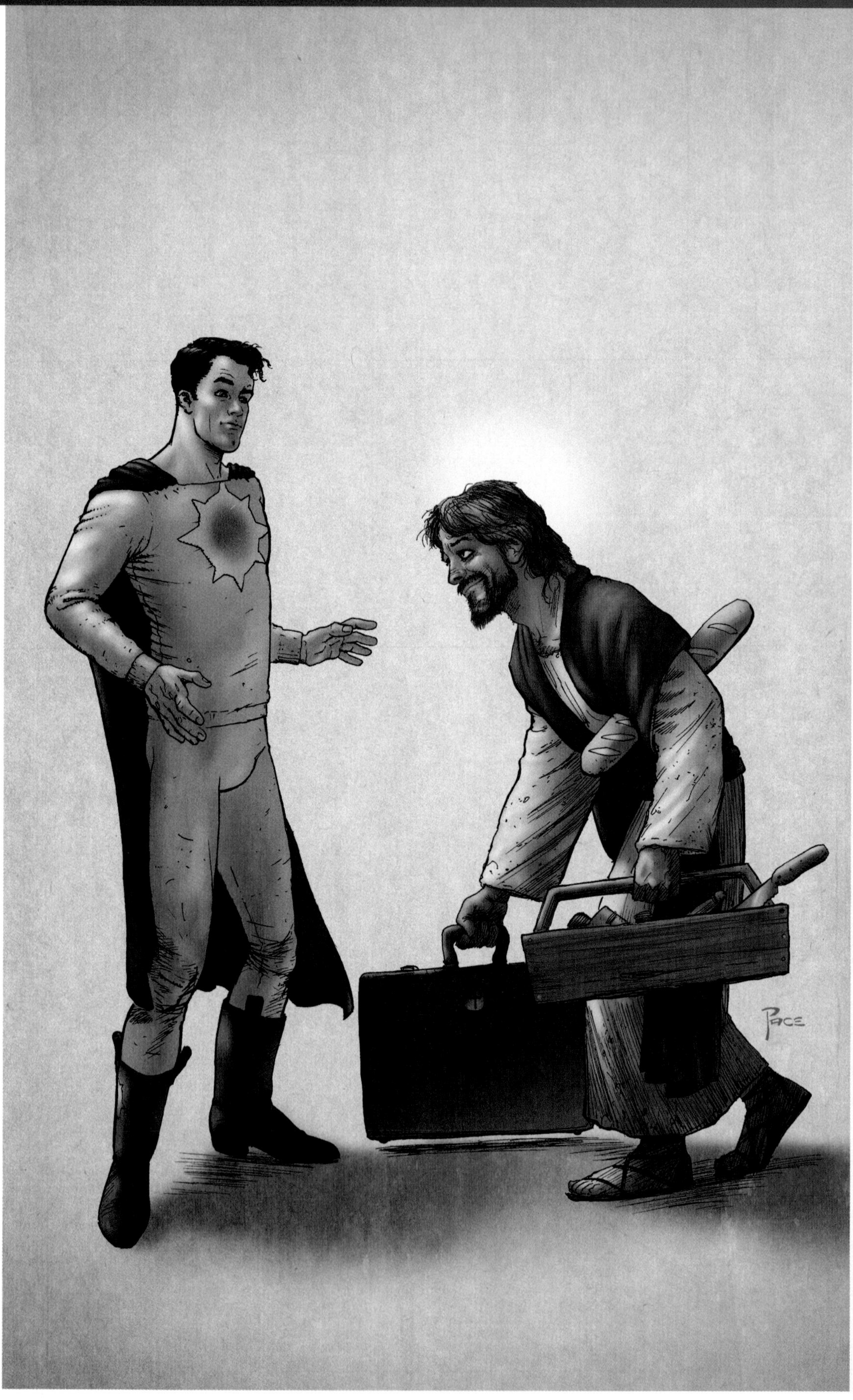
PACE

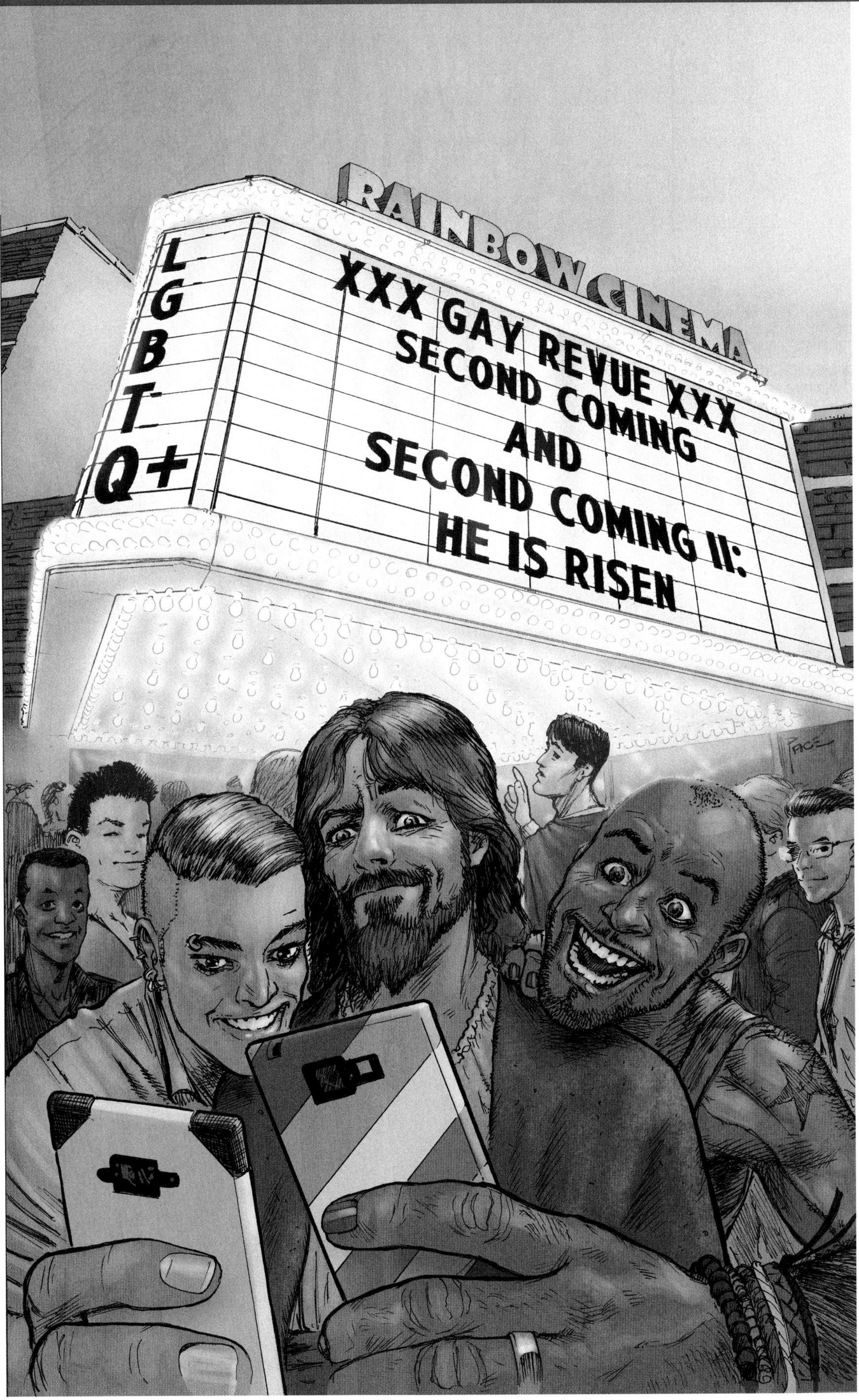
RAINBOW CINEMA
LGBTQ+
XXX GAY REVUE XXX
SECOND COMING
AND
SECOND COMING II:
HE IS RISEN
PACE

BIOGRAPHIES

AMANDA CONNER broke open the boys' club of comic book artists with her exuberant yet subversive sensibility. Her take on Vampirella, Power Girl, Captain Marvel and Harley Quinn has redefined the characters for a new generation of readers. Conner has also created work for television and advertising as well as *The New York Times*.

PAUL MOUNTS has earned accolades as one of the comic book industry's premiere color artists. In his 30 year career, he has worked on nearly every icon in the business, from a 130-plus issue run on *Fantastic Four* to the groundbreaking *The Ultimates*.

MARK RUSSELL is the author of not one, but two, books about the Bible: *God Is Disappointed in You* and *Apocrypha Now*. In addition, he is the writer behind various DC comic books such as *Prez*, *The Flintstones*, and *Exit Stage Left: The Snagglepuss Chronicles*. He lives in obscurity with his family in Portland, Oregon.

ANDY TROY has colored for Marvel Comics, DC Comics, Extreme Studios, and others, working on such characters as *Spawn*, *Batman*, *Captain America*, and *Iron Fist*. He lives and works in Huntsville, AL, where he used to play in the metal band Diamond White.

LEONARD KIRK began his comic book career with Malibu Comics. He has drawn numerous titles for Marvel and DC, including *Fantastic Four*, *Star Wars* and extended collaborations with Peter David on *Supergirl* and *X-Factor*. He, wisely, lives north of the border and recently drew a revival of the Canadian comics icon Captain Canuck and a return to the post-apocalyptic world of *Marvel Zombies*.

RICHARD PACE resides in Toronto, Canada, looking down upon the silly Americans to the south. From this perch, he has deployed his illustration skills on titles for Vertigo and Marvel and has also co-written Dale Keown's *Pitt* and *Batman: The Doom That Came to Gotham*.

ROB STEEN is the illustrator of *Flanimals*, the best-selling series of children's books written by Ricky Gervais, and *Erf*, a children's book written by Garth Ennis.